WAR, PEACE AND TERROR IN TH[E]

BOOKS OF RELATED INTEREST

War, Peace and Terror in the Middle East

Raphael Israeli

FRANK CASS
LONDON • PORTLAND, OR

First Published in 2003 in Great Britain by
FRANK CASS & CO. LTD.
Crown House, 47 Chase Side, Southgate,
London N14 5BP, England

and in the United States of America by
FRANK CASS
c/o ISBS, 920 NE 58th Avenue, Suite 300
Portland, Oregon, 97213-3786

Website: www.frankcass.com

British Library Cataloguing in Publication Data:

Israeli, Raphael
    War, peace and terror in the Middle East
    1. Arab–Israeli conflict – 1993 –   2. Arab–Israeli conflict –
    1993 –   Peace 3. Islam and terrorism 4. Middle East – History
    – 1979–
    I. Title
    956'.05

ISBN 07146-5531-7 (cloth)
ISBN 0 7146-8420-1 (paper)

Library of Congress Cataloging-in-Publication Data:

Israeli, Raphael.
    War, peace and terror in the Middle East / Raphael Israeli.
        p. cm.
    Includes bibliographical references (p.) and index.
    ISBN 0-7146-5531-7 (cloth) – ISBN 0-7146-8420-1 (pbk.)
        1. Arab–Israeli conflict – 1993 – Peace 2. Terrorism – Middle
    East. I. Title.

DS119.76.I822 2003
956.05'3 – dc21

                                                    2003048490

Typeset in 10.5/13pt Zapf Calligraphica by Frank Cass Publishers
Printed in Great Britain by MPG Books Ltd, Bodmin, Cornwall

*To my son, David
who taught his elders
compassion, humility and humanity*

Contents

List of Illustrations

Foreword

This book is a collection of articles written by the author, and for the most part published over the past few years, which are concerned with the fateful issues of war and peace in the Middle East; especially that evasive brand of war – terrorism and incitement – that usually escapes definition, but nonetheless has contributed greatly to the rising in the level of violence in that volatile area of the world.

Indeed, horrific words of incitement, followed by atrocious acts of terror, have occurred during the past few years and significantly eroded the hopes inherent in the peace process that had been initiated by Sadat and Begin a quarter of a century ago (1977) and driven it to an impasse. In fact, all the efforts to duplicate that feat between Israel and Palestinians have ended in frustration thus far, and it now seems that not only are we back to square one, but that a tremendous amount of ground work will have to be done before the situation is ripe again for a peace venture.

Though the Palestinian issue has been central to this set-back, it is nevertheless noteworthy that much of it has been fed, fomented and cultivated by rejectionists such as Saddam Hussein's Iraq and the Assads' (father and son) Syria; by the augmented and direct help of world Islamic terrorism; and, yes, even by Mubarak's Egypt, which has its own axe to grind in this issue. It is no coincidence that Palestinian recalcitrance and the outbreak of the Intifadah (2000) – which resulted in the undoing of the peace process – came on the heels of the Israeli withdrawal from Lebanon, which encouraged the Hamas and their peers to follow the Iran-sponsored Hizbullah model of fighting Israel into submission; or that the incitement to further violence, led by the Palestinian Authority, has been based on these themes; or that the current Islamic wave of terrorism worldwide has found strong and supportive echoes in the Palestinian street.

This collection of essays will focus on some of these themes with both the benefit of hindsight gained since the following articles were published, and the insight that the current world crisis has been occasioned by the terrorism and broadsides against Western culture which *al-Qa'ida* and its allies have launched. It is widely understood and believed that, in the wake of the present American campaign against terrorism, in which Muslim fundamentalists play the major role, but which some major Muslim countries may be willing to help quell, a new strategic thinking may emerge, which might reshuffle allegiances and alliances and produce a new world order.

Jerusalem
December 2001

Introduction
International Islamic Terrorism and the Demise of Peace

THE PREDICAMENT AND ITS TERMINOLOGY

When the horrendous act of terror at Oklahoma City unfolded before the incredulous eyes of Americans – who could not comprehend why a fellow American could be so filled with hate and motivated by evil as to eliminate dozens of his innocent countrymen – they sought solace in the law-enforcement system of the USA and its ability to bring the culprit to justice; but the whole horror and its ramifications did not transcend the American borders. Few looked for 'justifications' for the crime, or 'understood' the 'frustration' of the criminal; deeming mass killing on this scale an out-of-the-ordinary and aberrant form of behavior worthy of unmitigated condemnation and contempt.

But when, on 11 September, the terrorist act of the millennium wrecked New York and Washington, America woke up to a new reality of panic and disarray, because the perpetrators were guided from the outside, and the American justice system could not investigate and lay its hands on them within the perimeters of its territory. Hence, the process of seeking justice beyond American borders immediately took on the form of a world-wide war, which instantly became the concern of all nations. At the same time, however – precisely due to the international nature of this developing conflict – 'justifications', 'apologetics' and 'rationalizations' were offered which forced the American administration to feel its way as it went along.

President Bush was, at first, committed to 'punish' and 'bring to justice' the perpetrators; then he declared a 'crusade' against terror and against its heads who were 'wanted, live or dead'; then he gave the choice to all countries to either side with him or bear the onus of opposing him. And, finally, he resolved that terrorism had to be fought at its roots, and he prepared for an all-out war that disregarded collateral damage to civilians, and vowed to take it from one target to another until international terrorism was uprooted and defeated. While his initial reactions came from the hip and sounded more vindictive than rational, his later actions were more in line with a long-term determined and sustained policy of waging war and winning it.

Terrorism in its current manifestation did not begin in New York, nor did it originate in Afghanistan. It is essential not only to pinpoint the stage at which it emerged, but also to be aware of the vocabulary and definitions that articulate and govern it. It is also imperative to realize the world-wide import of its spread, bearing in mind that 56 countries in the world today, spanning the two continents of Asia and Africa, define themselves as Muslim, or as predominantly Muslim, and that sizeable Muslim minorities have been settling in the West in the past few decades, enabling some fundamentalist trends to take root there under the instigation and guidance of core Islamic fundamentalist countries such as Iran, the Sudan and Afghanistan.

Without attributing specific blame to Islam as a faith, or to Muslim countries as political entities, it is nonetheless a fact that many current domestic and international conflicts are led by Muslims, in the name of Islam, from Muslim countries, or under their wings, or by Muslim minorities under non-Islamic rule. This must signify something in terms of Muslim ideological involvement in terror, and especially the grass-root support it seems to have among large portions of the Muslim populace, notwithstanding Muslim governments' attempts at concealment. This means that President Bush's ultimatum to Muslim countries to identify themselves as either friends or foes has left them no choice but to mumble something about their friendly attitudes, while trying to suppress the spontaneous cries which hail Bin-Laden as a hero. Had the American President given them the choice between eradicating terrorism in their midst first, and then joining the coalition (not the 'Crusade', a word which is abhorrent to them), or incurring the wrath of the West, a different gamut of voices might have risen which would have made it easier for America to distinguish between friend and foe. This was not done, allowing many entities that shelter terrorists – such as Iran, Syria, Saudi Arabia and the

Palestinian Authority (PA) – to masquerade as 'allies' and anti-terrorists.

Before 11 September, the possibility was afforded to many countries that harbor terrorism to escape that label by imputing the horrors to 'suicide-bombers'; this term implied that the perpetrators who, by definition, were weak of heart and 'frustrated', were also, by definition, unstable and unpredictable, and therefore that little could be done to scuttle their schemes. But after the harrowing events in New York and Washington, the West began to point a finger at those bases in which the terrorists had been recruited, trained, indoctrinated, dispatched, financed and supported, and which had been, until then, immune to retaliation, due to fears of violating the sovereignty of the harboring nation or of 'harming the peace process' in the Middle East. By targeting the heads of the terrorist organization of *al-Qa'ida*, and by implying that other terrorist operators might be next, the USA has signaled to the world that these authors of horror and intimidation do not dispatch suicidal types to kill themselves – they are, rather, determined and highly indoctrinated murderers who kill and wreak terror on others, and might more appropriately be dubbed 'Islamikaze'.[1]

THE ORIGINAL SIN

Up until about three decades ago we used to divide the Muslim countries into monarchical/conservative/capitalist/moderate/stable/pro-Western (like Iran under the Shah, Libya under the Sanussi King, Saudi Arabia, Morocco, Kuwait, Jordan etc.) versus republican/revolutionary/socialist/radical/unstable anti-Western (like Nasserite Egypt, Syria, Iraq, Algeria and the two Yemens). However, since the Iranian Revolution in 1979, the line-up has been somewhat reshuffled; for the Islamic Revolution in Iran – which was planned for foreign as much as indigenous consumption – showed that Islamic radicalism under a revolutionary republican government, unlike Muslim conservatism under pro-Western wings, could escape Western tutelage, indeed rebel against it, and gain huge popular support. It also proved that, unlike the corrupt illegitimate rulers who had acceded to power and held on to it previously, the Islamic Revolution drew its legitimacy from Islam and the rule of the *shari'a*, and its leaders enjoyed a reputation for impeccable integrity, something that further increased their popularity.

Besides the tremendous efforts made by the Iranian regime to export the Revolution and to lend legitimacy to the Terrorism International that they were determined to lead and co-ordinate – and which would generate the globalization of terrorism that will be discussed below – one has also to account for the fact that Iran was the direct or indirect trigger for the four major wars that have plagued Asia since the 1980s. Although these wars did not always use Iran as their springboard, it can surely be said that Teheran was the foundation stone from which these wars have emanated and polluted the international arena in the past two decades. These wars were first centered on the Persian Gulf: the First Gulf War which pitted two Muslim countries, Iraq and Iran, against each other; and the Second Gulf War, triggered by the Iraqi invasion of Kuwait, in which a broad coalition of European and Arab countries were involved, led by the USA. Then, the center of gravity of the conflict moved eastwards and two more wars were fought. The first was caused by the Soviet invasion of Afghanistan, that is, a Communist Power versus a Muslim country; and then there was the Second Afghani War, in which the Americans and some of their allies tackled Muslim fundamentalists.

The Iranian connection is evident. The First Gulf War (1980–88) was launched by Saddam Hussein in direct response to the threat posed by the Iranian Revolution, which he feared might spread into his Shi'ite territory. While this was a clearly pre-emptive strike, it was miscalculated in the sense that Saddam had badly underestimated the stamina of Revolutionary Iran and its commitment to defend its territory; and what Saddam thought would be an easy walk into the Arab-populated and oil-rich territory of Khuzistan became – as in the First World War – a conflict fought in trenches which drenched both parties in blood and ended with both sides in almost the same position as they began – one million casualties, eight years and tens of billions of dollars later. Saddam had also eyed the Iranian sea-shore adjacent to his territory that would have allowed him a safe haven beyond the 30-mile narrow outlet to the Gulf which he had at *Shatt-al-Arab*, for the fleet he wished to develop to impose his hegemony in the Gulf. He thought that due to the isolation of Revolutionary Iran – which was perceived as posing a threat to all the American protégés in the Middle East – no one would mind if he gnawed at her territory; and this had become vital for him once his enmity with Teheran had exploded and the necessity to maintain a fleet that matched Iran's had developed.

Having failed in his attempt, and after having assured a *rapprochement* with America as well as a close partnership with Egypt and Jordan, and having 'pacified' the Kurdish north by using gas poison against its population, Saddam turned to the western side of the Gulf in order to achieve at Kuwaiti expense what he had failed to attain in the previous attempt against his sworn Iranian enemy. He invaded, thus setting off the Second Gulf War (1990–91), but was repulsed by the American coalition, and his dream remained unfulfilled. Therefore – taking into account Iraq's geo-strategic plight in the Gulf – Iraq is bound to try again and again, regardless who is in power, unless two conditions are filled: one, that the rivalry between Revolutionary Iran and Iraq is patched up, to the extent that any Iraqi leader would regard it as settled or that Iran no longer posed a menace to him; and, two, that the regime in Iraq is democratized to an extent that an accountable ruler would be reluctant to launch another round of war against his neighbors. The prospects on both grounds are dimmer than dim.

Experiencing similar concerns to Saddam, fearing that the revolutionary zeal of Iranian Muslims might spill over the Iranian borders into her Muslim Republics of Central Asia, the Soviet Union pre-empted Iran in a strike carried out on Christmas Eve of 1979 against adjoining Afghanistan, where Islamic fundamentalism was believed to be brewing. This time it was a communist power which took on the Muslims of that mountainous central Asian country,[2] where hordes of *Mujahideeen* (jihad fighters) soon assembled; these fighters were based in Peshawar, Pakistan, and trained, armed and financed by the CIA as part of its endeavor to topple the 'Empire of Evil'. Not all *Mujahideen* answered the call, others were being manipulated by the Iranians and had other axes to grind. It took ten years of harsh fighting to wear thin the overextended power of the Soviet Union and to convince her to withdraw in disgrace; something that probably facilitated the demise of the USSR. However, the Soviet retreat foreshadowed two major developments which were to haunt Afghanistan and much of Central Asia, the Muslim world and Great Power politics: the civil war in Afghanistan which ushered in the Taliban regime, and the phenomenon of the *Afghanis*.

The Taliban took over the leadership in Kabul in 1996 at the culmination of the hopeless civil war that for six years – since the evacuation of the Soviets in 1989 – had pitted various *Mujahideen* factions against each other in an effort to takeover the battered capital. This battle involved, as usual in Afghanistan: inter-tribal rivalries (the Pashtun majority against a coalition of Uzbek, Tajik and Hazara minorities); inter-faith controversies (the Sunni majority versus the Shi'ite minority); and contradictory loyalties to outside powers (the Pashtuns were supported by Pakistan; the radical and ruthless Gulbuddnin Hikmatyar was a client of the Iranians; and the forces of Shah Mas'ud, later known as the Northern Alliance, were sponsored by the West, and occasionally also by the Russians). The utter destruction of Kabul, and the impoverishment of the entire country, encouraged the young Pashtun scholars of Kandahar (the Taliban) – who had graduated from Pakistani *Madrasas* (religious schools) and were sustained by them – to launch a sweeping northern expedition to preserve the unity of the country, at the expense of Mas'ud's forces, which continued to resist them on their shrinking turf in the North.

The Taliban takeover, supported by Pakistan, and vastly popular throughout much of the country, was at first seen as a hopeful sign that the country was heading towards unity, stability and reconstruction; however, it transpired that the stringent Islamic puritanism of the new regime – which destroyed any signs of non-Islamic culture, oppressed women, defied the West and its civilization, and enforced an extreme form of Muslim conformism – soon began to lose some of its initial appeal. Moreover, when Bin-Laden's *al-Qa'ida* was expelled from the Sudan, upon American insistence following the disastrous 1998 bombing of American embassies in East Africa, the avowedly anti-Western Taliban accorded it shelter in their country, electing to support what they viewed as confessional integrity and devotion to their faith over any sort of pragmatic submission to American diktat; thus turning themselves into a pariah state.

The other outcome of the first Afghani War was the emergence of the *Afghanis* in inter-Muslim politics. These were the tens of thousands of volunteers from Arab and other Muslim states (mainly Saudis and Egyptians, but also Moroccans, Jordanians, Chechens, etc.), who had been recruited, armed, financed and trained by the USA and its proxies to help defeat the Soviets in Afghanistan. When that war was over, its graduates returned to their countries of origin, battle-hardened, immensely motivated and determined to produce Islamic regimes to replace the illegitimate and corrupt governments already in place. They caused domestic turmoil in Egypt, Algeria, Chechnya, Saudi Arabia and elsewhere, or enlisted in international Islamic endeavors in order to promote fundamentalist

Muslim regimes at home or in other Muslim societies, as well as an enhanced Muslim consciousness among Muslim communities in the West. For example, they were active in the service of Islam during the Bosnian War, and later among the Muslim Albanians in Kosovo and Macedonia. They were also in the Islamikaze training camps in Afghanistan under the Taliban, as well as in Chechnya and elsewhere in the Muslim world.

The most important and lasting international impact of the *Afghanis*, however, has been their enrolment into the *al-Qa'ida*; this was the direct cause and trigger of the second Afghan War, in which the Americans and their allies fought against the Talibans for giving shelter to terrorism, and in order to seize Bin-Laden and his collaborators. What this war has shown – though it is seemingly only remotely linked to original events in Iran – is that the Iranian Revolution, and the attempts to export it, is still alive and kicking. For, though at odds with Bin-Laden and the Talibans, the Iranians look with satisfaction on the 60 *al-Qa'ida* bases that Bin-Laden has succeeded in establishing world-wide, on all five continents, to fight the daily nitty-gritty war of reviving Islamic consciousness among Muslim communities everywhere, and to then move on to the next stage: action against their host countries. As has been evinced in this war, the *Afghanis* are the hard core of the fighters of *al-Qa'ida*, and its most devoted missionaries. These agitators have proved to the world that while Muslim governments have submitted to American pressures and threats, and in appearance have joined the American 'coalition' – or at least have given it their blessing or refrained from acting openly against it – the populace, media and public opinion in those countries have remained, to a great extent, pro-Bin-Laden.

THE GLOBALIZATION OF ISLAMIC TERRORISM

Until 11 September, and in spite of the occasional disclosure of the networks of international Islamic terrorism, the international community usually treated these revelations as 'exaggerations' or misplaced 'accusations', or as a figment of the imagination of their authors. Thus, when American investigative journalist, Steve Emerson, produced his one-hour television documentary about 'Jihad in America', showing the intensity of the Islamists' commitment among the Muslim immigrant communities in America –

including that in New Jersey which sheltered Sheikh Abdul-Rahman, the mastermind behind the first attempt against the Twin Towers – public opinion remained rather indifferent. Apparently, people react to actual disasters, not to potential dangers, however great they are. Emerson and other writers also described in detail the training camps of these terrorists in Afghanistan, and warned against the front 'charitable organizations' which spread all over the USA and collected money from innocent and unsuspecting common Americans for the 'orphans' or 'victims of aggression' in the Middle East, while in fact they used the funds for terrorist organizations. But all those disclosures did not convince the Clinton Administration to take crucial measures against these organizations, which, if taken in time, would have pre-empted many of the strictures of today. The half-hearted and toothless actions adopted then by American governments and services in fact facilitated the continuation of the terrorists' blooming on American soil; and the USA would, a few years later, become the victim of its own liberal and unmindful policies.

Thus, although there is nothing new in the globalization of Islamic terrorist activity, since it was initiated, activated and acknowledged by the terrorists themselves, it was the West, due to shortsighted policies, which refused to take cognizance of the situation as it was. This process of globalization took place over the 1980s and 1990s along three parallel but not unrelated courses: the Terrorist International, sponsored by the Iranian Revolution; the *Afghanis*, who became its most zealous agents; and, lately, *al-Qa'ida*, comprised of fanatic Sunnis, who disagreed with their Shi'ite competitors over the leadership of the world Muslim Revolution. In fact, *al-Qa'ida*, as well as the *Afghanis*, the main actors in Islamic terrorism internationally, had originally chosen to work from Turabi's Sudan – the first bastion of fundamentalist Sunni Islam in the 1980s – and then turned to Afghanistan when they were ejected from the Sudan. However, while the *Afghanis* were distributed all over the Islamic world, according to their nations of origin, *al-Qa'ida* was concerned from the start with building international networks funded by Bin-Laden's private fortune and money collected from other Muslim donors.

Iran, as the first agent of globalization, established the Hizbullah in Lebanon and used it as its international arm of terror, notably against Jewish and Israeli targets in Buenos Aires and London in the early 1990s, but most consistently on the Israeli–Lebanese border. As a result, the Israeli government was compelled by public opinion to undertake an early, unnecessary and perhaps fateful withdrawal which has led to, among other things, the *al-Aqsa* Intifada on the West Bank and Gaza, where the Lebanese model has been emulated by the Palestinians. Iran has also meddled in the re-Islamization of the Balkans (first Bosnia, then Kosovo, and now Macedonia), and hosted the annual co-ordinating meeting of all Islamic terrorist organizations in Teheran.

The *Afghanis* have lent another international aspect to Islamic terrorism, inasmuch as they have ensured the presence of their own combatants in practically all of the Islamic countries; these have not only stirred unrest in their own countries in attempts to topple their regimes, but also contributed to the rise of militant Islam in areas such as the Balkans, the Caucasus, Central Asia and Western countries; which, in turn, has produced the wave of terror we have been witnessing. The latest manifestation of globalization has been best expressed by the 60-odd *al-Qa'ida* bases found across the world, all of Bin-Laden's doing. *Al-Qa'ida* (literally 'The Base') refers not only physically to the hub of International Islamic terrorism, based in Afghanistan until new centers emerge, but also metaphorically to the core of the idea of Islamic revolution and confrontation with the West; this revolution will spread, conquer the world and rid it of Western–Israeli corruption. Hence, the inherent relationship between the two, and the usual Muslim rhetoric which invariably lumps them together.

The destruction of *al-Qa'ida* by the USA, has so far been confined to Afghanistan; to set out against all its 60 bases, especially as long as Bin-Laden and his operatives are alive, would neither be a quick nor a totally feasible endeavor. The operation's survival would then depend on American determination to pursue it world-wide, even as the cracks in the already tenuous pro-American coalition grow wider as the USA confronts Arab (for example, Iraq, Lebanon, Syria, Libya, Sudan, the PA or the Yemen) or other Islamic countries (such as Iran and Somalia).

CONCLUSION

The West and Israel have a major dilemma when fighting international Islamic terrorism: they cannot succeed world-wide unless they ally themselves with regimes in countries with bases that harbor terrorism, or that are in close proximity to those bases. However, these regimes are for the most part illegitimate inasmuch as they are autocratic, anti-democratic and at variance with their populace, which has been nurtured by anti-Western and anti-Israeli rhetoric and incitement over the years. What is the West to do? Attack the terrorists over the heads of the governments that ostensibly ally themselves with the West if they prove unwilling or unable to eliminate terror themselves (for example, Pakistan in Kashmir, Lebanon and Syria with the Hizbullah, or the Palestinian Authority with Hamas)? It is always tricky to prove whether governments that make fiery speeches against terrorism also do, or do not do, something to annihilate it. Even the formula of '100 per cent effort' which falls far short of the '100 per cent results' wording is not measurable.

Another aspect of this issue is the double game whereby the West promotes democracy, but as soon as Islam comes to the top as in Iran, Algeria, the Sudan or Afghanistan due to popular support, or makes gains as in Jordan, Saudi Arabia or the Palestinian Authority, it is the West which rushes head-on to support the illegitimate anti-Islamic governments in place and to throw in its fate with them (see Pakistan, Algeria and to an extent Saudi Arabia, to name only a few), thus disregarding popular sentiment. Maybe, instead of taking sides between fundamentalists and their oppressors, the West should encourage the democratic process and accept its consequences. If the current autocrats should win, though this is difficult to envisage, they will achieve legitimacy and perhaps become less autocratic; if the fundamentalists should win, then, as in Iran and in Sudan, the constraints of government might moderate them in the long run despite their commitment to Islamic legitimacy. It is noteworthy that this strategy did not work in Afghanistan, which elected Islamic puritanical extremism and sheltered terrorism. But then, at the very least, the West would know that it sets out to punish not only the leaders who harbor terrorism but the whole nation which has leant them legitimacy and support.

NOTES

1. The common term 'suicide bombers' is a misnomer; and this mode of terrorism is not unique to Islam, the Japanese Kamikaze at the end of the Pacific War (1944–45) had acted likewise. Hence, I have coined the phrase 'Islamikaze'.
2. Afghanistan has been invaded on a number of occasions over the centuries.

PART 1

Commitments, Ideologies
and
Incitement

1. Arafat's Peace*

When town after town on the West Bank and Gaza passed into
Palestinian Authority (PA) hands following the Oslo II Agreement
(1995) that was designed to facilitate the transition from Israeli
occupation to Palestinian self-rule, Yasser Arafat, president of the
PA, began to manifest some surprising traits in his statesmanship.
Most notable for someone viewed as a secular leader is his
profound Islamic commitment, which harks back to his
membership in the Muslim Brethren in Egypt during his formative
years. The issue of Islam is of particular interest, due to Arafat's
attempts to juggle between new-found pragmatism as a statesman
(who has, to all appearances, chosen the road of political settlement
with Israel, at least prior to the resumption of the Intifada in the fall
of 2000), and his innate propensity for doctrinal and vindictive
rhetoric. Arafat must strike a balance between his proclaimed
obligation to compromise – requiring him to set aside some of his
long-held Islamic convictions which had helped him mobilize
Palestinian public opinion behind him – and his need to placate his
most dangerous opposition, namely, Hamas[1] and the Islamic Jihad
(holy war), which refuse to shed the very same convictions Arafat
once held, continuing instead to embrace and profess them openly.

This essay will examine whether Arafat is in fact bound by one
particular set of principles (with the other being merely tactical
rhetoric), and whether he espouses any particular ideology only
when it appears to him at a particular time to best reflect his and his
people's interest. In other words, is there a way to read between the
lines of his ambiguous rhetoric and statements to gauge 'the real
Arafat'? Can one predict Palestine Liberation Organization (PLO)
and Palestinian policies based on Arafat's patently unclear
messages laced with double meanings?

*Originally published as, 'From Oslo to Bethlehem: Arafat's Islamic Message', *Journal of
Church and State*, 43, 3 (2001), pp.423–45.

THE DOUBLE-TALK OF REDEMPTION

True to his personal rhetorical tradition, Arafat pursued his Islamic discourse with eagerly receptive audiences when he oversaw the process of retrieving from Israel the West Bank towns of Jenin, Tulkarem, Qalqilya, Bethlehem and Ramallah in late 1995 and early 1996. In the process another town, Nablus, the hub of Palestinian nationalism in the West Bank, became the focus of an anti-Israeli explosion of sentiment associated with Arafat's rhetoric of redemption. After all, 'Nablus oblige', one might say.

The abandonment by Israel of Palestinian cities to Arafat's fledgling rule was traumatic to both parties, though it had something equally redemptive about it: it gave vent to all the tensions that had accumulated during 28 years of Israel's unwelcome domination. It created at the same time an ambiance of uncertainty, borne of the quasi-messianic expectation that Palestinian rule would inaugurate a new era of justice and plenty, coupled with the realization that existing social, political, and economic difficulties might seriously hamper this exciting experiment. One thing was certain: the historical scope and import of these momentous events. To rise to the occasion, Arafat had to cater to the predominant mood of excitement and hope by injecting into his speeches in practically all those cities the same redemptory themes: liberty, independence, Jerusalem as the capital, the continuation of jihad, struggle to victory.

Most of these themes are imbued with Islamic symbols and history. They are shrouded in an aura of myth, especially when Arafat himself posed, or came to be seen, as the Messiah-redeemer or *Mahdi* who would inaugurate this new era. Indeed, in every case, when traveling to the cities in question, Palestinian crowds awaiting him clamored cries of ecstasy upon seeing his helicopter approaching to land. Loudspeakers announced the coming of the chairman, and urged the masses to 'swear allegiance' to the president. In Bethlehem, where Arafat's inaugural visit coincided with Christmas celebrations, the entire landing ceremony, reviewing of the guard of honor, and world-wide broadcast of Christmas, were all announced over the Voice of Palestine radio and television stations as if they were all part of one great sequence.

Arafat's oratory in general leaves much to be desired. However, his habit of using repetitious phrases, easily-remembered slogans, a colloquial style of speech and popular imagery do touch deep chords in the souls of his audiences; he succeeds in creating an intimate discourse with them. He always addresses the masses that encounter him in personal terms, such as 'Brothers', 'Sisters', 'Beloved members of the family', 'Members of my tribe', etc.[2] Once he has introduced himself to his audience, he invariably invokes Jerusalem as a powerful unifying and mobilizing symbol. In every case, he lists each of the towns and villages so far 'liberated', and vows to 'march into Jerusalem' or to 'pray in Jerusalem' at the end of the peace process. He refers to Jerusalem as 'al-Quds a-Sharif' (Jerusalem the Noble), or 'al-Quds al-'arabiyya' (Arab Jerusalem), the former signifying 'all of Jerusalem' in Arab and Arafat's parlance, the latter designating East Jerusalem (the part of the city claimed by the Palestinians as their capital). Arafat also invokes the sacredness of the land. In Bethlehem, Arafat referred to 'our blessed land' that witnessed the birth of 'our Palestinian Messiah, Blessed be His Memory'. Thus, Arafat connects 'his' Palestine to the 'blessed land' with its messianic message, and then widens the scope of his Islamic commitment to Palestine to embrace Christianity as well, for the Christian Arabs of Palestine are as Palestinian as its Muslims, since Christ Himself was Palestinian. This ecumenical message, which makes Islam and Christianity (to the exclusion of Judaism) the twin divine revelations of Palestine, legitimizes Arafat as the curator and protector of the Holy Places of both faiths. It turns the PLO and its head into the representative and partner of world Christianity, as well as world Islam in Holy Jerusalem. Thus Arafat tries to portray himself as a better, and more universally accepted, ruler of the city than the Israelis.

Nothing epitomized this new garb donned by Arafat better than the well-publicized and widely reported visit by his wife Suha (a former Christian who converted to Islam as a prerequisite to their marriage) to the Church of Nativity with her newborn daughter, as if to proclaim that his Islam and her Christianity were happily wed together and jointly perpetuated in the persona of little Zahwa. Of course, Arafat would not admit to this union of the two great religions on unequal terms: his wife had to convert, after all, while he did not. Their daughter is Muslim, not Christian, because she was born of a Muslim father. But his *beau geste* of extending his loving care to Christianity in Palestine immediately attracted the interpretation that he coveted and had probably intended: the Greek-Orthodox Patriarch of Jerusalem declared to a delighted Arafat on that occasion, 'Here is the successor of Sophronius welcoming the successor of 'Umar ibn al-Khattab.' No one present or watching on television could miss the parallel. Reference was made, of course, to the submission of the Byzantine Patriach of Jerusalem, Sophronius, in AD 638 to the second Caliph of Islam, 'Umar ibn al-Khattab (634–644), who conquered Jerusalem for Islam and put an end to many centuries of Christian rule. Until the Crusaders established in 1099 the Christian kingdom of Jerusalem, the city was to remain, uninterruptedly, part and parcel of *Dar al Islam*, the universal Pax Islamica. This modern-day declaration of the patriarch was so melodious to Arafat's ear that he ordered all his media to publish it in their headlines. The public learned of his command only when an ill-advised and independent-minded journalist (the night editor of the daily *Al-Quds*, Mahir al-'Alami) refused to comply, and soon found himself arrested and interrogated in the dark basements of Jibril Rajub's security apparatus in Jericho.[3] Arafat's eagerness to widely publicize the patriarch's sycophancy did not stem from his intention to humiliate the latter, nor only because he was pleased by the flattering comparison with the Great Caliph 'Umar, but because such a statement confirmed his newly acquired, glamorous image as the new 'liberator' of Jerusalem.

Thus, Arafat was placed as the latest link in the chain of great Islamic liberators, which to date includes 'Umar as well as Saladin, who recaptured Jerusalem in 1187 and put an end to Crusader rule there. If one bears in mind the oft-made comparison in Arab and Islamic circles between the medieval Crusader State and contemporary Israel, one necessarily comes to the conclusion that exactly as 'Umar had occupied Jerusalem by peaceful means (namely, the surrender of the Christians), and Saladin by force (by the conquest of the city and the eviction or massacre of its inhabitants), so will Arafat now repeat that feat either by accepting the surrender of at least East Jerusalem by the Israelis, or by pressing his call for jihad in order to retrieve all of it. Many Palestinian circles (especially Muslim fundamentalists[4]) take delight in this parallel and are quick to draw conclusions from it. 'Umar and Saladin had been accepted as the legitimate rulers of Jerusalem following the oath of allegiance (*bay'a*) accorded them by the crowds. Now, as the loudspeakers were enjoining the populace to deliver the oath of allegiance to the president, the parallel became neat, complete, and inescapable. History had come full circle.

This outpouring of religiosity and Islamic symbolism by Arafat is consistent not only with his many speeches from Johannesburg to

Gaza, in which Jerusalem, jihad and other Islamic symbols have been repeatedly invoked, but also with Palestinian nationalist antecedents where Islam has played a prominent role. Indeed, since the 1920s, the Palestinian national movement has been headed by a religious leader, the Mufti of Jerusalem, Haj Amin al-Husseini (similar to Makarios, Archbishop of the Greek-Orthodox in Cyprus, or Bishop Muzurewa in Rhodesia). As such, it relied upon religious themes to shape the opposition to British rule and to Zionism. Moreover, in the 1930s, Izz a-Din al-Qassam, a Syrian Muslim who settled in Haifa, undertook extensive religious, political and educational activities in northern Palestine that soon lent prominence to his leadership. He then founded a militant group, the Black Hand, as an instrument of armed struggle against both British imperialism and Jewish Zionism. Al-Qassam called openly for jihad against both until the British killed him in battle in 1935.

During the Palestinian Revolt (1936–39), the Muslim Brethren, based in Egypt, established a number of lodges in Palestine that in later years grew into a fully-fledged network of the Brotherhood. The Muslim Brothers' activities later developed into a two-pronged activism (like al-Qassam's antecedent): struggle against British occupation and the Zionist menace. The 1948 War between Israel and the Arabs split the Palestinian–Arab population into an Israeli-ruled minority and a Jordanian-governed and Egyptian-governed majority on the West Bank and in Gaza respectively, where the Muslim Brothers continued to swell their ranks in spite of their frequent clashes with the authorities there. The occupation by Israel of the West Bank and Gaza in the 1967 War again brought the entire Palestinian population west of the Jordan River under Israeli rule. Paradoxically, the Muslim movements could thrive under Israeli rule, since it allowed them leeway in their overt activities so long as they did not contravene the law.

Conversely, Israel's penetration into the social, political and economic realms of life of Palestinians contributed to the destruction of the last vestiges of their old hierarchies and loyalties, and hastened their modernization, much to the outrage (and detriment) of Muslim fundamentalists who sensed that Israel was undermining their traditional Islamic society and turning it away from Islam. The seeds of a renewed open conflict between the fundamentalists and the Israelis were thus sown in the already fertile ground of the anti-Israeli sentiment prepared by the PLO and Palestinian nationalists who had also rejected Israeli rule over them for secular reasons. Hence, the eruption during the Intifada of Hamas, which was galvanized into a zealous Islamic group (by definition) encompassing most Islamic fundamentalist currents of the day. It is worth noting, however, that latter-day fundamentalist groups did not monopolize these elements of Islam. Even mainstream Palestinian nationalism, like most local forms of Arab nationalism, have made use of Islam to characterize enemies, to imply modes of action against them, and to define the nature of the Palestinian community and its struggle, thus linking key religious and secular concepts.[5]

For example, jihad is linked with the armed struggle of the PLO – the commitment to fight imperialism linked with the fight against Zionism (itself considered to be an extension of imperialism). Both concepts are joined together in a contemporary rendition of the first historical armed entry of the West into the Muslim world since the Crusaders. When the PLO refers to its casualties as *shahada* (martyrs), and to its guerrillas as *fedayeen* (self-sacrificers), it implies the redemption (in the Muslim sense of the concept) to be won from dying for one's homeland.[6] Similarly, the modern struggle against Jews, Zionists and Israelis (terms often used interchangeably) harks back to the old Muslim–Jewish enmity during the time of the Prophet. Thus, when Arafat made the pilgrimage to Mecca in 1978, he vowed to liberate Palestine, including Jerusalem, from Israeli occupation. Even the secular document of the Palestinian Charter (adopted in 1964 and amended in 1968) is interspersed with concepts that can be seen as Islamic, such as sacrifice, struggle and armed struggle; Article 16 itself refers to the issue of Palestine as a holy land with religious sites. At the Algiers Conference at which the Palestinians declared their independence (15 November 1988), Arafat referred to Jerusalem as a capital city, and he has been repeating that statement ever since.

PLO manipulation of Islamic symbols should be no surprise, for Islam is too important to Palestinian culture to ignore. However, while the PLO, and now the PA, handles Islam by controlling it, the fundamentalists are so passionate and so impatient that they would turn Islam into a way of life, thus challenging Arafat's secularism. So long as Arafat was struggling, like the fundamentalists, to achieve a state, he could afford to indulge in Islamic, as well as nationalistic, rhetoric, in order to mobilize the masses behind him. Indeed, Bernard Lewis has shown that Arafat's *nom de guerre* (Abu

Ammar), as well as his rhetoric ('Bismillah', 'jihad', etc.) has Islamic connotations. So too, have the names of the Palestine Liberation Army's regiments: al-Aqsa (refers to the mosque in Jerusalem), Hittin (Saladin's victory over the Crusaders), Ein Jalut (victory against the Mongol invasion), etc.[7] In other words, the profuse usage of Islam by Arafat has so compellingly depicted him as an Islamic leader – and not just a national leader – that he cannot disengage from that image in the process of achieving autonomy and statehood.

HAMAS CHALLENGE

During the months of negotiations leading to the Oslo Accords of September 1993, Arafat was remarkably reticent in his Islamic utterances, presumably because he had set out to attain a political-quantitative agreement based on compromise and ambiguity which otherwise might have evaded him had he insisted on the qualitative and unbending rhetoric of Islam. On the contrary, he spoke about recognition of Israel, not denial of her rights; of the end to war and violence, not of jihad, struggle and bloodshed; of negotiations and good intentions, not of endless *shahada'* and sacrifice. But no sooner had the agreement been signed than Arafat was attacked by groups of his own people for having abandoned his Islamic message and relinquishing the Islamic consensus that had previously united most Palestinians. Moreover, the polarization between Arafat and his opponents from Hamas and the Islamic Jihad grew so acute, and the tensions between them escalated so rapidly, that it was seen as only a matter of time before an all-out civil war erupted.

The challenge posed by Hamas to Arafat was no mere rebellion against his authority by an insignificant faction of the Palestinians. Rather, it was a viable and popular alternative offered to the Palestinian public that was just emerging from the Intifada. During that uprising against Israel, which tore apart the West Bank and Gaza from 1987, Hamas had carved for itself an important following in the Palestinian streets, precisely by being more demanding, violent and unbending than the 'National Leadership' sponsored by the PLO. And they achieved great success, not only in fighting the Israelis and inflicting heavy casualties on them, but also in building a network of welfare and religious educational institutions, in fighting crime, corruption and drugs, and in filling the vacuum of authority left behind by the withdrawing Israelis. What is more, in many of the Palestinian professional organizations (doctors, lawyers, accountants, teachers, etc.), as well as in student bodies in the universities of the West Bank and Gaza, all of which held elections even at the height of the Intifada, Hamas candidates often scored more highly than PLO members, thereby enhancing the prestige of the movement among intellectuals.[8]

The core of the Hamas program[9] poses no less of an ideological threat to the PLO political view than the challenge of the Muslim militants to Arafat's constituency. For while the post-Oslo PLO is committed, on record, to negotiate and to shun violence, Hamas, like other Muslim fundamentalists, holds an unbending view that only jihad – to liberate all of Palestine – will ensure the victory of Allah. They have also vowed that the land must be cleansed from the viciousness and impurity of its occupiers – the Israelis – since only under Islamic rule is there any possibility for other faiths to coexist. They claim that when Islam does not prevail, then bigotry, hatred, controversy, corruption, oppression, war and bloodshed follow, as evidenced by the existence of Israel. Israel is hated as an occupier who, due to its Jewish constituency (described as 'the scum of the earth'), also concocts plots to take over the world and corrupts societies from within. Hence the Muslim obligation, following the model of the Prophet, to fight the Israelis and kill them wherever they can be found, or at least ban them from Islamic lands if they refuse to submit to its beneficent hegemony.

Domestically, Hamas strives to establish an Islamic entity as part of the Islamic world that must be governed by the Caliphate. In such a state, 'Allah is the ultimate goal, the Koran its constitution, jihad its means, death for the cause of Allah its sublimest aspiration.'[10] Such a state is imperative because Allah had granted Palestine to His elected nation, the Muslims, as *waqf* (a holy endowment) until the end of all days. Therefore, Muslims cannot negotiate it away or strike any compromise over it, and any bilateral negotiation or international conference geared to that end is but a 'waste of time'. The only possible solution then is a Pax Islamica in which Islam reigns supreme and the members of the other faiths bow their heads in obedience to the generous provisions of the *shari'a* law. Jihad, the means of attaining such a state, ought not to remain a collective duty (*fard kifaya*), which would not be binding on every individual once the Muslim community as a whole has discharged it; quite the contrary, because the 'House of Islam' is aflame, it becomes incumbent upon every individual Muslim to extinguish the fire with his own bucket of water, namely, to fight jihad as a personally binding duty (*fard 'ayn*).

With such a radically different program from that of the official PLO, and in view of Arafat's inability to prove that his own version of national salvation is operative and effective, the temptation arose among Muslim militants to try the fundamentalist alternative. Success breeds success: after the Islamic Revolution in Iran and the Sudan, and its near-takeover in Algeria and Afghanistan, the winds blew ever stronger in the Hamas sails. Arafat, conscious of the challenge, tried on various occasions to harness Hamas to the PLO, and of late has attempted to press them to join the system by offering them participation in the 1996 elections for the Palestinian Legislative Council. However, exactly as they had rejected his earlier proposal to join the PLO, on the grounds that he was not allocating them sufficient seats in the Palestinian National Council commensurate with their real strength, they have now opposed the elections, claiming that participation would imply acquiescence in the Oslo Process, which they had rejected outright.

And so, the Hamas challenge continues to irritate Arafat and to pose a mortal danger to him in more ways than one: not only can Hamas mount lethal attacks on Israel, which would force her to retaliate and wreck the Oslo Process, but if they became popular enough (thanks to their stand against Israel), they may even dislodge Arafat and his PA. Indeed, in places like universities, Muslim militants have coalesced with Habash's Popular Front and Hawatmeh's Democratic Front to win over a majority of the student body opposed to Oslo and to Arafat's policies. Arafat, either eager not to be overtaken on the right by the Islamists, or to return to his genuine self, has taken over the fundamentalists' vocabulary and jargon. True, Arafat does not openly resort to the same overtly anti-Semitic language used by Hamas and other Muslim fundamentalist groups[11] (perhaps for fear of losing his Western support), but his militant Islamic message is no less acute and history-laden.

THE HUDAYBIYYA MODEL

Merely six months after the fanfare surrounding the signature of the Oslo Accords of September 1993, Arafat was on a visit to Johannesburg, South Africa, for the inauguration of President Nelson Mandela, his longstanding friend. Quite incidentally, and confident of the privacy and intimacy required for discourse with his local fellow Muslims gathered in the mosque of Johannesburg, he shared with them his thinking about the peace process that he had inaugurated with Israel, and entreated them to join jihad in order to recover Jerusalem. He also compared the Oslo Agreements to the Hudaybiyya Treaty concluded by the Prophet of Islam. When Arafat's words became known in the spring of 1994 with the release of a tape recorded by a reporter who attended that gathering incognito, a major storm swept Israel, with a part of its people feeling they had been duped at Oslo. As expected, the proponents of the Accords denigrated Arafat's words as insignificant rhetoric, while opponents seized them as 'proof' of his double-talk. Arafat himself, visibly shaken by the scandal that his words (meant to be uttered discreetly) had prompted once made public, explained via aids that his jihad meant 'peaceful means', and that he continued to be bound by the agreement made in Oslo.

However, careful observers in Israel and elsewhere continued to monitor his public addresses in order to determine whether his Johannesburg speech was a slip of the tongue, or part of a recurring pattern indicative of his genuine thinking.[12] This exercise has revealed that even when we do not know what Arafat says in the privacy of his councils, there is enough in his public parlance to suggest a recurring duplicity in his speeches in the Gaza Islamic College, climaxing in Bethlehem.

This is how Arafat was introduced on Palestine Television during a ceremony at Gaza's al-Azhar University on the day celebrating the *Mi'raj*:[13]

> This is the Commander, this is the man,
> His face is like a bright sunny day …
> May Allah grant him noble qualities of manhood …
> The leader of this nation, whom Allah watches over …
> Allah! Allah! Allah!
> Let us see Abu Ammar lead us to jihad … [14]
> In Jerusalem, in al-Aqsa we shall meet … [15]

And then came Arafat's turn to speak:

> My brethren, we are a sacrificing and fighting nation ... A Jerusalem *hadith* says: A group within my nation cling to my Faith and fight their enemies ... They cannot be harmed and they will win, with Allah's help. The Messenger of God asked, 'Who are they?' He answered, 'In Jerusalem ... in Jerusalem and its environs ... They stand at the forefront until Judgement Day ...'
>
> We are at the forefront, fighters at the forefront ... I said I saw a tunnel, and at the end of the tunnel are the walls of Jerusalem, with its mosques and churches ...
>
> And today, on the day Muhammad ascended to Heaven, we say: Blessed is he who goes forth from the mosque of Mecca to al-Aqsa.[16] We will enter the mosque and pray there, with Allah's help. Allah does not break his promise.
>
> Oh Brethren, the battle is long, very long and harsh ... The Palestinian people have always sacrificed ... generation after generation. We are at a war of 100 years ... a war in all spheres: political, military, a war of history and culture, of perseverance and survival, since the first Zionist Congress in Basel ...
>
> When the Prophet made peace with the tribe of Quraysh [at Hudaybiyya], 'Umar ibn-al-Khattab said: 'Stop! Had we known when we acclaimed you as Allah's Messenger, we would never have fought for you.'
>
> 'Umar even called it the 'despised peace' ... Our history is our best teacher, and no nation can be detached from its history ... We are a direct continuation of that nation and this land ... Bless you! Bless your struggle and your jihad on this land ... We shall press on to Jerusalem, capital of the state of Palestine ... This revolution began on 1 January 1965.[17]
>
> Fighters in this revolution ... are the sons of Izz a-Din al-Qassam ... [18] We renew our oath to the martyrs, and our oath of loyalty to Jerusalem, capital of our land in Palestine ... In the name of Allah the Merciful, we will redeem the downtrodden of the earth and make them leaders and heirs, and we will give them the land. We will bring victory to our Messengers and to the Believers in this world and the next, thus said the Lord.

Delirious crowds shouted: 'We shall give our blood and souls for you, Palestine!' Arafat continues:

I say that all of us are made for martyrdom. Hence, I say to all the martyrs who have died, on behalf of the martyrs who still live ... that we stand by our oath to pursue [the battle] ... Be patient, our men and women prisoners, be patient, Ahmad Yasin ... [19]

The same symbolism and vocabulary were repeated by Arafat in various gatherings in Gaza and elsewhere, culminating in the Christmas ceremony at the closure of 1995 in Bethlehem. Taken together with, and corroborating what had been said in Johannesburg, the following patterns emerge in his addresses:

1. Arafat purports to abide by the precedent set by the Prophet Muhammad in making the peace of Hudaybiyya ('History is our best teacher'). This means that expedient peace can be made with enemies, which can be broken when circumstances so warrant.
2. The fact that 'Umar had dubbed this peace 'despicable', even when sanctioned by the Prophet himself, could justify *a priori* its breach, again when circumstances justify.
3. Arafat learned from the experience of Hamas successes that blood-and-sweat discourses, with promises of protracted struggles and endless sacrifices, are paradoxically much more soothing, appealing and credible to the masses than empty pledges of a rosy life and easy victories. Harsh language not only justifies the martyrs of the past in this 100-year-war: it also mobilizes and encourages the new generation of *shahada'*. The Islamic calls for jihad (and the certitude of divine retribution as a result) were found by Arafat to be more cajoling to the hearts of the populace, and he invoked them repeatedly.
4. Jerusalem is the ultimate prize, the jewel in the crown of the Holy Land. It is the prime rallying point for Muslims from Johannesburg to Gaza. For Arafat, Jerusalem is primarily Islamic and secondarily Christian (Arafat saw in his dreams mosques and churches, not synagogues). This allows Arafat to play the role of 'Umar, the Muslim leader and savior, relegating the patriarchs of Jerusalem and the submissive Christian community to the role played by Sophronius and the Byzantines.
5. All Palestinians are potential martyrs (that is, likely participants in the coveted jihad of liberation) and, since all are likely to swell

his ranks, Arafat calls upon them to be patient. The head of Hamas, Ahmed Yasin (who had been lingering in an Israeli prison), is also one of those fighters-martyrs within the ranks, nominally under the one leader: Arafat himself. Hamas and PLO have become one.

The Prophet, 'Umar, jihad, martyrs, Jerusalem, the oath of allegiance: how do they all connect within Arafat's imagery? In order to understand the connection, the key concepts are Hudaybiyya, jihad and Jerusalem, which have become familiar words in every Palestinian household since Oslo, especially after the speeches in Johannesburg, Gaza and Bethlehem. Fresh from Oslo, Arafat in Johannesburg was not short of words had he wished to carry a message of peace to his Muslim audience or to convince them of his peaceful intentions towards Israel. He could have alluded to the many parallels in history, of sworn enemies who ultimately compromised and made peace. Instead, he delivered a martial speech calling for jihad, similar to the speeches reserved for Palestinian ears when urging his audiences to fight and make sacrifices. And he invoked Hudaybiyya and the other key concepts even before any substantial rift had occurred with the Israelis regarding the interpretation of Oslo or its implementation.

Why does Arafat need to stress the Hudaybiyya model? As reconstructed by eminent scholars specializing in early Islam,[20] the Hudaybiyya story unfolded in AD 628 when the Prophet of Islam, already solidly based in Medina, ordered his followers to the sanctuary of Mecca, which had become the center of Islamic worship. However, at Hudaybiyya on the approaches to Mecca, the Quraysh tribe (originally the Prophet's own) prevented the Muslims from entering the city. An agreement was negotiated and implemented, allowing the Muslims to come to Mecca the next year. The following year in 630, the Prophet, with his supporters, sought to conquer the city using, as a *casus belli*, the violation by the Quraysh of one of the terms of the treaty of Hudaybiyya (one which provided not only that the parties should refrain from battle during the coming ten years but also that no client tribes of either party should attack the other's). The conquest of Mecca (called *al-fath* in Islamic tradition) involved occupation of the city as well as taking control of the Ka'ba shrine,[21] which became the central sanctuary of Islam.

While there are many unanswered questions regarding this

event, the events at Hudaybiyya have become a model for generations of Muslims and the usage (sometimes manipulation) of the model by Muslim leaders – religious and political – suggests the resilience of that precedent when brokering peace with the enemy. Sadat of Egypt needed to legitimize his peace with Israel in 1979 through the Mufti of Al-Azhar, who drew the Hudaybiyya parallel.[22] Not only Arafat but others have also alluded to Hudaybiyya; for example, the Saudi Mufti was also quoted as justifying Oslo on the same grounds.

However, of greatest interest is the application given by Arafat and others of the various aspects of Hudaybiyya to modern-day conditions, such as the negotiations leading to that treaty; the significance of the agreement *per se*; parallel identification of today's parties with the Prophet who signed the original treaty, 'Umar who opposed it, and the opponents with whom it was signed, then Quraysh, now Israel; and the consequences of the treaty then and now. The question of Hudaybiyya's application and consequences is of great importance because of the various existing interpretations given to everything relating to the Prophet, including his Hudaybiyya venture. For example, Islamic tradition regards the Prophet as the most accomplished of men who could do no wrong, therefore his deeds and sayings ought to be followed to the letter, almost in blind emulation. Was 'Umar, another highly adored man in Islam, wrong then when he opposed the treaty? If so, why does Arafat wish so much to be cast in his image? Or perhaps he too opposed Oslo and signed it for tactical reasons that escaped the scrutiny of his interlocutors? These are pertinent questions indeed!

When the Prophet and his 700 followers were militarily stalemated at Hudaybiyya, the gateway to Mecca, they tried to convey to the Quraysh that they had come only to pray at the sanctuary. When the Meccans sent a delegation to negotiate, its head reportedly denigrated the Muslim army and immediately determined that the Muslims would not be allowed to go to the sanctuary that year, apparently for fear of losing face with the rest of the tribes of Arabia if they should yield to Muslim military pressure. They also probably suspected that the ultimate goal of Muhammad was military conquest of his native city, which indeed he moved to do eight years before expiration of the ten-year non-aggression Treaty of Hudaybiyya.

In Hudaybiyya, the Prophet did not offer any tough bargaining. On the contrary, 'he made concessions which related to the very essence of his prophetic mission.'[23] For example, he omitted the *basmal* (the ritual mentioning of the name of Allah in addresses and writings) from the text of the Treaty at the Quraysh's insistence. He also consented to return to Mecca any of the Quraysh members who would join the Prophet's faith. As a *quid pro quo*, Muhammad won recognition from the Quraysh and Mecca that his community at Medina was their equal.[24] Moreover, the Prophet was keen to avoid battle on two fronts (against the Jews of Khaybar on the one hand, the Quraysh of Mecca on the other) for fear of exposing Medina to the onslaught of the one from his rear if he attacked the other in full force. Therefore, he had to make those bitter concessions as a matter of expediency until such time as he could abrogate those concessions 'for the benefit of Muslims' (as indeed they proved to be).[25]

The Prophet had first to secure his Meccan flank when he attacked Khaybar. Once Khaybar was eliminated he could then turn against the Quraysh in Mecca. The Meccans, who had signed an alliance with the Jews of Khaybar, found themselves bound by two contradictory pacts: to run to their allies' aid if attacked by Muslims, as against their new commitment to lay down their arms and avoid hostilities for the next ten years. Then the Prophet turned against Khaybar under the protection of his treaty with the Quraysh, apparently impelled by his reckoning that, in view of Jewish and Meccan sympathies towards Persia, the Sassanid defeat in February AD 628 at the hands of Emperor Heraclius had finally tilted the balance in the Muslims' favor. Hence his calculation that the time was opportune to move against Khaybar and, in the meantime, to lull the Meccans with his seemingly conciliatory stance in Hudaybiyya.[26] The destination of Khaybar was also the compensation granted by the Prophet to his followers (such as 'Umar) who had been incensed by the Prophet's concessions in Hudaybiyya and who then found consolation in massacring, enslaving and pillaging the Jews of that imposing oasis.

In AD 630, the Prophet took Mecca and its sanctuary by assault. That conquest was consecrated by Islamic tradition as *al-fath*, literally the opening (that is, its opening to its new conquerors). While this was the *al-fath, par excellence*, all the later conquests of Islam in the Middle East were known as *futuh* (the plural of *fath*). Another derivative connected with this is the *miftah* (key) obtained by the Prophet from the guardian of the Ka'ba whom he then ordered to open (*fatah*) the shrine. Some theories connect the *fath* with the *opening* of the sanctuary rather than with the conquest itself, while others attribute the title of the *al-fath* to the Hudaybiyya expedition prior to the conquest of Mecca on the authority of 'Umar, who had reportedly said that 'there was no greater *fath* than Hudaybiyya.'

This *fath* is, in turn, connected to the oath of allegiance (the *bay'a*) given to the Prophet by his followers 'under the tree' at Hudaybiyya. There, the Prophet is reported to have had a vision in which he entered the sanctuary with his head shaved, opened it with the key, and then went to Arafa to perform rituals with the worshippers. This dream is borne out in a Koranic revelation:

> Ye shall surely enter the Sacred Mosque, if Allah will, in full security, having your heads shaved and your hair cut ... He has ordained you, besides this, a speedy victory.[27]

The entry to the sanctuary a year later for the *'umra* (minor pilgrimage), and the definitive takeover of the shrine by Muslims two years after that, are considered by some Islamic traditions as the fulfilment of the Hudaybiyya expedition.[28]

JIHAD AND JERUSALEM

The underlying justification for launching a war against an enemy is distilled by Islam in the quintessential notion of jihad. Etymologically, the word may have described an intellectual striving – and by extension, also a physical striving – for a cause. In Islamic *shari'a*, however, jihad has principally one meaning: a military action designed to expand the outer borders of the realm of Islam or to protect the boundaries of *Dar al-Islam* (Pax Islamica) from encroaching Unbelievers. This idea is founded on the notion that Islam is not simply one of the revealed religions but the prevailing faith, which has come to replace the other monotheistic religions. Islam constitutes the latest and subsequently most valid revelation.

Islam prescribes jihad as the only valid war because the Faith by definition requires all hostilities to be directed either against Unbelievers (hence the holy war to subjugate them) or against members of other faiths (including monotheistic) who do not accept the superiority and rule of Islam. The Faith is thus universal, encompassing all Muslims who are thereby enjoined not to fight against each other (internecine wars and rebellions or unrest are termed *fitna*). Thus, most wars waged by Islamic countries are usually dubbed jihad, and not only by fundamentalist groups or by religious leaders.

Theoretically, the duty of jihad is binding on the Muslim community until the entire world comes under Islamic rule. However, because most Muslim countries have desisted in practice, under various theological and pragmatic considerations, from pursuing this idea (which would otherwise have permanently pitted them against the rest of the world), jihad has been applied sporadically to describe certain wars, for example, those against Israel, Egypt's war in the Yemen in the 1960s, the Iran–Iraq War of the 1980s, and the current wars of terror by Hamas, the Islamic Jihad, and the Hizbullah against Israel.

Jihad does not necessarily have to be offensive and can apply to defensive wars protecting Islamic countries against aggressors. In this regard, and certainly in the case of the Arab–Israeli wars, Muslims would claim that since Palestine is part of their patrimony, and the establishment of Israel on that land therefore constitutes aggression, it is incumbent upon them to defend their land through jihad. When, at the turn of the century, new winds of liberalism and reform began blowing in the Islamic world as a result of Western influence, some apologists in Islam attempted to limit jihad to its strictly defensive scope or to the extension of assistance to persecuted or otherwise needy Muslims. But, again, identifying the aggressor against those Muslims remained problematic when done by Muslim interested parties. Some scholars detect a similar liberal train of thought in the early years of the Prophet's career, when he is said to have usually elected peaceful means over violence and war.[29] But the violent and war-like interpretation of jihad prevailed again when Muhammad launched his attacks against Khaybar and Mecca, and particularly after his death when Islam sprang out of Arabia and spread throughout the world via the Islamic conquests.

That violent interpretation usually continues to prevail in the modern world, especially in the jargon of the fundamentalists[30] and certainly in regard to Israel.[31] We have seen above that Arafat's repeated calls for jihad are usually focused on Jerusalem. There, jihad is referred to as a *qital* (battle), a 'struggle until victory', which demands 'sacrifices and martyrdom'. It is difficult, even if one should stretch one's imagination and generosity to the limit, to understand these words as 'peaceful'. Jerusalem as a mobilizing factor is given the role of Mecca in Arafat's use of imagery to parallel the history of the Prophet: Arafat also stands at the gates of the sanctuary and vies to pray there, vowing to enter as the victor. That is the reason why Caliph 'Umar, who is believed to have been in Jerusalem personally, provides the crucial link between the Prophet's history and Arafat's history-making.

Arafat could make the quantum jump from Mecca to Jerusalem, and use the one in parallel with the other, due to the historical precedent established by 'abd-al-Malik, who had erected the Aqsa Mosque and the Dome of the Rock (AD 691/92) as a substitute for the Ka'ba, then under the rule of Ibn Zubayr, his rival for the Caliphate. Indeed, people who made the alternative pilgrimage there circumambulated the Rock as they used to do for the Ka'ba in Mecca. Ibn Zubayr's reaction was as staunch: he blamed 'abd-al-Malik for daring to transfer the *tawaf* (circumambulation) from the House of Allah in Mecca to the *qibla* of the Children of Israel in Jerusalem.[32]

Arafat makes efforts to exalt and glorify the religious and political status of Jerusalem in the same way as the Umayyads, who are known for their building programs in the city and sanctifying the *Haram al-Sharif* (Noble Sanctuary). Some scholars believe, in fact, that the Umayyads had considered Jerusalem their capital or, at the very least, made it the political and administrative center of the district of Filastin (Palestine) in order to render it the equal of Mecca, if not its superior. We have a better understanding of present-day Muslim fears that 'Judaization' of those holy places might revive the Jewish claim to them if we add to that the fact that the Muslim rituals held at the Rock during the Umayyads 'were an echo of Jewish ceremonies' and evoked the ancient Jewish 'Temple of Jerusalem', or the 'Temple of David and Solomon' (as the 'Kings of the Children of Israel'[33]). Together with holding high the banner of Jerusalem as a holy Muslim shrine and as the capital of Palestine, Arafat would be ready to risk even open violence in order to thwart any Israeli attempt to resurrect the dead ghosts. Hence also the staunch claim advanced by Palestinian and other Muslim clerics that Israel and the Jews have no rights whatsoever to the Temple Mount, and any idea of sharing its sanctity between the two protagonists (as in the Tomb of the Patriarchs in Hebron) is dismissed out of hand with ridicule and contempt.

But, as we have seen, Jerusalem also conjures up in Arafat's mind 'Umar, who allegedly came to the city to accept Sophronius's surrender and the 'key' to the citadel without battle. Some say that 'Umar proceeded to Jerusalem from the camp town of Jabiya, in the Golan; others doubt whether it was 'Umar who accepted the surrender in the first place.[34] But there is no doubt that Islamic tradition took the trouble to insist that it was so, and for a reason: when Muslims arrived in Jerusalem they found a purely Christian city, with the Holy Sepulcher as the main site because it purported to have inherited the sanctity of the now-destroyed Jewish Temple. During the process of the Islamization of Jerusalem, a mosque was built on the Jewish Temple Mount. Later, when the Aqsa Mosque was built on the site, then (together with the Dome of the Rock) the whole complex came to be regarded by Muslims as the successor to the Temple: hence the *Haram*.

So, while the Christians had left the Temple deliberately in ruin, the Islamicized Mount became the destination of Muhammad's *isra'* (night journey) and the launching pad of his *mi'raj*. Tradition notes that the Caliph 'Umar went to the Temple Mount and to the Tower of David (a secondary site of Muslim ritual). After 'Umar prayed on the Temple Mount, he ordered the garbage that the Christians had deposited there over the centuries to be removed under the supervision of Ka'b al-Akhbar, a Jew who examined the measurements of the Jewish Temple and designated the exact location for cleaning. Thus, we have three authorities in Jerusalem: Islam, represented by 'Umar, the new ruler of the newly-dominating faith; the Christians, represented by Sophronius; and the Jews, represented by Ka'ba. 'Umar identified on the Temple Mount the place that the Prophet had described as the location where he landed after the *isra'* and from whence he took off for his *mi'raj*. Hence, 'Umar's personal involvement in visiting the city and giving the Temple Mount its Islamic meaning satisfies the secondary question of whether he was there at all.[35]

THE HISTORICAL REPLICA IN ARAFAT'S IMAGERY

Arafat's *modus operandi* has puzzled many observers who have been following the major milestones of this man's career and his semi-miraculous survivability. More than once, he was exposed to near-death situations: physically (for example, attempts on his life; a plane crash); militarily (for example, his escape from Israeli occupation in 1967; his stand in besieged Beirut in 1982; and, again, in Tripoli in 1983); and politically (for example, when expelled from Jordan in 1970; from Lebanon in 1982; and forgotten in Tunis following the fiasco of his support for Saddam Hussein during the Gulf War in 1991). He was bankrupt financially and diplomatically, to the point of being thrown into the 'waste-basket of history', but for the Israeli life-buoy thrown to him at Oslo that allowed him to peak again and obtain a Nobel Peace Prize on account of the Oslo Peace Process.

Arafat owes his resurgence of power, each time he was considered to have been doomed, in no small measure to his duplicity. This enables him to appear to be passionate and pragmatic concurrently, mercurial and calculating, disarmingly naïve and shrewdly plotting, furious and cajoling. At times he projects conciliation, at other times menace; he can indulge in fits of anger, and immediately after switch to excessive flowery rhetoric laced with milk-and-honey. He can promise peace and kindle the flames of war; declare his enmity to Hamas but also protect it with rage. There is no way to explain Arafat's duplicity, and the images he projects at different times, in different places, to different people, other than by the abyss constantly yawning between his self-perception as the life-long redeemer of the Palestinian people (until recently, he justified his celibacy by 'being married to the Palestinian cause') and the grim reality of extreme poverty, mounting unemployment, demographic pressures, an 'ungrateful' opposition, and the grinding helplessness and indolence encountered during his waking hours.

Arafat's moments of dream and vision carry him to the heights of the Prophet Muhammad, whose policies he purports to articulate, and of 'Umar, in whose footsteps he wishes to follow. But in his many more numerous moments of despair and frustration, he threatens, lashes out, or loses control. When the wings of vision transport him into the realm of the desirable and the coveted, then Hudaybiyya is for him the quintessence of the Prophet's diplomatic and political success; and Jerusalem the peak of 'Umar's strategic and political blueprint – in each case, political wisdom and prowess pre-empted war and violence. But when reality forces him to crash-land into the quagmire of problems which obstruct his very functioning and constrain the uplifting of his spirit, then he impatiently embraces jihad and reverts to his own true self. After all, the Prophet and 'Umar resorted to jihad when there was no other resource – that is to say, when their enemies refused to surrender to their will.

The temptation is great to draw step-by-step parallels between Arafat as he perceives himself, and his heroes, the Prophet and 'Umar. Arafat has apparently studied in depth the Hudaybiyya and Jerusalem precedents, and endorses them as models to be emulated. How else can one comprehend his frequent references to them, in all sorts of circumstances, private and public? He appears obsessed by them and convinced they must come to fruition under him; otherwise he could not be so forceful and passionate about them. After all, history is replete with examples of nations who were at war and made peace; why did he choose Hudaybiyya and Jerusalem, of all historical accounts, to exemplify or illustrate his own situations?

The similarities between the Prophet and 'Umar's plans and deeds (as understood and preserved in Islamic tradition) on the one hand, and Arafat's utterances and behavior (as we can best understand them) on the other, offer striking parallels:

1. Hudaybiyya was the place where the Prophet had his dream (*surat al-fat'h*, cited above), took the 'key', and with a shaved head entered the sanctuary in Mecca. Arafat's dream (recounted in the speech he gave in Gaza celebrating the day of *mi'raj*) also showed him the walls of Jerusalem, its mosques and churches (but, of course, no synagogues). One may assume that Arafat's complex about his bald head, which necessitates his perennial headgear, did not allow him to push the parallel as far as to include a shaven skull.

2. The conquest of Mecca by the Prophet (*fat'h*), or perhaps the Treaty of Hudaybiyya itself, which was also a *fat'h* by 'Umar's own authority, compares with Arafat's *Fat'h* organization, of which he was the founder and the head until it became the backbone of the PLO. Admittedly, his *fat'h* originates from the acronym *hatf* (*harakat tahrir Filastin* – The Movement for the Liberation of Palestine) which, when left in this order, would mean 'sudden death'. Hence the reversal of the ordering of the letters to produce the much more palatable '*Fat'h*', which means, precisely, conquest for the cause of Islam, with its significance accruing from Hudaybiyya and the Muslim conquests in general. Taken together with Arafat's Islamic *nom de guerre* and the titles of his military units already mentioned above, one

could understand the context in which Arafat's *Fat'h* came into being.

3. The Prophet had obtained the key to the sanctuary (*miah* which accords with *fat'h*), a symbol of dominion over the place, and so did 'Umar when he received the 'key' of Jerusalem from Sophronius as a sign of surrender. The recent 'surrender' of the Greek Patriarch of Jerusalem to Arafat in Bethlehem, carried with it a symbolic yielding of the 'key' of the churches of Palestine to the new master-protector of the Christians. Hence, the latter's insistence on the wide publicizing of this event.

4. The Prophet's lead at the head of his Muslim followers to launch jihad against the Unbelievers in Arabia, followed by the more extensive jihad which 'Umar conducted to expand *Dar al-Islam*, is continued by Arafat who incites his crowds, and is in turn incited by them, to lead them into jihad amidst shouts of *'Allah! Allah! Allah Akbar!'*.

5. Arafat delivered his fiery speech in Gaza on *Mi'raj* Day, the day on which the Prophet ascended to Heaven from Jerusalem, which was later to be conquered and consecrated by 'Umar and which will now be redeemed by Arafat, 'his successor' according to the Patriarch, who himself is Sophronius's successor.

6. The Prophet made 'peace' (actually a *hudna*, a ten-year armistice) with the Quraysh at Hudaybiyya, overriding the opposition of some of his most zealous followers, including 'Umar. Here, Arafat explicitly suggested the parallel in that he told his audiences repeatedly that Oslo equalled Hudaybiyya. Since he purports to follow the Prophet, one must then assume that the counterpart of the Quraysh as his interlocutors are the Israelis. If so, this statement would have far-reaching consequences:

   a. Like the Prophet, who made humiliating concessions in Hudaybiyya under the pressure of circumstances, so too has Arafat. Implicit in this is the assumption that, exactly like the Prophet, who knew when and how to extract himself from that humiliating treaty, so too will Arafat. This was his answer to the harsh critics among his Islamic opposition.

   b. The Prophet had pledged a ten-year armistice, but, when Muslim interests so necessitated, he entered Mecca as a victor two years after he undertook that obligation. Arafat's pledge to enter Jerusalem, to pray in al-Aqsa, and to attain victory, are precisely the parallel of the Prophet's vows and deeds.

   c. If the peace should turn sour (that is, if the Israeli partners, like the Quraysh, can be accused of having violated the Treaty), then nothing binds the Palestinians, successors of the Hudaybiyya Muslims. 'Umar himself had despised that peace because of its humiliating content, while the Prophet, who had also disliked it, had the foresight to adopt it, by necessity, as a tactic. But he also knew how to rise against it and abrogate it as soon as it was expedient to do so.

d. Many Western historians believe that it was the Prophet who broke the armistice of Hudaybiyya, because the Quraysh would not have dared to attack the Muslims who had become vastly superior to them militarily. Even within Islamic tradition this fact is acknowledged, together with the claim that client tribes of the Quraysh had attacked client tribes of the Prophet, thus justifying his abrogation of the Treaty. Western scholars believe that it was the Prophet who looked and found a pretext to move into Mecca. Muslim tradition contends that, of course, since the Prophet cannot be faulted, it must be the misconduct of his rivals that lay at the root of his military intervention in Mecca, in violation, as it were, of the Treaty. But even if we adopt the Muslim view in this dispute, how could Arafat know, six months after Oslo – when everything was proceeding according to the Accords – that Israeli, like Quraysh, would break her obligation to the point of justifying his jihad into Jerusalem, which he entreated his fellow Muslims in Johannesburg to join? That is unless, of course, he was looking for a pretext to abrogate the treaty, just as the Prophet did, regardless of whether or not the partner respects or violates the treaty. Or, unless Arafat was as far-sighted as the Prophet and foresaw the coming violation before it occurred.

7. Arafat's Hudaybiyya precedent was not lost on Hamas opposition, who were quick to push the parallel beyond its logic. The Prophet had temporarily appeased pagan Mecca in order to launch the onslaught on the Jews of Khaybar. But Hamas keep raising the spectre of Khaybar in their leaflets circulated on the West Bank and in Gaza, one of which ends ominously with the call, *Hanat Khaybar!* (The time of Khaybar has come!). The difference is that Arafat's Hudaybiyya has not yet failed completely, and in this scenario, it is Israel who plays the role of both Mecca and Khaybar.

8. The Prophet accepted his *bay'a* (oath of allegiance) 'under the

tree' in Hudaybiyya. One should note that Arafat's coming to Bethlehem and other West Bank cities was accompanied by calls to the populace to accord him the same *bay'a*. When they do, the parallel will be neat and complete.

We learn then that the choice of the Hudaybiyya–jihad–Jerusalem trinity by the astute Arafat is not accidental or inconsequential, but well perceived, if ill-conceived. Arafat, true to his Muslim convictions, finds common ground between his beliefs and the deep chords that he can play to instigate massive and passionate responses among his constituencies. In doing so, he not only rallies supporters from the traditional PLO around him (that is, those who regard him as the symbol of their national existence), but he can also cater to, and forestall, his Islamic opposition, who embrace precisely these very same Islamic symbols.

One may suspect that for Arafat, as for the Prophet at Hudaybiyya, it is of greater importance ultimately to placate his constituency than to please his interlocutors through his moves towards peace. He may make concessions, which his Hudaybiyya-based worldview might regard as temporary and tactical, but when the day of reckoning comes, there is no doubt where his heart will be. Experience has indeed shown that when Arafat clamped down on his opposition it was not because Hamas acted against his and their common enemy, or because of a disagreement on Islamic grounds. Rather, he moved against the Islamists when they posed a direct threat to his rule by creating disturbances and assembling rallies that went out of control; by denigrating him personally or mocking his visions of *grandeur*, and by pushing their social program to fill the vacuum left by his inability to provide security and prosperity.

The duplicity of Arafat's thinking and policy is attested by his instigation of the violent eruptions against Israel on the West Bank and in Gaza in October 1996; by his release from prison of Hamas convicts; by his persistent refusal to extradite to Israel the perpetrators of murders in Israel; by his procrastination in concluding the Hebron retreat of Israeli troops; by his pitting his security chief against Palestinians who live under Israeli rule in East Jerusalem; by his reported speech before Arab diplomats in Stockholm, in which he spoke of 'the impending collapse of Israel' and of 'flooding Israel demographically to bring it to its demise';[36] by the repeated declarations of Arafat and of some of his colleagues in the PLO leadership about the 'right of return of the Palestinians' (which corroborate the report about flooding Israel demographically); and finally, by the alarming press reports about Arafat's intentions to bring about a violent explosion in the territories if things do not work his way.[37] Each is an example of the duplicity underpinning his thinking and policy.

As we have seen, while Arafat pays lip service to peace and reiterates his commitment to the Oslo Accord in interviews with Israeli and Western media, he invokes the messages of jihad, impatience, blood and sweat, Jerusalem, violence and sacrifice when addressing Arab audiences like the Palestinians. This certainly outspeaks Hamas, who utilize the very same language, and it raises a plethora of questions about Arafat's sincerity in his purported quest for peace with Israel.

NOTES

1. Hamas is the acronym of 'Harakat Muqawama Islamiyya' (Islamic Resistance Movement), which became the umbrella organization, created virtually overnight at the outbreak of the Intifada in late 1987, in order to bring together all the local Muslim Associations of years past.
2. For vivid and detailed descriptions of these events, see *Ha'aretz*, 2 January 1996, sec. B3.
3. Ibid.
4. See, for example, *Al-Sirat Weekly*, 18 August 1989; see also the Hamas Charter as translated and annotated by R. Israeli, 'The Charter of Allah: The Platform of the Islamic Resistance Movement', in Y. Alexander (ed.), *The 1988–89 Annual of Terrorism* (Amsterdam: Martinus Nijhoff, 1990), pp.99–134.
5. Bernard Lewis, 'The Return of Islam', *Commentary* (Winter 1976, pp.39–49); N. Johnson, *Islam and Politics of Meaning in Palestinian Nationalism* (London: Kegan Paul, 1982), pp.8–15.
6. Johnson, *Islam and Politics*, pp.74–87.
7. Lewis, 'The Return of Islam'.
8. Incidentally, while those elections were taking place under Israeli occupation, no complaint was ever voiced regarding the 'impossibility to hold elections under Israeli guns', which would later be voiced when there was a question about general elections.
9. Israeli, Hamas Charter, pp.99–134.
10. Ibid.
11. See, for example, Esther Webman, *Antisemitic Motifs in the Ideology of Hizballah and the Hamas: Project for the Study of Antisemitism* (Tel Aviv: Tel-Aviv University, 1994).
12. For this and other videotapes, I am indebted to Mr David Ladeen and Mr Ygal Carmon of the Institute for Peace Education in Jerusalem.
13. *Mi'raj* is the ascension of the Prophet to Heaven, according to Islamic tradition. That ascension, which followed his mysterious nightly journey (*isra'*) on the back of his winged horse from Mecca to Jerusalem, is yet another proof of the link of Islam with that Holy City.
14. Abu Ammar is the name of an illustrious general in the early Islamic armies. Borrowing this title as a *nom de guerre* in itself suggests Islamic thinking on the part of Arafat.

15. Palestine television, 1 January 1995.
16. Wording used in the Holy Koran, describing the Prophet's night journey (*isra'*).
17. Official date of the establishment of the PLO.
18. Founder of the Islamic movement in Palestine in the 1930s; he became the first martyr in modern Palestine after being killed by the British.
19. Ahmed Yasin is the founder and the foremost leader of Hamas; he has been imprisoned by Israel for his alleged instigation of murders of Israelis.
20. See W. Montgomery Watt, *Muhammad at Medina* (Oxford: Oxford at the Clarendon Press, 1956); Gerald R. Hawting, 'Al-Hudaybiyya and the Conquest of Mecca', *Jerusalem Studies of Arabic and Islam*, 8 (1986), pp.1–23; Michael Lecker, 'The Hudaybiyya Treaty and the Expedition against Khaybar', *Jerusalem Studies of Arabic and Islam*, 5 (1984), pp.1–11; and M. Kister, 'The Massacre of the Banu Qurayza', *Jerusalem Studies of Arabic and Islam*, 8 (1986), pp.61–96.
21. Hawting, 'Al-Hudaybiyya', pp.1–2.
22. *Akhbar al-Yaum*, Cairo, 10 May 1979. The Mufti asserted in his *fatwa* that it is 'permitted to conclude peace with the enemy when Muslim interest is served. The Prophet had concluded peace with the Unbelievers of Mecca, in spite of the opposition to it, and he convinced its opponents of its validity'.
23. See Lecker, 'The Hudaybiyya Treaty', p.1. I am also indebted for this passage to my colleague Dr Ilai Allon of Tel Aviv University, who delivered a public lecture on this subject on 3 March 1992.
24. F. Buhl, cited in Lecker, 'The Hudaybiyya Treaty', p.2.
25. Muhammad Hamidullah and Sarakhsi on Shaybani, both quoted by Lecker, 'The Hudaybiyya Treaty', pp.2–4.
26. See M. Kister, 'Al-Hira', *Arabica*, 15 (1968); see also 'The Massacre of Banu Qurayza', *Jerusalem Studies of Arabic and Islam*, 8 (1986), pp.61–97.
27. Sura 48 (*al-Fath*), verse 27.
28. Hawting, 'Al-Hudaybiyya', p.3ff.
29. See 'Jihad', in H.A.R. Gibbs, B. Lewis, Ch. Pellat *et al.* (eds), *New Encyclopedia of Islam*, 2nd edn, 11 Vols (Leiden: E.J. Brill, 1960–2000).
30. See, for example, Sayyed Qutb, *Ma'rakatuna m'a al-Yahud* (Beirut, 1986); and Israeli, *Hamas Charter*.
31. See Webman,' 'Antisemitic Motifs'.
32. See Amikam Elad, 'Why did adb-al Malik build the Dome of the Rock?' in J. Raby and J. Johns (eds), *Bayt al-Maqdis*, Part 1 (New York: Oxford University Press, 1992), pp.33–57.
33. Ibid., pp.48–9.
34. H. Busset, 'Omar's image as the Conqueror of Jerusalem', *Jerusalem Studies of Arabic and Islam*, 8 (1986), pp.153–4.
35. Ibid., pp.164–8.
36. *Middle East Digest*, 7, 3 (March 1996).
37. Various articles, *Ma'ariv* (Weekend Supplement), Tel Aviv, 1 November 1996, pp.6–7.

2. Educating Palestinian Children*

'A nation is a group of people united by a mistaken view of the past and a hatred of their neighbors.'

Ernest Renan, *Qu'est-ce qu'une Nation?*

INTRODUCTION

The *International Herald Tribune* of 16 August 1999 carried a front-page article 'Rewriting Israeli History: Textbooks focus on facts', a shortened form of a piece which had appeared in the *New York Times* two days earlier. They were only a culmination of the flurry of articles in the Israeli press that reflected the deep revisions in Israeli textbooks occasioned by the new wave of 'New Historians', and the seeming immobilism in the Palestinian textbooks. The revisions are important obligations shouldered by both parties under the Oslo and Wye Accords to eliminate elements of incitement in their respective public-school systems.

Revisionism in Israeli textbooks had begun independently of, and prior to, Oslo as a result of some iconoclastic publications by young Israeli historians who showed that many established 'facts' and 'events' in Israeli modern history were one-sided, incomplete and distorted the truth. For example, accounts of the Palestinian refugees during the 1948 War, in which they were said to have all left the battle zone voluntarily, were found to be grossly exaggerated; the 'New Historians' found out that many of them were also expelled, while others ran away to secure their lives in the midst of hostilities. Other accepted assumptions regarding the process and

*Originally published as, 'Education, Identity, State Building and the Peace Process: Educating Palestinian Children in the Post-Oslo Era', *Terrorism and Political Violence*, 12, 1 (2000), pp.79–94.

the struggle of the establishment of Israel, such as the rapport of force between the numerous Arabs and the outnumbered Jews, have also been challenged by these historians. As a result, the Israeli Ministry of Education has initiated a revision of school textbooks in the past few years, in spite of the ongoing opposition of widespread circles to any changes in the established history.

In Oslo I (1993), Oslo II (1995) and the Wye Plantation Agreements (1998), Arafat undertook to eradicate the statements of hatred and incitement against Israel from Palestinian textbooks. The Oslo II Agreement states in Article XXII that

> Israel and the Palestinian Authority shall seek to foster mutual understanding and tolerance and shall accordingly abstain from incitement, including hostile propaganda against each other ... , shall take necessary measures to prevent such incitement by any organizations, groups or individuals within their jurisdiction.

In the same spirit, the PA reaffirmed in the 'Note for the Record' it signed on 15 January 1997, a commitment to 'prevent incitement and hostile propaganda as specified in Article XXII of the Interim Agreement'. And the Wye River Memorandum of October 1998 requires the PA to 'take all measures necessary in order ... to prevent incitement'.

The theme of the year 1994–95 in the Israeli school system was 'The Peace Process', geared to teach all Israeli school children that the era of peace has dawned. The new curricula were guided by a catalogue, approved and circulated by the Israeli Ministry of Education, which contained 900 examples of programs to illustrate the theme of peace to children from kindergarten to 12th Grade.[1] To what extent have Palestinian promises been fulfilled? To answer the question we shall examine Palestinian school textbooks, commissioned or adopted by the PA to see whether they are in conformity with the Authority's domestic and international commitments.

BACKGROUND

As long as the Palestinian entity existed only in slogans and in 'armed struggle', the education of Palestinian children was tackled mainly by the authorities under which Palestinians lived in various

Arab countries or under Israeli rule. In this regard, Jordan bore the brunt of that burden between 1949 and 1967, inasmuch as more than two thirds of the Palestinian people were under its aegis both east and west of the Jordan. The rest were either under Egyptian military government in the Gaza Strip, dispersed in the refugee camps of Lebanon and Syria, as a minority within Israel, or in search of their future in other diasporas in the Arab world or the West.

This meant that during the formative period of 1949–67, most Palestinian children who pursued regular schooling, even those in the United Nations Relief and Works Agency (UNRWA) school system, depended more or less on the curricula of the Jordanian Ministry of Education. Not surprisingly, the civic education imparted to Palestinian children under that system was of a general Arab–Islamic character, with special emphasis on loyalty to the Hashemite Crown, and a clear skirting of the issue of Palestinian nationalism. As in other Arab educational systems, it included a strong element of political indoctrination founded on sloganeering, memorizing, citations, repetitions and conformity, and little in the way of free thinking, creativity, imagination (in the sense of the imaginative, not the imaginary which was rife), and innovative spirit. Political education, either explicitly stated or implied, was geared to reinforce Arab and Islamic identity, to bring up children committed to Arab and Islamic causes, to Arab and Islamic unity and solidarity, and to resist the perceived enemies, be they abstract Imperialism or Colonialism, or concrete Israel and Zionism.

The question of multiple identities cultivated in the Jordanian system is by no means unique and stems from the three concentric circles in which any Arab finds himself/herself. First, there is the attachment to the locale (that is, patriotism) and distinguishes a Palestinian from a Syrian and a Libyan and is called *wataniyya*. Second, as an Arab, he/she would share a common ethnic descent, real or imagined, a common history, language and culture that nurture the myth of Arab unity and commonality of fate and destiny, what in Arabic is called *Qawmiyya*. And finally, the Islamic faith that is transnational and universal, the adhesion to the world wide Muslim congregation of the Faithful – the *Umma*. The tension between the three has been the main engine of Arab politics in the past century: while each territorial group has achieved its independence in the framework of a modern nation-state, attempts at unity have been made and unmade, but are maintained under the institutional symbol of the Arab League with its 22 member-states. Those for whom the Islamic identity is prevalent, like the fundamentalist movements, reject the existing 55 Muslim nation-states as divisive and strive to restore the old united Islamic Empire under one Caliph. One can find these tensions present in all Arab and Islamic societies, and the Palestinians are no exception.

When Israel took over the West Bank and Gaza in the 1967 War, it found itself constrained to maintain the legal and educational systems that had existed in those territories prior to the war, but it took the liberty to alter many passages in dozens of textbooks that it considered hateful, bigoted and inciting against Jews, Zionism and Israel. The extirpation of those passages predictably produced barrages of condemnation from interested Arab countries, Arab educators, Western countries and UNESCO, that Israel, as an occupying power, had no business in altering, censoring, rectifying, or otherwise correcting existing textbooks that had prevailed prior to occupation. Israel abstained, during the campaign of revision of those textbooks, from tampering with citations from holy Islamic sources, such as the Koran or the *Hadith*, even when they were considered highly offensive, but Arab and Islamic ire did not subside.

When the Palestinians gained self-rule in those territories following Oslo (1993), one of their main and immediate concerns was, understandably, to take renewed control of the future of their population and guide it into the new mold of Palestinian identity. Shaping the minds of Palestinian children, via textbooks and the state-controlled media, was considered a supreme priority.

Many reasons were implied for this urgency, which also occasioned the prompt restoration of the passages that had been obliterated by Israel during the occupation:

1. Palestinian children who missed school during the Intifada, which many credit for the Oslo Accords, now deserved to have their future chartered and guaranteed by the new PA;
2. The nascent Palestinian entity was searching for its identity, challenged domestically by Islamic movements, notably Hamas, and it became crucial to educate the new generation according to the Authority's prevailing vision of a Palestinian society in the making;
3. The new Palestinian entity would need increasing numbers of technicians, teachers, cadres, intellectuals and bureaucrats to

man its fledgling state institutions, its school system, its professional associations, its growing security apparatus and its economic management. Planning school curricula was considered vital for all those needs, and the new state ideology;

4. The Palestinian entity, which grew out of the Oslo Accords, was still locked into a bitter and prolonged struggle to achieve its full independence from an enemy unwilling to accord it all its aspirations. Since the foreseeable Palestinian future seemed tightly tied in with that struggle, it was necessary to define the enemy, to render society resilient in confronting it, and to shape relations with it. During the Intifada, Palestinian children viewed the Israelis as oppressive occupiers who usurped Palestinian lands, but their perceptions had to be different when dealing with a partner for peace, a neighbor, an employer, or perhaps even a legitimate political entity in its own right.

The textbooks examined here consist of 140 examples published by the PA during the years 1995–98. In the previous years of the existence of the Authority (1993–95), the Jordanian and Egyptian textbooks which had been in use under Israeli rule continued to prevail, but the corrections introduced by Israel were abrogated and the original defamatory text was restored. The new Palestinian textbooks are all the Authority's making, and reflect its educational policy better than the previous two versions. The textbooks under discussion cover the whole span of 1st to 12th Grades in humanities and social sciences that are loaded with values and therefore reflective of policy intentions. Subjects included are civic studies, grammar, literature, history, geography and Islamic studies.

BUILDING A NATIONAL MYTH

School education in the PA understandably provides answers to the questions about the identity, roots and history of the Palestinians. Enough evidence exists independently of the textbooks to sum up the elements of Palestinian identity since the 1920s when the Mufti of Jerusalem, Haj Amin al-Husseini, raised the vanguard of Palestinian nationalism both against the British occupiers and the Zionist contenders. Prior to that, when Palestine was part of the Ottoman Empire, it was divided into several *sanjaks* (counties) under the *Vilayet* (province) of Damascus, and not recognized as one political unit.[2] The local inhabitants consisted of several landed clans, some prominent families in the cities, a few nomadic tribes, and a melange of minorities and new migrants from Syria and Egypt. Certainly they did not consider themselves as one nation, their focus of identity being local, tribal, Muslim or Ottoman, or a combination thereof.

Nascent Palestinian nationalism, however, tries to lend depth to its history, either because 'old is beautiful', or because there is a necessity to contend with the Jews who provide a millenial recorded history of their link to that land. As there is no Palestinian historical record to satisfy that need, myths are designed, and school textbooks are a most efficient way to promote and diffuse them. Let us cite several examples and then try to make sense out of them:

> Dear pupil, do you know who the Palestinians are? The Palestinians are descended from the Cana'anites.[3]

> Jerusalem is an ancient Arab city, built by the Jebusite Arabs before Islam.[4]

> Jerusalem [introduces herself]: 'I am an ancient city, thousands of years old. I occupy a mountain plateau in the center of Palestine … My most ancient name, Jebus, is derived from the ancient Arabs, the Jebusites.'[5]

> At the conference … the Jewish claims and historical allegations in favor of their right in Palestine were noted, and the historical right of the Arabs over Palestine ever since the dawn of history was stressed.[6]

The claim to Palestine as Arab naturally delegitimizes those who today counter-claim it, and this theme will be discussed in more detail below. Here suffice it to note, that the repeated stress of the Palestinian educational system on the ancient Arab identity of the land is obviously geared to posit Palestinian antiquity without the need to produce any evidence to sustain the claim. By making Jerusalem introduce itself (above), in an innocent and straightforward fashion, addressing the third-graders directly, weight is added to the statement of its Arab identity, making evidence unnecessary.

Evidence by omission is another device used in the textbooks. Both PA Television and the school books use a map of the Middle East in which Israel does not exist and is replaced in its entirety by a country called Palestine. This is also the case for the privately-produced new atlas adopted by the PA education system. A sample of illustrations from various books show:

1. Under the words *our country Palestine,* a map of 'Palestine' replaces all Israel.[7]
2. A map entitled *Map of Palestine before and after the war of 1967* defines the area of the State of Israel as *the Arab lands conquered before 1967*, while the West Bank and the Gaza Strip are *Arab lands conquered in 1967.*[8]
3. Maps of the Middle East in which Israel does not exist and its area is marked as 'Palestine', appear in many pages of these textbooks.[9]
4. A map that accompanies the lesson *Palestine our Homeland*, encompasses the entire state of Israel and specifies numerous Israeli cities as Arab even though some of them date from biblical times: Safed, Acre, Haifa, Tiberias, Nazareth, Beit Shean, Jaffa, Jerusalem and Beersheba.[10]
5. A drawing shows a woman waving the Palestinian flag while in the background is the map of Palestine in the place of all Israel.[11]
6. Nineteen times in a geography book, maps mark Israel as Palestine.[12]

The Palestinian Television shows the same map as no.6, many times daily, at the beginning and the end of every news report. And so it goes for all geographical features of Palestine which bear modern Israeli names, some of which relate to biblical, clearly pre-Arab, locations such as the Valley of Jezreel (called Bani 'Amr Valley in the Palestinian textbooks and media).[13] Similarly, there are vows to return to Jaffa[14] which has been part of Tel Aviv for the past 50 years, and continued references to Israel as 'occupied Palestine' and to the Galilee as part of Northern Palestine.[15]

The substitution of Palestinian for anything Israeli, including Israeli industries which are not an intrinsic part of the claimed land (for example, *in Palestine there are two oil refineries … in Haifa and Ashdod*),[16] stands out, incidentally, not only in textbooks and the official Palestinian Television, but also in other media. For weeks in July and August 1996, the Jerusalem daily, *Al-Quds*, carried a daily page of chronicles of the history of the 'Palestinian-Cana'anite people'. In these chronicles, academics of the West Bank Universities explained how Israeli archaeological finds bolster the claim of the Palestinian-Cana'anites to age-old rootedness in the land. All these led to the celebration of the Summer Festival of Sebastya staged by the Palestinian Ministry of Culture in August 1996, where Arab youths dressed in robes bearing ancient Cana'anite figures brandished torches as they danced about the town square packed with PLO and PA administration officials. Others arrived atop horse-drawn chariots modeled on drawings found at the Israeli archaeological excavations at Meggido.[17]

On the same stage in the middle of the square, a dramatic passion was acted out with the Ba'al, God of the Heavens and Fertility in the Pantheon of the ancient Cana'anites struggling against Mut, God of the Underworld. Ultimately, Ba'al emerged victorious and the narrator took the opportunity to heap praise on the loyal Palestinian-Cana'anite nations: the Amorites, Girgashites, Jebusites and Perizites which had fought the Hebrew invaders across the Jordan.[18] This part is rather puzzling if one takes into account the numerous references in the Koran to God's Covenant with the Jews and His promise that they would inherit the Land [of Cana'an]; even more odd is the modern use of Ba'al, a pagan God, in a society where Islam is a serious contender for Palestinian nationalism.

This whole historical structure, which has been created, invented, imagined, adopted and elaborated by the Palestinians, raises several questions. First, there is the problem of the fashion in which this questionable concoction of events is instilled into the minds of children, not as an idea, option or theory, but as an absolute truth, as History, as their history, without criticism, evidence or sources. This is not without precedent: Saddam Hussein revived Hamorabi's heritage as his own during the first years of his rule (1975–90). In the Gulf War when he needed the help of other Arab and Islamic countries, he had to abandon his claim to antiquity. Sadat also repeated references to Egypt's, '7,000 years of Pharaonic history'. In both cases, those cultures were superseded by the Arabo–Islamic civilization that bears no resemblance to, nor claims descent from, them. Similarly, Jordan has been claiming the ancient heritage of the pagan Emorites, Edomites, Amonites and even Romans. In all these cases there is an attempt to construct a direct bridge to antiquity in order to gain legitimacy. However, in the case of the Palestinians, and to a certain extent the

Jordanians, this myth-building is also designed to deprive their rival, Israel, of legitimacy.

A striking characteristic of the Palestinian myth-building is not only the constant need to construct its past from imaginary building bricks, but in so doing to omit or refute others, denying their heritage and existence. The entire 1,000 years of two Jewish commonwealths in ancient Palestine are simply skipped over, and history is rewritten to erase any mention of the Jews. Or worse, pages of history are torn off, and the remaining pages are re-numbered so as not to disturb the smooth flow of events by the embarrassment of inquisitive questions.

The Palestinians could have generously and realistically admitted the existence of an ancient Jewish heritage which is past, and reclaimed the Cana'anite heritage as preceding it, but they do not. They construct their bridge to the Cana'anite past on an historical void, for fear that a recognized intermediary period where the Jews predominated, might threaten their way to the far end of the bridge. The omission of the Jews on the one hand, and the claim to Cana'anite descent on the other, seem inconsistent with each other: if the Palestinians descend from the Cana'anites, then the Jews in the intermediary period do not matter anyway because they do not interfere with the neat lineage. When the Jews are omitted, one suspects that either the Palestinian myth-builders themselves do not trust in their Cana'anite roots, or they acknowledge that their grounds are shaky forcing them to eliminate the contenders who stand on more solid historical ground. If a fever cannot be controlled, one may break the thermometer and eliminate evidence of a threatening temperature.

SELF-AGGRANDIZEMENT AND ENEMY DENIGRATION

Jahiliyya poetry in pre-Islamic Arabia – which attained high peaks of imagination, creativity and idiom – stood out in its purple verbiage of self-praise of the poet's own chief, family, clan and tribe and their feats of heroism and valor. It also used scathing, humiliating and abusive language to denigrate the enemy tribes and clans. This device is also applied by the writers of the Palestinian school textbooks. Apparently, those educators felt that beyond singing a people's praise and making up its history, they also had to dig a pit for their rivals/enemies to highlight a perceived chasm between the two. Maybe they sensed that rather than being overshadowed by the successful West and its perceived appendix, the Jewish State, both of which are not to their liking, they would rather minimize them to the extent possible, by castigating them, denigrating and diminishing them, in contrast with the lofty innate qualities of the Arabs in general and the Palestinians in particular.

A Palestinian textbook for 11th Graders[19] notes:

> In the present period ... of unprecedented material and scientific advances ... scientists in the West are perplexed by the worrying increase in the number of people suffering from nervous disorders ... and the statistics from America in this matter are a clear indication of this. (p.3)
>
> Western civilization flourished, as is well known, as a consequence of the links of the West to Islamic culture, through Arab institutions in Spain, and in other Islamic countries where Islamic thinkers and philosophers took an interest in Greek philosophy. (p.4)
>
> Western civilization, in both its branches – the Capitalist and the Communist – deprived man of his peace of mind, stability ... when it turned material well-being into the exemplary goal ... his money leading him nowhere, except to suicide. (p.5)
>
> There is no escape from a new civilization which will arise in the wake of this material progress and which will continue it and lift man to the highest spiritual life alongside his material advancement ... Is there a nation capable of fulfilling such a role? The Western world is incapable of fulfilling it ... There is only one nation capable of discharging this task, and that is our nation ... No one but we can carry aloft the flag of tomorrow's civilization. (p.12)
>
> We do not claim that the collapse of Western civilization and the transfer of the center of civilization to us will happen in the next decade or two, even in 50 years, for the rise and fall of civilization follow natural processes, and even when the foundations of a fortress become cracked it still appears for a long time to be at the peak of its strength. Nevertheless [Western civilization] has begun to collapse and to become a pile of debris ... We awoke to a painful reality and to oppressive Imperialism, and we drove it out of some of our lands, and we are about to drive it from the rest. (p.16)

It is noteworthy that although the argument for Islamic superiority and ultimate victory is clear, an allowance is made for 'natural processes' to unfold. Other fervent believers in Allah would rather impute to Him alone the decision and the timing of the Western collapse. One also wonders how the PA in fact expends tremendous efforts in the real world to find solace and seek favor in the West while teaching its school children that the very source of its sustenance is about to collapse.

With regard to Jews, Israel and Zionism, statements of vilification are even more straightforward. Israel, the immediate and most implacable enemy, does not deserve sparing: it is the source of Arab misery and universal evil. The Jews, who constitute the majority of its population, are corrupt by nature and cannot be expected to improve; the Zionist ideology which nurtures the Jewish state is the paradigm of racism and doomed to failure. Consider the following sample:

> One must beware of the Jews, for they are treacherous and disloyal.[20]
>
> Racism: mankind has suffered from this evil both in ancient as well as in modern times. For indeed, Satan has, in the eyes of many people, made their evil actions appear beautiful ... Such a people are the Jews.[21]
>
> The clearest examples of racist belief and racial discrimination in the world are Nazism and Zionism.[22]
>
> Israel's mean, brutal, inhuman, fascist, racist, genocidal, cleansing wars ... The Jewish gangs waged racial cleansing against innocent Palestinians ... large scale and appalling massacres, saving no women and children.[23]
>
> It is mentioned in the Talmud: We [the Jews] are God's people on earth ... He forced upon the human animal and upon all the nations and races of the world that they serve us, and He spread us through the world to ride on them and to hold their reins. We must marry our beautiful daughters with Kings, Ministers and Lords and enter our sons into the various religions, thus we will have the final word in managing those countries. We should cheat them and arouse quarrels among them, then they fight each other ... Non-Jews are pigs whom God created in the shape of men in order that they be fit for service for the Jews, and God has created the world for them.[24]

These passages derive from either ancient Islamic sources, considered irrefutable, or from speculation mixing wishful thinking with emotional distress in the face of formidable and successful rivals who refuse to disappear from sight. However, while Palestinian defamation of the Jews and Zionists can be understood in terms of the subjective sense of humiliation caused by a century of conflict and loss, it is much harder to comprehend fabrication of 'evidence' from the Talmud. Unless the writers of the text have themselves fallen into the trap of their own propaganda, it remains incomprehensible how educated people of obvious scholarly merit could posit a fake text when the authentic textual source exists. Worse, how could they hope to train a generation of scholars? Understandably, the writers of the text refrained from quoting a precise reference and hid behind a general attribution to the Talmud. Thus, instead of erecting a logical case based on evidence, the writers of the text seem to be content with mud-slinging, vilification and deprecation, assuming that by force of repetition some will stick and serve the purpose of political indoctrination.

JIHAD AND MARTYRDOM

Yasser Arafat, the Head of the PA, was introduced on PA Television during a ceremony at Gaza's al-Azhar University on the occasion of *Mi'raj* Day:[25]

> This is the Commander, this is the man, his face is like a bright sunny day ... May Allah grant him noble qualities of manhood ... The leader of this nation whom Allah watches over ... Allah, Allah, Allah!!! Let Abu 'Ammar[26] lead us to jihad.

And then, came Arafat's turn to speak to the crowds:

> ...Bless you! Bless your struggle and your jihad on this land ... We renew our oath to the martyrs ... I say that all of us are made for martyrdom. Hence I say to all martyrs who have died, on behalf of the martyrs who still live ... that we stand by our oath to pursue [the battle].[27]

The message of martyrdom and jihad carried and repeated by the Head of the PA on its official media must influence the textbook writers to internalize these symbolic and powerful concepts. When Palestinian politicians are castigated for this sloganeering for Holy War in an era of peace negotiations, they always insist that jihad is meant in its metaphorical and spiritual sense. Certainly, this word may have been made to designate an intellectual striving too, but in Islamic *shari'a* it clearly means a military action designed to expand the outer borders of the Realm of Islam or to protect the boundaries of the Pax Islamica from encroaching Unbelievers. Since jihad does not necessarily have to be offensive and can also apply to defensive wars against aggressors, the Palestinians, like other Muslims, can claim that since the Jews had attacked them in Palestine, they are entitled to thwart the attackers by jihad.

When, at the turn of the century, new winds of liberalism and reform began blowing through the Islamic world from the West, apologetic currents in Islam attempted to limit jihad to its defensive scope, and to that of extending assistance to persecuted, or otherwise needy, Muslims. Liberal thinking has also been detected by some scholars when, in the early years of Islam, the Prophet is said to have usually elected peaceful means over violence and war.[28] Still violent interpretation prevails in the modern world, especially among Muslim fundamentalists[29] and certainly as regards Israel.[30] All the more so when statements of jihad are coupled with *qital* (battle), *nasr* (victory) and *shahid* (martyr). It is difficult to envisage a spiritual jihad where people are enjoined to partake in battles and where martyrs fall in combat, especially in an era of peace where those powerful symbols were supposed to have been abandoned.

The textbooks in Palestinian schools do not lag far behind the statements of the leadership, reflected in the reports of the Palestinian Television and other state media, directly relevant to the prevailing ambiance of a continuing struggle, in which the enemy is vilified and made legitimate prey:

> Know, my son, that Palestine is your country … that its pure soil is drenched with blood of martyrs… Why must we fight the Jews and drive them out of our land? [*The text follows a map of Palestine that replaces all of Israel*]. There will be a jihad and our country shall be freed. This is our story with the thieving conquerors. You must know, my boy, that Palestine is your serious responsibility.[31]
>
> My brothers! The oppressors have overstepped the boundary. Therefore, jihad and sacrifice are a duty … Are we to let

them steal its Arab nature?... Draw your sword, let us gather for war with red blood and blazing fire ... Death shall call and the sword shall be crazed for such slaughter ... Oh Palestine! The youth will redeem your land ... [*the book then asks the following questions to emphasize the message that Israel, the enemy, is to be fought and defeated*]:

> What is the road to victory over the enemy that the Poet mentions?...
> The Poet urges the Arabs to undertake jihad. Indicate the verse in which he does so.[32] In your left hand you carried the Koran and in your right hand an Arab sword. Without blood, not even one centimeter will be liberated ... Therefore, go forward crying: Allah Akbar! [Allah is the Greatest!].[33]
> Muslims must protect all mosques ... and must wage a jihad both of life and property, to liberate al-Aqsa Mosque from the Zionist conquest.[34]
> Make use of the following expressions to make logical sentences: ...The Zionist Danger ... calling for jihad ... [35]

A Poem of Palestine
To Palestine greetings from Arab hearts
Who has stubbornly and successfully resisted the chains of the enemies
For me, the promise of martyrdom
And Jerusalem is my song.[36]

> If the enemy has conquered part of the land [of Palestine] and those fighting for it are unable to repel the enemy, then jihad becomes the individual religious duty of every Muslim, man and woman, until the attack is successfully repelled and the land liberated from conquest.[37]

These sample passages from a wide array of PA textbooks, point out the conviction which the Authority wishes to instill into the minds of its children, from an early age until adolescence, as to the necessity and inevitability of a prolonged jihad to liberate all Palestine from the Jewish–Israeli grip. The insistent demand that the children should be prepared to fight and die in the service of this dream, is unequivocal inasmuch as the textbooks do not offer any glimmer of hope for a peaceful settlement. Rejection of Israel,

Zionists and Jews, based on moral, political, nationalistic and religious considerations, is total and irreversible. A protracted and open-ended struggle is foreseeable. Success at the end of the process is promised if every Arab and Muslim regard it as his/her personal endeavor (*fard 'ayn*) and a commitment of the community (*fard kifaya*).

This approach is surprisingly identical to that of the Hamas.[38] Although the PA has been at odds with its formidable domestic rival for the soul of the Palestinian people, Hamas messages are unequivocally and uncritically echoed in the Authority's textbooks. While this partnership and collaboration might mitigate differences between the two contenders and make for a Palestinian united façade now, it may prove later to be dangerous when the 5th and 7th graders of today come of age and begin to make their political choices.

SIGNIFICANCE AND CONSEQUENCES

Declaring lofty principles and promulgating liberal-minded constitutions, agreements and treaties, is one thing, fulfilling them in the real world, is another. Despite the Oslo Accords, there is a question as to what extent do the school textbooks – *a priori* commissioned or *a posteriori* approved and adopted by the PA – reflect its thinking and policy. And if they do, are they in accord with the Authority's engagements, obligations and commitments, both domestic and international?

On the domestic front, it is evident that a state in the making must lay claim to its past, its own unique identity, myths and culture, to build social cohesion, construct a political consciousness and rally the masses behind it. It is less clear why such legitimate claims to the past and to a national soil, must delegitimize others and deny their future, and nurture a confrontational state of mind among the children, who must grow to accept or reject the counterparts of Palestinian nationalism as enemies.

Strenuous efforts are being made in Israel, with admittedly mixed results, to initiate peace education projects and educate Israel's children, both as a necessity and as an ideal and a value in its own right. Several Israeli–Palestinian institutions have been striving to inculcate those values into Israelis and Palestinian Arabs with various degrees of success.[39] But official Palestinian textbooks seem not only oblivious of these efforts, but they appear intent on perpetuating negative stereotypes and scuttling attempts at reconciliation and goodwill.

On the international front, it appears that the PA, rather than breaking new paths and making its impact on world public opinion, is bent on sustaining the current state of affairs. To be sure, the Palestinian textbooks do not operate in a void. They conform to much of the anti-Jewish and anti-Israeli stereotyping that has prevailed in the Arab World before and after the beginning of the peace process in the late 1970s. For example, when Egyptians accuse expert Israeli farmers, who help develop Egyptian agriculture, of poisoning Arab land and destroying the local farming industry, no one should be surprised that the Palestinian representative in the Human Rights Commission in Geneva accuses Israelis of injecting the AIDS virus into hundreds of Palestinian children. When Robert Garaudy, the notorious French anti-Semite and Muslim convert who denies the Holocaust in his 'scholarly research', is given a hero's welcome in the Arab world, it is no coincidence that denial of the Holocaust among Arabs/Muslims seems universal. Even the Arabs who have made peace with Israel have banned *Schindler's List* from their screens, though there is nothing Israeli or Zionist about it; the problem is that it does illustrate an event in the Holocaust. They overlook and deny the antiquity of the Jewish presence in Israel even when they allocate rooms in their museums to other ancient peoples in the Middle East who have long disappeared from the scene. They even attribute Israel's peace measures to dark schemes reminiscent of the *Protocols of the Elders of Zion,* calculated to take over the Arab world culturally and economically in the 'New Middle East'.[40]

These organized and institutionalized attitudes towards Jews and Israel, once given the official stamp of authority and approval by Palestinian textbooks, will encourage Palestinian children to express those feelings and attitudes in public, because it is legitimate to do so. This was the reason why Israel insisted, in both the Oslo and Wye Agreements, on the eradication from textbooks of the statements of hatred, but it remains to be seen whether or not a turnabout in the official Palestinian attitude will be implemented. So far, the only changes PA made in this regard, mentioned above, was to restore the negative stereotypes eradicated by Israel from the Jordanian and Egyptian textbooks on the West Bank and in Gaza.

Palestinian children absorb anti-Israeli and anti-Jewish stereo-types at home and from their environment, and bring them as part of their luggage of knowledge and conviction when they come to school. That body of knowledge and convictions is reinforced by the teachers who, regardless of their personal experiences and convictions, must impart the contents of the textbooks, through personal additions, interpretations and elaborations.[41] In the litera-ture dealing with political violence, it has been repeatedly demonstrated that verbal abuse and delegitimation of the enemy are necessary steps towards the use of violence against him. Conviction, authority and action converge in a deadly cocktail. This is the most worrying question: will they only remain part of a polit-ical indoctrination program which reflects public opinion and/or shapes it, or will they push the growing children of today and the adults of tomorrow, to transcend rhetorics into dangerous and ominous grounds of hostile action?

NOTES

1. For specific reading on this see Ruth Firer, 'From Peace Making to Tolerance Building', in R. Moses (ed.), *Psychology of Peace and Conflict: the Israeli–Palestinian Experience* (Jerusalem: Truman Institute for the Advancement of Peace 1995) pp.79–86.
2. See the important treatise by Haim Gerber, 'Palestine and other territorial concepts in the Seventeenth Century', *International Journal of Middle East Studies*, 30 (1998), pp.563–72.
3. *National Palestinian Education for Fifth Grade*, no.550 (Ramallah/Gaza: Palestinian Authority), p.19.
4. *Islamic Culture for Eighth Grade*, no.576 (Ramallah/Gaza: Palestinian Authority), p.50.
5. *Palestinian National Education for Third Grade*, no.529 (Ramallah/Gaza: Palestinian Authority), p.12.
6. A report on PA Television of 19 May 1998, on a conference where these themes were discussed.
7. *Palestinian National Education for Second Grade*, no.519 (Ramallah/Gaza: Palestinian Authority), p.21.
8. *Modern Arab History and Contemporary Problems, Part 2 for Tenth Grade*, no.613 (Ramallah/Gaza: Palestinian Authority), p.66.
9. For example, *Social and National Education for Fifth Grade*, no.549 (Ramallah/Gaza: Palestinian Authority), pp.81, 84, 88, 89, 103, 107, 109, 110, 120, 124.
10. *Our Arabic Language for Fifth Grade*, no.542 (Ramallah/Gaza: Palestinian Authority), p.64.
11. *National Palestinian Education for First Grade*, no.509 (Ramallah/Gaza: Palestinian Authority), p.11.
12. *Geography of the Arab Homeland for Sixth Grade*, no.557 (Ramallah/Gaza: Palestinian Authority), pp.12, 20, 23, 36, 48, 50, 53, 55, 61, 66, 72, 73, 75, 80, 81, 88, 90, 115, 124.
13. *Geography of Arab Lands for Twelfth Grade*, no.650 (Ramallah/Gaza: Palestinian Authority), pp.49, 55.
14. *Composition and Summarizing for Eighth Grade*, no.581 (Ramallah/Gaza: Palestinian Authority), pp.13, 20.

15. *Modern Arab History and Contemporary Problems for Tenth Grade*, Part 2, no.613 (Ramallah/Gaza: Palestinian Authority), pp.70, 91, 95.
16. *Geography of the Arab Lands for Twelfth Grade*, no.650 (Ramallah/Gaza: Palestinian Authority), p.186.
17. Yoram Hazoni, Editorial, *Azure*, 2 (1997), pp.3–5.
18. Ibid.
19. *Outstanding Examples of Our Civilization for 11th Grade* (Ramallah/Gaza: Palestinian Authority).
20. *Islamic Education for Ninth Grade* (Ramallah/Gaza: Palestinian Authority), p.79.
21. *Islamic Education for Eighth Grade* (Ramallah/Gaza: Palestinian Authority), p.95.
22. *The New History of the Arabs and the World* (Ramallah/Gaza: Palestinian Authority), p.123.
23. PA Television, 14 May 1998.
24. *The New History of the Arabs and the World*, p.120.
25. *Mi'raj* is the ascension of the Prophet to Heaven from Temple Mount in Jerusalem.
26. The *nom de guerre* of Arafat, borrowed from an illustrious general in early Islam.
27. PA Television, 1 January 1995.
28. See 'Jihad' , *The New Encyclopaedia of Islam* (Ramallah/Gaza: Palestinian Authority).
29. See Sayyid Qut'b, *Ma'rakatuna ma'a al-Yahud* [*Our Campaign against the Jews*], (Beirut, 1986); and R. Israeli, *The Charter of Allah: the Platform of the Hamas*, in Y. Alexander (ed.) *The 1988–9 Annual of Terrorism* (Amsterdam: Martinus Nijhoff, 1990) pp.99–134.
30. Esther Webman, 'Anti-Semitic Motives in the Ideology of Hizbollah and the Hamas', in *Projects for the Study of Antisemitism* (Tel Aviv: Tel Aviv University, 1994).
31. *Our Arabic Language for Fifth Grade*, no.542, pp.64–70. The map is on p.64.
32. *Reader and Literary Texts for Eighth Grade*, no.578, pp.120–2.
33. Ibid., pp.131–3.
34. *Islamic Education for Seventh Grade*, p.184.
35. Ibid., fn.35.
36. *Our Arabic Language for Second Grade*, Part 2, no.513, p.51.
37. *Islamic Education for Seventh Grade*, no.564, p.108.
38. See the Charter of the Hamas quoted above.
39. Non-government organizations like, 'Children of the Middle East', 'Flowers' and joint educational institutions like the Israel–Palestine Center for Research and Information are active in this domain in Israel.
40. Shimon Peres' book on the *New Middle East* was criticized in Egypt as '"conclusively demonstrating" that the old international Jewish conspiracy was still valid, even though its author is hailed throughout the Arab world as the champion of peace'.
41. For a good discussion of the education process see D.C. Phillips, 'The Good, the Bad and the Ugly: The Many Faces of Constructivism', *Educational Researcher*, 24, 7 (1995), p.7.

3. Peace, Peace and No Peace

INTRODUCTION

When Camp David II (July 2000) was convened to settle the protracted conflict between Israelis and Palestinians, one could not help reminiscing about Camp David I (September 1978), in which a similar valiant effort was made to reconcile Israel and Egypt and produce peace between them. However, when one looks at the way in which Egyptians conceive of this 'reconciliation' 20 years later, and the sustained levels of hatred, bigotry and rejection of Jews, Zionism and Israel that have become part and parcel of the Egyptian psyche, one wonders how these old stereotypes (that are common to most Arabs and to many Muslims around the globe) have survived the way they do in Egypt, especially as the Palestinians have come to know the Israelis more intimately over the years.

The anti-Israeli-Jewish-Zionist sentiments in Egypt and the rest of the Arab world are not the result of the Israeli–Arab dispute of the past 100 years. But they have certainly been exacerbated – indeed rationalized and justified – by the way in which the Arabs have come to understand, fear or suspect their Israeli rivals. Therefore, the peace process between Israel and its Arab neighbors – which had started at Camp David I and was predicated on the notion that Israel would give up lands in return for peace and normalization – did not work according to Israel's wishes. Those countries that received their territories in full, such as Egypt and Jordan, did not diminish one iota of their set attitudes towards the Jews and Israel,[1] and so it is with the Palestinians several years after the Oslo Accords (1993), where they undertook to desist from violence and incitement against Israel and the Jews.[2]

From the outset it was clear that Israel's partners for peace were far less interested in normalization than in retrieving their lost territories, and once they gained their desires, they desisted from reconciliation, something which highlights the different perspectives of the parties to these agreements. As far as Egypt was concerned, once the Sinai was back in the Egyptian fold (1981), peace with Israel was taken hostage and subjected to Egyptian-set standards for the expected behavior of Israel, which if not met would deny her the benefits of normalization. First, it was 'only the minor question of Taba', which if resolved to Cairo's full satisfaction, would produce normalization. Then, it was the Israeli bombing of the nuclear reactor in Baghdad (1981), the incursion of Israel into Lebanon (1982), and then the Palestinian issue, the Intifada, and the nuclear potential of Israel, that stood in the way to normalization which never came. In other words, even when there is a clear commitment by the Arabs regarding the 'end of the conflict', of the kind Israel has been trying to achieve with the Palestinians, there is no guarantee that normalization and reconciliation would set in, even after Israel pays the territorial price in full.

The Arabs know full well Israel's yearning for reconciliation and normalization, therefore that has become their choice weapon to coerce her to yield to their views and political attitudes. For example, after they retrieved their lands, which were the only trump card Israel possessed in the negotiations, they transformed the 'peace for territories' formula into 'peace for good behavior'. In this situation, it is more political for President Mubarak to retain the leadership in the Arab world in his capacity as the chief counsellor for peace negotiations with Israel, in order to keep his country's primacy in the region and to make Israel 'shrink back to its natural size', as the Egyptian hierarchy likes to say. And when it does, it would no longer be in anyone's interest to take it as a partner, let alone an ally.

Much has been said and observed about the nature of the Cold War that has prevailed between Israel and Egypt since Camp David I; while Egyptian representatives in Israel are pampered by Israeli society and its media, Israeli diplomats in Egypt have been practically excommunicated. In international events in Egypt (conferences, exhibitions) Israelis are not welcome, while Egyptian scholars, professionals and journalists invited to Israel, at its own expense, often do not so much as respond. The major farming projects established by Israel in Egypt not only are not rewarded by recognition, but often the Israeli experts are accused in the press of contaminating the Egyptian soil with a view to annihilating Egyptian farming. It is hard for Egypt, which prides itself on being the most ancient agricultural society in the world, to admit that it receives generous and advanced aid from the Jews and Israel, whom it seeks to diminish. Denial of the Holocaust, and the related prohibition of showing *Schindler's List* in the movie theatres, for fear that it might prove its veracity and elicit sympathy for the Jews and Israel, continues to haunt the daily agenda of many Egyptian writers. Vicious anti-Semitic attacks against the Jews, and the related denigration of the State of Israel, have become so common that even Shimon Peres' supremely conciliatory and moderate book about the 'New Middle East'[3] has been interpreted as 'proof' that the Jews wish to take over the world, this time economically, in line with the schemes stated in the infamous *Protocols of the Sages of Zion*.

However, these set patterns over the past two decades of peace should not preclude changes and developments down the years. It is therefore necessary to re-examine the issue at regular intervals to gauge whether, and to what extent, there has been any progress towards reconciliation. In this essay we shall report on the Egyptian press during the months spanning the turn of the century and the Millennium, and examine the changes that may have occurred. The findings enumerated below do not show, unfortunately, that either the articles or editorials in the Egyptian press, whether linked to the establishment or to the opposition, have been toned down or mellowed over the past few months compared to the past decades. These writings have remained grossly anti-Semitic, geared to diminishing Israel and denigrating it, to accusing it of all the ills suffered by the Arabs and the world, and to showing that no reconciliation is possible with it; even to leaving open the ominous prospect of the resumption of hostilities.

THE EGYPTIAN PRESS OF LATE 1999 AND EARLY 2000

The gravity of the positions adopted by the Egyptian press can only be emphasized against the background of the firm grip the authorities have on its demeanor, be it the 'free press' of the establishment, or of the opposition, which is usually more difficult to rein in. For example, none of them would dare to attack President Mubarak personally for fear of severe reprisals from the authorities. But as regards Israel, complete freedom, even encouragement on occasion, is allotted to all, and they compete in scorning, demeaning and calumniating her. The result is that academics and

professionals who write the condemnatory articles against Israel, or
are fed by them, boycott Israel without reservation. And, while
Israel annually commemorates the anniversary of the peace by
symposia, interviews, commentaries and special broadcasts, for
Egypt only Evacuation Day of Israeli troops from the Sinai is
celebrated.

It is no wonder, therefore, that whoever scans through Egyptian
newspapers these past few months, cannot but be surprised or
even deeply shaken by the intensity of the hatred towards Israel
that is reflected in them. For the initiated, however, nothing is
surprising or new, just disappointing and frustrating, and one can
assume that what was will also be, unless the Egyptian hierarchy
comprehends the irreparable damage caused to peace, to the bilateral relations with Israel and to the psyche of the new generation of
Arabs. For, exactly as Israel's full withdrawal from the Sinai has
become a precedent for the rest of the Arab countries to follow, so
will Egypt establish the precedent of pursuing campaigns of hatred,
in disregard to its commitments in the peace accords, and get away
with that. In practice this would signify that any Arab country,
including Palestine, would be able to accept any wording dictated
to it by Israel as a prerequisite for withdrawal, knowing full well
that it will immediately be ignored thereafter.

The themes that express this virulence seem unchanging,
though every time new twists and details are added from current
affairs and then incorporated for illustration. The most important
among them will be discussed and documented below. In this
ideologically loaded scheme Jews, Zionists and Israelis are inter-
changeable, inasmuch as Jews can transmit their innate ignoble
deficiencies to the Israelis, or Israel or the Jews can be portrayed as
responsible for Egypt's problems and Judaism and Zionism as
constituting world centers of dark plots aimed at undermining the
human order from within.

Israel is still shaken by the recent announcements from
Damascus which denied the Holocaust; how much greater is the
shock when this sickness of the mind takes place in Egypt, 22 years
after the Peace Accords were signed and signs of reconciliation
were thought to have begun to sink in. World events that have
nothing to do with Israel, like the David Irving trial in London,
have occasioned vicious hysterical attacks in the Egyptian press in
recent months, not against the denier of the *Shoah*, but against the
verdict of the British court of law. Although the press did not report

in detail the deliberations, debates, evidence and cross-examinations during the trial, the judgement of the court infuriated it. Similarly, when Haider won the elections in Austria and there was a chance that he might join the new government, the Egyptian press rejected with disgust Israeli and Western protests. The Stockholm Conference against the denial of the *Shoah* was also widely condemned in Egypt. Even such a humanitarian act as Germany's announcement of its plan to compensate Jewish slave laborers during the Nazi era, came under heavy fire from this press. When the Pope visited the Holy Land and he, together with the Church, begged pardon for their persecutions of the Jews in history, these gestures were rejected lock, stock and barrel, by the Egyptian press, as if the Jews, their peace partners, were condemned for ever to remain beaten, persecuted and living under oppressors of various sorts. Worse, when Israel came under severe attacks in Lebanon at the hand of Hizbullah, in the weeks that preceded its final retreat from there, accusations were hurled against Israel in the Egyptian press for its 'Nazi' policies that were aimed at 'genocide against the Lebanese people'.

THE MAIN THEMES OF HATRED

In February 2000, the Minister of Regional Co-operation, Shimon Peres, probably the most outspoken and influential champion of peace in the region, delivered a speech at the Davos Conference in Switzerland, where he mentioned that Israel did not wish to be the only 'island of prosperity and spot of cleanliness' in an ocean of poverty. The cataract of gutter language that was poured on him in the Egyptian press merits some remarks, especially those written by a senior writer, Walid Badran, in the establishment daily *al-Akhbar*. He said that Israeli society was racist and corrupt, where black Jews from Ethiopia were underemployed and discriminated against so that most of them lived beneath the poverty line, and therefore Israel had no lesson to teach others about fighting poverty. Peres' words at that conference have a totally different significance for this journalist: 'The spot of progress is no different from the spot on Monica Lewinski's skirt. In truth, it is a Western spot on the Arab garb, which one day will be totally expunged by a new detergent'.[4] Incidentally, in the English version of that article, published the next day in the mainstream *Egyptian Gazette*, it is emphasized that the 'spot will be removed by a powerful Arab detergent'.[5]

Nor does the Egyptian academic world shun the same language, all under the guise of pure scientific truth. Dr 'Abd al Wahhab al-Masiri, who published an encyclopaedic collection on 'Jews, Judaism and Zionism',[6] and claimed that Zionism had 'invented the Jewish people in order to impose its ghetto-mentality on the peoples of the world',[7] has inspired and served as reference to many a respectable journalist in Egypt. One of them, 'Abd al-Rahman Abu al-'Awf, a writer in the most prestigious daily in Egypt, *Al-Ahram*, cited this very passage.[8] In the same vein, this passage was mentioned in the Arabic London-based *Al-Hayat*. The Cairo Center for Political Studies, affiliated with the University of Cairo, convened a conference on this very theme (29–30 March 2000), to discuss that encyclopaedic masterpiece.

Anti-Semitic stereotypes are rife, especially in cartoon form in the Egyptian press. In one of them which appeared in the opposition *Al-Ahali*, a crooked-nosed Jew, holding a blood-dripping dagger, carries on his back a bag of spoils which carries the inscription 'the Arab lands', and on his head the double symbols of Zionism and Nazism, like inseparable Siamese twins. The hand that holds a powerful torch and projects a strong beam of light on the pictured miserable Jew, is identified as the 'Arab press', which claims the credit for revealing the true nature of the Jews. The cartoon came as a reaction to the protest that the Israeli Ambassador in Cairo lodged with the authorities there for the wild attacks against Israel in the Egyptian press, and the caption explains that the hideous Jew in the cartoon is none other than 'the Israeli Ambassador who launched a hysterical broadside on the Egyptian press'.[9]

Anti-Semitic stereotypes naturally link the atavistic deficiencies of the Jews with what has been happening today in Israel: 'Abd al-'Azm Hamad, an *Al-Ahram* writer, enumerates all the acts of corruption in contemporary Israel, especially the President Weizmann affair, and finds in them the decisive proof for al-Masiri's Encyclopaedia depictions, mentioned above, linking together the Jews and the Zionists.[10] Both, says he, are 'greedy, lusting for money and devoid of morality'. The 'Israeli personality' is imbued with these qualities, therefore:

> ... they would drag their feet before anyone negotiating with them, cheat, refuse to give up anything in their possession

until they are forced to do so, and even then only after they had caused confusion and chaos and spread around lies and false pretences regarding the right to rule that God has allotted them.[11]

The Jewish conspiracy to rule the world, which draws its inspiration from the *Protocols of the Elders of Zion*, also continues to occupy a prominent place in the Egyptian press these days. In cartoons, the Jewish octopus sends its tentacles to all directions, in order to suck the blood and the water of the Arabs, or to reach all the corridors of power in the world.[12] For *al-Wafd*, Israeli Nazism is like a new time bomb that threatens to destroy the world.[13] Thus, any international conference, symposium or convention that were not to Egypt's liking (such as the world conference on demography or the Gatt agreements) were described as a Western attempt to control the Third World, headed by the USA, which is guided by a Zionist gang who wishes to manage world affairs from the corridors of the White House, with the aim of causing destruction and chaos.[14] Similar Jewish designs to take over Canada, Europe and especially Sweden, were cited in other media.[15]

Anti-Jewish (and Christian) accusations concerning the Jewish penchant for forgery, which have accompanied Islam since its inception, still emerge now and then in the contemporary Egyptian press. Jews are accused of forging modern history, such as the story of the Holocaust. We have already mentioned the Irving affair, which, though its historical and human aspects did not interest the Egyptian public and were hardly reported, served as a launching pad for the Egyptian press to bedevil the Jews and the Zionists. Irving was seen as the victim of world Zionism which 'terrorised the world press and publishers, in order to prevent the publication of his books'.[16] The Jews were accused of exploiting their political, financial and media power to 'continue to spread their lies about the Holocaust and silence all those who reveal those lies to the world'.[17]

Thus, according to these accusations, using organized terrorism to cultivate the legend of the *Shoah*, the Jews have turned this story into a fact which ties down the hands of historians.[18] The Jews are also blamed for forging history in the face of existing scientific articles which have proven that there were never any gas chambers, or which have revised downwards the figures of the dead.[19] Abundant 'scientific documentation' has been produced by the Egyptian press to back these falsehoods.[20] Some papers have even claimed that Jews were not harmed during the Second World War, and that, quite the contrary, they profited from it, for had Japan and Hitler won the War, the Jews could not have continued to blackmail the world with their lies.[21]

However, one has to beware of blanket generalizations in this regard, in spite of the overwhelmingly incriminating evidence against the Egyptian press, if only because of the few courageous voices who have dared to distance themselves from this horrendous consensus, although their motivations are at times questionable. For example, Hazem 'abd al-Hama'in, wrote: 'even if the Jews have exaggerated the scope of the *Shoah*, its denial means aligning oneself with the camp of racists in Egypt and the USA, who support ethnic cleansing and the superiority of the Aryan race'.[22] This does not constitute a flat condemnation of the Nazi evil based on moral grounds, but a utilitarian approach which fears what might happen to the Arabs in the West. By contrast, Rida' Hilal, attacked the Holocaust deniers who, 'in their eagerness to mobilize the *Shoah* against the Jews, are sinning against all the principles of liberalism and enlightenment and find themselves in the same camp as the fascists and the Nazis'.[23] Dr 'abd al-Mun'im Sa'id, the Head of the Ahram Center for Strategic Studies, has also rejected the articles of the *Shoah* deniers for their 'disregarding the unequivocal fact that under the Nazi regime Jews were killed because of their Judaism'. He was also adamant that:

> Denying the Holocaust in order to negate the existence of Israel, could act as a boomerang, because it helps the racists of Europe, who also hate Arabs and Muslims, and exposes the Arabs as the allies of the extreme right, and the partners of murderers.[24]

Others, while acknowledging the Holocaust, dig up all manner of rationalizations to justify it. The notorious Egyptian anti-Semite, Anis Mansur, who had been paradoxically in the entourage of peace-maker President Sadat, and continues to be a very widely read columnist, has recently written in the government-sponsored *Al-Ahram*, trying to 'explain' why Jews are so sensitive to the loss of life in their midst during their 'acts of barbarism' against the Palestinians. He asserts that it is due to their small numbers in Israel, and in the world at large, compared to the hundreds of

millions of Arabs and over one billion Muslims, that they gain
support from world Jewry in particular, for if it were not for their
increasing casualties:

> ... it would become clear to the world that what happened to
> the Jews in Germany, Poland and Russia was justified. It is not
> true that all Jews want peace. There is a suicidal sect among
> them that does not desire to live. Thus, they kindle the
> people's hatred and hostility, and as a result the people turn
> against them. Although there are many intelligent people
> among them, they use their intellect to devise new ways for
> people everywhere to hate them and unite against them.
>
> Because the Jewish people are overcome by megalomania,
> they do not bow their heads in order to survive; they prefer to
> surface behind the steering wheels of the leadership in
> Europe and the USA, in order to evoke the world's sympathy.
> They were in the shadows, in the rear lines and in the dark
> alleys before the establishment of the State of Israel. They
> prefer an Israel surrounded by enemies to a ghetto that no one
> has heard of ... There are sects in Israel that view the Jewish
> State as a heretic one. They believe the Israelites deserve to be
> tortured and that what Hitler did to the Jews in the West is an
> appropriate punishment for their mistreatment of the Jews of
> the East.[25]

The author does not seem to be bothered the least that the
Holocaust preceded the 'mistreatment' in Israel of the Eastern Jews
by European Jews, since their encounter only happened in Israel
after the *Shoah*. In any case, the Jews are no longer able to countenance the 'stones and artillery of the Arabs' and will be forced to
emigrate to Europe and the USA. And he concludes that the Jews
are too intimidated to stay in the country, and are in a state of high
alert and eternal readiness; this serves as the melting pot that unites
their otherwise different skin colours, religions, schools of thought
and social strata. For without it 'nothing would remain of Israel,
with the exception of clerics, the elderly, the sick and ... [Ariel]
Sharon'.[26] This pathetic 'explanation' by someone who considers
himself, and is viewed by others, as one of the leading intellectuals
of Egypt, aims at clarifying for his readership the embarrassing fact
of why this odd Jewish state has been quite successful in spite of all
its built-in deficiencies. As on previous occasions, by swearing at

the Jews and Israel, this kind of hateful writing is supposed to provide relief for the otherwise unexplainable, blindingly obvious distinction between the democratic, prosperous and ingenuous tiny state of Israel, and the surrounding authoritarian, backward, corrupt and poor Arab countries. To all appearances, these Arab writers would rather pull down the Jewish State, which exposes their own frailties by comparison, than learn from it in order to increase their GNP 20-fold.

In fact, during the Intifadah that broke out on 28 September 2000, which brought about the election of Ariel Sharon to head the Israeli government, the maliciousness and vitriol against Israel, both on the street and in the Arabic press, only increased. Not only were Jewish shrines torched by Arabs in Nablus and Jericho while the Palestinians were watching, but in Ramallah a procession took place where a donkey dressed in the Jewish prayer shawl and with a swastika on his head was marched down the street, in an obvious attempt to demean and humiliate the Jewish faith, without any specific provocation. Some years ago there was an incident in Israel when a Jew in Hebron offended Islam by waving a poster in which the Prophet was pictured in the proximity of a pig. She was duly indicted and convicted by an Israeli court for anti-religious incitement, as would be the case in any civilized country. In Ramallah the perpetrators of this anti-Jewish abomination were considered heroes and they were acclaimed by their people, just as the arsonists of the Jewish sites in Nablus and Jericho were applauded.

The Egyptians, far from recoiling from these acts, on the contrary used Palestinian anger against Israel to prop up their own hatred of the Jews, and used the election of Sharon as an excuse to burst into a new wave of viciousness, which seemed to have no motivation for hurting the feelings of their rivals and the perverse satisfaction gained therefrom. Mustafa Bakr, Editor of the weekly *al-Usbu'*, described a 'dream' he had when he was delegated by the Egyptian government to serve as a bodyguard of Ariel Sharon on his visit to Cairo. The scene of the dream begins at the airport, and a pig – which is equally abhorrent to the Jews – is the star:

> After a short while the pig landed; his face was diabolical, a murderer; his hands soiled with the blood of women and children. A criminal who should be executed in the town square. Should I remain silent as many others did? Should I guard this butcher on my homeland's soil? All of a sudden, I

forgot everything: the past and the future, my wife and children, and I decided to do it. I pulled my gun and aimed it at the cowardly pig's head. I emptied all the bullets and screamed: 'Blood-vengeance for the [Egyptian] POWs, blood-vengeance for the martyrs.' The murderer collapsed under my feet. I breathed a sigh of relief. I realized the meaning of virility, and of self-sacrifice. The criminal died. I stepped on the pig's head with my shoes and screamed from the bottom of my heart: 'Long live Egypt, long live Palestine, Jerusalem will never die and never will the honor of the nation be lost.' I kept screaming at the top of my lungs until my wife put her hand on me. I woke up from this most beautiful dream and decided not to surrender to humiliation.[27]

CONCLUSIONS

These sorts of reports and commentaries have dominated the Egyptian scene in the past few months, a direct continuation of the Arab way of venting their anger and frustrations against Israel, regardless of whether it evacuated Arab territories, made peace or concessions, or showed its interest in regional cooperation. For Israel can do no good: if it refuses to give in, it is greedy and obstinate; and if it does, it is only because the Arabs have prevailed upon it. If it refuses to cooperate with the Arabs, it is due to its arrogance and foreign character; but when it does, it is accused of economic imperialism. When it fails, it is because of the innate misery and curse that Allah had brought upon the Jews; but when it makes some stunning breakthrough, that is because it is the client of America, and so on and so forth.

The above sample of hateful attacks against the Jews in the Egyptian and other Arab press is only the tip of the iceberg; the main body remains submerged under the water, unexposed to the scrutiny of the public, except for those whose duty or interest it is to follow these events and analyse them periodically. The Israelis in particular, who have had their fill of the conflict and want to see or hear nothing that disturbs their sweet dreams of peace, remain curiously and dangerously obtuse to this continuous litany of visceral hatred towards them, two decades after the bells of peace had rung in their naive ears. People of Western background find it difficult to realize that, while they mean well, it does not necessarily signify that their interlocutors reason similarly, and when their neighbors use modern terms like democracy, peace, civil rights, justice, lie, truth, fairness, concessions and negotiations, this does not necessarily mean that they conceive of those notions in the established Western fashion. Therefore, in this kafkaesque world there is no cause and effect: when you achieve peace, it does not mean reconciliation; when you wage hostilities, this does not amount to war; when you make concessions, it does not mean that you cannot go back on them when opportune times emerge; and when you pledge something it commits you only as long as this is convenient to you.

The infrastructure of anti-Israeli and anti-Jewish hatred, and the feelings of jealousy, helplessness, contempt and a total misapprehension that the Arabs evince, have been so deeply imprinted on Arab and Muslim consciousness for so many centuries – and more so with the onset of the Arab–Israeli dispute in which Jews showed their mettle for the first time and tackled Muslims and Arabs as equals – that it is hard to devise any easy way of turning things around. The peace process, if anything, has not mitigated these sentiments. Quite the contrary, it has woven together all those elements of hatred into a powerful fabric, and it is difficult to see how this might be weakened at the edges, unless the Arab countries first decide upon and then delve into a deep, courageous and determined process of soul-searching, from kindergartens to the press and academia. And it is very difficult to predict whether this will happen any time soon.

These incriminating materials against Egypt (and the rest of the Arab world) do not require much searching, or commentary according to one's political views or wishful thinking; they are so steady, vast, omnipresent, repetitive, prevalent and diffuse in all aspects of Egyptian society, for many years, in war and in peace, that no one can escape them – they are part of the infrastructure of education and socialization in Egyptian (and other Arab) society. Worse, there is no known serious attempt being made by the Egyptian authorities to mitigate these dangerous trends; therefore no one can venture an educated guess as to whether, and when, they might be uprooted. Quite the contrary, the fact that the hierarchy turns a blind eye, or may even be blinking with approval, is by necessity interpreted as official backing for these atrocious utterances. In turn, such articles by Egypt's appreciated and widely read writers, find currency in the rest of the Arab world. Therefore, it is not enough to raise the consciousness of the world to these hateful norms of human behavior, it is also imperative to arouse the conscience of those who care and those who can turn things around.

Much of the blame for this state of affairs lies at Israel's door, inasmuch as in order not to wreck the boat of peace, it did not deploy the requisite efforts to make any negotiations or concessions conditional on substantial steps by the Arab governments to control these waves of hatred. Camp David I did not put an end to Egyptian vilifications of Israel and the Jews in spite of Sadat's commitment to embrace such a policy, starting with textbooks of school-children where these ideas are systematically inculcated. In the Oslo and Wye agreements, repeated and emphatic obligations were imposed on the Palestinians in this regard, only to see them frustrated by reality.[28] But Israel, instead of taking firm steps as it did in the Haider affair, has adopted an inexplicably lenient attitude towards the Arabs; something that can only encourage them to pursue their anti-Semitic attacks.

This caving in by Israel is not appreciated in the Arab world as a strategy on her part to avoid conflict and promote dialogue, but is seen as either silent confirmation of their irrefutable calumnies which Israel must live with, or as a lever to squeeze more concessions from her under the threat of more scorn and libel. They look at Israel, smile under their moustaches and wonder how more reluctant and shy can the Jews be in defence of their national and personal pride in the face of the most outrageous attacks hurled against them. When the Jewish girl in Hebron dared to insult local Muslims by drawing a pig and waving it in their faces, the Israeli police considered this as creating a public offence, and arrested and jailed her for a few months. The Arabs took this action as a matter of course, because their faith does not bear denigration, even when it is individual and not government sponsored. If their insults against the Jews were to be judged by the same criteria, most of their intellectuals and spiritual and political leaders should be serving prison terms now. But they are not, in spite of the fact that they not only attack Jews on personal whim, but that they often represent the official anti-Semitic policy of their societies and authorities. The result is that there is nothing to stop their abuses of the Jews and Israel; and, as Israel disregards those daily abuses, this encourages more. Worse, while the Israeli government shows differential treatment on this subject – that is, the Arabs can say what they wish while the Jews are restricted – there is no escaping the conclusion that in Arab eyes Islam reigns supreme and untouchable, while Judaism is free prey for all.

NOTES

1. For the underlying themes governing the Arab views of Israel, see R. Israeli, *Peace is in the Eye of the Beholder* (Berlin/New York: Mouton Press, 1986).
2. See Chapter 2, 'Educating Palestinian Children'.
3. Shimon Peres, *The New Middle East* (Steimatzki: Bnei Brak, 1993) [Hebrew].
4. *Al-Akhbar*, 2 February 2000, p.6.
5. *Egyptian Gazette*, 3 February 2000, p.3.
6. Masiri, abd al-Wahhab, 'Jews, Judaism and Zionism' (Cairo, 2000) [Arabic] .
7. Ibid.
8. *Al-Ahram*, 13 February 2000, p.26.
9. *Al-Ahali*, 5 April 2000, p.7.
10. *Al-Ahram*, 24 January 2000, p.1.
11. Samir Rajab, *Al-Gumhuriyya*, 7 December 1999, p.2.
12. See, for example, the opposition paper *Al-Wafd*, 7 March 2000, p.8 and *al-Ahram*, 25 March 2000, p.8.
13. *Al-Wafd*, 26 February 2000, p.7.
14. See Mustafa Mahmur, 27 March 2000, p.24.
15. See, for example, *Al-Ahram*, 20 March 2000, p.7 and 17 May 2000, p.10; and also *al-Wafd*, 4 April 2000, p.8; the articles in *Al-Gumhuriyya* by its editor Samir Rajab,14 February 2000, p.12 and 5 March 2000, p.12.
16. *Al-Ahram*, 25 January 2000, p.26.
17. *Al-Akhbar*, 11 May 2000, p.22.
18. *Al-Wafd*, 13 February 2000, p.13; *Al-Ahram*, 19 April 2000, p.2 and the *Egyptian Gazette*, 20 April 2000, p.3.
19. Dr Sa'id al-Lawandi, *Al-Ahram*, 30 December 1999, p.6.
20. See, for example, the establishment weekly, *Rooz al-Yussuf*, 28 January 2000, pp.61–3.
21. For example, *Al-Hayat*, 31 January 2000, p.17; *Al-Akhbar*, 26 January 2000; *Al-Ahram*, 17 May 2000, p.10; *Al-Ahram*, 18 April 2000, p.6; the *Egyptian Gazette*, 17 April 2000; and more.
22. *Al-Ahram*, 19 April 2000, p.4.
23. *Al-Ahram*, 20 April 2000, p.4.
24. *Al-Ahram al-'Arabi*, 6 May 2000.
25. *Al-Ahram*, 13 February 2001. Cited and translated by the Middle East Media and Research Institute (MEMRI), Dispatch 188, 22 February 2001.
26. Ibid.
27. *Al-Usbu'*, Cairo, 12 February 2001; cited by Al Quds al-Arabi, London, 13 February 2001; translated and published by MEMRI.
28. See Chapter 2 above.

4. Arab and Islamic Anti-Semitism*

APOLOGIA

There is no doubt that, though the anti-Jewish sentiment that one detects in Arab and Islamic utterances has deep and ancient historical roots, it has been exacerbated in recent decades due to the ongoing Arab–Israeli conflict and the resultant bloodshed. And, as the conflict escalated, so did the anti-Semitic rhetoric on the part of Israel's rivals. One would have expected then, that as the peace talks progress between the Arabs and Israel, there would be a decrease in the intensity of anti-Israeli and anti-Jewish virulence among those of the Arabs who have succeeded in overcoming the psychological hurdle separating them from Israel. But it turns out that reality frustrates hopes, so much so that the very assumption that innate hatred and fundamental attitudes inherent in a religion or a culture, can shrink or be reversed in the face of a changing reality, is called into question.

SOURCES OF ARAB AND ISLAMIC ANTI-SEMITISM

Arabs in general have been using the words 'Jews', 'Zionists' and 'Israelis' interchangeably, despite their protestations to the contrary. The negative stance they usually adopt towards these terms and what they symbolize, stems from three strata of sources:

- The traditional anti-Jewish attitudes cultivated by the Holy Koran and other Islamic writings.

---

* Originally published as *Arab and Islamic Anti-Semitism*, ACPR Policy Paper No.104 (Sha'arei Tikva: Ariel Centre, 2000).

- An incremental layer of Christian anti-Semitic stereotypes which have seeped into the Arab world, either through the Christian Arabs who are part of the Arab national movement, or through the importation of such European writings *as The Protocols of the Elders of Zion*.
- As a result of the ongoing conflict in the Middle East, and the ensuing Arab need to dehumanize Jews in order to justify their annihilation.

The Islamic element in anti-Jewish attitudes of the Arabs finds its wildest and most vitriolic expression in the writings of the fundamentalist Muslims, foremost among them Sayyid Qut'b, the martyred head of the Muslim Brothers in Egypt, who has become, especially since he was executed by the Nasserite regime in 1966, the guiding light to all Muslim radicals in this regard. In his long essay entitled *Our Campaign Against the Jews*,[1] he toes the doctrinal line of medieval Islam, but his modern usage of the old doctrine extends and even transcends the original boundaries. For, if during the times of the Prophet there were already references to the Jews, which found their expression in the Holy Koran, and in the vast body of *Hadith* literature, in the modern times, and at the hands of radicals like Qut'b, the accusations against, and the condemnations of the Jews have gained in intensity and emotionalism due to the bitterness generated by the conflict. Hence, the tremendous intellectual land scholarly effort exerted by many Arabs and Muslims in general, but fundamentalists in particular, to develop this repository of irrational hatred into a rational and systematic 'scientific' doctrine.

Qut'b wrote his essay in the 1950s, and it remains an excellent example of this endeavor, when we consider that his work is profusely quoted by other Muslim radicals who have wide currency in the Islamic world. So much so, that the government of Saudi Arabia, the so-called 'moderate' Islamic State, which does not attract much scorn from the West due to its wealth and petroleum, found it necessary to re-issue that book in the 1970s, together with other anti-Semitic materials such as *The Protocols of the Elders of Zion*. Since Qut'b taught that the only divine truth left to humankind was Islam, it follows that all others, including Christianity and Judaism, are repositories of distortion and falsehood, not reflections of divine revelations. Therefore Islam, as the only one Truth, must retake its role of universal leadership in order to liberate mankind from their errors. Moreover, Jews and Christians, as purveyors of false revelations, were *ipso facto* insidious to Islam, as the current Jewish–Christian conspiracy against it proves. Therefore, no coexistence with them is possible. In his own words:

> Truth and falsehood cannot coexist on earth ... When Islam makes a general declaration to establish the lordship of Allah on earth and to liberate humanity from the worship of other creatures, it is contested by those who have usurped Allah's sovereignty on earth. They will never make peace. Then, Islam goes forth destroying them to free humans from their power ... The liberating struggle of Jihad does not cease until all religion belongs to Allah.[2]

In Qut'b's thinking the Jewish danger to Islam, and the West's assault against Islam, are one and the same, because the Jews are only a metaphor of the general danger to Islam's destiny, due to their basic dislike of Islam. The Jews intend to destroy it and they would use any means to attain that goal. According to Ron Nettler, who translated Qut'b's work:

> In a deceptively simple and highly readable style, Qut'b wove together Islamic historical, religious, political and emotional strands. In the resultant tapestry Islam's sacred sources came together in the focal point of the Jewish problem. With literary precision and religious acumen, Qut'b created a clear and prominent Jewish physiognomy on a tight-knitted fabric which promised great durability over the years. This promise was not frustrated.[3]

Qut'b indeed transmitted a message of eternal enmity between Jews and Islam, since the inception of Islam to the present day. It is a war that 'has not been extinguished, and its blaze continues raging in all corners of the world'. The Jewish conspiracy is designed to pry Muslims away from their faith. This is supported by quotations from the Holy Koran. Qut'b transposes the old stereotypes anchored in the Islamic tradition into the modern world, and finds Zionism as a contemporary expression of the old machinations of Jews against Islam, in much the same vein as *The Protocols of the Elders of Zion* which circulate in the Arab world and lend confirmation from independent Christian sources, about the nature of the Jews. In his essay, Qut'b elaborates on the natural disposition of the Jews:

> The Jews feel that they are cut off from the tree of life, and they just wait for humanity to meet with disaster. They suffer these same punishments repeatedly, in the form of dissensions among peoples and war, which the Jews themselves foment in order to make profits from them. Through these wars and disturbances they cultivate their continuing hatred and the destructiveness which they impose on people and which others impose on them. All the evil arises only from their destructive egoism.[4]

Translated into political terms, the Islamic grievances against the Jews, Zionism and Israel can be summed up in the following terms:

- Israel gave shelter to the Jews, whom the Koran had termed 'wretched people'. Jews are obviously not a nation, only a faith tolerated under Islamic rule (*dhimma*); therefore, their claim to a separate political existence amounts to an insult, as it were, to the holy tradition of Islam.
- The very fact that the Jews, who had lived for generations as *dhimma* people under the rule of Islam, have disengaged from its protective wings, defies and exposes to criticism the traditional Muslim allegation that the People of the Book had enjoyed equality, protection and benevolence under Muslim rulers. The massive exodus of the Jews from Arab lands to Israel belies Muslim contentions that fair treatment had been meted out to the Jews in their midst.
- Those same Jews who had been condemned to humiliation and misery in the Holy Koran, have dared, and even succeeded, although vastly outnumbered, in repeatedly defeating the 'Elected Nation of Allah'. Despite their assurances to the contrary, Arabs and Muslims in general regard today's Israelis as descendants of the Koranic Jews, hence the correlation between the two, which serves to aggravate Muslim sentiments against Israel.
- Palestine had been part of the Abode of Islam from the early seventh century through the Ottoman rule, until it was taken over by the British and then by the Jews in the current century. The inter-regnum of the Crusaders was a short-lived exception to that rule, inasmuch as they were eventually defeated by the

Muslims under Saladin, who restored the land to Islam. The Jewish usurpation of Palestine is thus considered as nothing more than an ephemeral crusader-like colonialist experiment, doomed to failure because it contradicts the logic of history. Thus, jihad (holy war) remains, as it has always been, a legitimate tool to be used by the Muslims to retrieve their land.

- A special status is accorded in this scheme to Jerusalem, not only as the core of the Holy Land but also as the place whence the Prophet made his ascension to Heaven.

As regards the European stratum of anti-Semitism borrowed by the Muslims, it is expressed not only in the *Protocols* and the Blood Libel which have found wide currency in the Arab and Islamic worlds in this century, but also in the references to the Shylock depiction of the Jews and Israelis. The Arab media, and even 'scholarly' books written by Western-educated scholars, delight in bringing up the following Christian-inspired themes:

- The 'International Conspiracy' of the Jews and world Zionism, are said to be aimed at undermining the world socio-economic and cultural systems, with the ultimate aim of bringing them under their domination.
- Zionism and world Jewry are often likened to an octopus which extends its tentacles whenever possible in a relentless drive to advance its ambition of enslaving humanity.
- In order to achieve its objectives, world Jewry allies itself to aggressive forces akin to it, such as colonialism and imperialism.
- The Jews in general, and American Jews in particular, are said to dominate and control the banking system, the media and the political arena. They plot behind the scene, concoct intrigues and support shadowy figures in order to advance their case.
- At times, however, Jews and Zionism are 'envied' by their Arab slanderers for their determination and *savoir faire*, and for their meticulousness of planning, devilish as it may be.

While both Islamic and European-inspired anti-Semitism have left their imprint on the Arab perception of Jews and Israel despite their irrationality, there has recently been an added rational element which is tied with the volatile fortunes of the Arab–Israeli conflict. So, while the basic anti-Jewish stereotypes provide the permanent infrastructure of Arab political thought, a process of development is discernible in the articulation of the anti-Jewish attitudes, in accordance with current political events. For example, any Israeli raid into Arab territory will be cited as characteristic perfidiousness and aggressiveness of the Jews, and any Israeli political triumph imputed to control of international politics. However, any defeat of Israel in the international arena will herald the awakening of the world conscience to the danger of Jewish evil. When the Israelis respond to Arab diplomatic initiatives, they are regarded as cowards who are overwhelmed by Arab power and righteousness; when they do not, they are accused of the legendary Jewish obstinacy.

Israel comes then to be regarded as a kinetic entity which reveals different faces under different circumstances: on the one hand, Israel lacks the prerequisites of a state, but on the other, it has the power to assert itself with the impact of a strong nation; whereas Israel could not survive without aid from its colonialist and imperialist allies, it can also manipulate world powers to its own ends; Israel is accused of 'Nazi arrogance', but it is nevertheless a shaky, ephemeral entity whose days are numbered. In order to cope with the unacceptable concept of an invincible Israel, which is constituted by evil and miserable Jews, its bad deeds and failures can always be interpreted as manifestations of its satanic character, while its successes or apparently positive steps can be either imputed to the powers standing behind it or to its arrogance or demonic propensity for secretly plotting and manipulating, as befits a Jewish state.

The layers which make up the Arab perception of Israel can only be differentiated analytically; however, in daily usage they appear so inseparably intertwined that it is often impossible to distinguish between them. When one reads systematically the Arab media or writings by Arab thinkers or Muslim fundamentalists, one is amazed by the wide array of accusations, scorn, condemnations and calumniations that are heaped indiscriminately against the Jews, the Zionists and the Israelis, drawing from all those sources simultaneously, and weaving all those claims and contentions into a powerful fabric of hatred, disgust, fear and suspicion. These accusations include, in fact:

- The racist and imperialist nature of Israel and Zionism, which are inherent in Jewish nature.
- Israel and Zionism undermine the world order, in accordance

with the millennial Jewish perversion as described in the *Protocols*.

- Zionism, by dominating the Jews, has made them the enemies of humanity. For, Judaism is only a faith and by instilling in them a sense of nationalism, it has distorted their vocation to live as a submissive and wretched minority under the generous wings of Islam.

- Apart from Zionism, which has poisoned the Jewish spirit, the Jews as such merit all the derogation and contempt the Arab vocabulary can wield of their own right. Jews are depicted as masters of trickery, cheating, plots and treachery. They are loaded with psychological complexes and fears: they have a sense of inferiority to others and of imaginary suffering. They masochistically torture themselves with these feelings and sadistically force others to share them.

- Their inner deficiencies are not the worse problems afflicting the world because of the Jews. Their international plotting and scheming, their concocting of wars and revolutions, their domination of key positions in politics, economics, media and world organizations places them well enough to subvert societies, to undermine political and economic systems and ruin the world morality.

ARAB AND MUSLIM ANTI-SEMITISM IN CONTEMPORARY AFFAIRS

When translated into the real world, namely when the images of the Jew and the Zionist have to be converted into policy towards them, the negative stereotypes are distilled into a few attributes which make them intractable. Jews are constantly perceived as incorrigibly and hopelessly corrupt, evil, greedy, immoral, intriguing and unconcerned with anyone but themselves. Amazing depictions of 'Israeli soldiers cavorting in al-Aqsa Mosque' or 'conducting sexual orgies' in the Tomb of the Patriarchs in Heron, are not arguments that one can debate or refute. They will probably go down as fact in some Arab history books, like the 'fact' that the bitter water of the Zamzam well in Mecca is 'the sweetest on earth', or that Jerusalem, in traditional Jewish perception, is the 'navel of the world'. For, what seems pure slander to Israel, are the authentic Arab perceptions in this regard, and they act upon them, as in their demonstrations of wrath and fury against what they have branded as Israel's deliberate burning of the al-Aqsa Mosque.

This ugly picture of the Jews which was, and one suspects still is, universally shared by many Arabs and Muslims, inevitably leads to the conclusion that the State of Israel – the creation of those very Jews – cannot be much different from its creators. They find 'evidence' for this view in the social inequity, discrimination, high crime rate, economic scandal and political dissent that the Arabs say is leading to the disintegration of Israeli society. The Jews, traditionally depicted in despicable terms in Islam and still portrayed stereotypically in Arab writings and cartoons, simply cannot be imagined as capable of maintaining a viable, let alone honest or decent, political life. These perceptions of the Jews and Israel dictate the choice of items that the Arab press publishes about Israel and the policies adopted by Arab states towards Israel. The careful screening of 'facts' and the outright fabrication of 'data' that fit their negative image of the Jews and Israel, generate contradictions that the Arabs choose to ignore. For example, while the Arabs keep repeating that neither Arab nor Islamic traditions ever called for hatred of the Jews as such, their verbal and graphic descriptions of the Jews are the most contemptible one can imagine. While they assert that the Jews in their midst have always enjoyed equal rights, Arab leaders are often exhorted by the press to improve their treatment of the remaining Jewish minorities, so that those who have migrated might return to their countries of origin and thus allow room for Palestinian refugees to be absorbed in their stead in Palestine. When Israel takes a firm stand in the occupied territories, it is oppressive; and when it shows flexibility and understanding, the Arabs claim that this is a maneuver to gain world sympathy for the occupation.

When Israel clings to its stated goals and policies, it is termed arrogant and high-handed; but when it is prepared to talk peace or to compromise, this is credited to effective Arab pressure, world pressure or Arab military prowess. When Israel evinces signs of weakness, it is clearly too unstable to rely on or to conduct negotiations with; but when it is perceived as strong, talks cannot be held either, since Israel is then seen as occupying a position of strength that can humiliate and intimidate the Arabs. If Western civilization and Jewish thought are taught in Arab schools in Israel, it means that the Jewish State is trying to erase Islamic and Arab tradition; at the same time, Israel is often accused of not teaching these matters in order to keep its Arabs illiterate and backward. Arab refugees are rotting in camps through Israel's fault; but when Israel makes attempts to resettle them, it is accused of obliterating the Arab character, or of eliminating (not solving) the Palestinian issue. If Arab villages in Israel or the territories are left without electricity or running water, this is deliberate under-development; but when Israel provides these and other social services, this is called sheer imperialism. When Israeli Arabs are integrated into the system, Israel is said to be uprooting them from their environment in order to make them forget their heritage; but if they are left alone to their devices, this is called oppression, apartheid, humiliation, exploitation, discrimination and second-class citizenry.

If an Arab prisoner dies while on a hunger strike, Israel is charged with mistreating, starving and torturing him; if he is force-fed, this constitutes barbaric treatment and coercion. When Israeli propaganda is perceived as fanning inter-Arab divisions, this is called an imperialistic divide-and-rule policy; but when it keeps silent in the face of inter-Arab or inter-Islamic infighting, it is accused, all the same, of adopting Goebbels' principle of 'non-interference in the growth of a young plant lest it be hindered'. The Arabs are entitled to wage war, launch propaganda campaigns, take loans, organize international festivals and conferences; but Israel cannot on pain of being accused of aggression, propaganda, indoctrination, plotting, sapping the resources of others, begging, and interfering in others' affairs; all innate qualities of the Jews. When the Soviet Union supplied the Arabs with airlifts during past wars, it was a friend and do-gooder, but if Israel was similarly supplied by the USA, it was begging and would have collapsed without this emergency charity.

The peace process between Israel and the Arabs, far from attenuating the intensity of anti-Semitic sentiment in the Arab and Islamic world, on the contrary aggravated it in many instances. For now, the Arabs and Muslims could claim, that even though they gave the Jewish State a chance to redeem itself from its inherently evil Jewish attributes, it has squandered that opportunity and proved how incorrigible it remains. Moreover, the victory of the Iranian revolution in 1979, has enhanced the Islamic anti-Semitism of the Muslim fundamentalists and widened the circle of the conflict in the Middle East. The entry of Iran, a non-Arab country and one that has no common boundaries with Israel, into the anti-Jewish club of the Arabs, on Islamic grounds, and Khomeini's vows to eliminate Israel, voiced in the most vitriolic anti-Semitic terms, have indeed exacerbated the anti-Jewish sentiments of the Muslims. For, from now on, not only direct clients of Iran, such as Sudan and the Hizbullah in Lebanon, would pick up the anti-Semitic gauntlet and amplify it worldwide, but fundamentalist movements throughout the Islamic world would begin copying and diffusing the anti-Jewish message on an unprecedented scale, using the same vocabulary and symbolism well beyond the Arab world.

And so, even in Egypt, which was the first Arab country to conclude peace with Israel in 1979, anti-Semitic onslaughts did not relent. Some of that output is edifying, especially that it reflects the thinking of mainstream Egypt rather than opposition groups which have refuted the peace process since its inception. Two cases in point are found in popular books: *The War of Survival between the Koran and the Talmud* and *The Jews: Objects of the Wrath of Allah*,[5] published in Egypt in 1980–81, namely two years after the conclusion of the peace, and which were reportedly much in demand during the Cairo Book Fair of 1981. Similarly, Anis Mansur, a notorious Christian anti-Semite and one of the closest aids to President Sadat, wrote a book entitled *The Wailing Wall and the Tears*,[6] in which he ridicules, slanders, condemns and calumniates the Jews as no other anti-Semite in recent memory has dared to do. For example, he wrote that 'Jews are enjoined by their faith to ravish all women of other religions'; that the secret constitution of the Jews – *The Protocols of the Elders of Zion* – encourages them to pursue the profession of obstetrician in order 'to specialize in abortion and so reduce the number of non-Jews'; that children in Israel kibbutzim are raised 'to hate everybody who is not Jewish'; that the Talmud advises Jews to kill all non-Jews; and that the soul of the Jews is full of hostility to all people without exception.

The apogee of anti-Semitism, the Blood Libel, also appeared in Cairo after the peace treaty with Israel, not to speak of denials of the Holocaust, the mass circulation of the *Protocols*, and viciously anti-Semitic attacks in both the mainstream press and the Islamic journals. Under the respectable guise of a 'scholarly' book, Dr Kamil Safan's *Jews, History and Doctrine*,[7] recounts as historical fact, and in considerable detail, the February 1840, Damascus Blood Libel, and affirms that 'similar cases went unnoticed by the chronicles or were manipulated by the Jews'. Another scholar, Dr Lutfi abd-al-'Adhim, wrote in *al-Ahram al-Iqtisadi* (the *Wall Street Journal* of the Arab world) on 27 September 1982, three full years after the peace treaty, a substantial article entitled 'Arabs and Jews: Who will Annihilate Whom?', which did not fall far behind Anis Mansur. Here are some excerpts:

> One of the assumptions that needs to be straightened out is the distinction made between Jews and Israelis ... for Jews are Jews; they have not changed over thousands of years: they embody treachery, meanness, deceit and contempt for human values. They would devour the flesh of a living person and drink his blood for the sake of robbing his property. They would not live in peace with Arabs. We lived under that illusion when some of our leaders declared the October 1973 War to be the last year. But I am absolutely certain that when Menachem Begin was signing those accords he was laughing at our naivete ...
>
> If we looked realistically into the problem, we would find out that it is one of a total war of annihilation waged by the Jews against the Arab nation. This war of extermination probably took its root from their assumption that the best way to wipe out the Arab nation, was through its humiliation, slander, character assassination, and the destruction of its present and past noble history. There was no better way to achieve that than dismembering the Arab nation, beginning with Lebanon, while the Israeli flag is hoisted in Cairo ... We do not mean necessarily that the Jews aim at the physical extermination of the Arabs; this is simply impractical, although they would have been delighted to do it. Rather, they intimidate them by such atrocities as Sabra, Shatilla and Deir Yassin ... There is no doubt that the Israeli master-plan strives to commit the same in Libya, Iraq, Syria and other places in the Arab world ... even Egypt would not escape this bloody and base Jewish scheme ... And there is no difference in this regard between the gangs of saboteurs ruling Israel and the Jewish lobbies across the globe ...
>
> Since I would rather be the killer than the killed (and I hope I am no exception in the Arab world), I cannot be expected to sit by and wait for the blood-thirsty and enraged Israeli dogs to dismember my body and bury the remains of the bodies of my wife and children ... Let me declare unequivocally that, yes, this is anti-Semitism, but since Arabs are also Semites, our

anti-Semitism is against Jewish Semites ... The Jews do not hesitate to resort to any means in their battle: they shot their own ambassador in London and killed Bashir Jumayyel in Lebanon, who had given them on a platter all they wanted ... I advise the Arabs not to be taken in by the appearance of protests in Israel and by the Jews around the world. All this is a well-orchestrated game where role-playing is effectively assigned ... The only difference between various Jewish circles is whether to kill their Arab victim under anaesthesia or attack it ferociously and drink its blood outright ... On the goal, all Jews are agreed ...[8]

This article was headed by a cartoon featuring a Zionist monster ripping children, presumably Arab, to pieces. Although the scholarly assumptions advanced by the learned author are echoed in the Arab press in general, it remains particularly alarming in that it not only presents deep-seated hatred of the Jews, but also summons Arabs to act upon the perceived threat that the Jews constitute, 'before it is too late'. Only one or two generations ago similar contentions and appeals in other anti-Semitic lands had ended in the mass extermination of Jews. And the fact that the Egyptian regime is either unable or unwilling to control this kind of violent rhetoric, which runs counter to its stated policy towards Israel, may be indicative of the predisposition of the Arab masses to absorb it. Otherwise, how can one explain the current *Shoah* denial in Arab lands, the siding of Arab and Islamic intellectuals with revisionist historians in the West who have been denying the *Shoah*, and even the banning in almost all the Arab and Islamic countries of the movie *Schindler's List*, which seemed to confirm the veracity of the Holocaust and to show some sympathy for its victims.

This virulence in post-peace Egypt does by no means exhaust the anti-Semitic sentiment in the Arab and Islamic worlds. If one peruses the writings of the Hizbullah in Lebanon, the Hamas in the West Bank and Gaza, and even the fundamentalist Muslims in Israel proper, one can find the same sort of anti-Semitic stuff, and worse. Moreover, while in those cases, radical movements take the lead in vilifying the Jews, and their views are carried by the media, including those of the mainstream, in Iran one can find state-initiated and state-led anti-Semitism of the worse kind. Paradoxically, the fundamentalist Muslims of Israel, through their representatives in the Israeli Knesset, and the leaders who have been elected as mayors of six towns and villages in Israel, have more leeway to express themselves politically than in any Arab country, except Sudan, itself a fundamentalist-run state. Nevertheless, taking advantage of the freedom of expression that is sacrosanct in Israel, they allow themselves to be openly anti-Semitic, and to even deny the *Shoah*, with impunity, something that in European countries like Germany, France or Sweden, they would have been convicted for.

When one comes closer to our days, one does not find solace. In a masterly article, Bernard Lewis, the dominant Islamic scholar of our time, enumerates the latest, and most disturbing, manifestations of anti-Semitism in the contemporary world. He asserts that Islamic anti-Semitism has conquered new grounds in recent years and risen to a new intensity. For, not only the old Christian anti-Jewish accusations (crucifying the Christ, well-poisoning, invented Talmudic quotations, conspiracies to take over the world, etc.), are reaffirmed and given an Islamic twist, but new ones are added to lash at the Jews, Israel and Zionism in the modern world, and to delegitimize them and struggle against them politically, culturally and religiously. He shows that much of the Arab media, on the left as well as those of the Islamic fundamentalist trends, acclaimed as 'heroic' the 1995 and 1996 'suicide' attacks of the Hamas against Israeli civilians. In a way, the hatred has been apparently transferred from the Jews *per se* to the Israelis and the Zionists, but the way these murders are justified leaves no doubt as to their anti-Semitic import. One of them, for example, said 'those who shed torrents of tears in mourning for filthy Jewish blood while sparing their tears when Palestinian or Lebanese blood is shed by the hands of the Jews, may Allah curse them'.[9]

The fear of the Arabs lest Israel overtake them economically, as it did militarily, also breeds their dislike for any economic cooperation with it even in the era of peace. Similarly, cultural exchanges are seen in the Arab nightmare as an attempt to undermine Islam from within and Judaize Arabic culture. Both items fit well with the *Protocols*, whose 'veracity' has now been rediscovered by the Arabs and the Muslims, among others, in the text of Shimon Peres' book about the New Middle East.[10] A prize was accorded, Lewis tells us, to a Masters dissertation at the University of Alexandria describing the Jewish economic role in Egypt, based on the *Protocols*.[11] Agricultural products of Israel are attacked in the Egyptian press for containing hormonal elements that kill men's sperm, and rumors circulate in Egypt and other Arab countries that Israel markets a chewing gum similarly treated, in order to harm the Arab's posterity and fertility. Jews are also accused of selling poisoned seeds in order to destroy Egyptian agriculture and poison its population.

These open, or implied, critiques of the peace with Israel, which has only brought dangers and disasters upon the Arabs, are coupled with the traditional Islamic negations of Jews and Israel in an uncompromising way, quite aside from those other accusations taken from European sources. The most abominable manifestations of that hatred can be found in the Hamas platform, which was published in 1988, and which takes Western anti-Semitism, adds to it Islamic or Islamized themes, and presents the whole mishmash as one coherent, sensible and well-documented doctrine. A few articles from that document will suffice to show the point:

- From Article Seven: The Prophet, Allah Bless Him ... has said: 'The Day of Judgement will not come about until Muslims fight the Jews; when the Jews will hide behind stones and trees. The stones and trees will say, "Oh Muslim, there is a Jew behind me come and kill him".'
- From Article Seventeen: The Muslim woman has a role no less important than that of the man in the battle of liberation ... The enemies have realized the importance of that role. They consider that if they can direct and bring her up the way they wish, far from Islam, they would have won the battle. That is why you find them giving these attempts constant attention through propaganda campaigns, films and the school curriculi, using for that purpose their lackeys, who are infiltrated through the Zionist organizations under various names and shapes, such as Freemasons, Rotary Clubs, espionage groups and others, which are all nothing but cells of subversion and saboteurs. These organizations have ample resources that enable them to play their role in societies for the purpose of achieving the Zionist targets and to deepen the concepts that would serve the enemy ... The day Islam is in control of the affairs of life, these organizations, hostile to Islam and humanity, will be obliterated.
- From Article Twenty-two: For a long time, the enemies have been planning, skilfully and with precision ... With their money ... they took control of the world media, news agencies, the press, publishing houses, broadcasting stations and others. With their money they stirred revolutions in various parts of the world in order to achieve their interests ... They were behind

the French Revolution, the Communist Revolution and most revolutions we heard and hear about ... With their money they formed secret societies, such as the Freemasons, Rotary Clubs, the Lions and others, in different parts of the world for the purpose of sabotaging societies and achieving Zionist interests. With their money they were able to control imperialistic countries and instigate them to colonize many countries in order to enable them to exploit their resources and spread corruption there ... They were behind the First World War, when they were able to destroy the Islamic Caliphate, making financial gains and controlling resources. They obtained the Balfour Declaration, formed the League of Nations through which they could rule the world. They were behind the Second World War, through which they made huge financial gains by trading in armaments, and paved the way for the establishment of their state. It was at their instigation that the League of Nations was replaced by the United Nations and the Security Council to enable them to rule the world through them. There is no war going on anywhere, without their having their fingers in it.

- From Article Twenty-eight: The Zionist invasion is a vicious one, it does not refrain from resorting to all methods, using all evil and contemptible ways to achieve its end. It greatly relies in its infiltration and espionage operations on the secret organizations it gave rise to, such as the Freemasons, the Rotary and Lions Clubs, and other sabotage groups. All these organizations, whether secret or open, work in the interest of Zionism and according to its instructions. They aim at undermining societies, destroying values, corrupting consciences, deteriorating character and annihilating Islam. It is behind the drug trade and alcoholism in all its kinds so as to facilitate its control and expansion ... Israel, Judaism and the Jews challenge Islam and the Muslim people. 'May the Cowards never sleep.'[12]

The Arab and Islamic anti-Semitic literature also rewrites history in order to vilify the Jews: for example, the Cana'anites are Arabs, therefore the Jews are usurpers of the land today as were their ancestors; Jewish history, including the ancient kingdoms of Israel and Judea, are obliterated from Arab and Islamic scholarship, and to the extent that ancient Jews are referred to, it is only in negative contexts such as deliverance from their oppression. Holocaust denials are rife, even among Arab citizens of Israel. Holocaust deniers in Europe, such as Garaudy, were protected, defended and welcomed with great pomp and honor in the Arab countries, even in those that have made peace with Israel. So, even though one hears from time to time some dissenting voices in the Arab and Islamic world that call for reason, they are usually silenced by the mainstream and the authorities, who wish to cultivate the traditional anti-Jewish sentiment, and to manipulate it to their purposes whenever it suits them.

In this light, or rather obscurity, one has to view current outbursts of anti-Semitism in the Arab world which have raised eyebrows in Israel and the West due to the putative peace process that has been unfolding in the past 20 years. In the middle of peace negotiations with Syria, *Tishrin* (a daily newspaper and organ of the ruling Ba'ath Party), lashed out at Israel at its weakest spot by denying the *Shoah*. This happened during the same week that Israel's heightened anxiety about Haider's party joining the government coalition in Vienna occasioned an outpour of sentiments and public debates which climaxed in Israel withdrawing its ambassador from Austria. This was done in spite of Haider's extreme caution and wish to appear democratic and humanistic; his decision to renege on his previous anti-Semitic and pro-Nazi statements; and his pledges to be politically correct in the future. The people of Israel ask, 'Why then should their government strive to complete negotiations with the Syrians, at a heavy price, and be so eager to send a Jewish ambassador to Damascus, while the regime is committed to persist in its anti-Semitism and promises not to relent?'

Nowhere else is the official stand adopted by the Syrian regime, exemplified by its giving asylum and protection to the notorious Nazi criminal Alois Brunner, better expressed than in the writings of, General Mustafa Tlas, its Defense Minister since 1972. In his preface to his book, *The Matza of Zion*, published in 1985, Tlas wrote:

> The Jew can kill you and take your blood in order to make his Zionist bread ... Here opens before us a page even more ugly than the crime itself: the religious beliefs of the Jews and the perversions they contain, which draw their orientation from a dark hate towards all humankind and all religions. I hope that I have done my duty in presenting the practices of the enemy of our historic nation. Allah aid this project.[13]

On 8 February 1991, at the Commission on Human Rights in Geneva, a Syrian delegate urged all representatives to read *The Matza of Zion* in order to discover the historical reality of Zionist racism. In 1999, still hoping to obtain a doctorate in Paris, Tlas declared:

> The assassination of Father Thomas [which lay at the base of the 1840 blood libel in Damascus] by the members of the Damascus Jewish community in 1840 is a known fact ... This event is authentic, for there have been in the history of the world sects and fanatical individuals who have committed inhuman acts.[14]

In November 1999, the Syrian literary magazine *Al-Usbu al-Adabi* published an article by Jbara al-Barguti entitled: 'Shylock of New York and the Industry of Death' (27 November 1999) in which he explains how:

> The Talmud instructions, soaked in hatred and hostility towards humanity, are stamped in the Jewish soul. Throughout history, the world has known more than one Shylock, more than one Thomas, as victim of these Talmudic instructions and this hatred ... Now Shylock of New York's time has come ... Israel's matza will continue to steep in blood, the spilling of which is permitted in the Talmud, in order to glorify the Jewish military. This happens because the Jews have more than one God, in contrast to their claim that they are monotheist.[15]

The same bewilderment can be raised with regard to the peace process with the Palestinians who, at the same time that they press Israel for more withdrawals in the name of peace, continue to teach their children, in their official school curriculi, fabricated 'quotations' from the Talmud which have no leg to stand on but denigrate the Jews and accuse them of the basest crimes. Children are internalizing those ugly and hateful stereotypes, and will end up acting upon them when they come of age. For if the enemy is delegitimized, as the Arabs do to the Jews in the most blatant and dehumanizing ways, then what is to constrain Palestinians, Syrians and other Arabs to avoid hostility and violence against the object of their hatred?

HOW JEWS ARE PORTRAYED IN THE ARAB PRESS
IN TIMES OF PEACE!

Figure 1: Jordan, *Al-Dustur*, an Amman daily, 1996.
After the evacuation of Hebron. Two years after the peace agreement.

Figure 2: Syria, *Al-Thawra*, daily newspaper of the regime, 1994.
During the negotiations with the Rabin government.

Figure 3: Egypt, *October*, an Egyptian newspaper, 1993. Cover page of the issue: 'The October War Was Not the Last …', 15 years after Camp David.

NOTES

1. Qut'b, *Ma'rakatuna ma'a al Yahud* [*Our Campaign against the Jews*] (7th edn, Beirut, 1986).
2. Ibid.
3. Ibid.
4. Ibid.
5. *The War of Survival Between the Koran and the Talmud* and *The Jews: Objects of the Wrath of Allah* (Cairo, 1982). Cited by R. Israeli, *Peace is in the Eye of the Beholder* (Mouton, Berlin and New York, 1985).
6. Anwar Sadat, *The Wailing Wall and the Tears*. Cited by Israeli, *Peace is in the Eye of the Beholder*.
7. Kamil Safan, *Jews, History and Doctrine*. Cited by Israeli, *Peace is in the Eye of the Beholder*.
8. Lutfi abd-al-'Adhim, *al-Ahram al-Iqtisadi*, 27 September 1982, pp.4–7. I am grateful to my colleague, Dr Norman Stillman of the University of Oklahoma, for this citation.
9. Lewis, Bernard, *Semites and Anti-Semites* (New York: W.W. Norton, 1986); see also Lewis, 'Muslim Anti-Semitism', *The Middle East Quarterly*, 5, 2 (1998), pp.43–51.
10. Shimon Peres, *The New Middle East* (New York: Holt, 1993).
11. *Protocols*. The infamous anti-Semitic tract published by Czarist Russia at the turn of the twentieth century, and since then a reference book for anti-Semitic authors.
12. Hamas Charter, see R. Israeli, 'The Charter of Allah: Platform of the Islamic Resistance Movement', in Y. Alexander (ed.), *The Annual of Terrorism* (The Netherlands, Martinus Nijhoff).
13. Mustafa Tlas, *The Matza of Zion*, cited in *France-Payes Arabs*, July–August 1999.
14. Ibid.
15. MEMRI Special Dispatch, No.66, Syria, 22 December 1999.

PART 2

War and Terror
in Action

5. The Problem is Not Saddam, but Iraq

APOLOGIA

For the past quarter-century problematic Saddam Hussein has been dominating Gulf politics and preoccupying the world with his whims and excesses, to the extent that the wish to eliminate him, or at the very least to remove him from power, has come to replace rational strategies of dealing with the permanent Iraqi threat of destabilizing that important area of the world. What is more, Saddam's hold on power does not seem to have diminished as a result of the wars he waged against his neighbors, or the sanctions he has been submitted to, or the miseries that his people have been suffering. He is now in a situation where he can relaunch his development of unconventional weaponry, free from the strictures of the UN supervision from which the Secretary General of that organization has helped relieve him.

In liberal democracies governments come and go, regimes change and statesmen rotate in their never-ending quest to satisfy the voters to whom they are accountable. Therefore, their stint in power is always temporary, they must act as fire-brigades to extinguish fires before the next elections, and they have neither the time nor the inclination to think decades or generations hence. But dictatorships, such as Saddam's, are longer-lived: he was there 20 years ago and will be there another 20 years, barring a violent death at the hands of other dictators who might disinherit him. To avert such a contingency, he created (like Assad the father in Syria, Gaddafy of Libya, Kabila of the Congo, and other tyrants) a republican monarchy where the son succeeds the father and continuity is assured. This means that while Bush Senior, Clinton, Thatcher, Major and Mitterand have passed into oblivion, and little or nothing of their legacy has remained, Saddam and his successors are sure to occupy the headlines in the years to come.

There prevails in the West the illusory hope that should Saddam be removed – and assuming that his clan and potential successors are also out of the way – some new democratic regime, elected, representative of the people and accountable to them, would automatically slide into place. But, as has been learned from recent experience, all the regimes that collapse after they were groomed as autocracy for generations, cannot become Western-style democracies overnight. So it goes for the Arab world, whose 22 states are all steeped in tyranny and corruption, born out of the permanence of power in the same hands, without alternation between rule and opposition, and even without challenge to the ruler. Even within relatively benign regimes such as Mubarak's in Egypt or the King's in Jordan, the ultimate focus of power is with the ruler, not the representatives of the people; the opposition is in prison, not in parliament; and no transition of power is envisaged unless the ruler leaves this world. There is no reason to believe that the Iraqis are any different.

When the West likes the incumbent regimes in these autocracies or can enlist them as its 'friends' (Egypt, Jordan), or providers of interest (Saudi Arabia, Kuwait), they are called 'stable', and stability is prized for its own sake as long as it can ensure continuity in the unhindered supply of those interests. Nevermind the bombast about democracy and human rights that are supposed to be upheld by a value-conscious West. But when those regimes are recalcitrant, or embrace an agenda that is not the West's (Saddam, Gaddafy, Assad, Turabi, Khomeini, etc.), then they are agents of instability, even when they are more stable in terms of domestic continuity than the others. It is this behavioral inconsistency on the part of the West which is targeted by Muslim fundamentalists all over the world, and exposed as 'hypocrisy', and is a major contributing factor to the rise of Islamist movements and regimes. If, following the abortive democratic elections in Algeria in 1992, the West hurried to turn its back on them because of the resulting rise of the Front Islamique du Salut (FIS), and supported instead the oppression of the military junta there, why should other Muslims in the Sudan, Libya, Iran, Iraq or Afghanistan embrace a Western path?

Thus, in Iraq as elsewhere in the Arab and Islamic world which refuses to fall into the Western fold, the choice is not between the current autocracies and liberal democracy – which is totally misunderstood there and can never be applied in its Western version – but between different degrees of autocracy. And from the Western point of view the dilemma is always to differentiate between the 'stable' and 'unstable' ones. Saudi Arabia is not a 'friend' of the West because it is any less autocratic than the others, quite the contrary; but because of the illusion of stability it projects. Conversely, Iraq and Iran are not 'enemies' of the West because of their regimes (in fact they hold some kind of elections, which are anathema to Saudi Arabia), but because of their perceived respective threats to Western interests, even when there is no unanimity between various Western powers. In short, if one wishes to analyse the potentials inherent in the Iraqi conundrum, one should cease looking at Saddam and his peers, and examine the geo-strategic predicament of the Iraqis, regardless of the regime that holds power there.

THE IRAQI PREDICAMENT

Whatever the psychological reasons underlying Saddam's personal megalomaniac ambitions, and regardless of the circumstances that allowed this cruel and ruthless man to seize power in Baghdad, one cannot overlook his visionary planning and his dogged determination to carry it out, against all odds. One thing is certain: not only has he outlived all those bent on eliminating him, domestically and externally, and not only has he gained prominence in the Arab world and the Gulf due to his violent anti-Israel stance, but he has demonstrated an acute understanding of his geo-politics, and has lent insight to the way the Arab world, and the West, have come to recognize his immense contribution, negative as it may be, to the make-up of the questions of security in the Gulf. He did so, not merely by his sheer overwhelming presence on the scene, but mainly by the series of adroit political maneuvers that he has adopted and the consistency with which he has been implementing them.

Already, in 1975, as Vice President to Takriti, but the strong man of Iraq (some have compared him to the strong-willed but young and unknown Nasser of the 1950s, who needed General Naguib as a figurehead), he began to show his mettle. Judging from the steps he would adopt for the long-haul, and his extraordinary capacity to concentrate on his goals at the expense of all the rest, he was then intent to attain *grandeur*, commensurate with his view of himself, of Iraq and the world; and he set out, step by step, to build up himself and his strategy. With considerable political savvy and personal charm, he maneuvered friends and foes to toe his line, cajoling, promising, threatening and arm twisting, but he never lost sight of his strategic goals, which were dictated to him not solely by his personal ambitions, but sorely by the constraints of his geography.

First, he had to unify his country around him by pacifying internal strife and providing national symbols attractive enough to rally his people behind his personal leadership. In 1975, at great political 'sacrifice', he signed an agreement with the Shah of Iran, recognizing Tehran's rights in the eastern half of the Shatt-al-Arab waterway, the confluent of the Tigris and the Euphrates, which for many years had been disputed between the two powers, with Iran claiming control of half the course and Iraq imposing its sovereignty over the whole body of water. The matter is of vital importance to Iraq, not only because of the vast quantities of water flowing through that semi-arid and steamy climate, but mainly because, as against the very long coast-line Iran enjoys, Iraq's access to the Gulf depended on unhindered and safe navigation along the lower reaches of that immense river. The 'sacrifice' that Saddam cunningly made, was to seemingly acquiesce in that great 'concession', in order to cash in on the Iranian *quid pro quo*, which was the cessation of the Shah's support to the Iraqi Kurds.

In fact, the perennial Kurdish uprising in northern Iraq, was part and parcel of the much wider and ongoing Kurdish unrest in the area of Kurdistan which had been a problem for decades. Half of their people (some 25 million today) were located in Turkey, which refused to acknowledge their national identity, even rejected their self-appellation as Kurds, in addition to banning the Kurdish language from their midst, and preferred to dub them the 'Mountain Turks'. Another 10 million of their brethren were equally partitioned between Iraq and Iran, with the rest in Syria and various diasporas. Since not much love was lost between Iran and Iraq, the Shah had allowed the Iraqi Kurds to find shelter in his Kurdish territory, and to use it as a launching pad for their activities against the Iraqi regime. Thus, Saddam's ploy to lure the Shah into that 'historic' agreement, was calculated to strengthen his grip on the oil-rich Kurdish north by pacifying it, at the horrendous price of inviting the Iranians into the *Shatt-al-Arab*; at least temporarily.

But Saddam, who comes from the Sunnite minority in central Iraq which ruled the Kurds of the north, was also at odds with the majority Shi'ite community of the south, which numbered around 12 out of the 20 million people in Iraq. The Shi'ites not only constituted the majority of the country and controlled the approaches to the Gulf, much of the agriculture and the immensely hallowed holy places of Najaf and Karbalah, where Caliph Ali and his son Hussein found their death and were buried, but were also the down-trodden part of Iraqi society – poor and destitute, despised by the ruling elite and under-developed economically, even in the days where the tremendous income from oil kept the country awash in cash. Bitterness there was deep and anti-Saddam sentiment ran high, as he ruled in the name of the Ba'ath Party, a 'socialist' and non-religious adept of Soviet-type 'democratic centralism', which could not cater to the needs of the Shi'ites and appeared to them sacrilegious for a deeply Muslim country. Saddam needed to erase all that by co-opting more Shi'ites into the large army he wanted to build, by opening up to them some of the avenues of power, and by initiating some economic development, short of which he could not count on them for the realization of his master-plan.

Saddam's blueprint also included his own personality cult, as the supreme commander and savior, to whom all Iraqis should turn in worship and adoration, so as to accept any hardships he devised for them without hesitation or complaint. He appeared in public in his military attire, always armed with a revolver at his waist. His increasingly larger portraits were posted in all public squares in towns and villages, and along public roads, and his underlings organized massive demonstrations of support for him. A mammoth arch-gate was erected in Baghdad, on the shore of the Tigris – prob-ably in imitation of the Saint Louis Gate, on the Mississippi bank – made of two intercrossing sabres held at their base by precise repli-cas of the two robust hands of Saddam himself. This campaign of self-aggrandizement, the like of which survives only in today's North Korea, has culminated in the inference that likens Saddam to Hamorabi, the great ruler and legislator of Mesopotamia, who had inspired great awe in the ancient world and thereafter.

It may well be that Saddam needed to cultivate his personal cult so that he could feel the adulation of his population and compen-sate himself for his deprived youth. But there is no doubt that he was emulating, indeed rivaling, his two political adversaries: Sadat of Egypt and the Shah of Iran. Sadat, who stood in those years, especially before his peace with Israel, as the foremost leader of the Arab world, constituted an obstacle on the road to Saddam's burning ambition to replace him in that role. Sadat, too, had posited himself as the successor of the Pharaohs, and boasted of the unrivaled 6,000 years of Egyptian civilization, as if Arab and Islamic culture had anything to do with it. Similarly the Shah, who contended with him on hegemony in the Gulf, had squandered untold amounts of money to revive Persepolis and the past glory of the ancient Persian Empire, of which he wished to be viewed as the heir. Saddam had an innate aversion to rivals. In Iraq, he eliminated, some say with his own hands, anyone who was suspected as vying for the leadership, or trying to pick up some of the crumbs of glory that the leader left in his trail.

Then Saddam turned to construct his main instrument of power – the military, which would not only ensure his grip on domestic power, but would also allow him to enforce his dreams of regional hegemony. That meant building a high-technology military industry that could produce missiles as well as nuclear, chemical and biological weapons. All this was attained via collaboration with European and South American private firms and governments who elected to overlook Saddam's growing threat and to channel their industrial, military and technological products to him in return for oil. However, this power had also to be projected where it counted most, namely in the inter-Arab arena. After Sadat had 'defected' from the militant camp in 1977, following his peace deal with Israel, and especially in the wake of the Camp David Accords of 1978 and the Peace Accords of 1979, Saddam moved in to take the lead of the Rejection Front, and he convened the first and then second Baghdad Conferences where Sadat was repudiated from the Arab camp for his 'treason'.

THE FIRST GULF WAR (1980–88) AND ITS AFTERMATH

Saddam needed to maintain the attributes of power he had labored to construct as well as the enhanced stature that he enjoyed in the Arab world as a result. He realized that in order to be credible he had to act, and to seem to act in the Arab interest, not only in the pursuance of his self-aggrandizement or of Iraq's primacy in the region. The Khomeini revolution in Iran (1979) provided him with the opportunity. Merely 18 months after the new regime settled down in Tehran, and fearing that the revolutionary passion of the Iranian Shi'ites might spill over into his own Shi'ite territory, where Khomeini was remembered and revered since his 15-year exile among the Shi'ites of Iraq (1963–78), Saddam decided to move. His objectives were fourfold:

1. He eyed the adjoining Iranian province of Khuzistan which, although Iranian-dominated was populated by Arab-speaking tribes. His coming, he hoped, as a 'savior', would not only be welcomed by those Arabs, but by the entire Arab world, which would rally around him in his struggle to retrieve Arab lands from Iran, the traditional foe of the Arabs.

2. He was advised that a move into Khuzistan would be an easy walkover, due to the turmoil engendered by the revolution in Iran, and the ensuing purges of the cadres in the previously mighty army of the Shah, which had left it decapitated and weakened. Such a move would also demonstrate to his Shi'ites at home, who began agitating as a result of the Khumeini Revolution, that the new Iran was but a 'paper tiger' that could be easily overrun by Saddam's emerging power. That, in turn, would hint to the Iraqi Shi'ites that they stood to benefit from supporting their new hero-leader who acquired fame and glory for their country.

3. Taking over that patch of land would double, in one sweep, Iraq's already fabulous wealth in oil production and reserves, allowing him to outstrip even Saudi Arabia, and to take over the leadership of OPEC with its corollaries: a determining voice in oil prices, global political and economic clout, and the rising stature of Iraq in world politics.

4. Moving into Iran at low cost, while the world would stand in support to him or at least remain indifferent to the fate of the much maligned new regime of Iran, would afford him, for the first time since Iraq's inception, a sea-shore of a few hundred miles, the lack of which had theretofore inhibited the build-up of Iraqi naval power in the Gulf. Such a territorial acquisition would give Iraq a secure boundary away from the threatening Iranian lines; would ensure the growth of Basra into a formidable naval and industrial base free from Iranian menace; would give him a total and unrestricted control of the mighty *Shatt-al-Arab*; and would enable him to build more deep-water ports on the Khuzistan coast.

The conditions seemed ripe for Saddam to achieve his goals. First, due to the excesses of the Iranian Revolution there was hardly any country, least of all in the West, that would shed a tear over Iran's plight in the war. Second, the rich monarchies in the Gulf felt directly menaced by the new revolutionary regime in Tehran, especially due to their own restive Shi'ite populations, lest the revolution encroach upon their domains. And, third, while Iraq was well-supplied by the Soviets and some Western countries, militarily Iran faced a world arms-embargo which incapacitated it in the long run. Thus, all Saddam had to do was to tear up his 1975 agreement with the Shah, and reclaim Arab – that is his – sovereignty over the entire *Shatt-al-Arab* waterway, his only outlet to the Persian Gulf, now triumphantly renamed the 'Arab Gulf'.

Saddam launched the attack in October 1980, seizing quick control of much of Khuzistan within a few weeks, to the point that his war aims seemed at hand at an amazingly low cost and high speed. But he had underestimated the ideological and patriotic zeal of the Iranians. After a few weeks of disarray, they fought back with a vengeance, substituting human waves for the equipment that was dwindling and never fully replenished. The heroic Iranian stand at Khurramshar, their equivalent of Stalingrad, marked the beginning of the end of Saddam's venture. True, Iran had neither the firepower nor the military hardware to threaten Iraq in any direct way, but neither could Saddam deliver the *coup de grâce* that he had relied upon. The war of attrition went on for eight years, a trench war not unlike the First World War in Europe, where the parties bled profusely but made no advances. But, in the meantime, Iraq could field-test its awesome arsenal of missiles and chemical weapons, which were still not sufficient to overwhelm the territory and population that Iran could field, both of which were three times the size of Iraq's.

All the while, Saddam not only was not condemned by anyone for his aggression, but he drew support from all quarters: the Americans, the Soviets, the Europeans and much of the Arab world. The Soviets and the Europeans sold him weapons, facilitated economic credits, and came to regard him as a bulwark against the spread of Islamic fundamentalism that they feared. The Arabs, especially the Gulf states, because of the same fears, continued to pour billions in 'loans' into Saddam's dwindling treasury, knowing that he would never be able, let alone willing, to repay them. Instead, he repaid them with lip-service, declaring that this was a second Qadisiyya battle, a repetition of that glorious campaign in the seventh century when the Arabs defeated the Iranian–Sassanid Empire and spread Islam into Persia. That meant that he stood in the forefront for all Arabs, in his bid to defeat that most dangerous and long-term enemy of the Arab nation, and they, in turn, owed him their unconditional support.

Desperate to win military, diplomatic and economic support from the USA, Saddam even veered back towards Egypt which he had humiliated in 1979 due to its peace accords with Israel, re-established diplomatic relations with Cairo, and edged closer to the Hashemite House in Jordan. Thus, by making up with the 'moderates' of the Arab world, who were also America's closest allies in the Arab world, he hoped both to isolate his arch-rival Syria, which supported Iran in the Gulf War, and to gain access to the USA. He and his new allies tried to project the image of a 'moderate' Saddam who 'really wanted peace', both in the Gulf and in the Arab–Israeli conflict. He emitted noises, that were interpreted as signals, that he was in favor of an Israeli–Palestinian settlement and that he was seeking equi-distance between the USA and the Soviet Union, his long-standing supporter. The Arabs who toed his line, from Egypt to Saudi Arabia, began echoing the blame against Iran as the 'aggressor', and the praise of Saddam as the 'peace-maker'. He wanted peace they said, but the Iranians were intransigent and refused his peace advances. They, together with the rest of the naive world, who failed to see the ploy of the dictator, conveniently elected to forget who had started the war in 1980, and who had used the most atrocious means of warfare on the battlefield.

Saddam's scheme had succeeded. He had abstained from opening a second front with Israel, which could have cost him his regime, in spite of Israel's devastating attack on his nuclear facilities in June 1981, which was universally condemned the world over. His reasoning was very sound: he could ill-afford a confrontation with Israel while he was stuck in the Iranian quagmire of his own making, for if a confrontation occurred he would be deprived of two lifelines that he had painstakingly erected during that long war. One was the access he had gained to the West, especially to the American administration, which thought it was cultivating a new moderate ally who would ultimately be lured away from the Soviet camp; second, he feared the loss of his only supply line via Aqaba in the Jordanian Red Sea which was at the mercy of Israeli guns two miles away.

When Saddam emerged from the war with Iran in August 1988, he claimed that he was victorious, whereas in fact he had gained only some insignificant patches of Iranian territory, but by no means attained his initial war aims. He had paid a terrible price: 200,000 casualties, a crushed economy, huge debts and a country to rebuild. But he had the aura of the victor, his stature was intact and his credit in the West was so high that even his barbarous attacks by gas against his own Kurdish population in Halabja in late 1988, and his systematic destruction of hundreds of Kurdish hamlets and villages, won him little censure from the world. Instead, he won praise for his 'moderation'.

Saddam immediately began re-equipping his million-strong army which had been battle-hardened during the eight years of war against Iran, and engaged in a vigorous diplomatic *démarche* to advance his position in the Arab and Western worlds. His repression of the Kurds at home, instead of being understood as a repetition of the 1975 ploy to free his hands domestically in order to move externally to expand his *lebensraum* across his borders, was left uninterpreted because it came to be regarded as his domestic affair. Having terrified dissidents within Iraq, he turned outward: on the one hand, he began reminding Israel that its 1981 attack had not been forgotten, and threatening that he had the capacity to use his missile and chemical weapons to 'burn half of Israel' (he never said what he would do to the other half), thus again assuming his position as the champion of the Arab and Palestinian cause. His huge army, which he continued to equip and train extensively despite his armistice with Iran, was enough of a guarantee to ensure the credibility of his menace and to turn him into a hero figure in Arab and inter-Arab politics.

On the other hand, he entered into a series of alliances in order to keep Syria isolated and to render irrelevant its bid for 'strategic parity' with Israel, which it had designed to ensure its role of leadership in the confrontation with Israel. His quadri-partite alliance with Egypt, Jordan and the Yemen was calculated not only to tighten the noose around Syria, but also to enhance his own image as a moderate and pragmatic Arab leader who put his faith in constructive inter-Arab diplomacy. His hatred of Syria was so great that he declared his support of dissident Lebanese General Michel Aoun in Beirut, who rejected Syrian occupation of his country and kept the Syrian Army busy there.

THE SECOND GULF WAR (1990–91)

Although Saddam had been severely bruised in his protracted war against Iran, he had emerged from it unscathed politically and psychologically. As the 'victor' in that war, in which he arguably defended the Arab cause, his aura was brighter than ever before. American senators, including presidential hopeful Robert Dole, who visited him in the spring of 1990, came out charmed with his 'reasonable, moderate and pragmatic' personality. The events in the disintegrating Soviet Bloc, with which the West was preoccupied, in addition to the fact that the West was made up of soft regimes which would not fight for anything overseas, gave Saddam the assurance that his way to the next adventure was open.

Saddam's ambition to control both the oil resources of his neighbors and their sea-shore, had remained his constant obsession despite the debacle of his war against Iran. Probably modeling his tactics on those of Hitler, he evaluated the geo-political situation around him: like Czechoslovakia, Kuwait was a small and weak country, easy to swallow and digest, especially since it answered both his ambitions for oil and sea-shore. There was a formidable enemy to the east – Iran, which had proved unbeatable during the war, so better join it than fight it this time. Replicating the Molotov–Ribbentrop Treaty, Saddam thought that, if and when necessary, he would rather appease that enemy in the east in order to concentrate on the south, first to 'return' Kuwait to the Iraqi fold, and then, if all went well, to sink his teeth into the juicy pear that was Saudi Arabia, another weak and rich 'sister' country. In short, what he had failed to achieve in the first Gulf War, he would attempt now on the opposite shore of the Gulf.

Saddam was very much concerned by Israel's military power, but he rightly estimated that Israel was too distant and had neither the means nor the interest to become involved in the Gulf region. Saddam therefore created an artificial argument with Kuwait over oil prices and the Rumeila oil fields in the buffer-zone between the two states, then spread around assurances that he had no aggressive intentions towards Kuwait, and vowed to his allies, including President Mubarak personally, that he would seek a 'peaceful solution' to the 'conflict' he had created. After all, he owed many billions of dollars to the Emir of Kuwait who had bailed Iraq out during its war with Iran. How could he be so ungrateful as to reward such help with aggression?

On 2 August 1990, Saddam struck militarily, in a blitzkrieg that baffled his foes and friends alike. He was condemned by most Arab countries, each for its own reasons. Syria was as frightened of the growing power of Saddam as it was delighted to partake of an all-Arab revenge against him. Mubarak, personally hurt that he had fallen into Saddam's net, had to admit that his alliance with Iraq and his intimacy with Saddam had been an act of naivete on his part. Saudi Arabia and the Emirates, shaken and scared for their lives, hastened to embrace any means to check Saddam's advance. The West, bewildered by Saddam's astuteness and aggression, humiliated at being outmaneuvered and outwitted by him, and fearful of the consequences of leaving in the dictator's hand an aggregate (Iraq and Kuwait) 20 percent of the world's oil reserves, decided to move – with much hesitation, just as Saddam had calculated.

Saddam, indeed, calculated that the USA, the most likely power to move against him, would be stunned, distant and irresolute. Unless it decided to act immediately with missiles and air strikes, before Iraq entrenched itself in Kuwait, it would take many months to assemble a military force equivalent to that deployed in Vietnam at the peak of the war there; namely some half a million troops. Besides, the Americans would find the desert conditions unbearable: dust, heat, Islamic puritanism, hostile Arab–Muslim environment, lack of alcohol and uncertainty as to the end of the conflict. Saddam immediately seized upon these difficulties to gain time. He ridiculed the American war aims: the defense of Kuwait's absolute monarch and his family who had systematically robbed the riches of his country for his private purposes. Was that the norm of democracy that America promoted? Americans did not come to Kuwait to defend legitimacy of rule as claimed, he asserted, but to keep down the price of oil. Otherwise, why did they not intervene when Indonesia invaded East Timor, Libya attacked Chad or Israel the West Bank and Gaza? Was it worthwhile for young Americans to fight and die for oil prices? The demonstrations in the USA against the war and for 'the return of our boys home' vindicated Saddam's war calculations and played into his hands.

While the USA was building up its forces in Saudi Arabia, Saddam was confident that the Arab–Muslim countries would ultimately succumb to the pressures from their population, which loathed the presence of Westerners in Arab lands, and especially their proximity to the Islamic holy places. Saddam discounted the role of the Arabs who rushed to Saudi help, realizing very well that they were there not to help their American 'allies', but to ensure their share of Saudi wealth should the aftermath of the war bring about the final demise of the Kuwaiti house, followed by the end of the Saudi ruling princes. After all, he reasoned, had Syria truly wished to assist the coalition as it pretended, it could have done that more directly and at lesser cost, by concentrating its troops on its border with Iraq rather than transporting them to Saudi Arabia.

Intent on holding fast to his Kuwaiti prey, Saddam assumed his most moderate posture when addressing the outside world: he wanted negotiations, he said, after he completed the occupation of Kuwait, not war; he would seek a peaceful settlement, he assured everyone, if the oil fields of Kuwait and the islands of Bubian and Warba were left in Iraqi hands; he was prepared to release all of his foreign hostages ('guests', he called them), if he was assured that no attacks would be mounted against him. His Foreign Minister traveled around the world affirming the peaceful intentions of his leader, and his message was heeded in some quarters. Indeed, a procession of senior statesmen came knocking on his door: Willy Brandt, Edward Heath, Yasuhiro Nakasone; all coming to beg for the release of their hostages, but at the same time satisfying the dictator's lust for the international limelight and his sense of self-importance.

To his people and to the Arabs, however, Saddam had another kind of message: steadfastness of the Arabs and Muslims against the New Crusaders who were scheming against the Arab home-land and the Islamic holy shrines. He incited the people of Saudi Arabia to rise up against their exploitation by the egotistical Royal House and class of privileged princes; and the people of Egypt and Syria to rebel against the collusion of their rulers with the West. Some of his agents were arrested in Egypt for plotting against the regime of his 'trusted ally' of six months earlier. Saddam's macho defiance of the West, and the USA in particular, won him tremendous popular support in the Arab and Islamic worlds. In Jordan, massive demonstrations in his favor, by both Arab nationalists and Muslim fundamentalists became daily routine, and King Hussein, probably Saddam's best friend and salesman, did nothing to curb them. The Palestinians heralded him as the new Saladin – the Muslim medieval hero who had united the Muslims and extirpated the Crusaders from the Middle East. The Mufti of Jerusalem delivered a sermon to the Believers to lend their hand to Saddam in his struggle against American imperialism.

To his people, who seemed to support him in spite, or perhaps because, of the squeeze of the international trade embargo, he pledged victory and a horrible defeat for the Americans who would be busy 'counting their corpses as soon as the war began'. He urged his people to 'eat dates and drink water', thus mocking the Western-imposed embargo on food. He encouraged his farmers to be self-sufficient, his urban population to consume less, and his soldiers to get battle-ready. Somehow, Saddam and his people refused to read the danger signs looming around them, and they remained confident in their right and capacity to deter any American attack. He was beaten ultimately by the Americans, although his defeat was much less terrible than it could have been, for the Americans desisted under pressure from the Arabs, who could not be seen as allied to a Western power which had entered the gates of Baghdad, the glorious medieval capital of the great Muslim Abbasid Dynasty.

Harsh sanctions were imposed on post-war Iraq, and vain attempts were made by the UN to curtail the development and production of weapons of mass destruction by Saddam's rogue regime. But the American war aims were basically not attained. For, even though Kuwait was nominally 'liberated' from Iraq, many people ask themselves what kind of 'liberty' it is to live under the absolute regime of a hereditary monarchy. The process of democratization that the Americans were promised would happen in the Gulf countries after the war, did not even begin. The backbone of the Iraqi Army was not broken, as the Republican Guards, who constitute the elite of Iraqi troops, were withdrawn to defend Baghdad and the regime, while the ragtag of Iraqi forces were allowed to be crushed by the invading Americans. And, finally, Saddam, who was personally targeted for elimination, escaped unscathed. His contemporaries – Bush Senior and King Hussein, Assad Senior and John Major, Mitterand and Baker – are all gone a decade later, but he is still around, healthy, self-confident and bursting with plans and programs for the future, and, most importantly, bracing himself for another opportunity to strike.

CONSTANTS IN IRAQ'S GEO-POLITICS AND STRATEGIES

Saddam has shown himself to be able to play to circumstances, while not losing sight of his ultimate goals; for what he cannot accomplish today he will try tomorrow. He tried against Iran ten years ago, and although he did not succeed he emerged strong enough to try again against Kuwait. He concentrated troops repeatedly, testing the degree of alertness of the USA and its allies, but always backed down when the danger loomed too great. He ostensibly 'accepted' the UN sanctions and program to destroy weapons of mass destruction, but he did everything to work under-cover, salvage his research and production capabilities under-ground, deny any existing prohibited weapons and work to build new ones. And when the UN supervising team became too insis-tent in its demands for minute inspection, Saddam did not hesitate to create an artificial crisis, and with the help of the UN Secretary General, he shrugged off the supervision altogether, under what triumphant Kofi Anan called a 'compromise'.

In the Arab arena Saddam has resumed Iraq's activity in the Arab League, relentlessly seeking to wrest its leadership from Egypt, by embracing rejectionist policies with regard to Israel and the USA. When the second Palestinian Intifadah broke out in September 2000, he became its champion and has vowed to pay indemnities to the families of the *shahids* (martyrs) who would lose their lives in the process. Among all Arab leaders he appears to the masses as the most credible and the most able and willing to act on their behalf. And the more turbulent and ugly the Israeli–Palestinian confrontation becomes, the more Saddam can draw dividends from the situation by pointing to Egypt and Jordan who have 'betrayed' the Arabs and turned their backs on their people while, conversely, exhibiting his material aid to the Palestinians, and tabling extreme resolutions in the Arab League against Israel.

Saddam is accumulating power and waiting for his next oppor-tunity, and if he is replaced, especially if this is done by force from the outside, his successors will not relent. He, or others after him, will wait until the Americans are ejected from their bases around the Gulf, as a result of the mounting Muslim wrath against them, and will not hesitate to replay his Iranian or Kuwaiti scenarios. There is no alliance of Arabs capable of threatening him, not only because infighting among Arabs is very unpopular among the pop-ulace, but also because any Arab troops strong enough to contain Iraq within its borders would constitute a menace to the very coun-tries (Kuwait, Saudi Arabia and the Emirates) that would host them. The reality is that the inequity between the strong but poor Arab countries, like Egypt, who might station their forces in the Arabian Peninsula, and the rich but weak monarchies needing protection, is too deep and too obvious to allow accommodation between the two in the long run.

From Saddam's viewpoint, his army is tenacious enough to absorb any Western or Arab attack and to survive it. Even if his industrial and technological base is demolished, he can rebuild it with his oil income during a period of ten years. Post-war Germany and Japan serve as hopeful models to him. Moreover, a war of this sort might rally the masses more tightly around him as long as he remains firmly in power. What if Saddam flees Iraq under duress? If the Americans and others allow him to survive, even at the price of relinquishing power, he may well try, like Napoleon on the island of Elba, to one day recapture his empire. But, as long as he is in place and retains power, he will try, again and again, to attain his strategic aim. And even if he falls, it is not certain that a more malleable pro-Western regime would replace him.

Lacking a tradition of democracy and rule by the people themselves, it is quite possible that he will be replaced by a new dictatorship, one that continues to contend for hegemony in the Arab world and embrace the same strategic goals. Another possibility is that Islamic fundamentalism, led by the Shi'ite majority in Iraq, might manifest itself, with or without collaboration with neighboring Iran. In view of experience in Algeria, Pakistan, Jordan and the West Bank and Gaza, where partial experiments of free democratic elections have given rise to strong Muslim fundamentalist movements, it is quite probable that if the Iraqis were to undergo the same experience, they might opt for such a regime. Public sentiment could then well shift to a strong identification with Islam, if the icon of Arab nationalism headed by Saddam is finally shattered.

The two Gulf wars have taught us that, paradoxically, stability in the Middle East is possible only in traditional authoritarian societies which crush any manifestations of democracy – be they monarchies, autocratic republics leaning on military power, or the new type of 'republican monarchies', where autocratic power is passed from father to son (Syria, Iraq, Libya). But these regimes, which sadly depend on the whims of one man and his inner group, can also wage war and take other destabilizing initiatives without any domestic public opinion being allowed to restrain them. It is a fact that in the twentieth century all wars were provoked by autocratic rulers, while democratic countries were drawn into these conflicts in self-defense. Unfortunately, however, grass-roots democracy does not seem to appear as a viable alternative to these dictatorships, and therefore not much hope can be pinned on achieving stability through democracy.

Regardless of who rules Iraq, it will be an authoritarian regime of one sort or another in the foreseeable future, for it is doubtful whether any of those groups who have been vying from the out-side to replace Saddam are either able to deliver, or committed enough to the ideas of a liberal democracy if they should succeed. An absolute ruler, with probably a military background, for lack of any other homegrown nursery for leaders, will have to rely, like Saddam, on his military power, and like him avoid accountability. Thus, although his legitimacy as a ruler will be clouded with doubts, he would not be in any worse situation than all the regimes in the Arab and Islamic worlds, which also lack legitimacy and escape accountability; exactly the recipe for the rise of a self-deluding dictator who breaks the rules of international conduct and turns his country into a rogue state. There are many dictators of this sort in the Third World (like Gaddafy, Idi Amin or Mobutu), but since they do not have the means to carry out their dreams across their borders, they confine themselves to carrying out their more modest dreams at home. But Iraq is fundamentally different.

Iraq is different because of its geo-strategic assets, its population and its location. Every Iraqi leader of reasonable composure and rational thinking, would be aware of the two immense resources that make the wealth of his country: water and oil. Water, afforded by the two large rivers of the Tigris and the Euphrates, which, since ancient times, had allowed the growth of successive Mesopotamian Empires and cultures in their rich and fertile valleys, continues to be a vastly important commodity in the contemporary Middle East, no less important than oil. The flow of the rivers which converge in the mighty Shatt-al-Arab waterway, makes the land of Iraq poten-tially very productive for agriculture and a blessed land for dense settlement of population in spite of its semi-aridity. Iraq has over 20 million inhabitants, who consider themselves descendants of ancient empires and heirs to great cultures and civilizations, who are relatively well educated and engender a large elite of intellec-tuals and entrepreneurs.

This literate class radiates throughout the Arab world; therefore, it is no coincidence that any ruler of Iraq would wish his country to be a beacon not only of culture but also of politics. And if it were not for the political and structural predicament that has been afflicting modern Iraq, it would certainly have wrested leadership from Egypt, which is poorer in resources, suffers from a terrible popu-lation explosion, and seems to be sliding into more impoverish-ment. The population of Iraq, far from facing the problems of density and impoverishment which characterizes congested Egypt, on the contrary can be potentially accommodated and comfortably fed in the vast fertile valleys of the great rivers. It can also easily raise a military force of two million men, ready for action in the service of the ruler.

Even though the country lacks cohesion due to its three ethnic components – the ruling Sunnites of the center, the Kurds of the north and the Shi'ites of the south – it can be held together in normal times by a strong but benevolent central government which is awash in income from the fabulous oil riches of the country. Indeed, it has been the oil which allowed Saddam to mobilize the national energy of his country towards implementing his schemes of *grandeur* and to hold it together. Anyone after him will have under his command that combination of population/water/oil revenue to consider, and no one would let the opportunity and temptation slip away between his fingers.

And then there is the all-important issue of location. All the components of power are there, only marred by the very narrow access to the Gulf that Iraq; and no ruler can avoid the thought that Iraq's potential to be a giant military and economic power should not be waived simply because of its geo-strategic inability to construct a large navy commensurate with its huge land army, in order to project its power into the Gulf and to stand up to its Iranian rival. And since safe naval bases will be needed to accommodate a large fleet, the perennial temptation to gnaw at adjoining territory, on either side of the Gulf, will remain overwhelming, especially as in either case it would yield the additional benefit of rich deposits of oil.

The conclusion from this reasoning is inescapable: to counter Iraq's designs in the Gulf, which will arise under any ruler, due to the given geo-political data, one would have to cut down to size Iraq's power and ambition against its neighbors, by neutralizing the elements which stir them out of control. For example, if the Shi'ite south could be made an independent entity, based on the port of Basra, and living off its rich agriculture, its trade routes and its Shi'ite holy shrines of Najaf and Karbalah, Iraq would not be able to pose any threat to its neighbors. It would turn Baghdad and its fiefdoms into a landlocked middle-size and homogeneous country, that would be so dependent on its neighbors as to dampen its territorial and regional ambitions. The Kurdish north, with its oil resources, could at long last enable those brave but unfortunate people to attain nationhood and to control enough resources to accommodate other Kurds from adjoining countries who wish to partake in living Kurdish statehood. The immediate neighbors need not be concerned, for if there is one independent Kurdish entity which affords open access to other Kurds, then those who chose to stay in Syria, Turkey or Iran will have to become reconciled to the idea of living there as an ethnic and cultural minority.

The second Gulf War was an opportunity to bring about the break-up of Iraq, but as has so often happened, the USA missed it, because it wrongly assumed that the UN sanctions and supervision of Iraq's disarmament would bring Saddam to his knees. This did not happen, the sanctions have proven to be ineffective and the disarmament program laughable. Saddam is at it once again. Therefore, perhaps the current world crisis occasioned by the war against terrorism, will present another opportunity to break up Iraq's power, if it can be shown that Saddam's shadowy terrorist apparatuses had a hand in the heinous attacks of 11 September 2001, against American targets in New York and Washington, and in the mass murder that resulted therefrom. The vast pool of outrage and horror that has built up against rogue states might have prepared world public opinion for such a decisive action.

6. Islamikaze and their Significance*

WHY ISLAMIKAZE?

Since the Hizbullah in Lebanon, and then the Hamas in the West Bank and Gaza, began launching human-bomb attacks against Israelis and others, the world has been stunned by this seemingly new pattern of terrorism where both the perpetrator and his victims lose their lives. The most current terminology in the Western media and in popular parlance for this kind of horrifying act has been 'suicide attack', due to the fact that, almost invariably, those who engage in this sort of operation know beforehand that they will die, and often prepare themselves for self-immolation in the process.

Much has been said and written about whether such acts of self-destruction amount indeed to 'suicide', as many outsiders would like to see them; or to 'martyrdom', as the perpetrators themselves and their instigators/operators hail them; or simply nationalistic 'heroism' on the part of those eager to venture cold-bloodedly into the enemy's den and inflict on him as many casualties and as much damage as possible, and are prepared to sacrifice their lives in so doing. This is not a matter of mere semantics, but of great importance in order to discern diverse notions and mindsets and their significance.

'Suicide' usually relates to a psychological or pathological disturbance under which an individual, eager to run away from his feelings about an overwhelming problem, or to 'solve' it, commits the ultimate act of killing himself. The 'problem' may range from romantic jealousy to professional frustration; from a banal disappointment to a burning sense of vengeance. The individual in question, unable to bear the pain, the shame, the embarrassment or

*Originally published in *Terrorism and Political Violence*, 9, 3 (1997), pp.96–121.

the confrontation involved; or to fight uphill to restore his dignity, his self-esteem, his place in society or his devastated ego, chooses to exit from life rather than sustain its vagaries.

Suicide may also be motivated by a strong sense of protest against an existing order or state of affairs that one is unable to either withstand or to alter, or by revenge on a person or group with whom/which one is disenchanted, but from whom/which one cannot disengage. In Japanese tradition, one sort of hara-kiri, the ritual suicide, was precisely geared to provide a respectful way out to people in such a dire need. The most important type of hara-kiri, however, was the ritual self-immolation that the samurai was ordered to perform by his lord, as an honorable self-inflicted punishment in order to escape a degrading and humiliating execution that he had 'earned' by his misdeeds or misbehavior.

Unlike the hara-kiri performers and others of their kind, the Japanese soldiers who were organized in 'Special Units', and were designed to blow themselves up with their enemies during the Second World War, were typically motivated by their devotion to their country and their Emperor. They became popularly known as Kamikaze,[1] the 'Winds of Gods', and they inflicted casualties, damage and terror on the American forces during the final stages of the Pacific War. These special units – which were trained, indoctrinated and sustained by the Japanese State – were in quite a different category from the hara-kiri or the conventional suicide performers, in the sense that they were not self-motivated, did not cater to their own personal instincts or needs and were part of a larger group of like-minded fellows. They felt that in their act they were performing an ultimate sacrifice for a cause, which not only had a political-ideological purpose, but also had a strong religious coloring (hence, Winds of Gods). And in so doing, they were prepared to sacrifice their lives without hesitation.[2]

It will be suggested in this article that the so-called Muslim fundamentalist 'suicide bombers' have nothing suicidal about them; they do not even resemble the hara-kiri of either the imposed or the voluntary type; but they come very close to the kamikaze in motivation, organization, ideology and execution of their task. It is therefore proposed here to adopt the appellation of 'Islamikaze' to describe them. In fact, a report from an Afghan camp where this kind of fighter is being trained, and which has come to be known as the 'Kamikaze Barracks', sports a slogan at its main entrance (made of whitewashed pebble and stone), which states:

'Jihad-Istishhad-Paradise-Islamic Kamikaze-Human Bombs'.[3] This is, in essence, the entire story.

THE PRODUCERS OF ISLAMIKAZE

We hear of the Hizbullah 'human bombs' exploding in Lebanon, or those of the Hamas blowing up Israeli buses. But little is publicized about the Islamikaze camps in Afghanistan where the latest technologies of death and destruction are imparted to the many volunteers streaming there from all over the Islamic world to train for their sinister missions. There are comparable camps in Lebanon, in Iran, in the Sudan and in any number of Islamic lands under conflict, but there is no doubt that lawless Afghanistan prior to the Taliban takeover must have constituted ideal grounds for such an endeavor.

These training camps for foreign Muslims are an offshoot of the long standing intake of volunteers from all over the Arab and Islamic worlds who went to fight on the *Mujahideen* side, at the instigation of the Americans and the Saudis, in order to undermine the Soviet grip there in the 1980s. Upon returning to their homelands at the end of the war, these so-called *Afghanis* often became the spearhead of Muslim opposition to the regimes in their countries. During the Afghan War, the Pakistani border city of Peshawar, which had been a remote backwater, grew into a major center that gave refuge to millions of refugees from the war zone. The city also became the staging area for *Mujahideen* counter-attacks against the Soviets, and also a teeming center of international illicit activity: arms deals of all sorts, spying grounds, drug trafficking, smuggling and terrorism.

It is no coincidence that some of the most recent spectacular acts of terrorism were either staged or directed from Peshawar, and it is in Peshawar that the blind Sheikh Abd al-Rahman – who was involved in the assassination of Sadat and later convicted for the New York Twin Towers explosion – met his operators prior to his journey to New Jersey to seek asylum from Egyptian authorities. And it is in Islamikaze camps such as those in Peshawar that terrorists from Algeria, Sudan, Egypt, Lebanon, Iran, Saudi Arabia and Pakistan are trained as Islamic death experts who later hijack, abduct, kill, lay explosives and commit 'suicide' attacks. While not many details have filtered out of those camps, the visit of the reporters for the Arabic weekly *Al-Watan al-'Arabi* (*The Arab*

Homeland)⁴ to the site of the 'Kamikaze Barracks' in Afghanistan sheds much light on the ideological and social make-up of the Islamikaze. The reporters, being versed in Arab and Islamic affairs, and presumably Arab and Muslim themselves, provide us with the following details:

1. The camp, located in a remote site in the vicinity of the Afghani–Pakistani border, is the site of extremely demanding physical training. For example, the trainees would run long stretches of the road every day, carrying bags of rocks or sand on their shoulders. This suggests, of course, that these people are not simply sent to their death, but are rather imparted skills for fighting and survival.
2. The instructors in this camp originate from Egypt, Saudi Arabia and Yemen, and are known for the toughness of their character.
3. The instruction for using weapons includes arms of all sorts and from various origins: Chinese, American, Turkish, and even the famous Israeli Uzi sub-machine-gun. The weapons span the entire gamut: from rifles and pistols to anti-aircraft Stinger missiles. This means that not only an abundance of these missiles is still available as a remnant of the Afghani War, but that the trainees are taught to handle them to down enemy aircraft, which is not necessarily the best or easiest way to commit suicide.
4. Instruction of the Islamikaze also includes urban guerrilla combat, sabotage, handling and concocting explosives, and mounting car-bombs; again a testament to the sophistication of these terrorists, but also to their perception of themselves as being much more a machine of death rather than a mere 'human bomb'.
5. The trainees are all designated, dispatched and financed by their home Islamic organizations. It is the foreign currency poured into Afghanistan to finance these courses, some say with the collaboration of the foreign currency-hungry authorities (at least until the Taliban takeover in late 1996), which keeps the Islamikaze camps going. The Islamic organizations and their sponsors – either governments or wealthy private benefactors – then determine where the hardened graduates of these courses are to act, and under what cover, and to what specific task they may be assigned.
6. Trainees come not only from Arab and Islamic countries, but also

from countries where Muslim minorities, or Muslim areas under non-Muslim rule, are deemed to be oppressed. Cases in point: Muslims in France (mainly North Africans), in Germany (mainly Turks), Palestinians (under Israeli rule), Bosnian Muslims, Chechnyans, Moros and others.

7. Graduates of these death courses later serve in such Islamic countries as Jordan or Egypt, or steal across the border into Pakistan, where they were set to remove Benazir Bhutto from power. Others went to Kashmir to help install an Islamic government. Many of them fought in Bosnia against the Serbs; and the expert saboteurs among them have set explosives in Delhi, Bahrain and New York, to cite only a few sample cases. This means that these young fighters are not necessarily dedicated to their own death but, rather, to wreaking havoc on their enemies.

8. The trainees are 16- to 25-year-old boys. Those who accede to the upper echelons of training, in preparation for Islamikaze missions, are subject to a particularly testing regime: they do not talk to each other and grow to become introspective and meditative. Side-by-side with taxing their physical endurance, they undergo endless sessions of religious indoctrination, mainly by Egyptian and Saudi *Ulama*.[5] The camp was founded and headed by a Pakistani scholar of this type. This means that those who go for straightforward Islamikaze missions are considered by their operators to be of a higher order who deserve the highest form of training, and that in preparation for their supreme act of devotion, they have to pave the last portion of their way to Paradise on their own.

9. The inherent weakness of the government of Afghanistan, and the infighting between contending groups for power there, enabled the foreign trainees, at least until the Taliban takeover, to both test their weapons and methods in real battle in real time, and all with impunity and without interference. This is unlike the situation in Lebanon, Syria, Iraq, Iran, Libya, the Sudan or Algeria, where such camps may be given to the scrutiny, or literally to the mercy, of the local authorities who manipulate them for their own purposes.

10. Each course lasts for a few months and costs approximately $3,000 per trainee. But both the instructors and their students also engage in the drug trade and smuggling in order to ensure the smooth functioning of the camps. Local Afghani warlords

collaborate with the camps in order to earn some illicit income for themselves while according, on their part, freedom of operation to the Islamikaze and their mentors. So, all rival camps in Afghanistan, from the now-deposed President Rabbani to arch-rebel Hikmatyar, could count on the camps in their areas of control for foreign currency income.

The convergence of this 'Islamikaze International' in Afghanistan; the number of volunteer trainees who flock to the camps there from all over the Islamic world; and the increasing cooperation between various Islamic movements who send the young Islamikaze to their death against both domestic and international targets, beg many questions:

1. Why in Afghanistan, and why to a lesser degree, in other Islamic countries?
2. How is one to account for this rather unique phenomenon?
3. What is the ideology instilled in the minds of the Islamikaze?
4. What can the West do?

AFGHANISTAN AND ITS CLONES

It seems rather aberrant that countries such as Afghanistan, Pakistan, Iran, Libya and the Sudan, which had enjoyed a close relationship with the USA and the West in the past, should turn so violently anti-Western, not only on the rhetorical level but also in the domain of terrorism. These countries share one common denominator, namely Islam that, *prima facie*, cuts through diverse ethnic, linguistic, national, political and social systems, and facilitates the growth of the network of international, mainly anti-Western, terrorism there. Moreover, if one takes into account the diffusion of the *Afghanis* and their likes in practically most Islamic countries, including those considered 'moderate' or 'pro-American' (for example, Egypt, Saudi Arabia, Pakistan, Jordan and Morocco), one could come to the erroneous conclusions that Islam necessarily equals terrorism, or that Islam by definition overrides all other considerations when it comes to international terrorism.

The reality is much more varied and nuanced, and it is tied specifically to local conditions in each country. The Islamikaze stand in most Islamic countries not as part of the Islamic order, but in opposition to it. They represent not the mainstream of Islam –

which is usually pragmatic and strikes compromises with the rulers in place in accordance with the Sunnite precept that 'better a bad ruler than political chaos' – but are more or less marginal groups in Islamic society. These groups may have sympathizers and supporters, but they themselves thrive on the disoriented, the disaffected, the disenchanted and the dysfunctional strata which cannot catch up with the rapid changes in society and which abhor modernity. They harshly criticize the regimes of their own countries, accuse them of corruption, submission to Western values, and subversion of Islamic ideals and tradition, and they often urge the toppling of their home regimes. In other words, unlike established Islam which seeks the gradual Islamization of society, peacefully and often in concert with the rulers in place, these radicals want everything here and now. Their passion is impatient.

The Islamists, as they are sometimes termed in the West, gather their force, their passion and their deep commitment around charismatic leaders, who provide them with a model of populistic sincerity, paternal devotion and concern, and scholarly wisdom and knowledge. They come to regard their enormously popular leaders as role models and they almost adore them as the epitome of rightfulness and as their source of guidance, not unlike the Jewish Hassidim *vis-à-vis* their rabbi. Setting themselves apart from the evil society that surrounds them, they wholeheartedly and boundlessly follow the word of their leaders as the ultimate interpretation of the will of Allah. Whenever need arises, these leaders can pronounce tailor-made *fatwas* to lend justification to the warranted action. One can understand how, propelled by this kind of relentless drive, enveloped by an approving and supportive environment, and guided by the semi-divine sanction of the leader-generated *fatwa*, a Muslim radical can also transcend the ordinary into the mystic and magnetic world of the Islamikaze.

In order to cultivate their self-image as the alternative to the existing order, these Islamikaze-prone revolutionaries not only boast their slogans of 'Islam is the solution', 'Islam is the alternative', 'Islam is the Truth',[6] but they also delegitimize the regimes under which they live, and the enemies against whom they are pitted, be they godless communists, the corrupt West, aggressive America and Israel, etc. Rhetorical violence against opponents and rivals sets the stage for their ultimate elimination. And if they cannot be eliminated by a face-to-face confrontation due to their (temporary) superiority in weaponry, then self-sacrifice by way of Islamikaze may become necessary.

Afghanistan became the choice site of activity in the 1980s following the 1979 Christmas Day invasion of the country by the Soviets at the 'invitation' of the communist regime in Kabul. This was, and still is, a country torn by ethnic differences,[7] and it was quick to organize popular resistance to the Soviets, with active American support along those lines. As long as the battle raged against the foreign invaders, and American aid abounded, channeled directly or via Pakistan, all factions were kept busy and happy. All prescribed Islam as their goal and way of life, and all vowed to extirpate the Soviets from the land at any cost and regardless of the time this would necessitate, much to the delight of the USA and the West in general. As the war escalated, the *Mujahideen* drew foreign participants from other Islamic countries (the *Afghanis* already mentioned) into the fray, and soon Iran, Saudi Arabia, Libya and private donors from the Gulf area raised enough money, bought enough weapons and recruited enough volunteers from practically the entire Islamic world to internationalize the conflict and make it a sort of 'Spanish Civil War', to which fervent Islamists flocked, this time to check Communist expansion.

But as soon as the Soviets tired of that endless war of attrition, as their casualties mounted and the vanity of the campaign became evident, they also realized that their goal of suffocating radical Islam in Afghanistan, lest it spread to their own Muslim republics, had backfired on them and increased its fervor and capacity to resist them. The Soviet withdrawal from Afghanistan, which coincided with the end of the Soviet Union and allowed the independent rise of the Islamic republics of Central Asia, signaled a new stage in the Afghani war.

While the foreigners who fought alongside the *Mujahideen* returned home and stirred up trouble in their own countries, the Afghani militias deployed their full forces and prepared to take over Kabul. The infighting that ensued left Afghanistan ruined and Kabul half-destroyed, in a senseless civil war which lasted from 1992 to 1996. The coalition government between the Tajik warlords (Rabbani as President, Shah Masud as Minister of Defense) and Hikmatyar as Prime Minister, seemed to offer, for a time, a similitude of hope for stability, until the Taliban, a Pashtun student militia trained and backed mainly by Pakistan, undertook to regain Pashtun dominance of Afghani politics with a view of reuniting the country under Islamic rule. It took them two years of fighting to capture most of the country and to pacify Kabul under their new order, namely as a strict *shari'a* state.

The significance of the Taliban victory in Afghanistan can range far and wide insofar as it reinforces Islamic regimes already in place, gives hope to other Islamic groups struggling in their own countries against regimes that they oppose (for example, in Egypt, Kuwait, Lebanon, Algeria, Saudi Arabia, etc.), or against Israel and the West (Hizbullah, Hamas, Islamic Jihad), and assures the incursion of radical Islam into Central Asia, thus widening its distribution and opening new avenues for its spread. And, exactly like Iran and the Sudan which have been maintaining state-sponsored training bases for Islamikaze, often with Saudi financing, state and private, so the new regime of the Taliban was able to embrace the existing Islamikaze structures in the country, and cultivate them both in order to serve the international network of terrorism and to manipulate them for its own purposes. And even though the Taliban failed, the end result from the Islamikaze point of view was the same. For regardless of who is in power, Afghanistan has been so thoroughly Islamized during the war[8] that it will not only continue to be a propitious ground for Islamikaze, but it will also play an axial role in the outward diffusion thereof.

WHAT MAKES THE ISLAMIKAZE TICK?

Perhaps the most intriguing question of all is why young men, with sometimes a promising future before them, apparently sane and healthy in every respect, would put themselves in jeopardy, and volunteer or be induced into an Islamikaze unit which is likely to put an end to their lives. Why don't they simply join a high-risk combat unit, if all their desire is to serve a collective goal of their nation/religion and at the same time satisfy their machismo? Are they subject to an underlying latent impulse to death? Are they exhilarated by mortal danger? Or is it the rosy promise, full of delight and clear of worry, awaiting them in the hereafter, which kindles their passion?

We have already discussed in the introduction to this article the question of the popularly used term 'suicide-bombers' and whether Islamikaze can be deemed suicidal. To remove any doubt regarding their motivations, one ought to consider the parameters that, from the point of view of Western psychiatry, define the requisite steps of the would-be suicide perpetrator.[9]

1. A thought about killing oneself.
2. The presence of a plan, that is, how to proceed, what are the precise steps to be taken, their sequence and timing, etc.
3. An energy level of the suicidal individual must exist, that is, his capacity to carry the plan out.

By contrast, in the case of the Islamikaze, it is the determination to kill the enemy which is the driving force; the plan relates to killing others and it is often prepared by the operators of the Islamikaze, not by him personally;[10] and he must be ready when sent by his operators, because unlike the candidate for self-immolation, he does not carry the burden of decision alone, and therefore he does not have to evince the same high degree of 'suicidal resolve'.

Psychiatrists say[11] that these cumulative three factors are among the most important for providing an indication of the likelihood of a suicide occurrence. Moreover, they say, suicide can be sudden, as in the case of major depression, or in compulsive individuals under conditions of extreme frustration; or it can be premeditated, as in a long-standing major depression where the individual has perhaps made a careful plan and meticulous preparations, such as giving away his most valued possessions, or may sometimes have written a note about his impending suicide. From a theoretical point of view, it is conceivable that a subconscious chronic suicidal agenda could motivate the death of the perpetrator in the case of an Islamikaze action, yet this seems highly unlikely. Although studies of German and Italian terrorists have indicated that many have been alienated, lonely, unsuccessful people, it is a far cry to claim that such people were actually suicidal. Furthermore, there is no clear-cut evidence that ethnic-nationalistic terrorists such as Basques or the IRA are of a similar mindset, and no relevant data are available for Arab and Islamic youth. That German terrorists committed suicide many years later in prison does not indicate that they were suicidal earlier in their terrorist careers.

In our case, the Islamikaze never go for a 'sudden' death; it is always premeditated and planned carefully, though not necessarily by them personally. However, while it is difficult to cite individual depression or frustration or compulsion in all these cases – because otherwise it is hard to envisage how this type of individual could enrol in an all-volunteer program designed by others, with a strategic goal to attain – it is also not unthinkable that these individuals may entertain their own private goal of killing themselves.

True, the Islamikaze do write 'suicide' notes (in our days in the form of videotapes), and may also pre-distribute their possessions, both signs of suicidal intentions, but in our case the interpretation of those signals ought to be vastly at variance with the classic suicidal syndrome. When an Islamikaze writes or records a note or a tape or a video, it is not usually geared to vindicate his act, to ask for clemency from the bereaved relatives and friends, or to 'punish' them by disappearing. Quite the contrary, the messages left behind are 'educational' in essence, formulated so as to provide role-models and positive examples to other youth who might be recruited after them. And in any case, the recording session is orchestrated by the operators, who then undertake the duty of propagating the 'legacy' of the deceased. In fact, all the deceased become martyrs and heroes, they are celebrated and cited in their community; and their relatives, far from evincing grief outwardly, on the contrary exalt with pride the honor that the departed had imparted to them. And when the Islamikaze dies in his mission, what is left to 'distribute' after him is a sort of 'pension', disbursed to the family by the operating organization. In other words, this is not a *pre*-death parting with belongings, but a promise to the families that they will not be forgotten *after* the death of the martyr. Due to their young age, these martyrs very seldom leave any property behind, but when they do, the belongings ascend to the status of 'relics', such as their pictures, which may become the object of worship-like adoration.

Given these outward distinctions between suicidal types and the Islamikaze, and due to the impracticality of clinical evaluation prior to the act of 'suicide-bombing' (much less subsequent to it), one is left with little or no basis for the reconstruction of the personality of the martyr or his biography before the act. Even in cases of failed 'suicide- bombing', or when the bombing succeeded but the perpetrator escaped death (which in itself invalidates that terminology in the first place), it is perhaps impossible to reconstruct his mind-set prior to the act because his survival – which may have been miraculous, voluntary or otherwise – does not diminish one iota either from his self-perception as a hero who has succeeded, even though he survived, or who tried at great risk to attain his goal but was foiled by outside forces beyond his control; or from the way others perceive him, not as a martyr if he did not die, but as a hero worthy of emulation by others.

If one could draw personal profiles of would-be bombers after their recruitment, perhaps their shared qualities, family backgrounds and socio-economic environment might hint at their predisposition to commit this sort of martyrdom. But again, since this is not suicide in the conventional sense, no individual can be tested for his intention to kill himself when he had, perhaps, never intended to do so in the first place, or before he in fact did it in the real world and for totally different purposes than suicide. From collected information to date[12] it would seem that people most likely to join these missions, or equally dangerous cults or revolutionary groups, share some basic characteristics which in themselves do not necessarily indicate psychiatric illness:

1. They are young and therefore have few life responsibilities: career, business, family, material possessions.
2. Many of them were not particularly successful in their lives: in study, work or interpersonal relations; or they have been relatively shunned by their families/friends/environment to the point of feeling isolated.
3. They are usually characterized by poor self-esteem.

It is evident that people of this sort might well find an alternative social organization, marginal, persecuted and problematic as it may be, in order to be recognized and accepted,[13] enhanced and appreciated. The new group gives them the opportunity to expand their own ego, and the newly acquired comradeship sustains their self-esteem and self-importance. They may be somewhat depressed and in search of easy solutions to their problems. Unsuccessful, perhaps self-despising, they find solace in becoming martyrs, thus almost instantly and mythically transforming frustration into glory, failure into victory and self-deprecation into public adoration. Perhaps this explanation holds for a certain percentage of these youths; perhaps others are duped. Perhaps still others are romantics or idealists (whatever that may mean); there is undoubtedly a spectrum of personalities involved. However, from a strategic point of view, the crucial issue is that a highly structured organization is shaping, molding and using these individuals for its own ambitions and sinister goals.

What is more, while adherents of cults find solace for their individual selves in their life and death, the Islamikaze fulfil a societal-family ideal, by preparing the grounds in Paradise for their entire family to follow. Their role as pioneers before their kin makes them precious in the eyes of the public, which views them and their surviving families with awe and admiration. This can hardly be said about cult or suicide victims. Moreover, if one is to summarize the popular songs about these martyrs, which are distributed *post mortem* on video, tapes and in brochures and posters; the host of orally transmitted stories of their heroism and self-sacrifice; and the repeated replay on stage of the saga of their martyrdom, much reminiscent of the Shi'ite *ta'zya*,[14] one cannot help noticing the enormous differences between these two kinds of self-inflicted death. Indeed, in the world of the Islamikaze:

1. The hereafter is lauded, not as an escape, but as a desirable fulfilment.
2. Paradise is depicted in exciting, plastic, worldly and pleasurable terms. Sex and wine, the two foremost taboos in Islamic society, are exalted in the popular literature of the martyrs as accessible and permissible in unlimited quantities, because in the hereafter everything is in abundant and limitless supply, and the restrictions of *shari'a* law do not apply.
3. The public which extols the martyrs stands as an approving and adoring audience, not as a traumatized or disgusted public as in the case of cult-instigated massacres or self-immolation.

THE ISLAMIC RATIONALE

The construct 'suicide-bomber' has been used by the Western media and the political community and, as such, it has had deleterious consequences: minimizing, trivializing and distorting a highly significant phenomenon. 'Suicide-bomber' implies a disposition to craziness, yet the term has not emanated from psychologically or psychiatrically responsible sources. Turning to an Islamic frame of reference for a definition, and perhaps a diagnosis, would then appear imperative if we are to comprehend the underlying motives of this sort of unparalleled mode of self-sacrifice. A venerated leader of the Islamic Jihad group in Gaza, Abdallah Shami, when questioned by an Israeli reporter about 'suicide-bombing', said:

> We do not possess the military hardware our enemy possesses. We do not have planes, missiles or even a cannon with which we can fight injustice. The most effective tool to inflict damage and harm with the least possible losses is

> operations of this nature. This is a legitimate method based on martyrdom. The martyr gets the privilege of entering Paradise and frees himself from pain and misery.[15]

The sheikh is then claiming that only dearth of weapons had caused his movement to use humans instead. He does not idealize or justify 'suicide bombing' as a goal unto itself. Moreover, while in conventional suicide the victim wishes to inflict the most possible damage on himself in order to make his task 'successful', here there is a reverse prescription to reduce the perpetrators' losses (and presumably to increase the enemy's). However, when there is loss, the perpetrator/victim is assured of life in the hereafter. To reduce the losses also implies that the operators of such acts do engage in 'economic' calculations, inasmuch as they strive to decrease the numbers of would-be martyrs for each operation, not in order to increase its efficacy, but in order to diminish the toll of their own casualties. Had death in itself been regarded as an ideal, even in the context of eliminating the enemy, then a maximum of participants in the operation, not the necessary minimum, should have been envisaged. This is similar to the kamikaze, our control group, where death for the Emperor, as much as it was idealized and irrational, still was tempered by the rational necessity to manage the available resources economically in order to put them to optimal use.

The build-up of the Islamikaze's ideological commitment, contrary to the stages of the suicidal type that we have seen above, is made incrementally of the following three elements: identifying the enemy; strengthening the value of jihad as the religious duty of every Muslim against the identified enemy; and then instigating the Islamikaze to show personal valor and self-sacrifice for the attainment of the prescribed goal.

The Enemy Looms Large

Radical Islamic movements in general have clearly identified their enemy: the regimes in the Islamic world which practice non-Islamic law; the West, which has been undermining Islam from within and corrupting it with its norms of permissiveness in order to destabilize and replace it; and Israel–Zionism – the Jews, who are intrinsically the enemies of Allah and humanity, in addition to their being an arm of the West in the heart of the Islamic world. The enemy must be depicted in evil terms so as to make it a free prey for Muslims to attack and destroy. Rhetorical delegitimation of their enemy is an essential step towards making the use of violence permissible, even desirable, against him.

Hence the systematic and virulent onslaughts of those movements against what they perceive as their enemies, domestic and external.

In the early 1950s, Sayyid Qutb, one of the great masters of radical Islam, published his book *Our Campaign Against the Jews,*[16] in which he warned of their evil subversion of Islam, and urged Muslims to go back to the Koran lest Islam be destroyed. Qutb described at length the Jewish propensity for plotting, for turning their backs on their own leaders, for hostility towards their prophets, for rebelling against Divine Will, for concocting revolutions and trouble everywhere, for instigating war and destruction, etc. He accused them of being egotistical and ungrateful, and of having forged their holy scriptures, and claimed that their innate hatred towards Islam stemmed from their hostility to the angel Gabriel who transmitted the Holy Revelation of the Koran to the Prophet of Islam.[17]

Those very attacks against the Jews are echoed, almost *verbatim*, by the Charter of the Hamas published in 1988:

> The Nazism of the Jews does not skip women and children … They make war against people's livelihood, plunder their money and threaten their honor. In their horrible actions they mistreat people like the most horrendous war criminals.[18]

Also:

> The enemies have been scheming for a long time … They accumulated a huge and influential material wealth which they put to the service of implementing their dream: to take control of the world media and news agencies, the press, publishing houses, broadcasting and the like … they stood behind the French and Communist Revolutions and most of the revolutions we hear about. They used their money to establish clandestine organizations which are spreading around the world in order to destroy societies and carry out Zionist interests. Such organizations are: the Free Masons, Rotary Clubs, Lions Clubs, B'nai Brith and the like. All of them are subversive spying organizations. They also influenced imperialistic states and made them colonize many countries in order to exploit the wealth of those countries and spread their corruption therein …[19]

The Muslim radical bent on violence finds the recipe for how to act against this abominable enemy in the form of a *Hadith* related to the Prophet:

> The Time [of Resurrection] will not come until Muslims will fight against the Jews [and kill them], until the Jews hide behind rocks and trees which will cry: O Muslim! There is a Jew hiding behind me, come on and kill him.[20]

Similarly, regimes in the Islamic world which are termed 'heretic' by the fundamentalists can become the target of the same kind of hatred and violence.[21]

The Doctrine of Jihad

As explained in Chapter 1, the underlying justification for launching war against such evil enemies, domestic and external, is distilled in the quintessential notion of jihad, both as a collective and personal duty. Let us listen to what the Hamas group has to say in this regard:

> When our enemies usurp our Islamic lands, jihad becomes a duty binding on all Muslims. In order to face the usurpation of Palestine by the Jews, we have no escape from raising the banner of *jihad*. This would require the propagation of Islamic consciousness among the masses on all local, Arab and Islamic levels. We must spread the spirit of jihad among the Islamic *Umma*, clash with the enemies and join the ranks of jihad fighters.[22]

According to this view, and along the lines charted by Sayyid Qutb and others before him, the Hamas view the war against Israel and the Jews as a religious war,[23] therefore Muslims ought to mobilize and swell their ranks and fight them to the finish, whatever the price. For, as one of their leaflets put it, 'Our struggle with the Jews is a struggle between Truth and emptiness, between Islam and Judaism.'[24] Sheikh Tamimi, one of the leading founders of the Islamic Jihad group, published a booklet entitled *The Obliteration of Israel: a Qur'anic Imperative*.[25] Moved by the sheikh's vow that 'we shall not accede to a Jewish state on our land, even if it is only one village',[26] young Palestinians joined his organization and were prepared to put their lives on the line for what they saw as a divine command. Thus, the jihad group recruited resolute

Islamikaze who embarked on operations designed to inflict on the enemy as many casualties as possible, often without planning their own escape. For example, during the Gulf War, one jihad recruit, instructed to set up and detonate a car-bomb on a busy street in one of the countries fighting against Iraq, told a *Times* correspondent that the fate he awaited in the afterworld was far superior to the 'rotten life he had at present'. But he added that his life was not all that miserable, for he was readying himself to die for his cause. He said that all lives were moving towards Heaven or Hell, and he chose Heaven.[27]

In spite of the wide variety of interpretations given to jihad in modern times, some of which are soft and subtle, it is evident that the Muslim radicals – including Islamic Jihad, the Hamas, the Hizbullah, and certainly the Islamikaze among them – are uncompromisingly dedicated to the violent version. They refer to many Koranic passages which assure the martyr (that is, the dead in the course of jihad), all manner of rewards in the next world.[28]

This is the reason why jihad has become the rallying slogan of many of those radical movements, as in 'Allah is the goal, the Prophet the model, the Koran the Constitution, Jihad the path, and death for the cause of Allah the most sublime creed.'[29] Death in the course of jihad becomes, then, an expected and even desirable outcome, especially when jihad is taken as the explanatory motive of history. Indeed, radical Islamic movements regard the present generation's struggle in the path of Allah as only one link in the chain of continuous jihad, inasmuch as precedent fighters/martyrs had opened the path and the living in each generation must follow in their footsteps, 'whatever time it might take'.[30] In fact, the Muslim Brothers' symbol is constituted by a copy of the Koran flanked by two swords, their explication being that force (jihad by the sword) defends justice as encapsulated in the Koran.

Hence, the powerful appeal for jihad, and for death in jihad if necessary, is reinforced by the Islamic legal prescription that all are liable to jihad except for the blind, the handicapped and the old, who cannot expend the requisite effort in the battlefield. In the macho-prone youth of the Islamic world, going to jihad is proof that one is not afflicted by those inabilities, Allah Forbid! One of the heads of the Muslim Brothers in Egypt[31] called upon the jihad fighters to brandish the banner of the Holy War until all Islamic lands were liberated and the Islamic State reinstituted. Similarly, Hamas leaders have repeatedly emphasized the importance of jihad by according to it the validity of a sixth Pillar.[32] In a *fatwa* circulated in the territories under

Israeli rule, spiritual leaders of the Palestinians have indeed determined that jihad is a personal duty binding on each and every individual 'until the usurper has been removed from the land by force of the sword'. They have rejected peace with Israel, if only because that would amount to cessation of the jihad and the obstruction of the road of jihad before the coming generations.

Martyrdom is the Remedy

The would-be martyrs belong within three concentric circles of identity which coincide with the three elements necessary to their ideological make-up: the public at large; their inner circle of like-minded activists; and the innermost nucleus of those ready for the ultimate sacrifice.

1. Exactly as the Kamikaze won the support of, and found sympathy among, the wartime Japanese public, so do the Islamikaze in their Islamic environment. Both publics were/are focused on their enmity and hostility towards their sworn enemy, thereby constituting the water from which these guerrilla-martyrs have sought sustenance. The clear identification of that enemy that they shared with their public, and the equally clear recognition by the martyrs that when they acted the public would stand behind them and revere them even if they failed, and much more so if they perish in battle, are the foundations for building the first element of the Islamikaze world view.
2. Islamikaze and Kamikaze alike belong(ed) to radical, battle-hardened and highly indoctrinated groups which vowed to serve the cause with unlimited devotion: the Muslim fundamentalists and the Japanese Armed Forces respectively. For the Muslims, jihad (as interpreted in Chapter 1) is the rallying point and the chosen path, and death in it promises in itself martyrdom and access to Paradise.
3. Above and beyond the commitment of the Muslim radicals to jihad, there is a chosen nobility, the best of the best, who prepare themselves for the superior form of sacrifice: the Islamikaze. Unlike the jihad fighters who fight in unison and seek comfort and courage in each other, but like the Kamikaze, the Islamikaze train alone for their mission and prepare themselves in glorious self-isolation for their task. Hence, the requirement of the ultimate degree of audacity, devotion, consciousness and piety.

It is this transition from jihad fighter to Islamikaze that needs elaboration. Let us listen, again, to a widely circulated tape extolling the Islamikaze:

1. Come on brother, join jihad
    Carry your machine gun from early morning
    And come Brother, join jihad. Choose one of the two:

    Either victory and a life of delight
    Or death, and a life with a Paradise girl[33] (refrain)

    Oh Brother, your country calls upon you
    Stand up and come to liberate her
    Oh, Aqsa Mosque, we are all mourning
    Your desecration by those cursed by Allah

2. But when the Muslims take notice,
    You'll bloom again like Jasmine
    Oh Brother! We have already endured humiliation
    Look at Sabra and Mia Mia[34]
    Manhood and zeal are lost
    Unless you pick up your machine-gun
    And join jihad[35]

The feeling of 'we have reached the ebb, we have nothing to lose' is exactly the impetus for exposing oneself to self-immolation, because while here there is only humiliation and suffering, 'there' the promise is great. Beyond this, one can detect in the song all three elements of the Islamikaze make-up: delegitimation of the enemy (the desecrators of Al-Aqsa, who are cursed by Allah), the call for jihad, which binds all Muslim fighters, and the final step of luring the predisposed to do so, to their death without fear. Let us look at another song of this sort:

The solution is inherent in your Faith, your Islam, your weapons
Oh Brother, persist in your way, with determination and resolve
How sweet to the ear is the voice calling for jihad
You better sing these lyrics of audacity
While handling the arrows in your quiver.
We shall crush the bastions of injustice
And turn them into ashes.
Then we shall brandish the banner of Faith
With pride and fortitude.

We have come to you, the landscape of our country,
Ready to defy death and to cleanse the impurities
Of the Zionist enemies.[36]

As Fat'hi Shqaqi,[37] the Secretary General of the jihad group explains, in a press interview regarding the 'suicide-bombings', in which he essentially repeated all the elements already discussed above:

> Our battle with the enemy inside Palestine is to open to all possible jihad methods and likelihoods, including martyrdom operations ... The enemy thought that by signing the Oslo Agreement he had closed the Palestine file and was about to liquidate it, a fact which demands from us a special effort to foil the plot. Hence the importance of martyrdom operations at this stage ... As to Iranian support, it consists in the main of help to the families of the martyrs and the prisoners ... Other than that, the Iranian support is just political and moral ...
>
> The young people who started Islamic Jihad in Palestine in the early 1980s were young people from secondary and primary schools ... I was one of the young people who felt extreme bitterness and sorrow following the 1967 defeat ... It shook us because it threw us into a bottomless pit ... During that time, I and others ... lost all balance ... We could not do anything other than cling to Allah as a means to get out of the impasse and restore our psychological balance ... The idea of Islamic Jihad emerged later and matured during our studies in Egypt in the 1970s ...
>
> As to Sayyid Qutb, his influence on our generation is beyond dispute ... The Islamic Jihad movement also works for the unification of the Arab and Islamic efforts towards Palestine while at the same time preaching Islam and its creed, laws, culture and discipline, and the revival of its cultural message to the nation and to mankind alike, and work for its emergence and triumph ... These objectives fall within the framework of our realization of the growing link and dialogue between the confrontation of Zionism and Imperialism and the revival of the nation, for it would not be possible for us to accomplish the Islamic revival plan without the question of the liberation of Palestine being the nucleus of such a plan and the area of its basic battle ...

The establishment of a truly independent Palestinian state with the existence of Israel is impossible ... The acceptance of a Palestinian state alongside Israel, besides not being possible, constitutes a dwarfing of the Palestinian question and conflicts with our revival plan ... Israel is an imperialist entity ... founded on expansionism ... It is also an imperialist base and an ally and partner of the West, and helps to facilitate the West's penetration into the Arab and Islamic fold, to dominate it and loot its wealth ...

It is true that the material balance of power is not in our favor. But this should not prevent us from striking a balance of terror with the enemy. Here lies the significance of the martyrdom operations, which prove that the unjust balances of power are not eternal ... and that we possess the option of fighting rather than surrendering ...

Change is undoubtedly coming, for it is a divine law and way. So it is better that change should find us steadfast in our positions rather than on our knees bearing the document of capitulation before the Zionist entity and NATO.[38]

The above citations from those directly involved in Islamikaze and their supporters certainly provide the Islamic rationale for their acts. What is missing is the formal religious-legal sanction lending a stamp of approval to these thoughts. Such approvals have been pronounced by several scholars in the form of *fatwa* (a religiously-binding verdict). One of them, Yussuf al-Qardawi, published a 2,000-word dissertation headed by the unequivocal judgment that 'Martyrdom operations in occupied Palestine represent one of the greatest forms of jihad for the sake of Allah.'[39]

The link that was missing, the *fatwa*, is necessitated by the fact that Islam usually proscribes suicide, since the soul given by Allah cannot be taken away by a unilateral act of a mortal Believer. Qardawi recognizes the Koranic injunction: 'Make not your own hands contribute to your destruction'; but he also acknowledges the consensus among most Muslim jurists to the effect that near-suicidal attacks by one man against a large number of the enemy are allowed when the perpetrator believes he has a good chance of staying alive, or if he believes he can inflict a substantial loss on the enemy, although his own death is certain. And he concludes:

> Calling these operations suicidal is an erroneous and misleading description. They are sacrificial, and heroic, and as

martyrdom operations they are totally detached from the concept of suicide. A suicider takes his own life, but this one in question kills himself for the sake of his religion and nation. A suicidal is a person who despaired of himself and of Allah, but this *Mujahid* is full of hope in Allah's mercy and beneficence.

Israeli society is a military society. [Hence the permission to strike at it.] Its men and women are soldiers in its army and can be summoned up for service at any moment. If a child or an old person is killed in these operations, this is not intentional but accidental. The necessities of warfare permit forbidden actions …

All we ask is that these martyrdom operations be carried out after careful consideration. It is best if they are undertaken through the collective intellectual effort (*ijtihad*) of reliable Muslims. If they decide that there is benefit in going ahead, they should do so and place their trust in Allah.[40]

WHAT CAN BE DONE?

Terror is the weapon of the weak. This, in itself, should have been cause for celebration, because usually the weak are supposed to succumb before the strong. However, played skilfully, the weapon of the weak is often more potent than that of the strong, for even when the latter wins in the struggles, it often loses (politically) and goes back to square one. Terror is not merely the use of violence against innocent people but also includes incitement and hostility, which when repeated consistently over long periods of time, create the necessary ambience to delegitimize the enemy as an abstract entity and to then act violently and indiscriminately against it.

Islamic terrorism, especially that perpetrated by the Islamikaze, adds a new complicating dimension. Because, as the *Wall Street Journal* put it:

In contrast to the close-knit, disciplined groups of the 1980s,[41] those posing the new threat are loose groupings of people of similar backgrounds and beliefs who see terror as a way to strike against their enemies … These groupings may engage in several assaults or may be assembled to carry out just one bombing … They may benefit from some links to a government, such as Iran, but operate largely on their own.

Some are well-trained but more often they are hardly trained at all … There is a common thread … attributed to the rise of Muslim fundamentalists who are using violence because of a variety of grievances and goals …

The rise of this informal web of terrorists is disturbing to law enforcement officials, partly because its activities are harder to detect and deter … Even if detected, the fundamentalist terrorists won't be easy to thwart because they are often organized in small local groups around the charismatic cleric … Even if one is jailed, there are others like him to inspire terror. These new terrorists can more than make up for their lack of experience by their zeal and willingness to take extreme risks … There is no question that the Trade Center bombers took enormous risks … To make a trigger for the bomb … they concocted … a substance so volatile that even bumping a flask could have blown them to bits. Professional terrorists [of another kind] prefer more stable materials. When they do carry out bombings and shootings the extremists may act out of a variety of specific motives. In many cases, there is broad resentment against Israel, and that nation's major backer – the US. In Egypt and Algeria, the Muslim extremists oppose their governments whose policies are anathema to them …

Terrorists' attacks around the world largely by Muslim extremists may grow … the fundamentalist extremists may gain adherents partly because of the fading appeal of the older terrorists groups … the new cycle of violence may be spurred by recent events, such as Israel's move to expel the 400 Palestinians and the plight of Muslims in Bosnia.[42]

This kind of attitude by a major Western newspaper does identify some of the motives of the Islamikaze activities, but it almost accepts them as a *force majeure* against which little can be done, except in a defensive manner: to foil the plots before they occur, by intelligence work.[43] This approach, which has been echoed by various European and successive Israeli governments, preferred to tackle the issue defensively, and in essence told the public (the prospective victims), 'There is nothing that can be done', 'Expect some more'. For this purpose, the appellation of 'suicide-bombings' was found appropriate. Indeed, by dubbing the Islamikaze a 'suicide', their stature was diminished to the level of the deranged few who are neither controllable nor predictable. Conversely, if they are defined as a lethal part of an organization which is indoctrinated, financed, organized, supported, trained by outside powers, countries, institutions or organizations, governments would also have to show cause why they do not act, and decisively so, against all those activities. The West did not move in a decisive and concerted fashion against the bases of Islamikaze and their protectors, for commercial, financial or diplomatic reasons, and Israel followed suit in order not to wreck the 'peace process', at least in the case of Hamas, Islamic Jihad and Hizbullah, or for fear of confronting the reluctant and reticent West.

In order for a battle against this kind of terrorism to be serious and effective, it has to acquire all the requisites of the world battle against drugs, namely, to be waged continuously, relentlessly, by all Western countries – even when they are not directly or immediately threatened by it.[44] This battle must be directed on four simultaneous fronts.

Deterrence

Deterrence, backed by a resolve to move in forcibly when deterrence fails. Thus fundamentalists have to know that for every act of terrorism, they, their bases, their countries of shelter, the organizations and countries supporting them, and their providers and benefactors, will pay a price many-fold higher than the damage they have caused. For we are facing ideologically-motivated groups who can only be curtailed by the prospective price they or their countries must be made to pay for their deeds. If these groups realized that their acts would generate utter destruction for themselves and their protectors, and might even backfire on them among the population among whom they live, they might reconsider. For besides the jihad imperative, there is also the pragmatic device of *hudna* (armistice), which applies when the enemy is stronger or when the damage inflicted upon you as retribution might cause your own demise. Better then to avoid another rout if you cannot win, or split even with the enemy, rather than bring upon Islam another humiliation.[45]

Deterrence means to project an image of resolve and unending determination on the part of the West, and to announce steps likely to force the Islamikaze and their operators to hide, to run for their lives, and to be busy in self-defense. For example: active pursuance, arrest, trial and jail of these people; self-restraint in aggrandizing the suffering they cause by their acts in order not to encourage them to commit any more; the announcement of harsh measures against all those who would be caught, before, during and after the act, including capital punishment and, in case of death, denial of a proper Muslim funeral in order to block their way to Paradise, etc.

Prevention

Prevention through intelligence (that is, defensive measures by the would-be victims) is the most widely pursued course by the West. Many more acts of terrorism are foiled than carried out. As an American expert was quoted as saying, 'those plots will be nipped in the bud, and we won't even hear of most of them'.[46] The point is that we need to be much more inquisitive, firm and demanding when it comes to suspects. It would always be immoral and illegal to encroach upon somebody's privacy, to restrict their civil rights or to expose them to unnecessary hassle; yet, one should also remember that we do allow, even encourage, the killing of others when it comes to what we perceive of as self-defense, and we do not hesitate to detain for questioning or to lay bare personal belongings on check-in counters in airports when we deem that necessary.

Examples of prevention: any assembly of terrorist organization of the above sort should be disbanded;[47] 'charitable' organizations which raise money for the Islamikaze should be closed, and their operators arrested and brought to justice. Prize money could be offered to turncoats who denounce their fellow terrorists; countries which shelter or support terrorists should be boycotted, etc. There should also be restrictions on freedom of movement; seizures of weapons and black money; the banning of the sale and the owning of inflammatory and explosive materials; support for groups and regimes who fight these terrorists; and extermination of opium fields in Lebanon, Afghanistan, Pakistan and elsewhere, which sustain some terrorist organizations. All these actions, besides the classic measures of prevention (searches, alarms, fences, guarding and watching, public alertness), can reduce the level of terrorism.

Punishment as a Deterrent

Deterrence that is not backed by effective and harsh punishment cannot succeed, because it gradually erodes at the edges till it fades. Punishment should be swift, massive and surgical, not as a 'revenge' for fallen victims but as a measure of retribution which posts a heavy price to be levied on terrorist acts, and as a deterrent to other terrorists when they know what awaits them. For example, capital punishment for those who have escaped the act of terror; arrest of leaders, instigators and operators of the Islamikaze, even if that signifies the breach of the sovereignty of the countries which knowingly give them shelter, even massive military action against bases where these terrorists train or set out for their operations; when arrested, tried and jailed, harsh conditions should be imposed on them, the rationale being that non-humane treatment is due to the inhuman blowing up of innocent people, etc. Media which support the terrorists, and countries and organizations which extol them, should be punished by restricting or banning all relations with them.

Information and Psychological Warfare

Part of the warfare must be psychological. Those who need to defend themselves against terrorism face a terrible dilemma: on the one hand, how to deprive the terrorists from the world arena of the media, which they often manipulate to diffuse their threats, plans, messages and even terms for a blackmail negotiation; but, on the other hand, how to alert the public to the jeopardy that the terrorists pose to civilized society. For, if the Islamikaze and their designs are publicized, the public might become more understanding, and even co-operate with the authorities in their bitter, at times cruel, battle with the terrorists; and this will, in turn, help galvanize public resolve, including the silent acceptance of casualties as the price of never yielding to terrorist demands.

Information should expose the terrorists' ugly face that is often masked behind slogans and innocent-looking organizations. Their vocabulary is often borrowed from the societies against which they struggle (words like democracy, liberty, civil rights), and they use that rhetoric to make themselves look humane and well-meaning; or they put up front names of charitable organizations which attract the public's pity and empathy. Here, too, self-restraint by the media can avoid a situation where the terrorist exploits generate heroic myths and correspondingly weaken public determination to fight back.

This battle also requires a consistent and sustained diffusion of broadcasts, movies and reports about the terrorists, their ideology, their commitments and the evil inherent in their *modus operandi*. Stories of arrested or recanting terrorists of this sort have to be brought to public attention on a regular basis as part of their education to withstand forthcoming trials. Muslim leaders and clerics who are prepared to condemn terrorists should be tapped and their voices amplified in the media. And, finally, strong, unbending and decisive action on the part of all governments is necessary to lead this battle to the finish until terror is eradicated.

NOTES

1. Kamikaze, literally Winds of Gods, was applied to a strong prevailing wind off the Japanese coast. Later, kamikaze referred to the storms that twice destroyed much of the invading Mongol armadas off the northwestern coast of Kyushu and forced them to withdraw in 1274 and then in 1281. To the Japanese of the time, the storms represented divine intervention by the gods. The myth of the Kamikaze was picked up in the Second World War to designate the units of human bombers trained by the Japanese army to throw into disarray the American armadas in the Pacific, see *Kodansha Encyclopaedia of Japan* (Tokyo/New York, 1983) p.126.
2. I am indebted for these clarifications to my colleague, Ben-Ami Shillony, a foremost expert on wartime Japan.
3. See *Al-Watan al-'Arabi*, cited by *Haaretz*, 28 June 1996, p.6b.
4. Ibid.
5. *Ulama* are Doctors of the Holy Law of Islam.
6. See R. Israeli, 'Muslim Fundamentalists as Social Revolutionaries', *Terrorism and Political Violence*, 6, 4 (Winter 1994) pp.462–75.
7. According to current estimates, the Pashtun (or Pathan) make up just over 50 per cent of the total population, and they occupy the southern part of the country as well as the adjacent border area with Pakistan where several million of them live. In the North, it is Tajik country with about 20–30 per cent of the population, and the rest are minorities such as the Shi'ite Hazara, Uzbeks, Turkemans and others.
8. See, for example, A. Gani, 'Afghanistan. Islam and Counter-Revolutionary Movements', in J. Esposito (ed.), *Islam in Asia: Religion, Politics and Society* (New York: Oxford 1987); J. Meirriam (ed.), *Afghan Resistance: the Politics of Survival* (Boulder, CO: Westview, 1984); E. Naby, 'The Changing Role of Islam as a Unifying Force in Afghanistan', in A. Babuaziz and M. Weiner (eds), *State, Religion and Ethnic Politics* (Syracuse, NY: Syracuse University Press, 1987); O. Roy, *Islam and Resistance in Afghanistan* (Cambridge: Cambridge University Press, 1987).
9. For the following discussion I am indebted to my colleague and collaborator, Dr Daphne Burdman, a Jerusalem psychiatrist, who has been pursuing research on Islamic terrorism.
10. It would be instructive to cite the case of Sufiyan Jabaree, who blew himself up with a six-kilogram explosive suitcase. He was 26 years old, an unemployed laborer. The Nablus man who had sent him on his mission, and had himself been captured by the Israelis, told his capturers: 'Hamas does not waste senior members with proven military successes on suicide missions. Our suicide bombers are merely human fuses replacing a chemical or electric device.' See Martin Gilbert, *Jerusalem in the Twentieth Century* (London: Chatto and Windus, 1996) p.355.
11. See note 8.
12. Ibid.
13. See the literature on Chinese Secret Societies, for example, Jean Chesneaux *et al.*, *Movements Populaires et Societes Secretes en Chine aux XIXe siecles* (Paris: Maspero, 1970).
14. *Ta'zya* is the Ashura Day massacre of Hussein, the son of the Caliph Ali, who was assassinated with all his retinue by Yazid, the son of Mulawiyya, the founding father of the Umayyad Dynasty in Damascus. That event, which occurred in AD 680 in the vicinity of Karbala, a city in southern Iraq, had triggered the transformation at the

end of the seventh century of Shi'ite Islam from a dissident political group into a religious movement. It is important to note that the whole idea of martyrdom, via individuals' act of 'suicide', has been ever since a hallmark of the Shi'ites, and it has been only lately that it was adopted by radical Muslims of the Sunnite denomination.

15. Israel TV, Channel 1 (Network in Hebrew) 18:00 GMT, 9 December 1994.
16. *Ma'raKatuna ma'a al-Yahud*, 7th edn (Beirut 1986).
17. Ibid., especially pp.20–38.
18. See Article 20 of the Hamas Charter. The translations of this and subsequent passages are taken from R. Israeli, 'The Charter of Allah: The Platform of the Islamic Resistance Movement', in Y. Alexander (ed.), *The 1988–89 Annual of Terrorism* (Amsterdam: Martinus Nijhoff ,1990) pp.99–134.
19. Article 22 of the Hamas Charter. See also Ahmad Rif'at, *Al-Nabi al Musallah* (London 1991) pp.120–48 and R. Israeli, *Muslim Fundamentalism in Israel* (London: Brassey's, 1993) pp.101–8.
20. In the most authoritative *Hadith* collection of Bukhari and Muslim. Cited in Article 7 of the Hamas Charter.
21. See, for example, the onslaught against Egyptian authorities by Shukri Mustafa, the head of a local Muslim group, in Ahmad Rif'at (note 18) especially pp.107–8.
22. See Article 15 of the Hamas Charter (note 17).
23. Ibid.
24. Leaflet No.70, circulated in February 1991.
25. Published and distributed in the territories under Israeli rule in the course of 1982.
26. Ibid.
27. See Bo'az Gannor, 'The Islamic Jihad: The Imperative of Holy War', *Survey of Arab Affairs* (15 February 1993), pp.1–2.
28. See for example, Surat *al-Nisa*, verse 74; Surat *al-Imran*, v. 169; Surat *at-Saf* v. 4; Surat *Muhammad* v. 4.
29. Article 8 of the Hamas Charter (note 18).
30. Article 7 of the Hamas Charter (note 18).
31. Mustafa Mashhur, *al-Jihad hua al-Sabil* (Jihad is the Path).
32. After the normative Five Pillars (Arkan) of Islam: the Shahada, Prayer, Fast, Alms and the Hajj.
33. In Islamic folk representations of Paradise, the martyr may freely mingle with the Virgins of Paradise (*huriya*), some say as many as 70 of them each, and after each act of sexual intercourse, the girls miraculously regain their virginity in order to give the martyr a continuous virginal pleasure. So it goes for alcohol, the other major taboo in Islamic society. In Paradise *shari'a* law does not apply, therefore drinks of all sorts are also available.
34. Palestinian refugee camps in Lebanon which had suffered during the civil war in Lebanon in 1975–86 and the Israeli incursion into Lebanon in 1982, and thereafter under Israeli attacks and Palestinian infighting.
35. I am indebted for this text to my colleague, Meir Bar-Asher. However, I am responsible for the English translation.
36. Like the preceding song, this is also a popular audio cassette distributed by Hamas sympathizers in the West Bank and Gaza. See preceding note.
37. Shqaqi was murdered in Malta in 1995, and the Jihad Group of which he was head accused Israel of that murder. He was a Palestinian who graduated from Bir Zeit College in the West Bank, in science and mathematics, like many other Muslim fundamentalist leaders. In 1968 he joined the Islamic movement, and in 1974 he enrolled as a medical student in Cairo, where he was arrested on account of his activity. In 1981 he returned to the West Bank and worked as a doctor, before he was detained and deported by Israel in 1988. Since then, he founded and headed the Islamic Jihad from Damascus until his assassination.
38. Excerpts from a long interview that Shqaqi gave to *al-Sharq al-Awsat* (the Middle East in Arabic), London, 17 March 1995, p.10.

39. See FBIS-NES-96-132, 9 July 1996, p.7. Leaders of the Hamas group also circulated in the West Bank and Gaza similar joint *fatwas* in this regard.
40. Ibid.
41. The Red Brigade, Action Directe, Bader-Meinhof and the like.
42. *Wall Street Journal*, 18 March 1993, pp.1, 8.
43. Ibid., p.8.
44. We should recall that as long as only Israeli airplanes were hijacked, and Israeli civilian objectives were attacked, the world turned its back and counseled 'to resolve politically the root of the matter'. Only when hijacking became universal, were world-wide precautions taken; when the World Trade Center blew up, the Americans moved; when French Metros began to explode, the French discovered terrorism; and so did the British, Egyptians, etc.
45. Incidentally, some Muslims (Palestinians, Egyptians and Saudi religious leaders), who accepted peace with Israel, have couched it in those terms of armistice, according to the precedent set by the Prophet at Hudaubiyya.
46. *Wall Street Journal*, p.8.
47. In the name of freedom of speech, Hamas, Hizbullah and other groups meet freely in the West Bank, Lebanon, London and the USA and these organizations exploit this state of affairs to plan, recruit and mount acts of terrorism in these countries.

7. Masquerade of Terrorism*

INTRODUCTION

Atrocious acts of terror have occurred during the last decades of the twentieth century, from hijackings of airplanes, boats and other means of ground transportation, kidnappings of civilians for ransom or political blackmail, the blowing up of buildings, malls, restaurants, airports, airplanes in mid-air, trains and buses, to attacks by gun-fire on individuals and groups. Atrocities of this sort were practiced in, around and about the Middle East since the late 1960s, but they soon spread to other areas of the world, until no continent or country was immune. During those years, terrorist groups, which smacked of Marxist-prone 'revolution' of some kind or other, mushroomed in all parts of the globe, from the Red Army in Japan, the Symbionese Liberation Army in the USA, the Red Brigades, the Action Directe, the ETA, the IRA and the Bader-Meinhoff in Europe, to the Shining Path in Peru and the various Palestinian rival groups of the PLO, the PFLP, the DFLP, the Abu Nidal group and their clones and splinter sub-groups.

Notwithstanding their different motivations, goals, scope of action, diffusion, means and targets of action, all those groups sought to sow fear amidst their enemy and to humiliate and intimidate him into surrendering to their demands. They took to long-haul military struggles in order to weaken the enemy by guerrilla warfare and constant bleeding, and attempted to capture the attention of the world media in order to air their grievances and attain their redress, or to obtain simply by terrorism what they could not achieve in the arena of the battlefield. But, although all these groups and organizations often collaborated and aided each other (like the Bader-Meinhoff involvement in the hijacking of the Air France plane to Entebbe in 1976, or the Japanese part in the

---

*Originally published as *The Terrorist Masquerade*, ACPR Policy Paper No. 132 (Sha'arei Tikva: Ariel Centre, 2001).

rampage at the Ben-Gurion Airport in 1972), they were never considered branches and arms of the same international networks. Moreover, while the acts of terrorism were often daring and required sophistication in planning and execution, they had always been the business of small groups, calculated to extract a demand or to inflict pain and damage on the enemy, while the perpetrators were planning and hoping to get away.

In most of the cases cited above, it seems that their ideologies have either worn out along the years, or the members of the terrorist cells have mellowed with age and change of status, or have shifted tactics and adopted peaceful ways to achieve their goals, or have been driven into oblivion due to effective eradication campaigns launched by the states concerned. Notable exceptions are those cases – like in Kashmir, Xinjiang, the Philippines and the Middle East – where persistent, unresolved ethno-national problems have complicated the issues at hand and contributed to their prolongation. At the same time, however, a new type of terrorism has emerged in the past two decades, triggered and nurtured by a certain interpretation of the creed of Islam, usually dubbed 'fundamentalist', which has lent new twists to the entire idea of terrorism. For now, it was no longer the followers of an ideological splinter group who purported to produce 'revolution' by terrorist means, but the adepts of one of the largest and most successful universal religions, which is the established faith in some 56 countries (namely about one-third of the total) across the world, spanning mainly the continents of Asia and Africa, but also counting among its 1.2 billion membership (that is, one-fifth of the world population) large minorities in the rest of the globe.

The massive return to Islam during the past two or three decades, whose roots and modalities have been discussed elsewhere,[1] has by necessity colored both the domestic struggle for legitimacy of governments within Muslim countries, and the lingering ethno-national strife between those countries and the rest of the world. Thus, on the one hand, one observes Muslim rule taking root in countries such as Saudi Arabia, Iran, the Sudan and Afghanistan, or struggling for the upper hand, *inter alia* via terrorism, in other places such as Algeria, the PA, Lebanon or Egypt; and, on the other hand, one cannot help notice that some of the international conflicts in which Muslim groups or countries are involved, such as the Middle East, Kashmir, the Philippines or Xinjiang, have also been tinged by Islamic ideology. The implications are vast: if thus far, conflicts were settled by negotiation and compromise, namely by quantitative means, once they are pushed to the religious domain – that is, as they become qualitative and not given to discussion and compromise – they also grow that much more difficult to resolve.

The Muslim groups and countries that have embraced this way – those we customarily call 'fundamentalists' – prefer the language of 'victory' over 'compromise', 'Holy War' (jihad) over negotiation, rejection over acceptance, exclusion over tolerance, the absolute Truth of Allah over human reasoning, and zeal over accommodation. In this state of affairs, terrorism, in the name of Allah, in His Path and for His sake, becomes not only permissible due to the unmatchable forces of the Western Satan and his underlings, but indeed inevitable. Only the vocabulary changes in this setting: jihad is never terrorism, but lawful battle, and the enemy's counter-attack is never legitimate self-defense or counter-measure, but always 'aggression', 'state terrorism', violation of the Divine Will, rebellion against the Divine Order. In this setting, when conventional terrorism is no longer efficient enough to deal the enemy painful blows, and necessity arises to afford unhindered access to the terrorist to strike his lethal blow at the enemy, then 'suicide-bombers' move into the picture, not to commit suicide, but to annihilate the enemy in earnest.

The misnomer of 'suicide-bombers' has been discussed elsewhere[2] and it is pertinent to our analysis of Islamic terrorism. Here, suffice it to mention that this mode of terrorism is not unique to Islam; the Japanese Kamikaze at the end of the Pacific War (1944–45) had acted likewise. We have also seen Indira Gandhi and then her son Rajiv die at the hands of such terrorists; and there have been a number of other isolated cases where the perpetrator was courageous/desperate/motivated enough to lose his life in the process of eliminating his valuable target. But it is in Shi'ite Islam, since the precedent of the 'Assassins' in the Middle Ages, that this form of self-sacrifice has taken root. It is no coincidence that it was among the Shi'ites of Lebanon that this lethal tradition surfaced once again in the 1980s, in the context of the Lebanese War; first against the American marines who landed in that quagmire to guard the peace, and then against the Israelis. Few in the West suspected that a generalization of this method would soon drag into the fray the Sunnite Hamas and Islamic Jihad who have also embarked on this road, with Western civilization in general as its prime target.

This is what dramatically changed the world scene on 11 September 2001, when it suddenly dawned on people that this ill-understood action by 'suicide-bombing' was not reserved for the Jews and Israelis only, nor limited to the Middle East and the Arab–Israeli dispute – but it was a well thought-out, patiently contrived and cunningly devised all-out war against the West, the Great Satan, for its 'corrupting' effect on the youth of the world; notably against those Muslims who were led astray by the glamor of the American material culture, and who tended to drift into the Western orbit of misdeed and mischief. Furthermore, the tragedy of the World Trade Center attested to the undreamt-of new reality where the 'suicide-bombers' are not individuals who act foolishly on the spur of the moment, but a coterie of several determined individuals who acted in unison to carry out a simultaneous series of hijackings for which they had been groomed for years, and who had even closely, precisely and cautiously programmed their harrowingly cold-blooded act of terror to coincide, in time, scope, space and horror, with the simultaneous and equally horrendous acts perpetrated by their like-minded fellow 'suicide-bombers'.

This drama has shown that not only did the perpetrators of these murderous acts not need the pretext of the Intifada (which began to unfold a long time after the preparations for the Twin Towers were under way), or the Palestinians (who currently plan and carry out their own 'suicide-bombings', without waiting for Osama Bin-Laden), but that the myth that used to link 'suicide-bombings' with economic under-development was without foundation. Neither Bin-Laden nor his operators, who could afford to study engineering and piloting in Europe and the USA, were exactly the impoverished types who, out of despair, depression or personal accounts to settle, would embark on this most horrible (and complicated) of atrocities. Explanations have to be sought, therefore, elsewhere; for example, in the powerful grip of Islamic ideology in general and its fundamentalist teachings in particular.

It is true that it is not Islam as such that has declared war on the USA and the West. For one thing, there is no single papal-like authority that can make such a declaration in the name of all Muslims. It is also true that one can cite verses of peace or war from any holy book, and manipulate Holy Scriptures, religious tenets, vocabulary and symbols to fill in tailor-made arguments. But one must also face several puzzling quandaries and attempt to resolve them:

1. Is it pure coincidence that all the hijackers and perpetrators of these horrors are Arabs/Muslims? And are the papers found on some of them, pointing to Muslim fundamentalist training and attachment, relevant?
2. If this horror has nothing to do with normative Islam, as we often hear it said, do we find in any other contemporary faith or system of belief any individuals or organizations who have launched or made common cause with a scheme of this scope and of this horrendous cruelty and inhumanity?
3. Why is it that Islam has given rise to so many groups of 'suicide-bombers', and to so many 'spiritual' leaders who openly condone this practice and lend legitimacy to it: Bin-Laden in Afghanistan, Sheikh Yassin in Gaza, Sheikhs Fadlallah and Nasrallah in Lebanon, etc.? Why is it that those adulated person-alities condemn acts of terror in general, but not those of their own doing or inspiration?
4. Why is it that most armed conflicts in the world today, and most acts of terrorism throughout the globe, are caused by, or connected to, Islam of one type or another, such as the Abu Sayyaf group in the Philippines, which kidnaps foreigners to collect ransom; to recurring arsons of churches in Indonesia, Nigeria, the Sudan and Egypt; to the ongoing genocide against the Blacks in southern Sudan; to the war in Kashmir; to the Hamas, Islamic Jihad and Hizbullah connection of the Arab–Israeli dispute; to the civil war in Afghanistan and Central Asia; to the heinous slaughters of civilians in Algeria and Egypt; and to the new wave of terrorism in America and Western Europe etc.? What is in fundamentalist Islam that is so bellicose and uncompromising as to sanction conflict, terrorism and 'suicide-bombing'?

These are some of the questions we will be tackling in the following pages, not only through examining their historical sources and their modern manifestations, but also by referring to some of the texts that have become hallowed in the modern Islamic world and are being consulted and cited as 'justifications' for these horrors. We have repeatedly heard the argument that these are 'un-Islamic' deeds performed by 'un-Islamic' zealots; and yet they all say and write, and are indoctrinated to believe, that they act in the name of Islam, for the sake of Allah. Are we then talking about a different Islam? If so, then how do we explain the vast popularity of the deeds and their perpetrators among the Muslim populace, after due lip service is paid, of course, to the 'deep trauma' that many Muslims say they feel in the aftermath of the Twin Towers slaughter? If the trauma were genuine, why is it that in previous smaller-scale murders of this sort, no outright condemnation was forthcoming from Muslim leaders?

In the wake of the Twin Towers horror, an almost universal cry of condemnation of this horrendous act was heard across the globe. One would have noticed, however, that except for the USA and certain of its closest allies, almost no one dared to condemn the perpetrators, under the pretext that 'clear evidence' was needed before one hurried to indict. When this argument is advanced by law-abiding regimes, one could still perhaps understand; but when it is particularly emphasized by the world of Islam, which does not count among its 55-nation membership even one regime ruled by law, this sounds like a rather flimsy pretext to avoid the need to act against the culprits. This is the reason that while almost all Muslim countries rushed to take cover by swearing allegiance to America, for fear of its wrath, a few of them have been accommodating in terms of joining the battle itself, or at least making their facilities available to the US fighting units, without restriction.

There is an obvious paradox: had the Muslim countries been so certain, as they claim, that no Muslim element was involved in the anti-American onslaught, then why are they reluctant to join the battle against the perpetrators? In fact, they know exactly where the terrorists had come from, that all those involved were Muslims, their doctrine Muslim, their financing from Muslim sources, their constituencies Muslim and their goal Muslim. These are the same Muslim governments which have fought the terrorism that threatened them (Mubarak against the Gama'at, Assad against the Muslim Brothers, Arafat against the Hamas); but when the same terrorism has been directed against Israel, the USA or the West, they have not acted against it, and have often even harbored it (for example, Egypt, the hijackers of the Achille Lauro; Syria, the Islamic Jihad and the Hizbullah; Iran, all the Islamic terrorist organizations; and the PA, the Hamas and Islamic Jihad, who day in, day out terrorize Israeli cities). Saudi Arabia and Libya subsidize the Hamas and other terrorist groups, and the Yemen refused to turn in the saboteurs of the American Navy ship, the *Cole*, in Aden.

One needs then to call a spade a spade, to identify terrorism not according to its victim but according to its perpetrator and mode of action. Whenever an organization trains, indoctrinates and dispatches groups or individuals to engage in wanton killing of civilians, for any purpose, it is a terrorist organization pure and simple, that has to be pursued and eliminated. No national or religious grievance, justified as it may be, can explain away or provide 'understanding' for acts of terror, and those who tolerate any kind of terrorism are bound to see it turned against themselves. There are civilized ways to struggle against 'injustice', 'oppression', 'occupation' and 'exploitation', which involve armed struggle against the armed forces of the enemy, if negotiations should fail; similarly, it is the duty of any country witnessing terrorism in the making, to take all necessary measures to avert it, through legal means if possible, but also through elimination of the culprits if necessary, after all precautions have been taken to minimize collateral damage to innocent civilians.

It will be the contention of the present work that while acts of violence that clearly take on the characteristics of terrorism, have to be identified and eradicated, one also ought to detect and recognize the ideological infrastructure which permits them to take hold in certain societies more than in others. While there are widespread acts of injustice, domination and inequality of opportunity around the globe, which generate terrorist movements (the ETA, the IRA, and the like), they are bound to recede when these grievances are laid to rest. What characterizes the latest wave of Islamic terrorism in America is that no specific demands were attached to it, like the payment of ransom, the adoption of a certain policy, the relinquishment of a certain territory, or the release of hostages. It was not unleashed as a warning or a bargaining position, or as a list of demands, the fulfillment of which would resolve the crisis and avert the horror, but as an irreversible punishment to be meted out, an expression of anger to be vented. This calls for investigation and unraveling, and this is what we shall attempt in the following pages.

SAMPLING MUSLIM REACTIONS TO THE NEW YORK
AND WASHINGTON HORROR

Unlike their governments, which lack legitimacy for the most part and do not reflect their public opinion, much of the populace in most Muslim countries reacted with jubilation to the disaster that befell the West following the attack against the Twin Towers and the

Pentagon on 11 September 2001. This is, of course, not necessarily indicative of the Islamic doctrine as such, or of the interpretation the Muslim masses lend to it in the world today, but it is certainly reflective of the depth of hostility towards the West, its wealth and values. Much of this hostility can be imputed to the way in which the policies, way of life and economic prosperity of the West are perceived by the unfortunate multitudes who live with oppression, misery, disease and illiteracy in those lands; but there is no doubt that a crude popular perception of Islamic doctrine has also played a significant role in this view of the world.

There is no way, of course, to gauge the predominant sentiment among the masses throughout the length and width of the entire Islamic world; but judging from press write-ups, and public demonstrations where pictures of Bin-Laden were displayed, slogans were brandished or shouted, and American (and Israeli) flags and effigies were trampled and then burned by crowds in delirium, and also the attacks against American institutions or businesses, one could make no mistake about the intensity of the feelings. Sometimes it is evident from the manifested support for the Taliban or for Bin-Laden, or from the waving of Islamic slogans, that the angry populace was transmitting a Muslim message of vindication, but at other times the virulent grievances sounded generally anti-Western and anti-American. In either case, it is certain that since Islam has remained the main focus of identity among Muslim societies, the anti-Western vitriol voiced among the masses, will almost always retain Islamic under- or overtones. There is also little doubt, that educated, Westernized and less-bigoted Muslims would feel and express sadness and horror at the sight of the tragedy; but, still, the seemingly prevailing mood among those societies was not one of mourning or identification with the victims and their families.

This should come as no surprise when one bears in mind, on the one hand, the harsh, even fanatic, reaction of Muslims world-wide to what they perceive as the profanation of their holy sites, or any slur to their culture, or the enthusiastic and self-assured way they go about spreading their faith and imposing it on others; but on the other hand, the unbearable ease with which they deny others' religious rights, and even step in to obliterate the religious heritage of other faiths. Similarly, it escapes no one's scrutiny that those who die in their clashes with non-Muslims, are immediately dubbed *shahid* (martyr), their funerals are tumultuous, emotional, vindictive and replete with shouts of revenge, even when the deceased had engaged in a visibly aggressive and unprovoked act of terrorism; while the death and destruction of others is jubilantly celebrated by dance, distribution of sweets and outright delight in the misery and havoc they had wrought on others. It is as if human happiness were a zero-sum game, where someone's glory must come at the expense of others' misfortune, and where any success of the West is regarded as a Muslim failure, and vice versa.

Mosques can be, and are, erected throughout the Christian and Jewish worlds, Muslim clerics are invited to officiate in national ceremonies of Western countries, as a matter of course, but no church can be built anywhere in Saudi Arabia or Afghanistan, Buddhist symbols are torn down by the Kabul government, and existing churches are torched or blown up in Indonesia, Egypt, the Sudan, Kosovo and elsewhere in the Islamic world, where the state religion is invariably Islam and no provision is therefore allowed or possible for other faiths. Moreover, Muslims around the world have grown accustomed to the fact that their rampages against other faiths go unpunished, and this encourages their belief that perse-cuting others is the natural state of affairs. For example, during the first year of the Al-Aqsa Intifada (2000–1) Muslim immigrants in Western democracies were involved in hundreds of cases of vandalism, desecration and assaults against Jewish sites and Jewish individuals and worshippers, the scope of which has been unprece-dented in Europe since *Kristallnacht*. Since not much was done to deter the vandals, it took a full year to calm tempers there, although in the Middle East itself, Jewish sites continued to be desecrated.

In short, there is a world of difference between Western values and the Muslim ones, at least those articulated by the fundamen-talists among them. While for the West terrorism is terrorism, and under no circumstances can there be any justification for loss of life of innocent civilians, Muslim fundamentalists – and one suspects also other Muslims around them – have found ample ideological rationalization for the wanton killing of civilians. Among the Palestinians, for example, although the Hamas supporters count for no more than one-third of the Palestinian constituency, polls among the populace show some 80 per cent support for acts of terror against Israeli civilians. These are precisely the numbers of the people who celebrated the New York and Washington horror in the streets of the West Bank and Gaza, and for that matter in the other Muslim cities and towns across the world. Years prior to this horrendous act of terror, Abdallah Shami, the Head of the Islamic Jihad group in Gaza, when questioned by an Israeli journalist about indiscriminate 'suicide-bombing' of civilians, answered thus:

> We do not possess the military hardware our enemy possesses. We do not have planes, missiles, or even a cannon with which we can fight injustice. The most effective tool to inflict damage and harm with the least possible losses is operations of this nature. This is a legitimate method based on martyrdom. The martyr gets the privilege of entering Paradise and frees himself from pain and misery.[3]

In these terms, not only does the killer have no qualms in killing anyone, by any method, due to his lack of arms, but he also delights in taking the shortcut to Paradise by doing so. And since the wanton murderer is 'privileged' to be dubbed a 'martyr', killing becomes 'legitimate'. This is the world of values of these terrorists, and this is the Islamic rationalization of these values. These notions, which are cultivated by entire networks of ruthless and heartless terrorists, as we have seen and heard in the Twin Towers tragedy, are also backed by the crowds who cannot resist the temptation to exhibit their jubilation in public. Worse, they are incited by politicians, journalists, clerics and intellectuals, who have no compunction in voicing their distorted and inhuman worldview in public, both in writing and orally. The following selection will exemplify this horrific state of mind, which allows this type of assassin to flourish and operate among a sympathetic population.

Maybe the most telling broadside against America, while it was still reeling from shock, merely one day after its unfolding, came from the Hamas movement in the Palestinian territories, those same people who murder civilians in restaurants, blow up school buses, re-enact in public those atrocities and brag about them. Typically for this brand of terrorist, the accusation is directed at the victim itself, which means not only that the act of terror and the mass-murder are justified in their eyes, but that they expected more to follow and that they might participate themselves in future butcheries of this sort. What is particularly sad and unreal about this is that one author, Atallah abu-al-Sabah, boasts the title of PhD – so he is a well-educated man, supposedly versed in humanities and perhaps trained to honor human life and human values as they are cultivated in the West. Here are some excerpts from his 'Letter to America', which he published in the organ of the Hamas in Gaza, *Al-Risala* (The Message, The Mission).

> I am confident that you will be facing for a long time to come the mirror of your history. Thus, you will be able to realize how oppressive, corrupt and sinful you have been, how many entities you have wiped out and how many states you have destroyed. Do you remember what you did in Korea and Vietnam? Do you recall how you turned Hiroshima and Nagasaki to piles of radioactive rubble, which contains death for the two destroyed cities, now and in the future? Not one single human being was left in those two cities that the fire has not deformed, nor a baby who was not torn to pieces, nor a bird that was not drowned in a sea of flames!
>
> Oh America, the sword of oppression, arrogance and crime! Do you remember how you smashed man's humanity? Do you remember how you mistreated the Blacks under your aegis? Can you describe for us the humiliation, disgust and contempt you meted out to those unfortunate people, whose only sin was that they were born to black parents? It was your white son who chained their necks in slavery, after he had hunted them down in Africa's forests and along its coasts. They were born free, but were enslaved in your virgin land …
>
> Did you ever ask yourself about what you did to the original inhabitants of your land, the Apache Indians? You trampled them under your white feet, and then used their name, the Apache, for the helicopter that carries death, destruction and annihilation to owners of rights, who dared to clamor for their right. This is a heinous and destructive conduct, which made us hate the Apache, before we could realize that they were themselves victims, just like us …
>
> Did you ever ask yourself what was the sin of the children of al-Amariyya[4] or Kana,[5] or the reason for the continuous injustice you have been bringing down on Baghdad,[6] Jerusalem and Jenin[7] and on all those who do not see eye to eye with you, or refuse to walk the road of those sycophant and emasculated [Arab] rulers that you treat as 'excellencies' and 'majesties'? America, did you ever ask yourself why do you produce cluster bombs, nuclear and hydrogen bombs, biological weapons for mass killings, and F-16 planes? Even should we accept the contention that you do it for your own

war preparedness, why do you put these weapons in the hands of every murderer, war criminal, and enemy of humanity, such as [Serbian war commander] Karadzic, [Prime Minister] Shamir and [Prime Minister] Sharon?

America, have you ever tasted horror, pain and affliction? These have been our lot for a long time, and they have filled our hearts, torn our guts and burned our skin. This has become daily routine for us, and carried out by your favorites with high proficiency. They indeed destroy our shacks in Jenin, and what has happened to us tonight there, is no different from what has happened to you …

Every so often Dick Cheney and his girlfriend, Condolezza Rice, set out to calumniate us, to castigate us, to incite against us. And we lined up and asked Allah to let you sip from the cup of humiliation, until Heaven responded. Now, America, consider whether you are able to forgo your fanaticism, your arrogance and your vanity … While we have accepted your mediation for the sake of peace … you have opened the gates of the Pentagon for every Jew to acquire a knife in order to slaughter us … You have planted yourself the seed of hatred for you … You did not think that the roots of those plants would grow to poke your eyes, even as they were placed on top of the World Trade Center … Those plants have also grown to hit at the heart of the Pentagon, the most heavily guarded facility on earth … Can't you see that the outgrown roots have reached the very eyes of your strong Secretary of Defense, Donald Rumsfeld, who thought he was immune to revenge for what he did?

America, why did you evacuate the Sears Building, the way we do every night in order to flee your laser-eyed missiles? Are you scared, just like us? Do the giants also experience fear and run for their lives just as the oppressed do? … It turns out that you are weaker than the weak, and miserable like all the refugees whom you forced out of their villages on the Palestine sea-shore, together with their wives, children and torn clothes … America, where is your famous CIA which can detect even ants on a rock? You did not see the grievances of those who have struck you … for your blindness could only see through the eyes of traitors and spies … America, where is your second eye, the Mossad, which you always made us believe could detect anything? …

Can we expect that this time you will reconsider and avoid attacking a drug factory in Khartum, or in Libya? Or will the appetite for revenge again blind your sight and lead you to discharge your wrath again on Al-Amariya or Bet Hanun [in the Gaza Strip]? What good did your Navy or ballistic missiles and nuclear reactors do to you? How have your satellites and AWACS, NATO and world leadership, come to your help? All those were paralyzed when the sword of vengeance got to your neck, in this unprecedented feat in world annals … You surely understand, that unless you repent from your corruption, you are bound to be hit once and again by the same perpetrators …

America, re-examine your decisions to cast hundreds of veto votes [at the Security Council of the UN], with a view of denying humanity its rights. Look at your humiliated face, and check whether it is not due to those votes. This will teach you to stand by justice and the righteous, even if they are weak, and then perhaps the dust of humiliation will be removed from your sad face …[8]

Along much the same lines, the Editorial of the same journal, also written by an educated and enlightened Dr Ghazi Hamad, calls America to task, stressing the rule that the 'punishment matches the crime', and wondering why the USA had not learned any lesson from the killing of her Marines in Lebanon, the destruction of her HQ in the Khobar Towers in Saudi Arabia, the explosion of her two embassies in Africa, the incapacitation of the *Cole* in the Yemen and the attacks against its forces in Japan and the Gulf. Thus, says the Editorial, America was bitterly 'reaping today what she had sown in the hearts of millions'.[9] These first projections of the blame on the victim, which showed no signs of sympathy for the families of the dead, and were probably boosted by the atmosphere of jubilation in the Palestinian street, soon gave way to denials that Arabs or Muslims could have had anything to do with the horrendous destruction. So, on the one hand, the Arabs were not displeased by the disaster that befell America; but, on the other hand, when they began to grasp the gravity of the horror and to fear the wrath of America's response, they ran for cover: they had neither seen nor heard, it was all the fault of others – America itself, Israel and all sorts of evil powers-that-be.

A columnist in the London-based Arabic *al-Sharq al-Awsat* put the blame squarely on President Bush and Secretary Powell. Bush, because he was 'hardly elected' to his post, and he needed the drama to draw behind himself the bi-partisan support of America, and Powell due to his military background which conditions him to conduct war, not diplomacy.[10] The next hypothesis was of course Israel/Zionism/the Jews, they being the 'most likely to benefit' from the slaughter. The Jews/Zionists, who 'control the world media, economy and politics', wished to press NATO and the Americans to 'surrender even more thoroughly to Zionist ideology', and to promote further the 'Zionist slogan of Islamic terrorism'.[11] World Zionism was accused by other Arab and Muslim journalists, who could see the imprint of the American–Zionist–Israeli 'holy alliance' on this affair, although they implied that the 'perpetrators' rushed to accuse 'international terrorism', by which they meant Arab and Islamic terrorism. One columnist advocated a firm stand from the Arabs, to wash their hands clean from any accusation, and to transcend their defensive stand and pass on to the offensive.[12]

Now that Israel was found to be the culprit, the act of terrorism becomes horrible, inhuman and unthinkable, epithets that fit in with 'legendary Zionist cruelty'. Another Arab writer claimed that only the Jews themselves would not be afraid to be caught, because no one 'would dare accuse them and incur the danger of being blamed for bringing upon them a new Holocaust'. Therefore, they are the only people who 'hide their crimes and are sure that no one would ask them to account for their deeds'.[13] The author did not explain, however, why the Jews needed to hide their deeds if they would not be held accountable in any case. Another Jordanian columnist was 'personally certain that no Arabs or Muslims stood behind this act', because it was the Zionists' organizations which were interested in perpetrating the crime in order to preoccupy the world while they destroyed the Aqsa Mosque;[14] while his compatriot imputed the deed to either Christian fundamentalist groups who support Israel or the Israeli Mossad, which reputedly pursues 'evil and dangerous avenues'.[15] The organ of the Muslim Brothers, *Afaq 'Arabiyya*, after exclaiming that 'no one in the East has shed tears for the Americans', castigated America for 'wishing to teach the world who is Allah', and for:

> ... preferring the monkeys [the Jews] over other humans whom they mistreated, for supporting homosexuals and interest [in banking, which is prohibited by Islam], and

forgetting that no one can escape Allah's punishment, and He indeed came from an unexpected direction and struck their hearts with fear.[16]

A Syrian columnist advanced the theory that this was a belated vengeance by the Japanese for Hiroshima and Nagasaki.[17] A Palestinian author, who admitted that there were many potential candidates for this act of terror, who suffered, like the Palestinians, from American and Western policy, nevertheless counseled the Americans to look for the perpetrators far afield from the Middle East, because 'not all those interested to counter American policy have also the means to perpetrate an act of this sort'.[18] Not a word of sympathy or compassion for the victims, just an expression of Arab helplessness in carrying out such a feat due to the scarcity of wherewithal at their disposal. A Lebanese reporter raised the idea that young computer hackers may have taken over the computerized air-control system and 'directed the airplanes to painful targets'.[19] Another reached the conclusion that since the Arabs did not stand to gain anything from the horror, they were not the likely perpetrators, but that others, like the Israelis, the Mafiosi, the Russians or the Chinese who oppose the American anti-missile defense program, or perhaps a fundamentalist group in the USA, must have concocted it.[20]

A pro-Arab British journalist, Patrick Seale, who was considered the court biographer of Hafez al-Assad, also joined the choir of denials in the Arab media. As against his doubt that Arabs or Muslims could have perpetrated this act, he posited the many 'massacres' committed in the past by the USA and Israel. He also embraced the theory that 'ecological terrorists' might have mounted the plot to deter the process of globalization. He elected to put aside the question of the immorality of 'suicide terrorists', and confined himself to inquiring about their efficacy, and evinces some understanding of acts of terrorism which impel desperate and oppressed people to seek vengeance, and to establish a 'balance of terror', which means that, for example, Palestinians threaten to kill Israelis, if the latter kill Palestinians, and that is an act of deterrence. Therefore, says he, there is no doubt that the perpetrators of the Twin Towers atrocity meant to establish a balance of terror with the Americans. He did not elaborate, however, upon whether Bin-Laden was appointed by the Vietnamese or the Japanese dead, or the Palestinians for that matter, to revenge them.[21]

The state-controlled Egyptian press, with some exceptions, condemned the attacks against the USA and also those Arabs and Muslims who had evinced joy at the misfortune that had befallen America, but it also used the occasion to call upon the USA to alter its policy in the Middle East. At the same time, many in the Egyptian media, including those toeing the government line, spoke about 'American and Israeli terrorism' and predicted the 'fall' of the USA from her superpower position. A columnist from mainstream *al-Akhbar*, who had in the past manifested support for Hitler, Ahmed Ragab, could not contain his joy over the disaster. He wrote:

> I know a person, extremely wealthy, scaringly influential, who rules like a tyrant, imposes his will but loses everybody's love. Suddenly, out of the dark, he was painfully struck on his behind. He turned around but only saw ghosts.[22]

The opposition press, which does not toe the line, but would not dare publish, for example, a personal critique of Mubarak, took the liberty to explode overtly in delight, as if human compassion had anything to do with political opposition to any rule:

> Let me state things directly and honestly: I am happy about what has happened to America, and I am elated about this high rate of casualties there. They can accuse me however they wish, but this will neither change nor diminish one iota from the happiness and delight that have taken me over, and no one can cause me to take back my words under any circumstances and for whatever reasons. All those innocent dead are the victims of the 50-year-long American barbarism and terrorism ... Just count the numbers of the victims of American weapons around the world and compare them to the figure of the killed in the US now, and you will discover that the latter is hardly 1 per cent of the former. Therefore, I have the right to be happy, I have the right to be joyful, for the Americans have finally tasted the bitter flavor of death.[23]

The editor of the same paper also insisted on his 'right' to celebrate, because that was the first step 'in the one-thousand-mile journey towards the rout of America by knock-out'.[24] Another columnist, this time a woman, whom one would have expected to show more sensitivity to human suffering, also states in no uncertain terms, her elation:

> I cannot hide my feelings, nor restrain my joy. For the first time in my life I can observe with my own eyes the collapse of American arrogance, tyranny, vanity and evil. For the first time in my life I am asking myself: Has Allah finally listened to the prayers of mothers and the supplications of the victims in Palestine, Iraq and Libya ... Am I expected to be hypocritical, like all the others, condemn the killing of civilians, express my sorrow about the American and other victims, and pray and donate blood for them? Why are we trying to satisfy the Master in the White House of our innocence? Throughout history we have never been caught red-handed with the blood of the innocent: Indians, slaves, Vietnamese, Palestinians, Iraqis. I want no alliance with America; I have had enough with the shame brought upon us in Iraq. I wish neither to pray for the Americans nor donate my blood to them. I do not want to condemn what has happened. It is America that killed them, as it had killed us in Iraq, and as it is continuing to slaughter us in Palestine.[25]

Other columnists called upon the USA to 'withdraw from the world, both as thieves and as policemen', and to choose between 'respecting other nations or die'. There were writers who stated that they were not happy for the death of civilians, but for the fact that 'America's horror had become a mop to trample upon.'[26] The peak of jubilation came, ironically, in the organ of the Egyptian 'Liberal' Party, which rejoiced over the rout that America suffered which demonstrated that she was a 'paper tiger'.[27] Very tellingly, one such 'liberal' author complained about the pressures exerted on him and his likes by the powers-that-be, to contain his joy:

> We were banned from demonstrating the happiness and delight we feel so as not to hurt American feelings, although in this case, expressions of joy are a national and religious obligation. For America is Israel's protector, and when we watch her crumble instantly, and her heroes run away in horror, to prohibit public jubilation is an unbearable burden. But we were deprived of it and forced to show sympathy to our executioners.[28]

Sarcasm too was resorted to by some writers in order to 'expose the hypocrisy of those who are now whining for the American losses'. One of them suggested that he could have hired the services of a professional weeper, but no one would agree 'even if he paid her $100 for each tear'. How could a columnist, he asks, who believes that 'America did get what she deserved for sucking the blood of other nations' escape the lies of the hypocrites who 'volunteer to shed tears, to donate blood and to put their intelligence apparatuses in the service of their cardboard Master'? And more: 'If you are killed by a thug, that is unfortunate; but if you are forced to attend his funeral, that is the peak of humiliation. Sorry, America, we have no tears left to participate in your sorrow.'[29] These unbearably horrific words were surpassed by another writer who described his watching live the horror as moments of:

> ... a beautiful and glamorous hell, the best and dearest of my life. I saw the towers, the walls, those symbols of power which constituted a modern and scary monster, penetrated by a courageous hornet ... The hornet stung that mythological monster, who looked horrific as he was hit, shouted and collapsed like a hell. All media who ply to America, broadcast once and again those pictures, that all the past and future generations will envy us for having been privileged to witness.[30]

These harrowing remarks were not criticized by anyone of stature in the Arab or Islamic worlds, because all those were busy containing similar outbursts of callous rage and furious indecency in their own countries, lest their 'national interest' be harmed by the exposure of those statements to international scrutiny. Many decent Muslims were certainly mortified by what had happened, but not all necessarily because of the human tragedy involved. Any number of them are embarrassed that so much killing has been occasioned in the name of their faith, or that so many violent movements across the Muslim world purport to represent Islam or to urge the believers to jihad against non-Muslims; others fear that the tragedy might backfire on them, elicit international hatred of Islam or lead to a negative blanket judgment being passed on it. And, if this is the situation in the countries most closely associated as 'allies' of America, how much more so in those overtly hostile to it, where words of compassion, or of criticism of the popular mood, are not even allowed – such as Iran, Iraq, the Sudan, Libya and Afghanistan – and among any number of other Muslim and Arab countries and organizations, notably Muslim fundamentalist groups in which hostility to the West is very deeply embedded.

Sheikh Yussef al-Qardawi, one of the senior spiritual leaders of the Muslim Brothers, and an authoritative doctor of the Holy Law in Sunni Islam in general, who was one of the first to sanction 'suicide-bombing', had argued that the martyr who goes to his death for the sake of Islam wages jihad as an active agent who seeks the extermination of the enemy of Islam, and is therefore justified in launching his attacks even though he might kill himself in the process. However, while in previous bombing incidents against Israel he was more permissive of the wanton killing of the enemy in general, the horror of 11 September apparently prompted him to effectuate some fine tuning to this rule: he said that the *shari'a* law was against indiscriminate killing, and that only enemy combatants who carried weapons were free prey for the Muslim jihad fighter, while innocent civilians were to be spared. He even stated that those who commit this sort of atrocity cannot be called Muslims. Nonetheless, this ruling is mitigated by so many caveats as to make it ineffective, or at the very least questionable. His main points were:

1. It is the West which has turned Islam into its enemy since the Crusades, by coveting Muslim lands and resources; while Islam, in his words, did nothing to justify its enemy status. What about the Islamic conquests in the Middle Ages, which threatened Europe and the entire civilized world at the time, or the present-day onslaught on Christians throughout the Muslim world, or the multitude of wars and acts of terror perpetrated in the name of Islam? He did not elaborate on these.

2. If the West attacks Muslim countries they cannot enter into any alliance with it, unless it is proven that they authored or sponsored the act of terrorism. The act of harboring terrorists does not mean that a country can be accused of participating in the murder. Just as one cannot attack Egypt or Algeria simply because Sheikh Abdul-Rahman, or some Algerian, have done something, so is Afghanistan exempt of any attack.

3. This attack against the USA is the fruit of hatred, whose roots have to be investigated, for if Bin-Laden is killed, another thousand like him will emerge. Is this what the world desires? Besides, neither the Taliban nor Bin-Laden could have had any responsibility for this.

4. The *shari'a* law forbids collaboration with non-Muslims against other Muslims. Such collaboration is a sin and an act of aggression. Moreover, *shari'a* law obliges every Muslim country to rush to the help of any other Muslim state under attack, with money and fighters.

5. It is also prohibited by Islamic Law to surrender a Muslim to non-Muslims, for this is opposed to common sense, since Islam does not recognize any geographic borders, race, color or language differences between Muslims. They are all one *Umma* (nation) dwelling in *Dar al-Islam* (Abode of Islam), united in its belief in Islam and in its Islamic fraternity.

6. It makes no sense that Pakistan should assist foreigners to invade its Muslim neighbor, no Muslim scholar would countenance such a prospect, and I do not understand why the Pakistani scholars of the Holy Law can allow this to happen.

7. If Bin-Laden should be proved guilty, I have no objection to having him handed over to Muslim justice in Egypt or Saudi Arabia. But who can prove that he recruited, trained, financed and dispatched the culprits? This would be very difficult, for terrorists exist all over the world and it is not inevitable that Bin-Laden or the *al-Qa'ida* should be involved.

8. There is no doubt that the Zionist entity is the one which stood to gain most from this crime; the USA supports Israel, and Israel is the greatest terrorist in the world.

9. There are two lines of terrorism: the one pursued by people who defend their rights and homeland, which is sanctioned by the Koran, as the Believers are enjoined to 'cast fear'[31] in the enemy's heart; this is the kind of terrorism practiced by the Hamas, the *Fat'h* and other Palestinian movements who defend their land. If this is terrorism, then this is the best kind of terrorism, because it is a jihad for the sake of Allah. The other kind of terrorism, which is illegitimate, is Israel's terror, which kills illicitly and desecrates Muslim holy sites. But even though the USA supports this Israeli terrorism, we should not attack civilians in the USA. We could, instead, boycott America and compel it to retreat as we did in Durban.

In other words, terrorism in the eyes of the venerated sheikh, who is looked up to by vast sections of Sunni Islam, is not a mode of operation that is absolutely forbidden under any circumstances, but it all depends who does the killing and against whom. When

Muslims fight for their 'rights', which they alone are authorized to determine, then a 'human bomb' is permissible even among innocent civilians; if the enemy of Islam defends itself against Muslim onslaught, it is he who is the terrorist, even when he uses more discriminatory modes of fighting than the Muslims would adopt. In either case, the definition of who is the terrorist, what is the subject matter that can be deemed as justifying Muslim 'suicide-bombing', what is the criterion for morality, right, justice, crime, etc., are all determined at the discretion of Muslim law, and not as matters of universal human rights or justice or by internationally agreed definitions and conventions.

What is appalling is that these points of view are not only shared by journalists who shape public opinion or are shaped by it, and Muslim fundamentalists in the Arab and Islamic worlds whose uncompromising anti-Western stance we have explored, but also by people who have intellectual pretences, such as writers and politicians, who set the tone of discourse in their societies. As has been already pointed out above, many Arab and Muslim leaders who nominally joined the American coalition, or have been knocking at its door, due to the promises it may hold, have set themselves on a collision course with their peoples and in the long run may have undermined their own regimes. But the others, who either openly loath America and its coalition, or see no prospects of joining it, do not mince their words when they analyze the events of 11 September. So much so, that an Egyptian movie critic, Samir Farid, wrote that he was 'ashamed of the commentaries I read in the Egyptian press ... in towns and villages of Egypt processions marched exclaiming the abominable slogan "We shall redeem you with our soul and blood, O bin Laden!"'[32]

Thus, the Chair of the Arab Writers' Association, found no other place than the *Literary Weekly* (Damascus), to give vent to his disturbing trend of thought which was considered worthy to publish in harrowing detail in a supposedly humanistic artistic journal:

> I ache for the death of innocent people, but the day the power symbols of America collapsed on 11 September reminded me of the daily funerals of so many innocent people in occupied Palestine ... of the day of the American–British aggression against Tripoli (Libya), when they tried to destroy the house of its leader while he was asleep, but they only succeeded in burying his daughter under the ruins; of the oppression of

peoples in Korea and Vietnam ... So, my soul was filled with disgust and bitterness towards a country which failed to register anything but a history of oppression and support to the racism of Nazi Zionism and apartheid in South Africa, a country which has itself founded its 'civilization' [quotation marks in the original] on the robbery of other nations and the imposition of tyranny, in the name of fighting tyranny ...

The American Administration, which is ruled by Zionist decisions and supports the occupation and racist deeds of the 'Israelis' [quotation marks in the original], have numbed my feelings. The American Administration has contaminated my soul, and when I saw the multitudes running away in terror, in the streets of New York and Washington, I was telling myself: 'Let them taste from the cup they have forced upon all nations and upon us in particular ...'

When the Twin Towers collapsed ... I felt as if I were extricated from the bottom of a tomb, as if I were hovering over the arrogant mythological symbol of American imperialism, which has covered up the crimes it had committed ... My lungs filled with pure air, and I breathed deeper than ever before ... even when I thought about the innocent who were buried under the rubble ... I was sorry that my humanity had been soiled by Zionist America and world Zionism ... But minutes later I learned new facts from the media: that Arabs and Muslims are accused as the culprits, and threats were voiced calling for revenge against them ...

This has returned me to the spiritual tomb where I was submerged by aggression, arrogance and distortion of facts. But my inner stamina which saved me from drowning, enabled me to breathe again over the surface: we shall live, be victorious and bring justice to the world because we are ready to sacrifice ourselves for our existence, our rights, justice and the world's humanity ... The American people has to wake up to the image that his policy has created of him, that is a dirty policy that does not bring respect to its initiator ... That moment of 11 September has to produce a re-examination of policy, strategy and ideas ... Maybe even the American brain will understand that military and economic power deprives him of true humanity ...

Americans have to understand that their commitment to support racist Zionism and its Nazi deeds ... causes the entire

Arab nation to rejoice when America suffers death and destruction ... The symbolism of destroying one of the five wings of the Pentagon and of killing 1,000 people there, is far more important than the fact that it continues to exist and to threaten other nations and especially Afghanistan and Bin-Laden. This means that it is enough that one person has decided to die for his honor, rights, nation, faith and civilization, in order to attain his goal even against a superpower and in the heart of its territory ... Consequently, if nations wake up and evince this kind of will power, and set out to resist tyranny, dictators, racists, arrogance and imperialists who drink their blood ... it is easy to imagine what will happen then ...

American policy causes hatred in support of racist occupiers, whose entire history is shameful, bloody, destructive, scandalous and full of plots against others. The hands of their leaders are soaked in the blood that was spilled by their racism, which had collaborated with the Nazis. The [Jews] distort history, religious faith and facts. They despise Gentiles and Prophets, crucify them, and treat other humans like animals which were born in human shape in order to serve the Jews ...

Something has collapsed in America, and this is the beginning of America's collapse as the sole superpower ... This collapse will be followed by the building of a new base for the victory of the oppressed and miserable people ... for all tyranny will come to an end, force will be routed by force, and there will be no limit to human will when it determines to take on the arrogance of force ...

Sure as I am that many of the victims do not deserve compassion, due to their belonging to the bloodsuckers of other people, one should not rejoice at the loss of human life. My humanity, that American and Zionist policy have attempted to numb, gains the upper hand in the final analysis over hatred and hostility.[33]

HYPOCRISY MASQUERADING AS A POLICY

In the face of these explosions of inhumanity, which were rather popular among the Arabs and Muslims, contrary to the reserve of their rulers who huddled to be embraced by the American coalition, the isolation and illegitimacy of the rulers grows ever more acute, insofar as they do not represent their public opinion on the one hand, and are unable to contain it in the long run on the other, to the point of being on the brink of being swept away when it erupts in earnest. One of the ways in which they try to walk the tightrope between popular resentment and their inability to respond to the American challenge to join the world war against terrorism (and their need to do the latter), is their attempt to draw differences between various kinds of terrorism. Theirs is considered, of course, 'national liberation', while moves of self-defense by the USA, Israel or any country that does not toe their line, is 'state terrorism', or simply 'true terrorism'. Even those who recognize America's legitimate anger are afraid lest it retaliate in 'illegitimate terms', thus hurting its own and others' interests.[34] All this rhetoric can be simply construed, however, as the third stage in Arab and Islamic reactions to the horror of 11 September.

The first stage was of unlimited joy and a bursting sense of revenge at the sight of what seemed a defeated and hapless America. Then, as the voices of harsh retribution rose among the American administration and public, and the growing evidence unfolded of Arab and Islamic involvement in the disaster, denial set in: suddenly the Arabs knew nothing and heard nothing, and all insinuations about their possible connection were categorized as 'bias' against them. Finally, when the culprits were named, and concrete plans started to crystallize regarding the targets for retaliation, differences between various kinds of terrorism were found, according to who performed them, not to the mode of their execution. In this fashion, the grotesque situation arose where some of the champions of terrorism began to condemn it (not its perpetrators), meaning the terrorism of others, and so they thought that they could gain the status of 'coalition members', and see themselves removed from the terrorist list of the State Department.

Due to this sequence of events, the Arabs and Muslims have been pressing for UN involvement – as they have an automatic command of one-third of the votes – to re-define terrorism and to commandeer any international measure taken against the perpetrators of the New York and Washington acts of terrorism. They do not hide their view that, if their position is adopted, they would be able to indict Israel for its 'crimes' which amount to terrorism in their eyes, while its brand of terrorism against Israel would gain international legitimacy, since in their view it is the Arabs who have 'always fought against terrorism'. Therefore, according to this logic, it would be futile to search for Arab or Muslim culprits. For, even if Bin-Laden threatened America, this does not make him any more susceptible in their eyes than, say, Prime Minister Netanyahu of Israel, who had once, in their view, 'threatened to burn Washington'.[35] The attempt to direct world attention away from the arrested Arab and Muslim suspects in America, and from the direct indictment of Afghanistan and Bin-Laden, naturally put many Arab and Muslim leaders on the 'Israel track', claiming that since the Zionists stood to gain the most from 'blackening the faces of Muslims across the world', they were the primary suspects as perpetrators of that horror.

TOWARDS A GLOBAL POLICY

President Bush was right in not only declaring a global war against terrorism, but also in coining a whole new vocabulary for dealing with it: its initiators were 'wanted', like in the Old West; they were to be 'smoked out of their hiding holes'; they were to be targeted, searched after and destroyed; their protectors who harbored them were to be punished, collateral damage and casualties notwithstanding; the war against them was to be sustained, protracted, determined and all-encompassing until they were caught, defeated, eliminated or brought to justice, and their bases destroyed, their finances dried up, their front-organizations disbanded and their supporters punished or otherwise coaxed to abandon them.

But that kind of policy cannot succeed unless it is global not only in its goals, ways and means, but also in its definitions, norms, standards and modalities. It is impossible to win, for example, if other acts of terrorism that do not concern America directly are dubbed 'local' (ETA in Spain, Corsica and France; the IRA against Britain; or the Hamas, the PLO, the Hizbullah or the Tanzim against Israel), and therefore unworthy of the global fight against terrorism. It is also impossible to win, if some acts of terror are accorded 'understanding' and various 'justifications'. Terrorism is a violent activity against civilians, for whatever reason; therefore, while one can 'understand' the struggle of the IRA or the ETA against the security forces of Britain and Spain whom they perceive as the occupiers of their countries, the moment they blow up car-bombs in the middle of Londonderry and San Sebastian, wantonly killing and maiming civilians, they become terrorists who should be combated without relenting.

A program for defeating terrorism will not succeed, if the vocabulary devised by the President of the USA is invalidated when it comes to places other than America. The USA has been rightly targeting the heads of the *al-Qa'ida*, using airplanes to bombard their bases, sending incursions into their territory to 'smoke them out', cutting off their sources of financing and supplies; but when it puts down and condemns the exact replicas of those actions, when pursued by others, as 'assassinations of leaders', as resorting to 'disproportionate force', as 'invading others' territory', or as 'depriving others of their lawful income', this does not sound like a universal war, that is launched on universally agreed standards, according to universal criteria. If the war is indeed one of good against evil, then evil cannot be allowed to masquerade as good, nor terrorism as a 'war of liberation'. If the clear and ironclad definitions voiced by President Bush are allowed to become eroded, because of temporary considerations, then the moral basis of the entire American campaign will grow so slim and shaky as to arouse domestic and international opposition to it.

When America searches for allies in its worldwide endeavor, the staunchest among them can only be counted among those democracies whose committed leaders have a staying power based on their legitimacy in government. Tyrants, monarchs, military juntas, who have no popular base to their rule, not only cannot pledge a long-standing and unrelenting support to America, but their very collaboration with the West arouses the opposition to both their 'participation' in the war effort, and also to their personal hold on government. The fact that the only committed allies of America are democracies, while the others shrink from 'attacking fellow Muslim states', demand 'evidence' of Bin-Laden's culpability, insist on novel definitions of terrorism which would sanction theirs (for example, the Islamic terror against Kashmir or Israel), only points to this trend of thought. Instead of President Bush categorizing the countries of the world into 'with us or against us', something that caused all of them to scramble for shelter under the wings of the virtual 'coalition', he ought to invite all the countries which fought terrorism and eradicated it to join in, while cautioning the others which did not, to straighten up their act, or else ... There would have been no stronger incentive for them to conform, and to embrace the American definitions of terrorism.

The fact that almost all terrorist movements in the world today are Muslim, and all the universal organizations and networks among them are the produce of fundamentalist Islamic thought, ought to cause us to review not the 'root reasons' for this terrorism, as the Saudi Prince suggested to the brave Mayor of New York who refused to sell out his principles; but to review the childish, uninformed and untruthful declaration by many Western leaders that 'Islam is a religion of peace.' If it is peaceful, why are so many atrocities done in its name? Every Muslim and Western leader repeats the mantra that 'the acts of terror are un-Islamic'. If they knew anything about the division of the world into *Dar al-Harb* (The Abode of War) and *Dar al-Islam* (The Abode of Islam) that is brandished by the Muslim fundamentalists today to justify their jihad (Holy War, including terrorism) against the non-Muslims, maybe their spines would shudder at the thought that this core concept is part and parcel of political Islam, not a new invention of the fundamentalists.

At the same time that Muslims across the globe trample American flags and intimidate Americans with horrific acts of terrorism, long lines are formed in the Muslim world to apply for student visas in the West or ask for outright immigration there (yes, that hated West). But those who grant the visas are not aware, or pretend not to understand, that those young students and the rest of the migrants, while they may innocently wish to study or to better their lot economically, are the very stuff that will turn its acquired knowledge against the countries that were courteous enough to dispense it to them, and the very masses who will go on the rampage against democratic governments that gave them shelter. After all, most of the suspects arrested by the FBI are Egyptians and Saudis, from the very countries that are supposed to be the USA's closest allies in the Muslim world. The fact that America failed to act against Mubarak when he gave shelter to the terrorists of the Achille Lauro and denied it, or against the Saudis who disburse huge sums of money to support the Hamas, could have been interpreted by their citizens dwelling in America and elsewhere that license was given to acts of terror, or at least that the USA would look the other way when the terrorists were citizens or originals of the 'moderate' regimes befriended by America. In the year of the Intifada, hundreds of cases were recorded in all Western democracies, of desecration of Jewish sites, of torching synagogues and destroying cemeteries. Those same Muslim migrants, if not checked, will turn against their new governments and compatriots, as the events of 11 September have shown.

NOTES

1. Bernard Lewis, 'The Return of Islam', *Commentary* (Winter 1976), pp.39–49.
2. Raphael Israeli, 'The Islamikaze and Their Significance', *Journal of Terrorism and Political Violence*, 9, 3 (1997), pp. 96–121.
3. Israel TV, Channel 1 (in Hebrew), 9 December 1994, 18:00 GMT.
4. The hundreds of civilians who were accidentally killed in a bomb shelter in Baghdad during the American bombings of the Gulf War (January 1991).
5. The hundred or so civilians killed by an Israeli stray bomb in Southern Lebanon during the Israeli operation there in Spring 1996.
6. The continued bombings by the USA and the UK of Iraqi targets in the no-flight zone established there in the aftermath of the Gulf War.
7. The retaliatory raids by Israel, using American-made weapons, against Palestinian targets.
8. *al-Risalah* (PA), 13 September 2001, cited [in Hebrew] by MEMRI (The Middle East Media Research Institute), *Terror in America*, No. 1.
9. Ibid.
10. *Al-Sharq al-Awsat* (London), 14 September 2001; extracted by MEMRI [Hebrew], *Terror in America*, No. 4.
11. *Al-Dustur* (Jordan), 13 September 2001; ibid.
12. Ibid.
13. Ibid.
14. *Al-Ra'i* (Jordan), 13 September 2001; ibid.
15. *Al-Dustur* (Jordan), 13 September 2001; ibid.
16. *Afaq 'Arabiyya* (Egypt), 19 September 2001.
17. *Tishrin* (Syria), 13 September 2001; ibid.
18. *Al-Ayyam* (PA), 13 September 2001; ibid.
19. *Al-Safir* (Lebanon), 13 September 2001; ibid.
20. *Al-Sharq al-Awsat* (London), 13 September 2001; ibid.
21. *Al-Hayat* (London), 13 September 2001; MEMRI No. 5.
22. *Al-Akhbar* (Egypt), 17 September 2001; MEMRI, No. 8.
23. *Al-'Arabi* (Egypt), 16 September 2001; ibid.
24. Ibid.
25. Ibid.
26. Ibid.
27. *Al-Ahrar* (Egypt), 14 September 2001; MEMRI No. 8.
28. *Al-Ahrar* (Egypt), 17 September 2001; ibid.
29. *Al-Usbu'* (Egypt), 17 September 2001; ibid.
30. Ibid.
31. The Arabic term is *irhab*, which translates the modern word of terrorism.
32. *Al-Hayat* (London), 3 October 2001.
33. *Al-Usbu' al-Adabi* (*The Literary Weekly* – Damascus), 15 September 2001; MEMRI No. 10.
34. See, for example, the article by Dr Adnan 'Amran, the Syrian Minister of Information, in *Al-Sharq al-Awsat* (London), 21 September 2001; ibid. No. 11.
35. Ibid.

8. Exporting Islamic Violence to Western Democracies*

THE NEW WAVE OF ANTI-SEMITISM

Since the al-Aqsa Intifada erupted in the Middle East in late September 2000, an almost simultaneous wave of violent anti-Jewish and anti-Israeli sentiment has accompanied it in the Western democracies, initiated and executed mainly by locally nationalized Arab or Muslim immigrants, long-established or recent arrivals, legal or illegal. Due to the ubiquity in space, synchronicity in time, and similarity in style and content of these events, one wonders whether they were all triggered and managed centrally, or spread by emulation from one part of the globe to another.

One also questions why, beyond the Arab and Muslim worlds, these eruptions are limited mainly to Western democracies, and whether it is so because of the large concentrations of new immigrants of Muslim/Arab descent there; or due to the openness of Western societies and political systems which tolerate such demonstrations; or to the existing anti-Semitic infrastructure there that instigates, or encourages, or joins forces with the demonstrators; or by reason of the perceived support of those countries for the Jewish State; or as a result of the influence and high standing of the strong local Jewish communities which the demonstrators seek to challenge.

Indeed, all these questions are intertwined in more ways than one, and have come to the fore in the recent wave of seemingly anti-Israeli eruptions, in the context of the Arab–Israeli dispute, but which very often belie deeper anti-Semitic strata.

What is more, Arab and Muslim politics in those Western countries are gradually becoming part and parcel of the local scenes

*Originally published as 'Anti-Semitism Revived: The Impact of the Intifada on Muslim Immigration Groups in Western Democracies', *Jerusalem Viewpoints*, 455 (2001), pp. 1–8.

as the populations with those ethno-religious origins have been growing rapidly due to a high birthrate. The consequence is that their impact on the politics of their countries of shelter will further increase as the many young are coming of age and becoming more vocal than their parents who had been too busy searching for employment and survival, and who had been – for the most part – disenfranchised due to their status as foreign workers.

Thus, politicians of all parties, especially in areas of heavy concentrations of Arab/Muslim immigrants, are on permanent lookout to enlist the support of these nationalized citizens and listen to their special concerns, be they domestic in the fields of education and religious and social services, or foreign as regards the relations of their new Western homes with the Arab and Muslim worlds.

This process, which has dramatically increased in the past decade, has had immediate large-scale repercussions:

1. The long-established Arab/Muslim immigrant populations have become politically active as they have learned to translate their numbers into political clout and to make their political support conditional upon satisfaction of their demands. (Indeed, local Muslims in Britain reportedly targeted pro-Israel candidates in the June 2001 parliamentary elections.)
2. The strong Muslim/Arab communities established in the Western democracies often use their leverage to clamor for easing immigration controls on their kin who wish to join them and further increase their numbers.
3. Paradoxically, these new immigrants, formerly unable to voice their views and bring their influence to bear under the authoritarian regimes in their home countries, are now using their democratic power in their new lands to exert pressure on their governments to rally behind and support the poor and undemocratic regimes that they left behind.
4. Domestically, these new immigrants are clamoring for equal rights and tapping the resources of the host countries to support their absorption in their new homes and to benefit from the high-quality social services these nations offer their citizenry in general; but at the same time they import with them their own understanding, biases and emotional approach to the Middle East dispute, and strive to align their new countries with those views.

5. As they grow in numbers and influence, they not only assidu-
    ously assert their views, but they also begin to erode the longer
    established and highly regarded local Jewish communities
    which usually wield a very visible influence on the economic
    and cultural domains and stand at the opposite political pole as
    regards the Middle East. The result is that, despite tremendous
    Jewish efforts at dialogue with their Muslim/Arab compatriots,
    antagonism between the two communities sets in.

6. Although much of the developing tensions between the two
    denominational communities can be traced to the wide gap
    existing between the usually more educated and prosperous
    Jews and the poorer and more frustrated new Muslim/Arab
    immigrants, a large part of it must be ascribed to their usually
    antagonistic positions regarding the Middle East.

7. While Jewish support for Israel is normally dignified and within
    the boundaries of law and legitimate dissent and demonstration
    in democratic societies, the Muslim newcomers, who are not
    versed in these niceties upon their arrival, tend to perpetuate
    the tradition of violence and open outrage that they bring with
    them from their countries of origin, resulting in clashes,
    eruptions of rage, and acts of force, intimidation, arson,
    beatings, and the entire gamut of fury and passion resorted to in
    the Middle East.

IMPORTED FURY FROM THE MIDDLE EAST

In what has become routine, the Israeli government, in conjunction
with the Jewish Agency, has been issuing a monthly report on anti-
Semitic outbreaks around the world. Usually, this report centers on
anti-Semitic propaganda and other hate literature in European and
other Christian societies where traditional anti-Semitism has been
rife. It details the anti-Jewish threats, desecrations of Jewish sites,
acts of violence against Jewish targets or individuals, manifestations of Nazi or neo-Nazi ideology and practice, Holocaust denial,
allegations of the universal 'Jewish conspiracy', and suchlike. In the
past few years these reports have been 'enriched' by Internet sites
which cultivate xenophobia, in general, and anti-Semitism, in
particular.

A special section of the report is devoted to concrete steps in
legislation, memorial-building, prosecution, education, physical

protection of Jews and their sites, and information campaigns that the governments of those anti-Semitism-prone countries take to minimize and control the sentiments and manifestations of anti-Jewish rhetoric and action.

These are routine reports and yet, when one reads through the many pages and the multitude of anti-Semitic eruptions, one cannot help wonder at this high concentration of events in the Christian world at the turn of the twenty-first century, and merely half a century after the Holocaust. Furthermore, the report does not encompass, for some mysterious reason, the daily occurrences of anti-Semitic vitriol in the Arabic press throughout the Arab world and beyond, including in such countries as Egypt and Jordan which have signed peace accords with Israel. Moreover, had these monthly reports looked routinely at the school textbooks with which generations of Arab children are being educated, one would begin to comprehend the connection between education and hatred and its violent manifestations.

However, since there are practically no Jews left in Arab and Islamic countries, the anti-Semitic rhetoric there is directed against Israel, the product of the Jewish people, and against Zionism – their movement of national liberation. Thus, Arab/Muslim immigrants to Western countries for the most part carry with them the anti-Semitic luggage which they had absorbed by education in their motherlands and cultures; and their renewed encounter with Jews in their new host-countries permits them to vent their inherited sentiments and express them in both anti-Jewish and anti-Israeli terms. The fact that most Jewish congregations in the West voice their support for Israel and general Jewish causes makes it convenient for the Arab/Muslim immigrant communities there to combine the two and they often fail to distinguish between them.

With the al-Aqsa Intifada breaking out on the eve of the Jewish New Year (28 September 2000), which rallied Arab-Muslim immigrants in Western countries around the Palestinian cause, and the parallel concern of the Jewish communities in those countries for the safety and welfare of Israel, both sides were set on a collision course, giving rise to an almost unprecedented level of rhetorical and physical violence on the part of the Muslim immigrants, legal and illegal, against Jews and Israel.

This outpouring of sentiment and violence was further aided by several factors:

1. The period of the Jewish High Holidays is particularly prone to heightened tension because Jews – even those who do not usually identify themselves as such or do not actively participate in Jewish life – are drawn to synagogues of all Jewish denominations, where Jewish piety as well as Jewish awareness and communal concerns are voiced and expressed.

2. In most Western countries, and independently of the Intifada, there are enough anti-Semites and hate groups to provide material for the monthly reports of anti-Semitism worldwide. Groups such as the Black Muslims in America are all too ready to put their experience, networks, Farrakhan-style anti-Semitic passion, funds, eager audiences and national resonance at the disposal of their fellow demonstrators.

3. Upon the outbreak of the Intifada, the Muslim/Arab communities in those countries found fertile ground to demonstrate their fury against Israel and Jews, in combination with the active support of their natural allies, the locally established anti-Semites. Thus, under the guise of anti-Zionism, violent events unfolded in the streets and on the campuses of practically every Western country that shelters Arab/Muslim communities, much to the horror of Jewish congregations which immediately sensed the anti-Semitic import of those manifestations.

4. Local circumstances in each country, such as the nomination of Senator Joseph Lieberman to the presidential ticket in the USA, or pro-Israeli declarations by the Prime Minister of Australia, or words of sympathy towards Jews expressed by some European leaders in view of the desecration of Jewish sites in their countries, only fueled anti-Semitic outbursts there; in consequence, anti-Israeli rhetoric and acts of violence resulted.

ONSET OF THE INTIFADA IN THE WEST

According to the August 2000 Report – that is, prior to the outbreak of the Intifada – the Beit Aharon Synagogue in Brooklyn, New York, was torched on 31 August, following rock-throwing, an incendiary bomb and window-breaking during the preceding month. August–September 2000 saw a mounting wave of aggression against Jews, their cemeteries and synagogues in: Sweden (12 September); Russia (17 and 27 September); Italy (18 September); France (24 September); England (6, 7 and 12 August and 29

September); Lithuania (two cases of desecration); Germany (one case); Russia (one case); Ukraine (one case); Norway (Holocaust denial and desecration); and Ireland (one case). These acts of defamation or desecration were accompanied by intense anti-Semitic propaganda on walls, Internet sites and in posters and fliers, especially after Lieberman's nomination.

Acts of this sort were even reported in Bolivia and in Belgium. On 29 September in Brussels, muazzins in the mosques urged worshippers to go out and 'take vengeance against the Jews in retaliation for the events in Israel and the Palestinian territories'. On 30 September, one day after the outbreak of the Intifada, a rabbi was assaulted by unidentified youths on his way back from synagogue in Brooklyn. Tear gas was sprayed in his face before he was beaten, while the assailants screamed: 'This is for the Palestinians!' On the same day a Hassidic Jew was stabbed in New York City. The aggressor said he was Palestinian and told his victim to 'get out of here!' Some steps were taken by governments in the Czech Republic, Sweden, the USA, Germany and Russia to contain these violent eruptions of anti-Semitism, but the worst was to come.

The October 2000 Report detailed an alarming increase in anti-Semitic outbreaks. The, by now, routine desecrations, assaults, arson and Holocaust denial, and the unexpected joining of forces between Arab/Muslims and local anti-Semites, were now backed by open incitement, almost unprecedented in peacetime, against the Jews and Israel.

On the day after the Intifada erupted, rocks pelted the windows of Kehillat Yaacov Synagogue and the Great Synagogue of Fieldgate Street in London. On 1 October, an Arab driver attempted to run over Jews on their way to the Aubervilliers Synagogue in Paris, followed by Arab youths who threw water bottles at the walls of the synagogue. On the same day Arab youths approached a large group of Jewish holiday worshippers and pelted them with chestnuts in the vicinity of Ohaleikha Yaacov Synagogue in Paris. Only the police presence and intervention kept matters from getting out of hand. On the same day, other Arab youths were reported hurling rocks and abuse at Jewish worshippers both in Creteil, a Paris suburb, and Villeurbanne, a Lyon neighborhood, better known for its basketball team. Jewish New Year notwithstanding, other Arabs in Antwerp, aided by local skinheads, abused Jewish worshippers with insults and curses, and one raised his right hand in a Nazi-style salute before they were constrained by police.

TIMING OF THE RIOTS

This flurry of heightened anti-Semitic activity peaked in Western countries in the coming days as the events in the Middle East kept escalating. Thus, the spiral of violence rose rapidly in both places, as the Jewish Holidays passed from the New Year to the Ten Days of Awe leading to the Day of Atonement (Yom Kippur).

It is interesting to note the choice by the rioters of these most holy of days in the Jewish calendar, which, of course, reflected the realities on the ground in the Middle East. Why the Palestinians elected precisely those days, exactly as Sadat had done in the 1973 October War against Israel, may be a matter of speculation. Either the Palestinians believed like the Egyptians before them, that the Jews would be busy praying and fasting, and therefore less alert and more vulnerable, or both thereby expressed their contempt and derogation of Jews by denigrating their holidays.

Conversely, during the holy month of Ramadan, which was celebrated by Muslims, including Palestinians, in the middle of the Intifada, the Palestinians decreased their level of violence and expected Israel to follow suit, both out of respect for their holiday and out of exhaustion from the fast. Israel complied on both scores, since it had no desire or stake in the continued riots in any case, and the hostilities tapered off. Thus, turning the heat on and off at their whim only helped to demonstrate that the 'spontaneity' of the Intifada was controllable after all, and that the respect others duly owe the Islamic faith and its believers is not necessarily rewarded in kind.

ASSAULTS ON DIASPORA JEWISH COMMUNITIES

As the Intifada gained force, the rate of anti-Semitic occurrences increased. In central Lille, France, swastikas were spotted on walls with the equation: Star of David = Anti-Arab. On 2 October, in Rue Gresser Synagogue on the 19th Arrondissement in Paris, a bottle was tossed at the building and abusive and menacing telephone calls were received at the synagogue in the middle of the morning prayer. The same day, in Britain, a *fatwa* was issued by a Muslim cleric and placed on the Internet, calling for jihad against Israel and Israeli interests.

Sheikh Umar abd-a-Rahman, the blind Egyptian cleric who had

masterminded the Twin Towers explosion in New York and has since been serving a prison term, was quoted that day as urging his believers to launch jihad against Jews wherever they could find them. That same night, three firebombs were tossed at the entrance to the synagogue and Jewish community center in Dusseldorf, Germany, while an anonymous call received by the Nice (France) Fire Department warned of a ticking bomb at the local synagogue. Similar warnings and acts of violence against synagogues were recorded that same night – which can only be compared to the infamous 1938 *Kristallnach* – in Malmo, Sweden, in Brussels and in Schwerin, East Germany, where an elderly Jewish couple was assaulted and the woman seriously injured. That same night the Jewish cemetery in Schwaebisch Halle in Germany was desecrated and swastikas were painted on the Buchenwald Concentration Camp Memorial near Munich, and on the Old Synagogue Memorial in Halle, Germany.

The next day, on 3 October, a synagogue in the Villepinte neighborhood in Paris was hit and partly burned by three firebombs. In the Campinas suburb of Sao Paulo, Brazil, thugs threatened to kill the policeman on guard near the local synagogue. In Thessaloniki, one of the most 'Jewish' cities of the Balkans under the Ottomans and modern Greece, a huge demonstration was held opposite the offices of the waning Jewish community. In Florence and Venice, Italy, threatening phone calls were made against Israel and the Jews. Again in Malmo, Sweden, where a large community of Arab refugees has found shelter, the Jewish cemetery was desecrated on the night of 3–4 October.

The next day a large demonstration, led by the Italian Fascist Forza Nueva, took place in central Rome. The Jewish cemetery in Potsdam, Germany, was desecrated and its Jewish symbols abused. That same day the leaders of the German–Jewish community received letter-bombs and threats to their lives. Threats and anti-Semitic insults were also received at a Jewish day school in Paris. Radio 786, an Islamic radio station in Cape Town, South Africa, broadcast inciting messages against Israel and called for the 'liberation of Jerusalem from the Zionists'.

On 5 October, a Jewish boy was attacked by Arab teenagers near the Or-Yossef Jewish day school in the 19th Arrondissement of Paris. The next night rocks broke windows at the Kreuzberg Synagogue in Berlin, followed by the desecration of the Bar-Yohai and Or-Aviv Synagogues in Marseille, France, where graffiti proclaiming 'Death to the Jews' and 'The Jews are Murderers' was sprayed on the walls. Attacks on Jewish targets also occurred in Toronto and London, Ontario and in Montreal.

On 6 October, students leaving the Tenouji Jewish school in St Ouen, north of Paris, were pelted with rocks. The same day, the Jewish newspaper in Sao Paulo received abuse against Jews and threats to blow up the local Jewish Federation facilities and the local Israeli Consulate, as well as the Israeli Embassy in Brasilia. Ominously, the threats were signed by Osama Bin-Laden and the Hizbullah. Words of abuse, which compared the Jews to Hitler, and a threat to blow up the Jewish Museum in Rio de Janeiro, were received by e-mail on the screens of Israeli and Jewish institutions in town.

In Panama, the Arab community released a communiqué condemning Israel and the Jews, in response, they said, to the unfolding events in Palestine. The communiqué stated that 'Jews are murderers of anyone who opposes their aspirations to rule the world.' The Latin American Ciudad de Libre Opinion Internet site posted a call to 'oust the genocidal Zionists' and to support the Palestinian cause. On 7 October a picture was added to the site showing Palestinian youths hoisting a red banner with a black swastika in its center. The caption under the picture read: 'The Jewish occupation forces have murdered 47 Palestinians and shot to death 12 children', and quoted Iranian President Khamenei's summons for jihad against Israel.

On 7 October there was a large demonstration opposite the UN buildings in Geneva where calls were heard for jihad against Israel. An incendiary bomb was tossed at the Aubervilliers Synagogue northeast of Paris, where local Arabs threatened to blow up the building on the approaching Yom Kippur. Firebombs were hurled at a Jewish restaurant in the 19th Arrondissement in Paris, and rocks smashed its windows. Later, Arab youths attempted to force their way into other Jewish restaurants in the area amidst insults and curses. In a suburb of Lyon, the La Duchere Synagogue was attacked with rocks and the worshippers had to be evacuated in police cars. Threats by Arabs followed to torch or otherwise harm Jewish houses of worship on Yom Kippur. In London, on the same day, the Reform Synagogue at Edgeware was hit by rocks and its windows broken, and at the Elstree Borehamwood Synagogue in London, the Ark containing the Holy Scrolls was crushed and some of the scrolls were burned by arsonists. That same night firebombs were thrown at the windows of synagogues on Upper Berkeley Street and Seymour Place in London.

Dozens of other Jewish targets were attacked in similar ways in the coming days in Marseille (7–8 October), Lyon (8 October), Leicester, England (8 October), Birmingham (8 October), London and the Bronx in New York on the eve of Yom Kippur. The campaign against Jews continued in Daghestan (Russian Federation); Ottawa, with slogans crying 'Glory to Islam'; Montreal, where Muslims screamed 'Death to the Jews'; and five similar attacks in Toronto and its vicinity during the first week of October.

On Yom Kippur, 9 October, a synagogue was torched in Harrisburg, Pennsylvania, ironically bearing the proud name of Ohev Shalom (Lover of Peace). On the same day a synagogue in the Clichy S/Bois suburb of Paris was torched and its worshippers sent home. So it was at other synagogues and Jewish facilities in France (five cases in Paris, one in Lyon and one in Strasbourg). Indeed, during October, more than 100 anti-Semitic incidents occurred throughout France, including the burning of a synagogue in Trappes on 10 October. In Tashkent, Uzbekistan, a synagogue was also burned to ashes and its Torah scrolls destroyed. All this occurred in so-called civilized countries, where freedom of religion and worship is supposed to be safeguarded by constitutions, legal systems and law-enforcement authorities.

CHARACTERIZATION AND SIGNIFICANCE

These widespread pogrom-style outbursts of anti-Semitism, which are probably unprecedented since the Holocaust, happened in mostly democratic and pluralistic countries, notably in France and Britain, which are committed to human rights and freedom of worship. Nevertheless, the law-enforcement authorities seemed to stand by haplessly, helplessly and hopelessly before this violent wave which surprised them in its scope and intensity. The detailed incidents described for the first week in October were repeated throughout the following months, albeit with varying degrees of violence and shifting emphasis from one country to another. However, the patterns of violence, which seem to have been guided, cultivated and fed centrally, invoke some thoughts and categorizations that can be useful in sorting out this immense worldwide wave of anti-Semitic outpouring.

Although expressions of anti-Jewish and anti-Israeli sentiment were rife throughout the Christian world well before the Intifada, and independent of it, it is evident that the quickly mounting spiral of violence that broke out is indicative of an existing infrastructure of anti-Semitism in practically all of the infected countries, and it was used, expanded and solidified by the Muslim/Arab rioters to their own ends.

It is also evident that the unprecedented scale and intensity of the rampages against Jewish targets in the Christian world could not have reached this level of its own volition, since no Christian country, not even Russia and Ukraine, would have dared to revert to this medieval style of rampant and open anti-Semitism, for fear of American retribution. However, when combined with Arab/Muslim anti-Semitic outrage, disguised as anti-Zionism, the Christian anti-Semites, not least in the great democracies of France, Britain, Germany, Canada and the USA, used Western tolerance for anti-Israeli sentiment to legitimize and widen the anti-Semitic base in their countries without incurring any severe criticism or vigorous crackdown on the part of the authorities.

Once quiescent 'legitimacy' was accorded to these outbursts in Western Europe, other anti-Semites in North, Central and South America, Australia and Eastern Europe raised their heads to join in the rampage, 'celebrating' the widespread pogroms against the Jews as of old, with impunity.

The countries most affected by these rampages, where native anti-Semites converge with large immigrant Muslim/Arab populations, are France, Britain and Germany, in which the populations of foreign Muslim workers are the largest: North African, Pakistani and Turkish, respectively. These manifestations of hostility and intolerance have highlighted the increasingly burdensome issue of Islamic penetration throughout the Western world, first via legal and temporary residence for the purpose of work, and then via illegal infiltration with the intention to stay.

In the long run the demographic balance will be affected, especially in countries of high immigration such as Canada, the USA and Australia; just as it already has been in Western Europe, which accords political asylum to refugees from Islamic countries. More ominously, it means that these immigrants, both the already established and the newcomers, including the illegal among them, import to these countries of shelter their hatred for Israel and the Jews.

Once the demographic balance has tilted far enough, this is likely to undermine the enviable status that these Jews enjoy in those countries out of proportion to their numbers. The Arabs/Muslims are determined to dethrone the Jews from that position of privilege and to seize primacy from them, both by the sheer numbers that they will bring to bear in those democracies, and by violence and intimidation towards the Jews themselves.

This, in turn – again in conjunction with local long-time anti-Semites – will signal to the general population that Jews are 'dangerous' to befriend and be involved with, and therefore their neighborhoods and company ought to be avoided. It is easy to foresee the sentiments of anti-Semitism that will erupt when common people, who never particularly liked Jews in the first place, or who were envious or afraid of them, are made to feel that their undesired neighbors have become a cumbersome liability.

The attacks launched daily against Israelis since the onset of the Intifada are calculated to make life in Israel intolerable and drive the Israelis to despair, to abandon their hard-won prosperity, their remarkable democracy, and their phenomenal technological advances, so as to pave the way for their departure. Similarly, the Muslim communities worldwide, who view world Jewry as the main life-artery of Israel, are harassing the Jewish communities by attacking their religious and cultural centers and symbols: synagogues, cemeteries, restaurants, day-schools and community centers, in order to render their lives untenable and force them to go. In effect, in Sydney and Paris, London and Cape Town, from Ukraine to Panama, these hundreds of acts of arson, assault, murder, beatings, anti-Semitic slogans and posters, and calls to Muslims to join in jihad to liberate Jerusalem from the Zionists, are two sides of the same coin, which have rattled cities and towns both in Israel and world-wide, all in pursuit of the same objectives.

The globalization of information has caused the universalization of Arab and Islamic sentiment and solidarity. In a paradoxical way, the local media in each Islamic country provide immediacy of awareness and identification with the Palestinians and help break the local siege of censorship on information. International Arab and Muslim concerns are hijacked by activist groups who not only transmit messages instantly regarding the oppression of Palestinians and the dangers that the Jews pose to the Muslim holy places, but also help raise funds, urge co-religionists to demonstrate (violently if necessary) in support of those causes, and even provide instructions on how to join terrorist groups or concoct explosives. Thus, what happens on the ground in Gaza or Nablus has immediate reverberations on the streets of Melbourne and London, Kuala Lumpur and Sao Paulo; not to speak of the Arab street from Rabat to Baghdad, or the Islamic street from Teheran to Jakarta.

With regard to the reactions of the authorities in the countries that are the arenas of this violence, doubts arise as to the firmness of the governments in place when it comes to clamping down on Muslim minorities. They may hesitate lest the violence turns against them, or are wary not to antagonize Islamic countries with which they maintain economic relations, or are simply cognizant of the mounting voting power of those growing minorities in their midst when elections come. There is even a suspicion that some officials, with the tacit support of their constituencies, may elect to look the other way. Otherwise, it is hard to explain how dozens of acts of violence are repeated daily across the major European and North American nations that pride themselves on respect for human rights and the enforcement of law and order. Had Jews assaulted mosques or Muslim individuals in those countries, and certainly if anyone had torched Christian churches, public outrage would have surely compelled the governments to take harsh measures, as was the case in the 1980s when daily terrorist bombings in Parisian stores and metros led to unprecedented police control of the street of that city.

The consequence is that Jewish communities in Western democracies, which have always prided themselves on their individual and collective safety – and even more so those under regimes in Eastern Europe and Latin America where public order leaves much to be desired and anti-Semitism remains rampant – now fear for their lives. Informal and unarmed Jewish self-defense groups have sprung up to defend their property and police presence has been increased in violence-prone areas. Jews move out of 'dangerous' neighborhoods or eliminate outside emblems of their Jewishness: *mezuzot* disappear from their doorposts, *kippot* are hidden in pockets, and Star of David jewelry is concealed underneath clothes. Some even emigrate, either to Israel or to other destinations around the globe considered safer.

PROSPECTS FOR THE FUTURE

This wave of violence has had a far-reaching impact on Jewish communities world-wide, due to a combination of their intimidation, fears for the future and helplessness in the face of inaction or ineffective action by local authorities. These communities face the following choices:

1. Retreat from the outer and public manifestations of their Jewish identity and attempt to melt into the general population so as to escape public scrutiny and hide themselves from persecution, discrimination and humiliation.
2. Revert to the old formula of being Jewish indoors and anonymous outdoors, in order to practice their Judaism clandestinely and avoid raising any suspicion as to their alien identity which might warrant slur, hatred and hostility on the part of the general population.
3. Stand up and struggle, proudly but at a cost, against the anti-Semites, both local and immigrant Muslim/Arabs, by openly asserting their identity and their support of their faith, community, people and the State of Israel; mobilizing to their side the authorities who are generally supportive of their cause; and using the legal means available to pursue their detractors in long, costly, exhausting and unpopular campaigns.
4. Abandon the local scene altogether and tie their destiny to the Jewish State where, in spite of its problems, at least there is an infrastructure of Jewish pride and safety, also at a cost.

Jewish communities world-wide usually tend not to make clear-cut choices in this regard, and simultaneously adopt an amalgam of these strategies. They send family members to settle in Israel or purchase a home there as a safety measure for doomsday. Individuals among them will intermarry outside the faith and disappear from the community head-count. Others, in a desperate effort not to rock the boat, keep silent about their Jewish identity but nurture links to their Jewish roots. Still others, especially in places where they enjoy the cooperation of the local authorities, or are self-confident and strong enough to resist their detractors, stand up and fight, either as individuals or through their powerful institutions, for maintaining both their privileged status in their countries as well as their strong links with Israel.

In view of the unlikelihood of a quick fix in the foreseeable future to settle the Arab–Israeli rift, which seems to be gaining in intensity, it is likely that anti-Israeli sentiment will continue rising and spreading in the countries where Muslim/Arab communities are taking root and becoming part of the socio-political scene. Concurrently, local anti-Semites will continue to translate their unfashionable anti-Jewish attitudes into more legitimate and acceptable anti-Zionist and anti-Israel bashing. This is the common denominator around which the anti-Semites and the Arab/Muslim communities converge. Therefore, Jews at large and Israel specifically can expect these kinds of violent eruptions to recur in the future, with growing intensity and efficacy, and should brace themselves, jointly and severally, to counter them.

9. A Manual of Islamic Fundamentalist Terrorism*

INTRODUCTION

In June 1988, at the height of the first Intifada declared by the Palestinians against what they viewed as Israeli occupation and repression, a text was published as an appendix to an issue of the Muslim fundamentalist organ *al-Islam wa-Filastin* (Islam and Palestine), which carried a very detailed and intriguing analysis of what it took to become an 'Islamikaze'.[1] The term had been coined in 1996, when the making of the new brand of Muslim terrorists in Afghanistan was described, which argued that it was a fallacy to dub these people 'suicide-bombers', because their primary concern was to kill their enemies, not themselves, sacrificing themselves only in the process. Typologically, they come closest to the Japanese kamikaze of the Pacific War in the Second World War, and therefore it was suggested that this term should be combined with Islam into this new word.[2] When the above Arabic text came to my attention, after the term 'Islamikaze' had been coined and diffused, *post-factum* justification was added to support the article, which established a linkage between the outer-objective definition of Islamikaze, and the inner-subjective terminology suggested by the Arab–Muslim writer of that text.

A.J. Wensinck has demonstrated the resemblance between the Christian and Muslim doctrines of martyrology, down to small details and to the parallel development of the two. He has also shown that the ancient roots of both go back to the Jewish monotheistic concepts of death and martyrdom for the sake of God (*kiddush Hashem*), and also took in philosophical and ascetic elements from Hellenic tradition, all anchored in the pre-

* Originally published under the same title in the *Journal of Terrorism and Political Violence*, Winter (2003).

monotheistic pagan world.[3] Incidentally, even the etymological transition from the Qur'anic *shahid* as a witness, into the self-sacrificing martyr of later times,[4] already pointed out above, can be traced in Christian tradition as well, inasmuch as the 'witness' to the deeds of God in the New Testament, developed into the concept of the martyr.[5] Even in the rewards of the martyr, both traditions are similar in so far as in both he is promised an eternal life of bliss in the highest position in Paradise, close to God Himself and above the righteous and regular pious Believers. In both, the martyr is assured of exoneration for his sins and from the torments of the Day of Judgment; and there is the idea of the martyr as the mediator who intercedes before God on behalf of other Believers in order to alleviate the burden of their sins.

Understandably, during the lifetime of the Prophet, and then during the expansion of Islam, which sprung out of Arabia and launched the jihad for the conquest of the world (*fat'h* – incidentally also the name of the major component faction of the PLO, which set out to conquer Palestine–Israel), the jihad fighters were in their prime and their status in society attained its highest level ever. The martyrs who perished in battle acquired precedence over all other Believers. But when the Islamic Empire settled down and the fighting zeal receded, at a time when the expansion of Islam was pursued more by Sufi mystics than by illustrious conquerors, the question of martyrdom through other avenues than fighting came to the fore. For example, if the mystic missionary put himself in the service of Islam at great risk, by traveling great distances and penetrating uncharted territory, then why was his brand of martyrdom any less than the classic fighter who died in combat? Then, interpretations of martyrdom as the supreme spiritual state of the Believer, who knows how to control his worldly desires and rein in his ambitions and personal interest, began to advance to the forefront as worthy forms of martyrdom. Ghazali, the eminent medieval mystic (d. 1111), was quoted as saying that 'Anyone submitting (Islam = submission to the Will of Allah) totally to Allah in his battle against his desires, is himself a martyr.'[6]

ROOTS OF THE ISLAMIKAZE

In the contemporary Middle East, due to the vicious conflict which puts Arab–Muslims in opposition to Israel, and due to the sustaining support which the USA (and to a lesser extent the rest of the West) are perceived as extending to Israel, there has been a revival of the old notions of martyrdom. It is true that all the Arab casualties of the half-dozen wars that broke out between Israel and its neighbors during the second half of the twentieth century, were considered martyrs. However, it was the Hizbullah in Lebanon which gave this belief the greatest impetus in the last two decades of the century, as a martyr was no longer defined as a Believer who accidentally died in battle, with 'martyrdom' being automatically thrust upon him as a result. A new model of martyrdom was introduced, of the Believer who defied death actively, and was ready, if not eager, to die in the process of destroying the enemy; namely the Islamikaze-type. The Hizbullah is, of course, the direct product of Shi'ite Islam, the same brand of Islam that rules Iran; therefore, one has to look at the trunk in order to comprehend the branches.

Central to religious beliefs in Iran, as well as in other Shi'ite communities, is the re-living of the legendary suffering of Hussein in Karbalah in AD 680, before he was annihilated with his followers by Yazid, the son of the Umayyad founder, Mu'awiyya. The re-enacting of that horror – dubbed *ta'zya*, a sort of passion play, which is displayed on 'Ashura day by processions of the pious who beat and hurt themselves in an orgy of supreme masochism – is considered the apex of identification with the suffering of Hussein. Suffering as a theme unto itself, including self-inflicted bleeding and death, become a way of life for the devout Shi'ite, a method of expressing selfless sacrifice in honor of the assassinated son of Ali, the first true Imam and successor to the Prophet (superseding the three 'imposter' Caliphs who were in power before him). The bitterness of the Shi'a – the even downtrodden and persecuted branch of Islam (in fact a branch of them in Lebanon called itself the 'downtrodden on Earth', as a sign of distinction, not complaint) – is best expressed in the anger and rush for self-sacrifice on the one hand, and the posthumous glorification of the martyrs after their death on the other. So, young Iranians were encouraged to clear mine-fields during the first Gulf War (1980–88), with 'keys to paradise' hanging on their innocent necks; their parents were congratulated, not consoled, by family friends for the martyrdom of their children; and all these horrendous sacrifices were immortalized in the memorial for the martyrs in Tehran by a water fountain colored blood-red, which symbolizes and eternalizes the endless flow of suffering and blood.

Naturally, those groomed in that culture cannot be expected to recoil from the ultimate act of suffering; that is, death. Quite the contrary, the stream of the Islamikaze has never dried in Iran, and it is diverted to flow in other lands of Islam. The attractive rationale reads:

> The skies are shrouded in black, rivers of tears are flowing, Hussein arrives in Karbalah to sacrifice himself for Allah. This is the 'Ashura story, tend your ears to listen to its sadness, let your tears flow for the King of the Martyrs, because he will bring you to Paradise.[7]

These are the lyrics to one of the songs found in the mourning 'musical-passions' that are re-enacted in Iran and elsewhere to commemorate the martyrdom of Hussein. These re-enactments, and the generally militant demands by the Shi'ites for their rights and for justice went into abeyance or adopted a low profile for centuries (a state of *intidhar* – namely waiting and expectation), due to the principle of *Taqiyya* (dissimulation), which was adopted after the mysterious disappearance (not death) of the Twelfth Imam (hence Twelver Shi'a), as a defensive measure of self-preservation in a hostile environment. The expectation of the return of the absent Imam provided the entire rationalization and driving power behind Twelver Shi'ism, inasmuch as it encouraged the Believers to suffer and wait, as the more they waited and suffered, the closer his return was deemed (like the 'pangs of the Messiah' in Judaism). But if anyone, at any time, claimed to be the Imam, he was immediately repulsed and condemned as an imposter, and treated accordingly.

The last decades of the twentieth century, however, witnessed an ideological and political quantum jump effected by the Shi'a, under the revolutionary impulse of Ayatullah Khomeini and other mullahs. The nature of the change, which has taken the Shi'a from passivity and expectation to activity and aggression – namely, making the human will predominate over fate or over the 'natural course of events' – is indeed nothing short of revolutionary. This is inherent in Shi'ite theology which recognizes the head of the clerical hierarchy as the *marja' taqlid*, the supreme reference who commands the emulation of the Believers. In fact this major figure, who gains his superior status through his scholarship and religious authority, is the supreme *Mujahid*, the 'striver' to interpret the will of the Hidden Imam who is the actual ruler of the world. The

Mujahid thus acquires the power of a legislator among the Shi'a, and his rulings are the law. This is the reason why Khomeini spoke about *wilayat faqih* (the rule of the jurist), for only such Heaven- and Imam-inspired jurists, who are the upper echelon of the mullahs, could be clairvoyant enough to detect the Truth and pass it on to others. Khomeini himself wrote that 'only the mullahs are able to take people to the streets and motivate them to die for Islam, and bring them to beg that they be allowed to spill their blood for Islam'.[8]

The new activism brought about by the Islamic Revolution in Iran has taken up the tragic death of Hussein – which used to be viewed as a murderous and cowardly act sustained by that greatest of martyrs, and remembered throughout the years by the low-profile followers of the Shi'a – has been rendered into an active declaration of war against injustice, that has to be initiated out loud and pursued in earnest by Hussein's followers. In this context, Hussein becomes not someone to be mourned, but a heroic leader in battle and a model worthy of emulation on the way to Paradise. He, the paradigm of martyrdom, will intercede on behalf of his followers to ensure the admission to heaven of the new generations of martyrs. Hence, we learned of the flocking of millions of adults and children to the mosques in Tehran when the war with Iraq broke out and a call for volunteers to the front was sounded by the government. The demand for martyrdom by far exceeded the needs of the military. Children were urged to go to the front without their parents' permission, and were used to clear mine-fields in a deadly trance into which the naïve and unsuspecting young and inexperienced minds were easily encouraged. They expressed their happiness at 'rushing to Paradise in unison with their friends', under the promise that in Paradise too they would be able to unite and pursue their worldly worry-free life.

The eagerness for death through martyrdom in that culture often prompts young Iranian demonstrators to join processions covered in their death shrouds, as if to signify that not only do they defy death, but they are also ready for it. They were swept away by the magic rhetoric of their leader, whom some saw as the Imam – that is an incarnation of the Hidden One – when he said that life was illusory and merely a corridor to the real life in Paradise, there-fore it was not worth living. The activization of the martyrdom of Hussein, which in Iran has involved a real change in the *ta'zya* ceremonies on Ashura Day, has also transcended Iran's boundaries and been made a model for other Shi'ites, such as in Lebanon, where Hizbullah in particular and the Amal Shi'ites in general, have adopted the same style. Moreover, the Hizbullah – the active long arm of Iran in its quest to internationalize the Iranian Islamic Revolution – has been adopting a militant and aggressive stance in its pursuance. It not only routinely uses violence on the Israeli–Lebanese borders, but it is known to aid terrorism across the world against Israeli and Jewish interests (such as the blowing up of the Jewish Community Center and the Israeli Embassy in Buenos Aires) and for its close cooperation with the Palestinian Intifada, both in coordinating joint operations against Israel and in direct involvement in arms supplies, instruction in violence and terrorist warfare.

Above all, however, the doctrine of the Islamikaze – that is, active death in martyrdom – was revived by the Hizbullah in Lebanon. The first acts were performed in the early 1980s against American and Israeli presence in Lebanon, but as the Israeli presence in the southern part of that country continued, these operations were intensified until they became the routine trade-mark of the violent encounters between Israelis and the Hizbullah, usually at the initiative of the latter. It took another decade or so before that mode of action was emulated by other Muslim terrorist groups, most notoriously the Sunnite Hamas, and to a lesser extent Islamic Jihad. All it took for the transition to take place was for fundamentalist Sunnite scholars, such as Sheikh Qardawi – whose doctrine was mentioned above and will be discussed below in more detail – to provide the missing link between the 'natural' vying for suffering that fundamentalist Shi'ism has inherited from the *ta'zya* tradition, and the practice which pushed martyrdom to the top of the ways in which an individual could strive to emulate the slain Imam Hussein. Sunnite scholars also linked the general Islamic hallowed idea of martyrdom and its rewards not with the goal of self-inflicted pain but with the aim of inflicting damage onto the enemy, even at the cost of one's own life. The long succession of *fatwas* delivered to fill this gap, which will be cited and discussed below, has indeed provided rationalization to the mostly Sunnite Islamikaze groups for their deadly attacks.

PALESTINIAN ISLAMIKAZE

It is quite amazing indeed to watch the Sunnite fundamentalist groups adopt the Shi'ite ways, not only by embracing the Iranian and Hizbullah mode of operation (something that has been evinced in the collaboration of Iran and the Hizbullah with the Hamas and the Islamic Jihad, and the latter with the *al-Qa'ida* network), but also by creating their own version of the supreme sacrifice and suffering inherent in the *ta'zya*, only in reverse. In the field of battle and terrorism for the sake of Allah, we have seen 19 members of the *al-Qa'ida* committing collective Islamikaze acts within one hour of each other on American soil, on 11 September. *Al-Qa'ida* fighters in Afghanistan defied death in the face of American airpower, as do Hamas and Islamic Jihad operatives in the PA, or the fanatic Gama'at in Egypt, or the Abu Sayyaf group in the Philippines, or the Muslim terrorists in Kashmir and India Proper, or the fundamentalists in Algeria who slay their own compatriots with the same senseless and blind zeal as they do foreigners. This universalization of Sunni Muslim terrorism has been accompanied by a growing daring in the operations, and its frequency and diffusion make it almost banal. The massive Islamikaze attack of 11 September, with probably more to come, and especially the almost daily attacks taking place in Israel against its civilians by Hamas and Islamic Jihad, have rendered these harrowing acts routine, to the point that there is a risk that they will become accepted as 'part of life', as if they were God-ordained and impervious to human preventive initiative.

Even more worrying, however, is that the non-Shi'ite fundamentalist groups do not content themselves simply with getting closer to the Shi'ites in terms of audacity, sophistication and the spread of Islamikaze worldwide. They are able to capitalize on being Sunnis like most of their compatriots and draw other groups like the *Tanzim* or the Popular Front among the Palestinians, who are not avowedly fundamentalists or Muslim zealots, into the circle of self-sacrificing terrorists. It is quite extraordinary to watch members of the Marxist-oriented Popular Front talking of jihad and *istishhad* (martyrdom) when they set out for their operations. They realize the high status of the Islamikaze in their society, and since they act against the same enemy as the Hamas they seem to have no compunction about gaining popularity through using fundamentalist vocabulary and discourse. The Sunni Islamikaze are edging towards their Iranian model not only ideologically, as we shall see in the following pages, but even in their mores and patterns of behavior. For example: the headgear worn by members of Hamas, parading in the streets of the PA, under the permissive eyes of its security forces and often in collaboration with them; the video cassettes they leave behind as their will and parting speech for their loved ones, but which are often used by their operators as a 'patrimony' to preserve, and as an 'educational' tool to recruit others; and the slogans, the citations from the Holy Scriptures, and the words of praise about martyrdom and the martyrs, are all ominous imitations of the Shi'ite model.

Most intriguing, however, is the counter-example of the Sunnite *ta'zya* in reverse, widely and repeatedly practiced by the Hamas, and perhaps by others too. We have seen that Shi'ite martyrdom is closely associated with suffering and bitterness, initially out of passive identification with the supreme martyr Imam Hussein. Then, following the Islamic Revolution, which pushed the protest into the domain of action, the *ta'zya* grew more aggressive and a rallying point to the martyrs; yet it remained essentially a self-pitying, introspective, self-sustained, self-consoling and 'within-the-family' sort of affair. Within the Hamas and the Islamic Jihad, a new pattern has developed in which the terrorists re-play, re-emphasize, boast about and delight in the suffering they inflict on their victims. Indeed, every now and then – especially when the PA fails to intervene from fear of the populace, and especially following major acts of terrorism which have left dozens of Israelis dead or maimed – local chapters of the Hamas set up processions to mark the event. Wearing headgear of the hallowed *shahid*, they shout slogans of martyrdom, Israeli and American flags are burned and puppets representing Israeli and American leaders are stabbed by a frantic crowd. When they arrive at the end of the procession they fire volley after volley into the air with the illegal weapons they should not possess or be handling in the first place, and then the harrowing orgy of 'celebrations' begins.

We have become 'accustomed' to the horrendous sights of outlandish displays of jubilation when there is no one in sight to rein them in by Palestinians, and other Muslims when the news breaks of a 'successful' terrorist attack against America (as in the Twin Towers and the Pentagon) or against Israel or Jews at large. On these occasions, they distribute sweets, dance in the streets, and cry out 'Allah Akbar!!', the war-cry of Muslims in general, as if to attribute to Him those great deeds against their sworn enemies; or they perform the repetitive ritual of burning the flags of their victims or trampling them under their feet. What the demonstrators are unable to do to their enemies in person, they perform symbolically, praising Allah for His intercession on their behalf. But few outsiders have paid attention to the makeshift stages, erected at the end of these processions, which bring the celebrations to their climax. Often, the latest target they destroyed, for example an Israeli bus loaded with dozens of passengers on board, is meticulously reconstructed in paper, cardboard and cloth, painted so as to imitate the original, and then set ablaze to the lunatic cries of delight from the watching crowds. All the while, the perpetrators of the actual horror against the real Israeli bus, or more often their successors, who wish to cultivate the 'heritage' of the deceased Islamikaze, run around the stage in a frenzy, shooting long bursts of ammunition into the air, as if possessed by some unworldly power. They shout blood-curdling war cries, repeatedly invoke the Power of Allah, smash the burned carcass of the bus and stab with their bayonets the 'remnants' of the slain 'passengers'.

Even these horrendous scenes, which rely upon a different sense of reality than that known to civilized people, can be 'improved upon' by the Hamas. In Nablus, during the Palestinian Intifada that broke out in October 2000, a most disturbing 'exhibition' was presented for the general public in the city public square, in which replicas of the blown-up limbs and body pieces of Israelis who had perished in a restaurant attack by Hamas Islamikaze, were displayed in inhuman detail. It was only reports by the deeply disgusted foreign correspondents, and the protests of the Israelis, who did not want to relive that horror by seeing it replicated on the screens, that convinced the PA to move the exhibition indoors – not to close it down and arrest its promoters. Once again the thermometer was broken, but the fever refused to vanish. It is understood that by making these scenes widely available to Muslims, to the point of rendering them into a sort of popular street theatre, the organizers came to elicit respect and esteem for the deceased heroes, to encourage the *shahids* of tomorrow who are bound to emulate them, and to facilitate recruitment of new Islamikaze in the future – even among the majority of quietist Muslims, most of whom do not belong to the fundamentalist hardcore.

In other words, unlike the inward-turning stories of suffering re-enacted by the Shi'ites for the sake of commemoration, identification and self-hardening, in order to stand the excruciating things to come, the Hamas hardens its crowds and cultivates its audiences by boasting about the gruesome suffering inflicted upon their enemies. This change of focus – or a *ta'zya* in reverse – emanates from the difference between the universal Shi'ite doctrine of *istishhad* as the ultimate way to identify spiritually with Hussein, and the attitude of the Hamas, whose most urgent goal is to bring down its enemy. According to Palestinian thinking the most atrocious injustice has been done to them by Israel by its very birth and continued existence, for its presence in their midst and vicinity exposes their own helplessness and haplessness. They and Israel had begun from the same departure-point half a century ago, but while their sworn enemy has progressed, settled down its refugees, and prospered and advanced to the forefront of modernity and technology, they are still rotting in refugee camps for the third generation; the gap between them and Israel keeps yawning, and their refugees have remained dependent upon UN flour supplies and foreign aid (ironically, mainly American and Western, and less Arab and Islamic).

There is nothing more humiliating to the Palestinians than this. They therefore hate Israel, who shows them what they have failed to achieve by not following its example; and they spurn America, to whom they must turn as beggars to improve their lot. In consequence, rather than striving to equal Israel, in order to eliminate their dependence on America, they would rather attack them both in order to bring them down and wipe out the constructive model which constantly exposes them to shame. This is the reason that, when the Oslo process was at its hopeful beginnings, it was the fundamentalist Hamas who rejected it, lock, stock and barrel, for fear that it might reinforce and eternalize the superior stature of Israel, which they could neither bear nor be reconciled to. The ensuing demonization of Jews, Zionists and Israel, and the legitimization of ruthless attacks against them – as demonstrated in the recurrent Islamikaze onslaughts in Israeli streets and cities, aimed at intimidating the Israelis and wrecking their economy – are part of the mechanism of this externalized *ta'zya* in reverse, which is focused on the suffering inflicted on the enemies, rather than extolling their own suffering and sacrifice. The Twin Towers horror, also inflicted by Sunnite Islamikaze (the *al-Qa'ida* is one of their organizations), can therefore be interpreted in the same vein. Bin-Laden himself, not to speak of other Muslims throughout the world (see Chapter 1), was shown delighting in the humiliation of America and the role he played in helping to bring her down, as he had hoped.

The paradox is that while in Shi'ite Islam, notably after the end of the First Gulf War (1988), acts of Islamikaze had been restrained after their peak in the 1980s, it was precisely then that they were picked up by the Hamas and other Sunnite groups. In Lebanon, where it all started, the Hizbullah leadership had come to the conclusion that the exaggerated use of over-zealous youths for such acts had often ended in the death of the perpetrator without inflicting enough casualties on the enemy to justify that sacrifice. The Head of the movement, Sheikh Fadallah, has even issued a *fatwa*, allowing acts of Islamikaze only on special occasions.[9] Sheikh Na'im Qassem, the Deputy Secretary of Hizbullah, translated the guideline of his spiritual leader into specific directives, which he issued to the organization and released to the public in a press interview:

> First, one must obtain the authorization of an accredited Mufti. Anyone seeking to sacrifice himself, especially by car-bomb or blowing himself up, must first consult with a Lawyer of the Holy Law, because the soul is dear and can be expended only for the sake of the Islamic *Umma*. Secondly, after the religious authority delivers its verdict, the political leadership of the movement must deliberate on the political and military merits thereof. For when the same goals can be obtained without self-sacrifice, we do not send any Islamikaze to his death. The Islamikaze act is efficient only when other means are not deemed [by the leadership] to attain the same results.[10]

True, when the Islamikaze martyrdom was adopted by the Palestinians in the 1990s, there were tremendous debates among Palestinian scholars of the Holy Law whether they should be sanctioned. Dr Hamza Mustafa, the Head of the Shari'a College at al-Quds University, and himself a member of the Jerusalem-based Supreme Islamic Council, was emphatic in a press interview:

> Allah has determined that whoever commits suicide will end up in Hell. It is clear that suicide is unreservedly prohibited, because his soul is not his private property but belongs to Allah. There are those who believe that when suicide is committed as part of an act of war against the enemy, it is not forbidden, but most believe that suicide is prohibited in any case.[11]

A perception crystallized in those days, claiming that while the tiny Islamic Jihad group did opt for Islamikaze bombings as part of its world of self-sacrifice,[12] the larger and more popular Hamas did not encourage its membership to engage n this kind of operation. Sheikh Jamil Tamimi, one of the leaders of the Muslim Movement in the West Bank, for example, was often quoted as totally opposing these acts, not only due to the loss of life involved, but mainly because of the categorical prohibition against self-immolation in Islam. He did, however, recognize that some Muslim scholars permitted this sort of operation in the context of war and of struggle against the enemy, though he emphasized that he personally was opposed to this interpretation.[13] At the same time, however, Izz a-Din al-Qassam,[14] a hallowed name and symbol for both the Hamas and the Islamic Jihad, was cited as urging his followers to martyrdom, because 'martyrdom is only the beginning of the road … Jihad is either victory or martyrdom'.[15] 'Victory or martyrdom' was adopted as a slogan and battle-cry and naturally encouraged people to sacrifice themselves. Indeed, after the first Islamikaze act perpetrated by Islamic Jihad against Israelis in Beit Lid in 1994, one of the Gaza mosques' loud speakers proclaimed: 'Islamic Jihad has announced long ago that we have hundreds of volunteers for martyrdom, ready at any minute to hurt the Zionist enemy and burn the land under his feet.'[16]

THE MANUAL OF MARTYROLOGY

So while no one of authority in Islam permits suicide *per se*, those who allow, indeed urge, the martyr to sacrifice his life, use the commonly held view that the soul belongs to Allah in order to justify facilitating its return to Him. We are not talking here of a suicide, nor an accidental or incidental death incurred during battle – which is commonly dubbed *istishhad* (martyrdom) even when the martyr did not willingly embrace it – but a *'amalyya istishhadiyya* (an *act* of martyrdom), meaning that the individual has taken the conscious decision to sacrifice his life for the Islamic cause. In this case, the martyr has considered his act imperative for the achievement of his goal; he has 'purposely thrown himself to his death, confident that he is rushing to Paradise'.[17] And, since he neither wished for nor prepared any way of retreat, he has no other choice but to perish together with his targeted, or incidental, victims. Even the above-described Islamic Jihad's eagerness for martyrdom is, however, limited by the prohibition on killing innocent people, and the essence of the matter then becomes the definition of who is right and who is wrong, who is innocent and who is the culprit. At any rate, the struggle of the Islamikaze has become so sustained, that differences between Hamas and Islamic Jihad on the one hand, and the nuances distinguishing the innocent from the culprit on the other, have become completely blurred. Moreover, as already pointed out, other Palestinian organizations who have thus far had nothing to do with the Islamikaze, have been embracing martyrdom.

The author of the *Readings in Islamic Martyrology*,[18] which will be dealt with extensively below, indeed addresses himself to these basic dilemmas. He cites Shari'a sources which negate suicide, from the Koran, to the authoritative collection of *Hadith* edited by Bukhari, and finally decrees that it is unlawful for any Muslim to commit suicide – by poison, jumping from a high place, stabbing, suffocation, or the cutting of the main arteries in the hand or neck – under the threat of Hell punishment. He determines that Islam prohibits suicide out of despair, to avoid suffering due to illness or injury, or because of debt, poverty, fear, disaster, imprisonment or torture. Killing others can only be undertaken 'justly', according to Koranic injunction, for adultery, murder, apostasy and desertion of the company of the Believers.[19] By avoiding generalizations and overarching and abstract principles, and by keeping strictly faithful to the detailed cases of prohibition mentioned in the sources, the writer of *Qira'a* thus prepares his readers to conclude that everything that is not expressly forbidden is allowed.

The most fascinating aspect of these prohibitions is that they rest on the strict requirement grounded in the Koran[20] requiring respect for the sanctity of human life and the superior role of humans in Allah's creation. It is fascinating because it stands in stark contradiction to the seemingly unbearable facility with which the Islamikaze kill themselves; much more others. The resolution of this contradiction is the whole innovative import of the new convoluted interpretations undertaken by fundamentalist Muslim scholars. Man was created, according to the *Qira'a*, with the belief in Allah imprinted in his heart, and all his strength and spirit are devoted to the ordering of the created world. In order to guide man to follow the right path, Allah sent Prophets, apostles and His Messenger Muhammad, together with the Koran and the Sunna. Hence, the purpose of man on earth is to worship Allah (*'ibadat Allah*), which is more important even than human life. However, these two themes of the sanctity of human life and the worship of Allah are not contradictory.

This world is the scene of the struggle between good and bad, between the worship of God and the worship of Satan, the choice between a life of belief and the option of disbelief. The right choice by man of Truth in this world will bring him to eternal life in Paradise. Namely, if man devotes his life in this world to the worship of Allah, he will end up with eternal life in the hereafter. Thus, the laws of jihad not only do not contradict the prohibitions of self-immolation and of killing others unjustifiably, but are even complementary to them. And this is precisely what makes Islam a perfect religion in terms of its regard for human life: namely, the preservation of human life on the one hand, but also self-sacrifice for the sake of Allah. For, contrary to other doctrines which permit killing in the pursuit of material benefit, Islam supports the value of human life. And contrary to the theories that regard human life as a supreme value, Islam advocates the value of the worship of Allah. For, in the final analysis, according to this logic, setting up human life as the supreme good, permits injustice to persist without opposition, thus *eo ipso* violating human dignity. Conversely, the worship of Allah, which applies the tenets of enforcing justice and upholding right (*iqamat al-'adl wa-ihqaq al-haqq*), in itself constitutes the delicate balance between these two values. This kind of balance, which exists only in Islam, makes it the supreme human and cultural model in existence.

Naturally, when the author of this dissertation posits the worship of Allah as supreme, and the way of jihad as the apex of worship, he inescapably comes to the conclusion that any Believer who follows divine guidance with regard to jihad and emulates the Prophet in this respect, must evince his willingness to die for Allah.[21] To support his conclusion, the author cites a famous *Hadith*, in which the Prophet undertook to die for Allah, come back to life and then die once again.[22] This means that there was no bigger goal in the Prophet's own existence than to die for Allah, and to do so repeatedly. Therefore, this tenet constitutes, in the author's mind, a divine guideline that applies everywhere at all times. Hence, the necessity for Believers to embrace the road of self-sacrifice (*tad'hia*) and spiritual devotion (*badhl a-nafs*), becomes the central motif in the author's concept of jihad. He recounts many episodes from the life of the Prophet where the latter proved his devotion to these themes in his jihad against his enemies.[23] This had necessitated the

Prophet's readiness, indeed eagerness, to die in the course of jihad; and this should be the standard behavior for all Muslims who seek battle at the highest level of risk, who are eager to take part and sacrifice themselves. For this purpose, the author recognizes three kinds of battles, which must be ranked in accordance with the level of risk involved:

1. Where the chances of either dying or emerging alive are even. In this case, the surviving fighter would deserve honor (*karama*), and if he should perish, his death would be considered martyrdom (*shahada*). An illustrious Muslim fighter, Khalid ibn al-Walid, was quoted as wondering every day of battle whether he was escaping from the day of *karama* or that of *shahada*. That meant that dying in this fashion was a winning proposition in either case.[24]

2. Where the balance of power is not in the Muslims' favor, the Muslim fighter needs to display much more audacity to overcome the enemy against all odds. Once again, in many of such battles, in which the Companions of the Prophet (*sahaba*) participated, the Messenger of Allah provided a personal example by fighting valiantly and very close to the eye of the storm, in defiance of the dangers the enemy posed to him. Such harsh battles, where some of the *sahaba* made the ultimate sacrifice after they sustained so many multiple wounds that their corpses became unrecognizable,[25] of course became the ideal of combat to be followed by other Believers.

3. A third category of battle is when self-sacrifice is not only hallowed, as in the previous examples, but imperative as the only way to win it. This is where the act of jihad, itself highly regarded and lavishly rewarded in Heaven, transcends into the domain of an act of martyrdom (*istishhad*). The difference between standard self-sacrifice and spiritual devotion on the one hand, and this sort of conscious and deliberate act of martyrdom on the other, is that in the latter case a special strategy is adopted by a particular group of Muslims in order to rescue the entire Muslim Army or the whole of the Muslim *Umma* from dangerous straits, or to disrupt the enemy's war plans or to sow disarray in its ranks; or their strategy is geared to hurt the enemy's morale and boost the Muslims', or to bring such a disaster upon the enemy as to increase his losses and to decrease those of the Muslims.

One does not have to guess much in order to realize that the latter mode of combat is assuredly the highest and most adulated, and conforms typologically to the Islamikaze *modus operandi* that we have been dealing with in this work. We learn from the author of this treatise that he regards the Islamikaze not as a current, normal and routine strategy to fight the enemy in the battlefield where massive armies are deployed, but as a tactical device to be used when regular conventional battles are of no avail or about to be lost, and only when no other avenues are open to the Muslim armies to win the battles. In this context we may digress to find grounds to interpret the Twin Towers disaster, or the daily attacks by the Hamas and Islamic Jihad against Israel, once the Palestinian Intifada had failed to bring Israel to its knees. It is also noteworthy that when Yasser Arafat was at the end of his wits, when he realized that his declared campaign against Israel was falling flat on its face, and he despaired of gaining anything in his campaign of terror, he personally joined the fray by stating before delirious and equally despairing crowds, that he was ready to be a *shahid* for the sake of 'liberating' Jerusalem, and he repeatedly urged his followers to launch the jihad to realize the evasive dreams of the Palestinians.[26]

Once again, in this ultimate model of self-sacrifice, it is the Prophet himself (or his *sahaba*), who stars personally and makes daring self-sacrificing moves to save the entire Muslim strategy from failure in the battlefield – when the choice was self-sacrifice, namely martyrdom, in order to attain the victory of the Muslim armies, unless victory could be assured without it. From instances of this sort, drawn from the personal histories of the most worthy Muslims at the time of the Prophet, the author infers the implicit permission for Muslim fighters to sacrifice themselves for the public interest.[27] This is the stuff that the present day Islamikaze hang on to, to justify their acts of martyrdom. The author makes a very concrete connection between the two: he says that while today the Islamikaze can carry explosives on their bodies in order to carry out their mission, in the times of the Prophet the audacious fighter threw himself on the swords of the enemy, but that both modes of action are essentially the same. Similarly, just as in early Islam, when valiant Muslim fighters had to dismount their horses which were no match for the elephants of the enemy, and had to face those immense and frightening animals with only their bare swords in their hands, even though they were trampled upon and slaughtered, so today, an Islamikaze can defy planes and tanks with his body, and perish under their weight, or blow himself up on a mine-field in order to facilitate the passage of his fellow fighters into enemy territory, or their retreat into safety at the price of sacrificing himself. In both cases, the gates of Paradise are wide open to receive the new martyrs.[28]

Thus, the author of this treatise, which grants license to acts of Islamikaze, builds his argument tier after tier: first, he declares the value of the worship of Allah over the value of human life; then jihad as the supreme form of worship; and, since jihad involves self-sacrifice, three levels thereof are identified, the highest and most commendable of which is the *act of martyrdom*. All those stages are widely and soundly grounded on the precedents set by the Prophet himself or his Companions, whom the Believers hold in high esteem and therefore cannot dismiss the model they pose for all generations to come. Moreover, from examples in early Islam cited by the author, where self-sacrifice was not absolutely necessary,[29] one can deduce that the very defiance of death in the face of the enemy, in a battle for Islam and for Allah, is seen in itself as a worthy act which enables the deceased fighter to enter into the realm of Paradise. Moreover, as the author quotes the Prophet determining that jihad is the 'top of Islam's honey', he asserts that the act of martyrdom is the 'top of Jihad's honey', thus concluding that the higher the risk of perishing in such an act, the more precious is the martyr's status in the eyes of Allah.[30] To illustrate his point, the author cites a sprinkling of *Hadith* which demonstrate that, in the eyes of the Prophet, defying death for its own sake is in itself a worthy act, even when it is not absolutely necessary to achieve victory for Islam. For example, he cites the case of a Muslim fighter in the fateful battle of Badr, who took his armor off before the battle and was killed as a result although he won praise from the Prophet for his audacity.[31]

The author of the treatise does not avoid confronting the contradiction between his sanctification of death and the Koranic injunction to preserve life and escape peril. Once again precedents from the time of the Prophet and his Companions are cited: for example, of the fighter who literally committed suicide by single-handedly attacking an entire Byzantine column; whereupon a discussion ensued about whether this hero did not go to his certain death unnecessarily. For the author, again through a tortuous manipulation of *Hadith* accounts, the real peril is not death in battle, but in turning one's attention to material life and neglecting jihad activity.[32] The same goes for the explicit Koranic prohibition on committing suicide;[33] the author has to perform an intellectual summersault in order to circumvent the issue and manipulate it to prove his point. He says that while both suicide and an act of martyrdom require the express act of will on the part of the Islamikaze, what matters is not the act, but the intention (*nia*) of the martyr; this is what determines, in the final analysis, the quality of the act. Once again, the literature of the first Muslims is invoked as example and precedent. A case in point is the martyr for Islam who appears on the Day of Judgment and claims that he fought for Allah, but Allah reminds him that his courage was displayed only so that it could be said of him that he was courageous, whereupon he was dragged away on his face and consumed by the fire of Hell.[34]

This twist in the argument is extremely important, for it leaves the final judgment to Heaven; as even when a man performs acts of extreme audacity and is considered by peers, eye-witnesses and contemporaries as a hero of Islam and a well-deserved martyr, it is up to Allah to scrutinize his intention and decide otherwise. Conversely, a man may be considered by other humans to have committed a despicable suicide, but when Allah examines his intentions, he might be rewarded with the highest degree of martyrdom and status in Paradise. And this is precisely what sets suicide, a flight from the vagaries of life, apart from an act of martyrdom, which is a human response to the call of Allah to sacrifice oneself for the sake of the religion of Allah and to inflict loss on the enemies of Allah. The question remains as to whether martyrdom is the domain of the elected few who can cultivate the requisite pious intention, or whether it is a choice available to every willing, individual Muslim. The author suggests an analogy with the laws of conversion. Muslims are allowed to renege on their faith outwardly, says the essayist, under duress or threat against their lives, as long as in their hearts they do not budge from their creed.[35] However, insists the author, as against that permission (*rukhsa*), there exists also personal resolve (*'azima*), which is admittedly more difficult to pursue and to experience; this consists of the refusal to abandon the faith even in the face of certain death. Those who choose this course out of their own resolve, in spite of the allowance made by the *shari'a* in cases of imminent peril, of course attain the highest levels of martyrdom and reward.[36] And, since in every operation against the enemy there is a danger of death, the whole issue is one of the degree of the threat. Any act of martyrdom

of the Islamikaze kind carries with it certain death, though everything is ultimately in Allah's hand, and this is what places it at the
apex of martyrdom.

A SUMMARY AND A WARNING

This is, in a nutshell, the Doctrine of Martyrdom as viewed by the
author of *Qira'a*. The problem remains to discern the circumstances
under which this weapon is to be used, and to detect the enemy to
be targeted for such lofty operations. First of all, the act of martyrdom is an expression of jihad; but since this act is not necessarily
initiated or legitimated by an Islamic state, and is often necessitated
as an act of defense against an enemy who has invaded Muslim
homes and territory, it behoves individual Muslims to act by force
in order to redeem their rights. Therefore, unlike state-led jihad,
which is the duty of the entire Islamic polity, in this case it becomes
an individual duty (*fard 'ayn*, already mentioned above), to be
performed by the Muslims who are closest to the enemy and have
access to him. In the case of Palestine, which is the arena being
specifically discussed by the author, he focuses on the duty of jihad
against the combined Judeo–Western onslaught which constitutes
a threat to Islam. There, he says, physical attacks against Muslims –
expulsion, killing, wounding and imprisonment; concern over the
take-over of Muslim Holy Places to be replaced by Jewish ones; the
Judaization of Muslim land and the violation of the honor of
Muslim women; and, especially, the expansion of [Israel], which
serves as a launching pad to conquer more Muslim countries, and
forms a base to 'diffuse Jewish corruption, westernization, humiliation, enslavement and exploitation of Muslim society', are current
daily events.[37]

These perceived combined actions by the enemy amount, in
Islamic perception, to a declaration of war of annihilation against
Islam; something that impels any Muslim to take up jihad without
waiting for permission from non-existent authorities. Therefore:

> The Zionist enemy must be attacked by all means permitted
> by the Shari'a, and all possible efforts ought to be expended to
> that end, not only by the Palestinians but by the entire Muslim
> *Umma*. For Zionism is not a local enemy, it is a universal one,
> it is the sword that tears apart this blessed land.[38]

This analysis by necessity leads the author to conclude that the actual battle falls into the third category which makes acts of martyrdom imperative and entails an individual commitment by every Muslim to engage the enemy. The current danger to the Muslim *Umma* is great, both due to the rifts and splits within Muslims on the one hand, and the combined power of the Zionist enemy and his allies on the other. According to the author, the situation of the Muslims today is worse than during Crusader times; therefore jihad in Palestine acquires its own character and requires acts of martyrdom to take precedence over all other modes of warfare. For him, all the pre-required conditions to launch such acts exist in Palestine with regard to the Zionist enemy, particularly when all other conventional military avenues have proved insufficient or ineffective, due to the military superiority of his tactics, equipment and technology. Even laying explosives within enemy targets would not help, due to his vigilance or due to the random effect on victims, who may turn out to be women and children.[39]

On the other hand, he says, in an act of martyrdom, the explosive is focused on precise targets that cannot be missed. Moreover, due to the interception of weapons and explosives by Israel before they could be activated, it becomes imperative to use the little there is in the most focused and infallible manner, through the Islamikaze. From these harsh words of the essayist one can draw many sad conclusions:

1. The precise targets chosen for these acts of martyrdom, which are supposed to spare children and women, seem to be ignored by the perpetrators, since most of the victims have been women, children and aged people.
2. The more counter-terrorist attacks succeed in paralyzing the terrorist organizations (what we call the infrastructure of terror) such as the Hamas and the Islamic Jihad, the more their members will be pushed to resort to acts of Islamikaze.
3. The more frequent the acts of Islamikaze, the more evident the failure of the organizations in the overall campaign.

Another advantage that the author seems to ascribe to the acts of Islamikaze, is their effect on morale:

> By Allah's grace, one or two fighters succeed in breaking into the lines of the enemy, then attack a group of the enemy's

forces by an act of martyrdom, thereby inflicting on him heavy damage and tottering his morale in the face of the indestructible fighting spirit of the martyrs.[40]

He also asserts that by this kind of operation, the entire Islamic *Umma* is rescued, as its casualties are minimized, the enemy's are maximized and his ability to retaliate is weakened. The destruction of any part of the enemy force means the corresponding saving of lives of hundreds of Muslim women, children and aged, and extricating them from his bloody grip. All this is certainly worth sacrificing a few fighters for. It is imperative, however, that those who embrace this road should do it with *nia*, namely not an escape from life and its vagaries, but with the intention of jihad for Allah, in order to kill the enemies. This is, in fact, he concludes, the best and most economical possible way to engage in jihad in Palestine under the prevailing circumstances.[41]

To sum up this completely amazing doctrine, which first pays lip service to the value of human life, but then posits the value of worship of Allah above it, and then jihad as the highest degree of worship, it may be said that it actually overlooks, dismisses and belittles the entire humanistic concept of the sanctity of life as it is understood in Western tradition. Even though the injunction to self-sacrifice in jihad is divided into three levels of necessity – unnecessary if there is an equilibrium of forces with the enemy; desirable when the rapport of forces is in the Muslims' disfavor; and imperative when perilous danger threatens the community – one cannot escape the impression that this edifice of rationalizations is geared to dwarf human life in the final analysis and make it subservient to religious fanaticism. This is borne out by the fact that the author lauds self-immolation in the process of the act of martyrdom, even martyrdom for its own sake, and even when it is not needed for the success of the operation, for he seems to say that death for Allah, as long as that is the intention, has a special significance and is to be considered the highest form of martyrdom. In fact, he is actually speaking about the sanctity of death, which in a very roundabout, paradoxical, way stems from the basic assumption of the sanctity of life. His reluctance to bind Muslims in general to such a harrowingly demanding injunction is, however, noteworthy, and he limits it to the few who have attained such a degree of self-sacrifice as to be able to commit it without hesitation, and who would be rewarded in the higher reaches of Paradise.

One characteristic of this treatise is its fundamentalist approach to the sources and their interpretation: it harks back to the times of the Prophet and his Companions, quotes the Koran and the *Hadith* profusely, and almost disregards the 13 centuries of subsequent *shari'a* developments. For, had he surveyed the entire span of Muslim Law, it is doubtful whether he would have come to the ultimate conclusion that every 'true Muslim' must be ready, eager and willing to sacrifice his life in the cause of jihad. He himself complains in his essay, on more than one occasion, about the attempts made throughout history to 'hide the true meanings of jihad and martyrdom'; therefore, it was only natural for him to go back to the sources and squeeze them to extract and justify his fundamentalist interpretations. For him the 'true Muslims' are those who follow the radical interpretations, in contrast to those who have been spoiled and diluted by Western and modern foreign ideas and who are no longer faithful to the pure creed.

Even so, the *Hadith* cited by the author are not always accurate and sometimes are turned around so as to illustrate the point he wants to make, even when it is not certain that the original, or the most authoritative version, had been intended to have exactly that meaning. It is interesting to draw some comparisons with other versions which appear in books by other scholars such as Ibn al-Athir; but this is beyond the scope of this study. At any rate, it is clear that because some radical Muslim movements who have sanctified self-sacrifice are accused of adopting Shi'ite theology, the author is obviously making an effort to stay within the bounds of the Sunna, even if it is the most puritanical and strict interpretation thereof. In the context of universal Muslim combat for survival, which the author describes as the context in which Islamikaze acts are imperative, one is led to believe that without the supreme act of martyrdom, there is no other way to rescue Islam from its demise. Paradoxically, as we have indicated above, it is precisely the perceived impending danger to Islam which forces the martyrs to commit their fanatic act of self-immolation; and it is their desperate act of self-sacrifice which signals that they have failed to transmit their message in some more acceptable and less horrific way.

NOTES

1. Raphael Israeli, 'Islamikaze and their Significance', *Journal of Terrorism and Political Violence*, 9, 3 (1997), pp. 96–121.

2. Ibid.
3. A.J. Wensinck, 'The Oriental Doctrine of the Martyrs', *Med Akad, Series A*, 6, 1 (1921), pp. 1–28.
4. Ignaz Goldziher, *Muhammedanische Studien* (Halle: University of Halle, 1989), p. 387.
5. Wensinck, p. 9.
6. Cited by Wensinck, pp. 5–6.
7. Amir Taheri (a former pre-revolutionary Editor of the daily *Kaihan*), *The Spirit of Allah* (Tel Aviv: Am Oved, 1986), p. 148 [Hebrew translation]. See also Mahmoud Ayoub, *Redemptive Suffering in Islam*, pp. 148–58; Emanuel Sivan, *Muslim Radicals* (Tel Aviv: Am Oved, 1985), pp. 192–5 [Hebrew].
8. Amir Tahiri, p. 55. See also Hamid Algar, *Islam and Revolution* (Berkeley, CA: UC Press, 1981), pp. 329–43; and Martin Kramer (ed.), *Protest and Revolution in Shi'ite Islam* (Tel Aviv: Tel Aviv University), p. 29 [Hebrew].
9. Report by Guy Bechor, Arab Affairs commentator of *Ha'aretz*, 6 December 1995, p. b2.
10. Ibid.
11. *Ha'aretz*, 23 January 1995, p. 6a.
12. Meir Hatina, *Palestinian Radicalism: The Islamic Jihad* Movement (Tel Aviv: Tel Aviv University, 1994), pp. 79–80.
13. *Ha'aretz*, 23 January 1995.
14. Izz a-Din al-Qassam was the founder and hero of the Islamic movement in Palestine in the 1930s, and engaged in battle both against the British Mandatory forces and the Jewish self-defense groups, until his death in combat in Samaria in 1935. His name was picked up by the Hamas, upon its foundation in 1988, and given to the military arms of the organization.
15. Hatina, *Palestinian Radicalism*, p. 82.
16. A citation from a leaflet distributed by Islamic Jihad, *Ha'aretz*, 23 January 1995, p. 6a. The leaflet was reportedly headed by a citation from the Repentance Sura in the Qur'an which promises Paradise to those who kill and are killed in the battles of Allah.
17. *Qira'a fi Fiqh al-Shihada* (Readings in Islamic Martyrology), the very subtitle of this work, was published in 1988 as a special addendum to *al-Islam wa-Filastin* that appears in Nicosia, Cyprus, but has been the ideological supporter of the Islamikaze operations against Israel. See *al-Islam wa-Filastin*, 5 June 1988, p. 9.
18. See note 17.
19. *Qira'a*, p. 3.
20. The Cow Sura, verses 28–36.
21. *Qira'a*, p. 4.
22. Citing Malik ibn Anas, *Ahadith al-Jami' al'Saghir*, in *Qira'a*, p. 4.
23. Ibid., p. 7.
24. Ibid., p. 8.
25. Ibid., pp. 8–9.
26. Palestinian Authority Broadcasting, shown on Israeli Television, 24 January 2002, 20:00 News Bulletin.
27. *Qira'a*, p. 12.
28. Ibid.
29. Ibid., pp. 10–12.
30. Ibid., p. 10.
31. Ibid., pp. 10–12.
32. Ibid., p. 10.
33. Qur'an, Women Sura, verse 29.
34. *Qira'a*, p. 6.
35. The Bee Sura, verse 108.
36. *Qira'a*, pp. 10–11.
37. *Qira'a*, p. 7.
38. Ibid.
39. Ibid., pp. 14–15.
40. Ibid.
41. Ibid.

PART 3

Peace and Its Demise

10. The Oslo Delusion*

Since the onset of the Oslo peace process between Israel and the Palestinians (1993), an entire structure has been erected which has no foundation; an entire set of axioms has been woven which assumed that once they were addressed, negotiated and agreed upon, the fundamental problems pitting the parties against each other would become soluble. For example, it was, for a time, assumed that Israelis and Arabs depended on outside mediation to negotiate, and the various Camp David conferences were cited as 'proof'; while in effect the Sadat Peace Initiative (1977), and the Oslo Accords (1993) were the result of secret and direct bilateral negotiations between these parties. Another assumption that was repeated *ad nauseam* in all international forums posited that the Israeli settlements were an obstacle to peace, while they proved not to be so in the Israel–Egypt Peace Accords (1979), and even in the ongoing Israel–Palestinian negotiations. In any case, when the discussions faced crisis or were aborted, it was due to other issues dividing the parties, such as Jerusalem and the right of return of the Palestinians, not specifically the settlements. If anything, the case can be made for the argument that without the settlements, which lend urgency to the issue of territory, maybe it would have been that much more difficult to coax the Palestinians to go to the negotiating table in the first place.

Foremost among these assumptions was the untested fixation which posited that the Palestinian issue was 'the core of the Arab–Israeli dispute', as if it were impossible to resolve other problems without first addressing this or, conversely, as if resolving this would usher in solutions for all the rest. The fact is that the Egyptian–Israeli and Jordanian–Israeli Peace Accords (1979 and

*Originally published as *The Oslo Delusion: Or the Collapse of Axioms*, ACPR Policy Paper No. 126 (Sha'arei Tikva: Ariel Centre, 2001).

1994, respectively) were signed, for what they were worth, regardless of the continued festering of the Palestinian issue, and that the threats from Iraq, Syria or Iran do not appear to diminish when the prospects brighten for an Israeli–Palestinian settlement. If anything, the Palestinian issue, far from constituting the incentive behind the ongoing Arab and Islamic enmity towards Israel, has been the pretext and rationalization for their continuing hostility. Instead of urging the Palestinians to settle with Israel, they put shackles on their hands through coaxing, threats and promises of ultimate victory if they should wait for outside deliverance. In fact, two decades into the peace accords between Israel and Egypt, the cold peace persists, visits of Egyptians to Israel are curtailed by Cairo, anti-Semitic and anti-Israeli campaigns prevail in the government controlled media, and Israel, the Jews and Zionism, independently of the fortunes of the Israeli–Palestinian track, are treated with scorn and abuse, not much unlike the pre-peace period.

Until the 1967 War, which catapulted Israel into the stage as a power to be reckoned with, the very existence of the embattled Jewish State, within its dangerously impossible boundaries, attracted much of the Western world's sympathies. For in the Arab–Israeli equation, the Arabs were numerous, overwhelming, wealthy and powerful, while the fledgling Jewish nation seemed small, resourceless, teetering on the edge, threatened and besieged. It appeared to owe its survival to its pioneering and innovative spirit, and to world Jewry and its Western benefactors. But, following Israel's stunning victory in that war, roles were inverted: Israel now appeared as the conqueror, the expansionist, the victor and the successful; while the hapless Arabs gladly took on the appearance of the defeated, the victims, the conquered, and the humiliated, who needed the world sympathy to deliver them from the claws of Zionism. It was then also expedient on their part, with the active support of intellectuals in the West, including Israel itself, not to speak of the diplomatic and military support of the Communist Bloc, to narrow the equation of the conflict to the Israel–Palestinian arena, where Israel appeared more threatening, oppressing and evil as ever, while the occupied and underdog Palestinians warranted the support of the world, materially and morally.

Against that backdrop, the Palestinian national struggle attained its apogee; the PLO and Yasser Arafat became household names, both in the chanceries of the world and in the living rooms of practically everyone. It was in those years that the myth was cultivated that the Palestinians were the 'core of the conflict' and the rest of the Arab–Israeli dispute was made subservient and hostage to them. So much so, that through a long process of guilt-cultivation among the Left in general, and self-flagellation by the Israeli Left in particular, which prompted them to revise the basic ethos of Zionism and question the very validity of the Zionist enterprise, they lent credence to the Palestinian claim that Israel had been born in sin and that unless that wrong was redressed, the Arab–Israeli dispute would remain insoluble. The moral burden was then shifted from the negativist and politicidal broadsides of the Arabs against the existence of Israel to the latter's obstinacy to deny the Palestinians what it had itself struggled to achieve: a place under the sun, recognized by the world community.

The steady erosion in Israel's stance in the world, when faced with this systematic onslaught on its decency and *raison d'être*, ultimately produced Israeli governments who were ready to go to Madrid, Washington, Oslo, Cairo and Sharm e-Sheikh to engineer a peace accord with the Palestinians, precisely after the latter had evinced their commonality of purpose with Saddam Hussein whom they enthusiastically raised on the pedestal during the Gulf War and its aftermath. The reversal in Israel, and in consequence in the USA, was so complete that the order of the day became a quick, complete and comprehensive settlement of the Palestinian issue. By shouldering that responsibility alone and exonerating the Palestinians themselves, and other Arab countries from the search for a solution, Israel was soon left in solitude like a thorn in the desert, to produce the panacea. And the deeper Israel delved into this impasse, the higher the expectations were from her to deliver. In other words, most of the concessions were Israel's while the Palestinians neatly aligned themselves on the receiving end, as if they had no responsibility to shoulder and no self-reckoning to undergo. Any snag, any friction, any misunderstanding, any prolongation of the debate, were then systematically laid at Israel's door, due to her 'procrastination' and lack of 'good faith'.

Chief among those concerns which caused the negotiations to stall once and again, were Jerusalem and the unexpected insistence by the Palestinians on the right of return for their refugees. Contrary to Israel's conclusion, since 1967, that Jerusalem would remain 'forever united under Israeli sovereignty', the Palestinians meant business when they stood by their resolution that their

Palestinian state must be crowned by Jerusalem as its capital. Thus, another of Israel's long-held assumptions was found to have no leg to stand on. It became clear that Israel's self-delusion that it could attain peace with the Arabs and at the same time maintain the whole of Jerusalem under its rule had evaporated. Similarly, all the 'understandings' – according to which the Palestinians were supposed to have internalized and digested the unfeasibility of the repatriation of their four million refugees to Israel proper – proved to be deep and irreconcilable misunderstandings. With these two fundamental assumptions vanishing, the gaps between the parties grew truly unbridgeable.

Probably the most disappointing among the collapsed assumptions was the realization that the substantive change that Oslo introduced in the relations between Israel and the Palestinians, namely that differences were to be settled peacefully by way of negotiations, proved totally illusory. In fact, as an immediate result of the signing of the Accords, the intensity of Palestinian violence against Israel dramatically increased in comparison to the era preceding it. Distraught Israelis were told that they were asked to make the 'sacrifices for peace', an interesting innovation for an embattled people who had been urged to make sacrifices for survival during the preceding decades. It also soon appeared that the PA which was supposed to ensure the peace and rein in the terrorist groups under its aegis, was turning a blind eye to their anti-Israeli activities, at times even condoning and aiding them, sometimes condemning the acts of violence, not their perpetrators, as if they were natural calamities, and often blaming them on the Israelis themselves.

This enabled the Palestinians to pursue, simultaneously, a two-pronged policy of negotiating with the Israelis while at the same time allowing a controlled level of violence to prod their interlocutors to submit to their demands. For a time, this behavior raised doubts about whether the PA exercised effective control over its citizenry, especially when Arafat condemned the acts of violence, declared that he had no part in them and that they were perpetrated by the 'enemies of peace', and vowed to avert their recurrence. But it turned out that he could move decisively against them, notably the Hamas, when they posed a danger to his rule. Otherwise, he lauded their martyrs and even participated in their funerals, as in the case of the 'Engineer', Yihye Ayyash who was eliminated by Israel. Moreover, Arafat himself never desisted from his incitement against Israel and from calling for a holy war (jihad) to liberate Jerusalem from her. His campaigns of incitement, which ran contrary to his commitments in Oslo, were reflected in the official Palestinian media and in the Authority's school textbooks.

The Israeli government went along with this line of thinking, claiming that the PA's '100 percent efforts' to prevent terrorism did not necessarily mean '100 percent success'; thus letting Arafat off the hook. Moreover, by calling the Hamas terrorists 'suicide-bombers', it implied that these were unpredictable and insane people who acted alone and therefore could not be stopped. The Israeli public was asked to brace itself for more acts of this sort, and they did occur. Had the Israeli government acknowledged that the terrorists were trained, financed, indoctrinated and dispatched by an organization within the PA (Hamas or Islamic Jihad), it would also have come under pressure to move decisively against their bases and eliminate them, something it would not do in order to preserve the 'peace process'.

And so, the reciprocity that was embedded in the Oslo Accords, and which is inherent in any contract or treaty between parties, was gradually eroded, with the Palestinians overlooking their obligations and the Israelis overlooking their partners' oversight. Paradoxically, the Palestinians, who were on the receiving end of the deal and should therefore have been interested in implementing the agreement to the letter, soon learned that they could still make Israel deliver its part even when they procrastinated on theirs; while the Israelis seemed so eager to finalize the deal and prove that the Oslo strategy was sound, that they became more and more forgiving, until they unwittingly contributed to the collapse of the Accords. Indeed, Israel had committed itself to evacuate territories gradually, in return for Palestinian pledges to eliminate terror and incitement, collect illegal weapons, cut the Palestinian Police to the agreed size, and extradite criminals who found refuge in its territory. Much of this was not done, yet the demand that Israel should evacuate territory was constant. Netanyahu's innovation in the Wye Agreements of October 1998, was to specifically link Israeli withdrawals with Palestinian implementation of their obligations, and was summarized in the catchy phrase: 'When they give they will receive, if they do not give they will not receive.' But soon the Labor opposition to his rule began mocking that slogan and unilaterally accusing Netanyahu, not the Palestinians, of obstructing the peace. All the Palestinians had to do, then, was to demonize

Netanyahu with the Israeli Left's support, and to wait him out until he was dethroned and replaced by Barak.

When that happened in May 1999, the Palestinians were elated and their expectations were raised. The new Prime Minister energetically and confidently re-launched the peace process, assuming that the Palestinians would accept with gratitude his far-reaching concessions which violated the taboos that previous Israeli governments had imposed. Instead, the entire Oslo process blew up in his face. Only now did he finally realize that, regardless of who leads Israel in the negotiations, its maximal concessions for the sake of peace would remain far beneath the Palestinians' minimal demands, short of which there can be no agreement between the parties. That realization, which started with Barak's sobering up in Camp David II (July 2000), came to full bloom when the Palestinians decided in late September 2000 to back it up with large-scale acts of violence which delivered the *coup de grâce*, and finally buried all the assumptions upon which the Oslo Accords had been erected. It was realized that what was at stake was not a quantitative issue of assets and territory, which could be negotiated and settled through compromise around a negotiating table, but a value-loaded and qualitative matter which could not be negotiated away and which touched upon the very existence of the Jewish State. Moreover, as the Palestinian stance on these matters is endorsed by the Arab and Islamic worlds, and powerful doses of religious vocabulary and symbols are injected into this already difficult debate, the dispute becomes anything but soluble.

The Middle East has experienced a wide gamut of situations between the two poles of war and peace, therefore one is not necessarily only the absence of the other. In other words, one does not have, perhaps, to achieve some sort of utopian peace as a prerequisite for terminating a state of war. Hence the need to define what peace is. Is peace value- and culture-bound? Is it enough to agree on words which have an accepted dictionary meaning, or is one bound to deal with the agreed upon terms in their relative cultural dimension so as to avoid the pitfalls of misapprehension and misinterpretation, which produce frustration and bitterness? Aren't the gray areas of armistice, cease-fire, truce, interim agreement, disengagement, and the like, more realistic a pursuit than the elusive total peace; just as agreed armistice lines, no man's lands, separation and demarcation lines, and demilitarized zones, seem more down to earth than constantly contested and challenged boundaries and international borders in this part of the world? Not only Israel's borders with the Arab world are indeed a subject of constant controversy, but among Arab states themselves territorial disputes abound: Iraq–Kuwait, Algeria–Morocco, Morocco–Mauritania, Syria–Lebanon, Yemen–Saudi Arabia, etc. So, Israel's disenchantment with temporary or ongoing territorial arrangements with its neighbors ought perhaps to occasion some rethinking.

EYESORES AND DISSONANCE

One day in January 2001, at the height of the al-Aqsa Intifada, the Israeli press carried the picture of a procession in Ramallah, which paraded a donkey wearing a Jewish prayer shawl and a Star of David in the shape of a swastika. The Israeli public was deeply shaken, regarding this act of profanation and abuse as a continuation of the torching of the Jewish synagogue in Jericho and Joseph's Tomb in Nablus during the initial stages of the current upheaval. In all those cases, what transpired was a Palestinian determination, born out of frustration and hatred, to take revenge on Jewish religious symbols, knowing full well the hurt and anguish they would cause among the Israeli public. The angered and disappointed readership of the papers was reminded that, when in 1997 a settler from Hebron held up a poster in public in which the Prophet Muhammad was reviled by the drawing of a pig in his proximity, she was arrested, tried for anti-religious incitement and incarcerated for three years. That event, which rightly caused Muslim outrage, was condemned, across the board, by Israeli politicians and religious leaders, who understood the sensitivity of such provocations. Israelis therefore expected to see a similar reaction on the part of the Palestinian authorities and their religious hierarchy, but in vain.

This phenomenon of poking the Jew in the eye in order to demean him by diminishing his national and religious symbols, has been repeatedly manifested in the age-old desecration of Jewish sanctified objects, such as the Israeli national flag, or parchments of the Torah, or anything the Arabs could lay their hands on. The burning of the flag, which is usually done in conjunction with the American flag throughout the Islamic world, has grown into a ritual whenever dissatisfied mobs gather to air their frustration against Israel or the Jews. More ominously, even more respectable gatherings, such as the annual commemoration by the Egyptian Lawyers Association of the peace their country signed with Israel in 1979, have adopted the custom of burning the Israeli flag at the height of the ceremony. 'They are angry and frustrated', we are told, and therefore we are asked to 'understand'. The current Intifada erupted during the Jewish High Holidays and no respect was paid to them by the Palestinians. Violence was launched against the Israelis across the width and length of the West Bank and Gaza, worshippers at the Western Wall were pelted with rocks, and the police were constrained to stop their prayers for fear of their safety. But when Ramadan set in, it was the Israeli Police who protected the right of the Muslims to worship freely on the Temple Mount, and it was taken as a matter of course that the Israeli authorities should handle Arab disturbances with extra care so as not to arouse Muslim sentiments.

The result is that the Muslims under Israeli rule or in the neighboring Palestinian territories have become accustomed to thinking that their lofty faith deserves the respect of everyone, as of right, while other religions, especially Judaism, must absorb without protest all the scorn, humiliation, calumniation and abuse they might care to heap on them. Thus we find the Chief Mufti of al-Aqsa Mosque in Jerusalem, who was appointed by Arafat, denying any Jewish link to the Temple Mount and refusing to recognize any remote Jewish right there, while aggressively declaring the place as a Muslim *waqf*; namely claiming that the Muslims alone have the exclusive claim to that compound. And, lest the Jews advance the argument that the rubble of their Holy Temple is buried under the Mosque, he declared that the validity of the *waqf* also extended seven stories above and seven beneath the actual level of the contemporary Muslim buildings. The experiment in sharing that the Israelis had instituted at the Tomb of the Patriarchs in Hebron since 1967, far from serving as a precedent and model of tolerance, on the contrary sharpened the acuity of the totally negative stance of the Muslims towards the Jews.

The total deprecation of the Jew as such in the Arab and Palestinian thinking and media is not new; it has accompanied the fortunes of the Arab–Israeli conflict since its inception. It has Islamic, anti-Semitic and specific roots which are linked to the immediate grievances of the Palestinians in view of their dispute with Israel. It is evident that in a confrontational situation no one expects the parties to love one another or even to develop empathy towards one another. However, even in a state of hatred, where there is contempt and deprecation of the rival, there must be some measure of respect for facts and reality, for otherwise one begins to project on the other one's own defaults and to indulge in such an exercise in self-delusion as to end up harming oneself and one's own interest. One may take the basic deficiencies of the enemy and inflate them so as to score propaganda points. But when one invents 'facts' and 'events' that have no leg to stand on, one by necessity creates a devil larger than life with which no accommodation is possible. Because then, one becomes trapped in one's rhetoric and understandably abhors any settlement that the satanic one has fabricated.

We are not talking about Goebbels-style libel and calumnies, which are stated in the belief that if lies are repeated often enough and insistently enough they end up becoming the recognized 'truth', but about the fabrication of verifiable delusions, and the manufacturing of 'histories' to elevate oneself and deprecate the others. In the first category one is reminded of the legendary 'map hanging on the Knesset wall' which allegedly depicted the coveted boundaries of Israel 'from the Nile to the Euphrates'. There are Palestinian members of the Israeli Knesset (those mistakenly dubbed 'Israeli Arabs'), who could confirm as firsthand witnesses the vanity of that claim, but the Palestinian leadership would not let the facts confuse it. It is said that when Sadat visited the Knesset in November 1977, some of his aids unabashedly asked to see the map for themselves and could not be convinced that it had never existed. Of late, the Palestinians have discovered another 'irrefutable proof' of their allegation when they spotted the two blue stripes on the Israeli flag which, for them, represent those two rivers. Go and explain to them that the stripes are taken from the Jewish prayer shawl, that same artifact that they desecrated when they paraded a donkey wearing it in the streets of Ramallah. Incidentally, on a previous instance, Arafat presented in a press conference the coin of the Israeli ten agorot (dime) that carries an ancient historical stamp, as 'proof' of the territorial ambitions of Israel.

To the second category belongs the invention of the myth which uncritically relates the origins of the Palestinians to the Canaanites as a fact of history. If this was done only in order to create a normative national myth which would cement their claim on the land

in a remote past, one could perhaps nod with a smile of understanding. But when they, at the same time, deny the existence of
one millennium of documented Jewish history in that land, with its
two commonwealths and exiles, just in order to brand the Jews as
liars, forgers of history and usurpers of the truth, and they end up
believing in their own concoction to boot, this is self-delusion pure
and simple. Or when they invent a 'text' and claim in their official
publications and textbooks that it is a 'citation' from the Talmud,
and they repeat that with conviction, this is nothing short of a
pathological deficiency which deceives them and prevents them
from comprehending their enemy or sensing his true nature,
motives and ambitions.

In June 1967, as the Arab Air Force lay in tatters, President
Nasser of Egypt was assuring King Hussein on the telephone that
Israel was being beaten and decimated, and urged him to join the
glory of victory, which he disastrously did. During the 1973 War, it
was Sadat who assured his Arab audiences that the Americans were
fighting side-by-side with Israel, hence the temporary difficulties
that his armies were experiencing in the Sinai. And when his attack
was repulsed, and his troops were trapped by Israel's pincer
maneuver, he still claimed that he had vanquished Israel and won
a victory. In both these cases, it is not that the leaders did not
receive adequate reports from their subordinates in the field, but
they were constrained by their shame culture to deny defeat and
create an illusory world of success, against an enemy that had
always been depicted as cowardly, weak, dependent on others and
shunning battle. How else could they explain to themselves and to
their audiences this incomprehensible reversal of events? The end
result was that when they woke up from their delusions they felt
deeply humiliated, and were inexorably bent on vengeance in
order to redress the wrong. That is hardly conducive to reconciliation and peacemaking in the post-conflict era.

There are two contradictory aspects to these distortions which
feed Arab beliefs regarding the Jews and Israel. On the one hand,
they harbor a natural propensity to demean the enemy, to deprecate and despise him, but at the same time also to impute to him
supra-natural demonic forces. For one has to explain the enemy's
occasional successes which seemingly run counter to his inherently despicable nature. Therefore, only if Israel is linked to a great
power, for example, can its military or technological prowess be
explained; when an Arab defeat is imputed, not to Israel's courage

or *savoir faire* – for that does not fit their image of the cowardly Jew – but to some mysterious weapon that Satanic Israel has ways of attaining by Satanic means, that provides a plausible, if incorrect, rationalization to hang on to. Then, the shame and humiliation becomes more bearable, pending devising a way of avenging it.

In this state of affairs, where Jews are inherently evil, the scum of the earth, cruel, devoid of human feelings, scheming, greedy and treacherous, anything that can be attributed to them, even the most incredible and outlandish, is possible. Similarly for the State which they created, which is by necessity tinged and stained by their murky and negative character. Therefore, there is no limit to the imaginary atrocities that Israel can be blamed for and there is no boundary, in time or space, to its evil-doings across the world. Muslim authors accuse Israel of having caused all wars by undermining all societies in order to conquer them from within, and denounce the Jews for having instituted both capitalism and communism, and taking over the media and financial centers, so as to enslave the world. *The Protocols of the Elders of Zion* – which is considered worn-out anti-Semitic propaganda, citation of which is a punishable crime in most Western societies – fares well and is alive and kicking in contemporary Arabia, including Palestinian writings, political platforms, propaganda incitements, media commentaries, school textbooks, popular stereotypes and religious sermons. Therefore, any lie, story, accusation, libel or calumny about the Jews and Israel is easy to diffuse and quickly absorbed, and finds fertile grounds on which to grow, bloom, prosper and multiply.

These are not necessarily lies that are concocted in propaganda offices, that are notoriously part of the ministries of 'national guidance' in the Arab world, but simple delusions and wishful thoughts that are imagined on the spur of the moment in a public square, in a classroom, in an editorial room, at the rostrum of a university or the pulpit of a mosque, or in a political speech. And this is enough to ensure their instant propagation as a verified and irrefutable gospel. And the more the story sounds unlikely or unreal, the more easily it is circulated and the more 'authoritative' it becomes. In this mental make-up, where reality and imagination are intertwined and indistinguishable, what is unfeasible in the real world becomes a fact of life, once the mind that wished it, imagined it to be so.

Hence, the horror stories about the Jews and Israel that we hear and read, day in, day out, in the Arab media, in sermons in the mosques, in political speeches, in 'scholarly' textbooks, and in general Arab discourse, among the Palestinians in particular. They are not only the fruit of premeditated viciousness, but the produce of popularly crafted stereotypes, beliefs and rumors, which have become part and parcel of the mental make-up of the Arabs, especially now during this time of Israeli–Palestinians strife. The Jew, the Zionist and Israel are the negative models to be looked at and hated, because they are the devil personified, and their demonization makes them legitimate prey for attack, humiliation and the channeling of anger and frustration. This is the picture constructed for the eyes of their children, soldiers, refugees and media consumers because it is truly believed that it reflects truth and reality. The Arabs need that negative image of the Jew in order to aggrandize themselves, by comparison, as the 'noble Arab nation' and the 'righteous Palestinian people', following the 'lofty Faith of Allah', who face the cunning but undeserving Jews, the treacherous and rebellious Judaic faith, and the heartless and wild Zionists.

The Blood Libel, for example, is a sum total of those innate Jewish depredations and perfidy. Mustafa Tlas, the Syrian Defense Minister for the past 20 years, has made an 'academic' career out of this abomination which he never tires of peddling to his eager Arab audiences and to his revisionist audiences in Paris as a 'fact of history', based on his 'research' and 'experience'. Denial of the *Shoah*, and the concurrent praise of the European revisionist historians who champion the same, are current in the Arab world, including among intellectuals and academics who ought to know better.

It may well be that all these patterns of behavior emanate from naive or simply misinformed data that the Palestinians and the rest of the Arabs are constantly fed. More serious, however, is when these anti-Semitic utterances are covered by a religious cloak, which makes them not merely devices of hatred for Arab/Muslim self-preservation (something that could theoretically be altered via education, enlightenment and open-mindedness), but absolute statements that are backed up by citations from the Holy Koran or the *Hadith*, or from latter-day luminaries of Islamic fundamentalism that render them divine-like, immutable and eternal. Like the Hamas and the Hizbullah, Arafat personally often engages in religious rhetoric, calling upon his followers to join the jihad to liberate Jerusalem, or lauding those who fall in attacks against Israel as martyrs. Whether the anti-Jewish statements are taken from Islamic or Christian anti-Semitic sources, they become axiomatic, they do not require verifications or criticism, and once pronounced by a public opinion-maker or a cleric, they are recited like mantras verbatim and *ad nauseam* throughout the Arab and Islamic world. The fact that they fit neatly with the perceived demonic picture of the Jew that is familiar to them is proof of their validity.

If they are valid, then it is incumbent upon the Arabs and the Muslims to spread the word throughout the world – both in order to explain their plight in their confrontation with such an enemy, and to warn others to beware the Demon incarnate. It is therefore imperative to deny any link between these unworthy people and the Temple Mount (or the Noble *Haram al-Sharif* in their parlance). Since the current Jews are the descendents of those who had invaded the land of the Canaanites, the forefathers of the Palestinians, why should Arafat and his people concede anything to them today? The Arabs are frightened by any act of the Jews that seems benevolent because that destroys the irrevocably negative image they have of them. For example, when Israel dispatched a team of agricultural experts to Egypt, and they did a very useful and laudable work, they were accused by the Egyptian press, followed by the rest of the Arab world, of spreading diseases in order to contaminate Egypt's land and ruin its farming. The rationale is clear: how could miserable Israel, populated by those Jews that were born for humiliation, extend any help to the most ancient and experienced farming culture in the world? Something does not add up, therefore it is better to deny that they are of any use and accuse them of ill will. Since no Egyptian leader dares to come out against those calumnies, they are taken as valid and true.

Similarly, in the West Bank and Gaza, where Israel introduced modern agriculture and raised productivity manifold, you can only hear a long litany about the destruction that the Zionists inflicted on Palestinian agriculture in order to bring about their impoverishment. The six universities allowed by Israel when it ruled the territories, the many training courses for medical, educational, legal and other civil servants that were run by Israel over the years, are all denied, because Israel is only bent on the destruction of the Palestinian infrastructure. Some time ago, a rumor was circulated in the Arab world about a chewing gum emanating from Israel which had the power to enhance sexual lust in women. That was calculated, of course, to drive Arab women to sexual corruption in order to destroy the values of Arab and Islamic society. Many thousands of Palestinians go to Israel for medical treatment, including during the days of the Intifada, but the official Palestinian line of argument is that it is better to fly their casualties to Baghdad and Amman in order to rescue them from the Zionist mortal danger. The main thing is not to have to acknowledge that the Jews are sometimes capable of doing good deeds, that they stand in many countries in the forefront of philanthropy and human rights, and that the aid that Israel is giving to dozens of Third World countries is sought-after and appreciated.

In May 1983, the Palestinians accused Israel of having 'poisoned' schoolgirls in the West Bank, who were in fact fainting in a wave of mass hysteria. The affair was taken up by the rest of the Arabs and Muslims, then by UN bodies and the Western press, which was wondering 'how the Jews who had experienced the gas chambers could now treat the Palestinians the same way'. Cries of genocide flew from all quarters, until an international medical inquiry team came up with the explanation of mass hysteria. But the Palestinians did not budge, they had adopted the much more 'plausible' theory that the Jews had schemed to 'sterilize' young Palestinian women in order to affect the demographic balance which was ticking adversely in their disfavor. This calumny was duplicated in 1996 by the Palestinian Ambassador in Geneva, Mr Ramlawi, who accused the Jews of 'once again' ... 'true to their genocidal designs against the Palestinians', injecting 300 of them with the AIDS virus. Even though the Palestinian delegate could not substantiate his claim, the fact that it was not firmly refuted by anyone present, save the Israeli delegate, was 'proof' enough for the Arabs of its validity. Israel is 'known' for its genocidal schemes, therefore there is no need to prove them, and even if the accusations are false this time, they will be true another time.

The moral depravity of the Jews is evinced in their systematic 'desecration' of Islamic Holy Places, in particular the al-Aqsa Mosque. Since the 1970s Israeli men and women soldiers have been accused in the Palestinian and other Arab press of enjoying drinking and sex orgies within the Mosque compound. It is interesting to note that the two taboos in their puritanical culture (alcohol and sex) are given liberty when they are projected onto the enemy. When the al-Aqsa Mosque was burned by a lunatic Australian tourist in 1969, Israel was directly blamed by the Palestinians and the entire Muslim world of being behind the arson. The fact that the arsonist was apprehended and sentenced, that he was Christian, and that it was the Israelis who rushed to extinguish the fire, did nothing to exonerate the Jews from their guilt, because it is in their 'nature' to carry out acts of profanation. Similarly, when Israel reopened an old Hasmonean tunnel in the Old City of Jerusalem in September 1996, that was good enough reason for the Palestinians to cause a conflagration which ended in many casualties, because they spread the rumor that Israel was purposely digging under the Mosque in order to destabilize its foundations. No assurance that the tunnel was parallel to the mosque and at a safe distance, could alleviate Arab suspicions.

The al-Aqsa Intifada also began on the Temple Mount when, using the pretext of the visit of Ariel Sharon the day before, Palestinians erupted into violence during the Friday prayers of 29 September 2000, in what appeared as a premeditated attempt to obtain through the use of force what they failed to achieve during the Camp David Conference the previous July. A pretext, because had they wished to keep this quiet; in spite of what they regarded as a 'provocation', they could have contained their 'anger' and 'frustration', otherwise what would prevent the Israelis too, at any time they are angry and frustrated, from causing a conflagration? The question here is one of maturity and responsibility: the Palestinians are supposedly rational people who would not irresponsibly break loose and cause hundreds of casualties to themselves and to others just because they are frustrated. But this pattern is not new: anything Israel does, even an act of self-defense against overwhelming force, is provocation and aggression, but anything they do, even the most murderous and cowardly attacks, is a commendable act of bravery for which they often win the title of *shahid*. They pit children, armed with rocks and bombs, in their hundreds, against Israeli soldiers, and dub their unprovoked attacks jihad; but when they are hit in the ensuing test of force, then the Israelis are the cruel enemy who shoots indiscriminately at teenaged Palestinians. It does not occur to them that, had they not sent children to the front, they would not have been hurt, exactly as they could avoid the entire Intifada had they contained their repeated 'days of rage'.

These days of rage are, in their eyes, merely the legitimate expression of their rejection of Israeli occupation. They have the right over any territory they consider theirs, to the exclusion of all the others. And if the others resist, they are dubbed 'Nazis'. One would assume that Palestinian (and other Arab) intellectuals and educated people would not only understand the difference between what the Nazis did in Europe and what they are subjected to under Israeli rule, but that they would refrain from using that comparison, knowing how offensive it is to the Jews. But, perhaps it is precisely because of this that it is so widely used in the media, politics, religion and education. To 'prove' this, there has been a flurry of Palestinian accusations against the Jews, especially focused around the theme of 'poisoning', a blunt reversal of what had been done to the Jews by the Nazis, and a reversion to the old European anti-Semitic theme of well-poisoning. Suha Arafat delivered an impassioned speech in December 1998, in the presence of Hillary Clinton who was visiting Gaza with the President, in which she accused Israel of having systematically poisoned Palestinian lands and waters. The lack of reaction on the part of the American First Lady only emboldened the speaker to continue in her broadsides, and the audience to believe them.

These depictions fit perfectly with the image the Palestinians have of the Jews and Israel. Furthermore, following the reports about Western troops who were exposed to depleted uranium ammunition during the Kosovo venture, and the suspicion that they may have been inflicted with cancer, the Palestinians also picked up that new avenue of attack against Israel. Reports were vented for a while in the Palestinian press that the Israeli bullets that killed or maimed them during the current disturbances, were made of uranium, in order of course to poison the innocent Palestinians and to harm their health in the long run. Those reports receded when no evidence was provided and the Israeli military denied any use of that sort of ammunition. But the pattern was clear: this was no different from the previous blaming of Israel for having 'poisoned' the Jenin schoolgirls and injecting Palestinian children with HIV-positive virus.

This concentration of hatred and venom against the Jews and Israel has ceased to provoke sharp reactions in the world, and most Israelis are not even cognizant of it! Small wonder that the Arabs regard it as a confirmation of their veracity. While one could claim that the underdog Palestinians have no other way to vent their anger, one is advised to look at the same intensive use of this vocabulary in Egypt after 22 years, and in Jordan after 6 years, of their peace accords with Israel. The infrastructure of deprecation and disdain for Israel not only has remained intact, but has become so deeply ingrained in Arab thinking and mental make-up that there is no point in asking them to forego it by signing an 'end of the conflict' statement. Egypt and Jordan have signed it, but to no avail.

Breaking the thermometer will not cure the fever. Assuming that violent rhetoric, which delegitimizes the enemy, produces physical violence when the opportunity arises, Israel must maintain its power of deterrence if it wishes to survive. For the Arabs have never hesitated to use their power to the maximum when they thought they could overwhelm Israel, while it is the latter who exercises restraint even when attacked, in order to avert a Palestinian holocaust of major proportions.

For the Arabs, it is always a jihad, a war to the finish, without limits or constraints. At times it is expressed in terms of annihilation: 'throwing the Jews into the sea', or sinking them in a bloodbath, or Saddam's vow to 'burn half Israel' with his weapons of mass destruction; at other times it appears in more euphemistic terms such as 'battle until victory', 'cutting them down to size' or sending them to 'drink the water of Gaza' (or of the Dead Sea, which is as deadly). Their inability to achieve that in one stroke, in a 'mother of all battles' as Saddam had pledged, prompts them to derive pleasure from smaller feats which point to that direction. For example, while Israel has never dared to use unconventional weapons in combat, its bombing by missiles from Iraq during the Second Gulf War (1991) drew tremendous support from the Palestinians and the rest of the Arab street, which came to regard Saddam as the new Saladin who will deliver the *coup de grâce* to the hated Zionist entity. Short of that, murdering innocent Israeli passers-by, mutilating corpses of their victims and dragging them into streets, or luring Israelis into their domain and ambushing them, have been their way to achieve, in the meantime, a long series of small total annihilations. On the symbolic level, the torching and destruction of Jewish synagogues and Holy Places, the digging up of tombs and crushing of bones, the burning of Jewish books and Torah parchments, and the trampling, tearing, stabbing and then setting ablaze of Israeli flags and effigies provide them the same partial satisfaction.

THE INEXTRICABILITY OF THE DISPUTE

Viewed in this light (or rather obscurity), one can see that the long-term goals of the parties are not symmetrical. It is not the case that both parties seek a settlement and a compromise: the Palestinians (and the rest of the Arabs) want victory, justice and restoration of

Arab splendor and hegemony; while the Israelis have a much more modest ambition of security and being accepted and recognized by their neighbors. In the total war that the Arabs, mainly the Muslim fundamentalists among them, are ready to wage, every means is sacred and no means is abhorrent: jihad, unconventional war, annihilation, using children, lying, calumniating, inciting, murdering, oppressing their own people and sometimes executing them, self-deprivation, and what not. Admittedly, some of these methods are also used by Israelis in self-defense, when faced with a situation of no choice in this ugly battle. But, at least appearances of, and concern for, morality are kept. Many Israelis who were thought of as hurting unjustly Palestinians were prosecuted and serve their term (long or short) in jail; in the PA killers are hailed as heroes. The Israeli military often conduct investigations to monitor abusive behavior of its troops, and punishments (heavy or light) are often imposed on the culprits; and many outstanding officers have paid with their careers for their abuses. No parallel to this has come to light in the Palestinian (or Arab) camp.

When Baruch Goldstein committed his abominable act in Hebron, he was universally, and as a matter of course, condemned by all camps of Israeli politics; but when Yihye Ayyash, the super-murderer, was killed, Arafat attended his funeral, and words of praise were showered on him from all quarters. We have never heard a Palestinian leader condemn any perpetrator of crime against Israelis. At the most, they would condemn the *act* of murder or terror as if it were a natural calamity, but they would never have the guts, or the nerve, to condemn the perpetrators, much less by name, unless the act was directed against the Authority itself. In any case, the statement would be diluted by a general condemnation of violence 'on all sides', or 'against civilians', meaning that terrorism against Israeli soldiers is valid and to be expected. Worse, in not a few cases (for example, the Beit Lid horror in 1994 where 21 Israeli soldiers commuting back to their units on a Sunday were decimated by two bombs), the PA and Arafat himself have imputed these acts to Israeli provocateurs with the intention of smearing the good reputation of the Palestinians or of justifying retaliation against them.

Often, these atrocities are dismissed by the Palestinians as part of the excesses on the part of 'extremists on both sides'. But there are no two sides to this story. True, there are individual lunatics and fanatics, like Goldstein and Popper, or settlers who, unjustly and unprovoked, harm or kills a Palestinian, but one would be hard pressed to find in Israel a mainstream organization like the Hamas, or even the *Fat'h* Tanzim, whose stated purpose and *raison d'être* is to indiscriminately kill the enemy. And, if such a group is suspected to exist in Israel, it would be hounded, hunted down and monitored by the Israeli security apparatus, and often brought to justice when it transgresses the boundaries of law. There is no organization in Israel which systematically places bombs in market places and in buses, just to kill or maim citizens; there is no leadership, religious or otherwise, which supports such acts, and there is no prize, fame or popular following to sustain the perpetrators. No Israelis stab Arabs in the streets and no Palestinians have been murdered in Israeli restaurants or buses. Palestinians can circulate in full safety in Israeli streets, hotels, hospitals, beaches and universities (admittedly with the unpleasantly intervening security checks and roadblocks); but should Israelis dare to visit, or even to stray by mistake, into Palestinian territory, they risk their lives.

With this kind of moral make-up, in a leadership which claims to be fighting for independence, peace and good neighborliness, one should not be surprised by unpredictable and puzzling modes of behavior. They can argue, with the generous assistance of the Israeli Left, that Sharon's visit to the Temple Mount had triggered their anger, because he was the 'butcher of Sabra and Shatilla', and they rationalize thereby the ensuing orgy of killings. If we were to follow that logic, then every time Arafat – the man who has been directly responsible (not indirectly, like Sharon) for killing thousands of Israelis and Arabs – sets foot somewhere in Israeli-controlled territory, an effusion of Israeli anger should decimate entire Palestinian villages.

This is the reason why every time Israel is close to a settlement with the Arabs, be they Syrian or Palestinian, and after it makes far-reaching concessions (short of total surrender) for the sake of peace, the Arabs back down and retreat. Israeli negotiators, and many a Western observer, are stunned with disbelief, unable to comprehend the 'Arab propensity to miss yet another opportunity'; for they would rather wait for the whole, for the sake of satisfying their honor and sense of justice, than bend to the humiliation of accepting a part, which signifies that they have reconciled themselves to injustice. Justice is whole and indivisible, therefore they educate their children to claim it all and to deny their rivals any part of it; and when they report on their clashes with Israelis, there is never an understanding of the other's pain, losses and ambitions. In Israel, there is a whole political camp which sympathizes with the Palestinians, diffuses their grievances and expresses them in the media. No trace of that is found on the Palestinian side, and if there should be one, the 'culprit' would be condemned, arrested or worse – gunned down or executed. In 'moderate' Jordan, those who visit Israel, entertain any links with her, or come out in favor of peace and normalization, are excommunicated by their communities and, more ominously, are excluded from their trade unions, which means in effect that they are denied the right to work and make a living.

After every incident, Palestinian spokesmen are allowed to voice their grievances in the Israeli media, where the damages and casualties inflicted on the other side are reported, while the Palestinian media never interview any Israeli, or anyone critical of them, and disregard the casualties and damages they have inflicted on the others. In this way Israel is always presented as the aggressor who pesters the lives of Palestinians for no reason; and the feeling is cultivated among the Palestinians that they are the innocent victims who can do no wrong. The very notion of being a 'refugee' derives from this situation; inasmuch as this ceased being only a socio-economic status and became a state of mind. Thus, the Palestinians will be the eternal poor victims to whom the world owes everything. They make children, but the UN has to feed them. They build 13 different security apparatuses, but the donor countries have to finance them. They are dipped in corruption, but the Arabs and the Europeans have to foot the bills. It does not occur to them that if they had rolled up their sleeves and applied themselves to work, construction and peace, they would have solved all those problems in the past 50 years instead of perpetuating them and throwing the blame on others.

This is often interpreted as a result of the humiliation, the conquest, the oppression and the travesty of justice occasioned by Israeli occupation. But the historical record shows that these attitudes are as old as the relations between Jews and Muslims/Arabs, or at the very least since the re-establishment of the Jews in Palestine in modern times. In the times of the Jerusalem Mufti, in the 1920s through the 1940s, the Jews in Palestine were a minority, certainly not conquerors or oppressors, and very often close to extinction due to the Palestinian onslaughts on them (1929, 1936–39 and 1947–49). The Jews survived and prospered, but the

Palestinians refuse to alter their attitude of contempt, exclusion and hatred towards them, or their victim mentality. It seems absurd and paradoxical that, even as the negotiations between the parties are being held, attention is focused on the Temple Mount instead of on resolving fundamental issues. The Israelis, who are supposed to be the cruel oppressors, the champions of force, etc., are the ones who are ready to withdraw and share sovereignty over the Mount, as if they were the losers in this struggle; while the weak and conquered are those who behave with intransigence as if they were the victors, and they insist on total and exclusive sovereignty over the holy shrines. This is a reversed logic, the like of which one cannot find elsewhere.

What allows the defeated and occupied Palestinians to behave as if they were the victors and the occupiers is the strength and self-assurance of their Arab and Muslim history, culture, traditions and legacy, of their 200 and 1,200 million followers, respectively. It is no coincidence that at crucial moments Arafat clings to the claim that he represents all of them, even though no one has delegated that power to him. His pretense goes even beyond, as he also demands the right to represent the Christian world, for Jesus Christ was Palestinian, and his own daughter, the fruit of his marriage with the Christian, Suha, is the perfect combination of those two worlds under his aegis. The Jews did not have the nerve to advance the argument that they ought to watch over the Christian Holy Places in the Holy Land because Jesus was Jewish; therefore it is the Palestinian claim that is under consideration, while the more nat-ural, and more credible, Israeli guarantee for the safety of the Christian shrines under its aegis, is not even heard. Israel cannot be entrusted, as far as the Arabs are concerned, with anything that might hint to its permanence or continuity, since it is a Crusader-like fleeting entity. From the peaks of Arab and Islamic history, Jews are looked down upon as an inferior and unnatural religious group, not worthy of statehood, and certainly not of acceptance and recog-nition by the Arabs and Muslims.

The Arab and Muslim contempt for the Jews, which is deeply engraved in their historical and political consciousness, is fed by the inexplicable gap presumed between Jewish inferiority and the curse that was cast on them by Allah and History, and their rather stunning success as a modern state in the Middle East, in spite of their minority status and their long record of evident persecution and seeming rootlessness. Particularly incomprehensible and unacceptable to Arabs and Muslims is the status of the Jewish communities in the Western countries, especially in the USA, where they enjoy a far greater influence in the economic, cultural, scientific and political domains than their small numbers would warrant. Especially humiliating to Arabs and Muslims is the fact that the Muslim community in the USA, with its large Arab component, equals in numbers, and certainly in years of existence, its Jewish counterpart, but is nowhere near it in terms of impact. Due to the considerable assistance that American Jews have extended to Israel, it has become imperative in Arab thinking to weaken American Jewry in order to help cut Israel down to its 'natural size'. Hence, their attempts to reduce this influence, then achieve parity with it, then eliminate it and replace it – both in America by means of Islamic/Arab growth and awareness, and in the Middle East, by presenting the Arabs as more worthy allies than Israel.

The Arabs have begun attaining the first phase of parity with the Israelis via the various peace processes. It is not the case that the Arabs have become tired of war and have converted to Isaiah's prophecy of universal peace. Egyptian intellectuals, since the 1970s, have floated the notion of letting Israel merge into the Arab world by peaceful means, sort of 'giving them enough rope to hang themselves'. Sadat was the first to understand that without formal peace with Israel he would not be able to ward off the then Soviet threats from the west (in Libya) and the south (in Ethiopia), nor could he obtain American assistance to rehabilitate his economy or modernize his troops. By effecting a turnabout in 1977, he indeed attained near-equality with Israel in the USA, and turned his country into an American ally. During the Second Gulf War, it was the Arabs, including the intransigent Syrians among them, who became America's war partners, while the Israelis were asked to sit by quietly and absorb the missiles showered on them by Saddam. After the war, it was Arabs, including those who sided with Saddam (Jordan and the PLO) who were forced upon Israel in Madrid, thus setting off the roller coaster of pressures against Israel that would produce Oslo and its aftermath.

Today, the American military holds more frequent and more visible joint maneuvers with Egypt than with Israel. The latter, the supposed 'strategic ally', who was repeatedly assured strategic upgrading and funds for the concessions it was made to accept, was abandoned by President Clinton in the twilight of his rule, without making good on his promises and after having set a dangerous baseline for future negotiations between Israel and the Palestinians, though he knew that neither the Israeli Knesset, nor the Israeli public, were ready to stomach these far-reaching departures from existential red lines. This was accomplished by rewarding Palestinian violence, by overlooking their disregard for their obligations under Oslo, Sharm e-Sheikh and Arafat's various pledges, and by being totally ignored, snubbed and thwarted by Palestinian negotiators. This was made possible when Israel legitimized the PLO in Oslo, raised funds for it, armed it and submitted territory to its control, and introduced Arafat to the White House. The end result was that, far from toeing the line of peace jointly with the Israelis, the Palestinians have gathered enough self-confidence to push the Israelis aside, to gain their own access to the corridors of power in Washington, and to aspire to replace Israel there. But no enhancement of the peace process occurred as a result.

Were the Arabs to solidify their position of parity, and then gain an edge over Israel in Western chanceries, on the political, moral and international levels, they could then move to overwhelm it, again with its generous help. Because, while the Palestinians, and the Syrians, like the Lebanese and the Egyptians before them, insist on their complete and uncompromising rights (for example, as regards Jerusalem and the Temple Mount), Israel resorts to compromise and 'understanding'. Like the Solomonic trial, justice rests with the firm and unflinching, not with the hesitant and spineless. Similarly, the right of return of a refugee to his home sounds much more credible, and draws much more support, than the counterclaim of those who are prepared to yield part of their country, their holy places and their very security, 'for the sake of peace'. How can one convince anybody of one's right to his home if one is also prepared to yield the basement thereof? In negotiations, the mediators always seek the middle ground between declared positions, and those who advance concessions will be pressured to concede more in order to meet the recalcitrant party closer to his stance. Barak had started with far-reaching compromises in Camp David II (July 2000), and he was refuted by the Palestinians who would not budge, as they had learned that they could get more if they stonewalled; better yet, if they shoot and kill in order to show their determination. Because then, in order to appease the obstinate, the mediators and the other party would rush to offer more concessions. Do we need a better lesson a mere two or three generations after Munich?

The Arabs have then learned that unless they can get their whole desire fulfilled, better to avoid any compromise settlement that might freeze the present balance of parity and scuttle their efforts to revert to their aggressive policy once new opportunities are open to them. In fact, after Egypt signed the peace treaty with Israel 22 years ago, it did not desist one day from its anti-Semitic propaganda nor from its stated wish to diminish Israel and reduce it to a more controllable scope that would ensure Egyptian hegemony in the area. That was necessary in order to keep alive the infrastructure of hatred that can be mobilized once again when the day comes. Similarly, all those who hoped that after the concessions they obtained in Oslo, Wye and Camp David, Palestinian hatred and incitement would be scaled down, were soon to discover that they were scaled up, and lately garnered with open hostilities and shooting to boot. We are told that they are 'angry' and 'frustrated', therefore they are justified in their uncontrolled outburst. They were made to promise in those peace conferences to desist from violence, and they did under duress. But exactly as you cannot extort from a person a pledge to stop breathing, you have to take as a premise that any Arab assurance to alter or amend their attitudes towards Jews and Israel has no viability nor longevity, regardless of what Israel might concede.

The Arabs are ready to sign a treaty with Israel only if it leaves them enough leeway, and promises a firm enough potential, to bring about Israel's demise. Hizbullah first demanded Israel's withdrawal from Lebanon; then an unconditional withdrawal, so as to leave the border area in chaos and Israel on its toes; then the Shab'a Farms; then the liberation of Lebanese prisoners of war, followed by Palestinians and other Arabs; and now they are talking about the return of all occupied Arab territories. To make their point, they kidnapped Israeli soldiers and an Israeli national in Europe, and their men daily scale the Israeli fence in order to defy its guards, while the Lebanese authorities refuse to deploy their soldiers along the border for fear that they might be misconstrued as 'defending Israeli territory'. Lebanon, Egypt and the rest of the Arabs will continue to hound Israel until it relinquishes its strategic assets in the West Bank and the Golan, gives up its unconventional weaponry and establishes a hostile Palestinian state at a stone's throw from its heartland. Syria, likewise, will not be content to get the Golan Heights; it also covets Israel's water sources, so that the Zionist State could be helplessly reduced to Arab mercy. This is the Israel with which the Arabs wish to make peace.

One of the most offending elements that the Arabs find unbearable is Israel's tremendous achievements, in the space of 50 years, and against all odds, in the fields of government, economy, society, science and technology, which stand in deep contradiction with the negative and contemptuous image they have of the Jews and Israel. Hence the urgency of redressing that balance. Not, Allah forbid, by revising upwards the convoluted data they have been treasuring to fit their concepts and beliefs, but by pulling Israel downwards to make it concur with the distorted knowledge they possess. If Israel has been successful economically, then instead of learning from it how a developing nation can make progress, they accuse it of Neo-Imperialism in order to take over the Middle East. Even Shimon Peres' book, which envisioned a 'New Middle East', for the benefit of all its inhabitants, was greeted in Egypt as 'new evidence' of the validity of *The Protocols of the Elders of Zion*, this time via economic means. Thus, instead of learning how they can attain a GNP 20 times larger than theirs, in order to extricate their people from poverty, the Arabs would do everything to boycott Israeli goods, to limit their commercial relations with the Jews, and anything that would reduce Israel rather than recognize its edge.

And if there is no way to impose their way on Israel via peace talks, they resort to violence: a daily and draining Intifada which sets aflame every city and village in Israel, terrorizes its people, kidnaps and maims people, and car-bombs urban centers; all calculated to make life in Israel untenable and drive the Israelis to despair, and to abandon their property in order to pave the way for their own departure. World Jewry, which is conceived as the main life artery of Israel, is also similarly harassed. In addition to the Intifada in Israel, Muslim/Arab communities throughout the Western world have launched violent attacks against their neighboring Jewish congregations. In Sydney and Paris, London and Johannesburg, hundreds of events of this sort have shook cities and towns which had seemingly nothing to do with Middle Eastern events: synagogues have been torched; Jews have been assaulted; cemeteries have been desecrated; Israeli flags have been burned or trampled upon; anti-Semitic slogans have been voiced; and jihad summons have been uttered, urging Muslims to join in the liberation of Jerusalem from the Zionists. Unlike parallel Jewish gatherings for the support of Israel, which were held with dignity and composure in the synagogues, without any disturbance to the public order, the Muslim demonstrations were violent and scary.

These manifestations of hostility and intolerance highlighted throughout the Western world the increasingly burdensome issue of the Islamic penetration there mostly via illegal immigration. This means that the demographic balance will be affected in the long run, especially in countries of high immigration such as the USA, Canada and Australia; just as it already has done in Western Europe, which accords political asylum to refugees from Islamic countries. More ominously, it means that these immigrants, both those already established and the newcomers (including the illegal among them) import to their countries of shelter their hatred of Israel and the Jews. This in itself is likely to undermine the enviable status that the Jews enjoy in those countries, out of proportion to their numbers. The Muslims are determined to eliminate this primacy, both by the sheer numbers they will bring to bear in the local democracies, and by violence and intimidation towards the Jews themselves and by signaling to the general population that Jews are 'dangerous' and that they and their neighborhoods should be avoided. It is easy to foresee the sentiments of anti-Semitism that will be raised when common people who never liked the Jews in any case would be made to feel that the latter have become a cumbersome liability.

In our days, the globalization of information has caused the universalization of Arab and Islamic sentiment and solidarity. In a paradoxical way, the local media in each Islamic country provide immediacy and help break the local siege on information. International Arab and Islamic concerns have been hijacked by activist groups who not only transmit instantly messages regarding the oppression of Palestinians and the dangers that the Jews pose to the Muslim Holy Places, but also raise funds, urge co-religionists to demonstrate, violently if necessary, in support of those causes, and even provide instructions on how to join terrorist lodges or to concoct explosives. Thus, what happens on the ground in Gaza or Nablus has immediate reverberations in the streets of Melbourne and London; not to speak of the Arab street from Rabat to Baghdad, or the Islamic street from Teheran to Jakarta.

Had the Arabs been able to isolate Israel from the world and turn it into another Gaza, instead of lifting themselves to its level, then the demographic pressure, corruption, poverty, chaos and backwardness would have exercised their adverse impact and eroded the Jewish edge. The way to attain this is to press for the 'right of return', cause disorder and initiate shootings in order to thwart tourism, to disrupt production and normal life, and cause irreparable damage to Israel, even at the price of self-inflicted harm, for they have not much to lose at any rate. This is exactly the soft point that they have detected in Israel: this prosperous, advanced, modern and industrious country, which attracts foreign investment, especially in the high-tech domain, needs tranquility and stability. Indeed, the greatest proponents of the peace delusion are the industrialists, who have paradoxically become associated with the ideological socialist left in Israel because they both expect to derive the greatest benefits from it. These are precisely the characteristics of a 'soft state' which is no longer ready to defend its strategic and cultural assets if they levy too heavy an economic and human price, thus lending top priority to immediate short-term 'peaceful' gains at the expense of the long-term existential interests of the country and the Jewish people.

Another paradox is, that it will be precisely the concessions for the sake of economic growth that will engender the next rift with the Palestinians and the Arab world. For a great part of the Palestinian and other Arab wrath against Israel stems from its success, which exposes for all to see their own incompetence in comparison. They have a hard time explaining to themselves and to others, how a small and persecuted people, which has been in their eyes, for many centuries, the paradigm of misery and humiliation, has dared and succeeded, in a relatively short time, against the odds of war and of a difficult starting point, to achieve goals that the Arabs can only dream of attaining. This is something they cannot bear, and the more the Jews are successful and prosperous, the more the hatred, born out of jealousy, will increase. There is no basis to the worn-out assumption that economic development in the Arab world will blunt extremism and make Israel acceptable to them. We have already noticed that it is much more important for them to pull Israel down than to elevate themselves to its level. The hypothesis which posits that loans and allowances for development could override ideological and doctrinal considerations is not only incorrect but also patronizing and condescending and does more harm than good.

Thus, the right of return from the Palestinian point of view, which is calculated to bring Israel down, is the supreme test case: if it is accepted in one variety or another, then all is well, because that would trigger the process which will end with the removal from the scene of all the values of the Jewish State which pose an inimitable challenge to the Arab world. They understand full well that a mass return of Palestinians to Israel, together with the million Palestinian Arabs already living in Israel, would turn the country into another Gaza, hence their insistence on becoming full-fledged citizens upon their return to the land. One wonders, why should they want to be the citizens of a state they hate and complain about regarding its oppression, unless they want to dismantle it from within? And then, when they gain the majority and make the land into another corrupt, poor, backward, dictatorial and overcrowded country of their liking, Israel's sin of her unwarranted and humiliating excellence will be wiped out. They also understand full well that all the symptoms of successful and democratic Israel will persist only as long as the Jewish majority leads it, and will vanish when the Arabs take command and control. The fact is, that in spite of their legendary wealth, not one of the 22 Arab countries has succeeded in adopting Western culture, government, economics and mode of life. Better then not to achieve a settlement than see a recognized and accepted Israel pursuing her course, as this can only deepen Palestinian and Arab humiliation.

Successful and westernized Israel, like the West itself, is deeply hated by the Arab and Islamic worlds. It is in the nature of things that the backward and the poor should detest those whom they cannot resemble. Therefore, Israel and the West are always intertwined. One can hear in campuses around the world that both are Neo-Colonialist or Neo-Imperialist, enemies of Islam and of the Third World. In these demonstrations the Israeli and American flags are always burned in tandem. Israel is the corrupting Western arm in the heart of the Arab and Islamic world, that does the groundwork of undermining Islam, of corrupting its youth with foreign values, music, pornography and permissiveness. Hence, the commitment to fight them both relentlessly and ruthlessly, even at the price of self-perdition.

The Arabs' ultimate demand is for 'justice' ('peace with justice', a 'just peace'), as if justice were absolute and not in the eye of the beholder. Justice (*'adalah* in Arabic, which is also, incidentally, an Arab civil rights group in Israel) is for the Arabs linked to the notion of balance between the two saddlebags on the camel's back, short of which the camel cannot march at length to cross the desert. Justice is also connected to honor, and the maintenance of honor hinges on the ability of a man to protect his property, and his women, and his proven capacity to retrieve them if they are violated. Otherwise, his reputation is irretrievably compromised. Thus, one's honor is constantly on the line, and it is tested by a man's daring in the service of his honor. An Arab will not rest until the wrong done to him is redressed and his property is recuperated. Then, justice is done, and one can go back to functioning normally. There are no objective criteria to define the feeling of right or wrong, or the encroachment on one's honor; they hinge upon the subjective sense of the wronged individual.

When the Arabs, the Palestinians included, demand justice, they mean their justice, that is, the return of their rights and property as they perceive them, regardless of whether, what and how, others might advance disclaimers in historical, legal, logical or human terms, for all these are irrelevant. First, the Arabs must get full satisfaction, in accordance with their sentiments and convictions, their right must be recognized and stated, and only then they might show generosity and give something back out of their own volition, not as a result of coercion or force. Thus, the whole notion of compromise does not come into play, because if something is yours, you must obtain it first. Sadat in his speech at the Knesset in November 1977, the Syrians in their negotiations with Israel, the Hizbullah in Lebanon, and now the Palestinians in the peace process, have all demanded a total Israeli withdrawal before the negotiations can proceed, or at the very least an Israeli commitment to retreat at the end of the day. Not because, as some diplomats have thought, the Arabs wish to obtain the result of the negotiations before they even begin, but in order to signal that their belongings are not subject to negotiation. They are theirs, period.

The Palestinians, like the rest of the Arabs, sense in their deepest consciousness that the Holy Land in general, and Jerusalem in particular with its innermost sanctum, the Temple Mount, have been the exclusive patrimony of the Arabs/Muslims since they became included in the *futuh* (holy conquests by Islam) and were bequeathed to them by Allah, for all generations to come, as a *waqf* (Holy Endowment) land, never to be parted with or negotiated away. Hence, the right of return is not only a human and political need, but also a religious duty which imposes on them to struggle and pay any sacrifice so as to snatch the land from its usurpers who have subtracted it from Islamic dominion. This is particularly valid with regard to the *Haram al-Sharif* (the Temple Mount) which was the very site of the Prophet's mystical nightly visit (*isra'*) and ascension to Heaven (*mi'raj*). Thus, only after this right of theirs is recognized, as a matter of course world-wide (what they call 'international legitimacy'), may they evince *ex-gracia* generosity and allow others to collect some crumbs from their table. Until then, all means are allowable to retrieve the loss by peaceful means if possible, through violence if necessary, for in any case its holy character prescribes jihad.

Theoretically, the right of return could be implemented by dividing the land between Muslims and Jews, and allowing each of them to return to his part of the land. However, by acquiescing in this solution, the Muslims would be lending a stamp of consent to the existence of the Zionist entity in the Holy Land, something that is to be totally rejected. Hence, Arab insistence that the Arab returnees to their land must enter Israeli territory, for only then can they, together with the Israeli Arabs, effect the demographic shift which will overwhelm Israel by democratic means. Never mind the complaints that Arabs are discriminated against in Israel and by Israel, and the contradiction between this repeated grievance and the eagerness of so many Arabs to become nationals of the oppressive Zionist regime, together with the Israeli Arabs who are already suffering under the yoke of that oppression. This is not a hidden agenda, it is stated clearly; Israel has simply to bite the bait and believe that the right of return of the Arabs into its territory will produce peace. Israel's refusal to bite is one of the major reasons for the Palestinians' frustration and anger, for which Israel certainly owes them an apology.

The Islamists among the Palestinians add many more arguments to rationalize their right of return, beyond those advanced by other Arabs and Muslims. The Hamas platform, for example, claims that when Islam was not in charge in Palestine – for example, under the Crusaders, the British and the Jews – the country knew only friction, conflict, war and bloodshed; while under Islam, love and fraternity, peace and tranquillity have reigned. Hence, the urgency to return Palestine in its entirety, including what is now Israel, into Islamic hands. Then, the Jews can revert to their 'natural' status as *dhimmis* under the generous and protective wings of Islam, as long as they recognize and accept its superiority as the latest, and therefore the most valid and updated, divine revelation, which has supplanted all its predecessors. Then, they must be content with whatever the Muslim masters grant them.

This is the essence of tolerance under Islamic rule, which is not to be confused with pluralism. In Western terms, a tolerant society is a pluralistic one where everyone is equal under the sun, and no one culture, religion, race or ethnic group is superior over all the others. Namely, one is tolerant in spite of his difference from the other and without passing any value judgement on one or the other's group. But in Islamic belief – under which if one is not a Muslim one is either an Unbeliever, or at most a protected *dhimma*, whose juridical, political and social status is inferior – tolerance means to accept the other *in spite* of his inferiority. This understanding of tolerance not only is not likely to produce an egalitarian and pluralistic society under Islamic rule, but is likely to perpetuate a patronizing condescendence towards the non-Muslim. This is precisely the socio-political framework to which the Muslims would like to return the Jews (and the Christians) if they could. This is what they would do if they could take over Palestine through the right of return.

Thus, the peace conditions offered to Israel by its Arab neighbors do not evince a mature and open recognition of reality and of the rights of others. It is no coincidence that even in the Arab countries that signed a peace with Israel (Egypt and Jordan thus far), the populace has not accepted the terms: normalization has been hampered by large and dominant groups in Arab civil society, and the peace has remained one concluded by the ruling elites. All Israeli attempts to trigger a process by which the Arabs will come to respect the Jews as their peace partners and share holy places with them, or land claimed by both, have been in vain. Furthermore, these Israeli concessions and offers for compromise, have raised the threshold of Arab demands, since what is conceded becomes the basis for the negotiations for a new 'compromise', that is concession, etc. When Israel declared its willingness to return all the Golan to Syria, Damascus also demanded the shores of the Lake Tiberias; when Israel was ready to return Arab neighborhoods in Jerusalem, the Arabs demanded all East Jerusalem, including the Temple Mount and the adjoining Jewish Western Wall. And when Israel exhibits its readiness to discuss these claims, the incredibly belligerent demand is advanced for the right of return in order to deliver the final *coup de grâce* to the Jewish State.

BACK TO THE BEGINNING

If there is not sufficient maturity to accept Israel, much less to conclude peace with it, there is no urgency for Israel to rush into a settlement which can only prejudice its most vital interests. A long series of 'agreements' have been signed: Oslo I and Oslo II; Cairo Accords I and II; Camp David Conferences I and II were convened; Sharm e-Sheikh meetings I and II were held, and Taba and Eilat, and Wye and Washington, and no concrete and palpable results could be shown. If there are so many agreements, maybe there was none? Israel and the Arabs did sign, under external prodding, masses of papers, and raised expectations for the upcoming era of peace, but the result is frustration. Israel did not take a break to examine the consequences, to test the ramifications, to make further concessions conditional, equal and parallel to steps to be taken by its peace partners. For example, normalization should not have been left until after Israeli withdrawals were completed, but a long-term phased withdrawal should have been made to hinge upon the gradual internalization and implementation by the Arabs of their obligations. Israel has demonstrated in all stages of negotiations with the Arabs a dismal misunderstanding of Arab purposes, overlooked Arab violations of their commitments, and pursued withdrawals in spite of clear Arab indications that they had no intention of honoring their engagements. And, when Israel at times stopped to reflect upon the process, or slowed it down, it was accused by the Arabs and the world of hampering the peace process, compared to the euphoric assurances it publicized, and the high expectations it raised, regarding a new era or a new Middle East, every time some 'agreement' was reached.

When the right-wing government of Netanyahu (1966–99) attempted to slow down the pace of Israel's unilateral retreats and concessions after the Wye Conference (1998), by floating the slogan 'The Palestinians will get only if they also give', he was ridiculed by the Israeli left-wing opposition and accused of destroying the peace process. Arafat heard and understood that all he had to do was to sit out the Israeli government until it would be ousted and replaced by a more forthcoming Labor government. That happened in May 1999, but the newly elected Barak government soon learned that its proposed concessions not only would remain one-sided, but they would also generate more and more pressing demands for more concessions. This lesson was learned and internalized by Barak during the second Camp David conference in July 2000. Faced with the outbreak of Palestinian violence, precisely when Israel attained the peak of its concessions, which enjoyed neither Knesset nor

popular backing, Barak was stunned; he had staked his entire political career on this peace. He could either admit his monumental
error and retire in disgrace, or entrench himself deeper and more
perilously, in his lost positions, and offer even more concessions.
He elected to do the latter in spite of the fact that his right-wing
opposition did support any of the strong-handed reactions he sporadically adopted to counter Palestinian violence.

The collapse of the peace process forces Israel not only to reconsider the whole *démarche* in the light (or rather obscurity) of
Palestinian demands, but also to forge an alternative that will be
acceptable to the Israeli public, whose support is essential for the
endorsement of any settlement. There is no choice, then, but to
revert to square one. Israel must define its vital strategic and
national assets, announce them, define the red lines that are not to
be crossed under any circumstances, and stand by them regardless
of what the Arabs like or dislike, accept or reject, exactly as they do
not base their ambitions and demands upon Israel's wishes or sen-
sitivities. This is normal; each party is responsible for its dreams and
nightmares. For we have seen that all Israeli attempts to 'understand', to be considerate, to share, to compromise, have been thrust
back in its face and have only stimulated scorn, anger, contempt
and more demands. Paradoxically, in the present ambiance of an
oriental bazaar, where everything is up for grabs, and every item is
open to bargaining, only maximal and uncompromising demands
can bring one closer to what one wants. If you are intransigent,
your interlocutors and mediators will knock on your doors, beg
you, coax you, appease you and do everything to satisfy you. Try to
be nice, accommodating, responsible and understanding, and you
are sure to invite more pressure to give in.

Thus, Israel's stated desire for peace ought not to obscure its
interest. Again, paradoxically, by compromising before the negotiations even start, Israel cannot attain peace. Quite the contrary; by
embracing conciliatory attitudes without any retribution, Israel can
only invite more pressures for a compromise. The best proof is
what happened in the West Bank and Gaza following the far-reaching concessions Israel offered at Camp David. It became evident
that if one begins negotiations from a position of begging and sup-
plicating, signaling a need for peace at any price, spinelessness, lack
of resilience and a propensity to move back and forth at the whim
of one's interlocutor, one is likely to encounter increasing and
tougher demands, than if one had shown determination to stand

firmly, to wait out the partner, not to yield one inch without proper *quid pro quo*, and indeed no urgent interest to reach a settlement. At the same time, however, Israel must consistently indicate its interest in, and desire for, peace, a peace of reciprocity, which is tested along a protracted period of time, without rush, after long deliberations and considered reasoning, insisting that the agreed upon is implemented before any further step is effected.

Before anything else, Israel must demand evidence for the political will of the Arabs to make peace, which she must welcome; and she must pledge its commitment to respond to such advances and reward them. Israel must also insist that no negotiation is possible when violence, incitement, education to hatred, and other measurable indicators are pursued. Israel should not accept any excuse or pretext from the Palestinians or the rest of the Arabs that anything within the purview of their obligations lies beyond their authority or their ability. The ludicrous Arab proclamations of 'we are not responsible for the protection of Israel's borders', or 'someone is "angry" or "frustrated"', or even that 'some authority exerts 100 per cent of its goodwill, which does not mean 100 per cent efficacy', are unacceptable. Just as reciprocity is expected of Israel, Israel must demand that obligations under an agreement are absolute under any circumstances, and that every party is 100 per cent responsible for what is happening within or from its territory. Second, the Arabs must declare their will to share, like normal human beings, historical and religious sites that are important to both sites. If they insist on exclusivity on the Temple Mount or the Tomb of the Patriarchs, for example, it is they who should be excluded until they comply, and not the Israelis who are willing to share. If they disturb the order in those places, or desecrate them, like they did in Joseph's Tomb, they will have to be removed without ceremony from all sites where they have demonstrated their unworthiness to rule or have access.

The oft-repeated slogan that 'they understand only the language of force' is pretentious, patronizing and insensitive, because they too could say the same about the Israelis and then the parties would find themselves, once again, in the domain of argument and one-upmanship. Israel ought to render the language of talk, negotiations, sensitivity, sharing, trust, respect, hope and reward for good deeds into the cornerstone of its culture of contacts and negotiations with the Palestinians and the rest of the Arabs, and expect the same from the Arabs. These values and techniques of discussion will not emerge overnight, certainly not among leaders such as Saddam Hussein, who projects hopelessness and aggression. At any rate, all those who thought that the Palestinians were the heart of the conflict, and that a resolution to their plight would terminate the entire dispute, should rethink their concepts and look beyond the horizon. While Saddam is indeed a cruel, ruthless and bellicose leader to Israel and most of the rest of the civilized world, he symbolizes a great hope for the Palestinians and many other Arabs, a sort of modern Saladin, who holds the key for their salvation. Saddam's ability to break the UN and US sanctions in recent months is only a hint of what awaits the Middle East in the years to come. Therefore, it is premature at this point to talk about the peace that is to descend on Earth should the Israeli–Palestinian dispute be somehow resolved, much less if it is not. It is to be hoped that with a strong and firm Israel as a prospective partner, the Arabs will come to understand that short of a profound, indeed revolutionary, revision of their traditional views about the Jews and Israel, and their acceptance of their Jewish rivals as their partners in peace, in full equality, they can only hurt themselves. Israel's slogan should then be: 'Only if you change will you receive, if you don't, you won't.'

11. Oslo is Dead,
Long Live Brussels!

APOLOGIA

The current renewed outbreak of violence in the Middle East, in which the hitherto main broker – Washington – is now reluctant to dirty its hands, leaves the European Union as the only other alternative to get negotiations going again, even if there is not much promise, at this point, of a quick result. For there is always hope that when the guns are silent, the muses may be aroused by determined, fair, imaginative and purposeful mediators. This is precisely the role that Europe can play at this crucial moment of truth, before things get worse and the damage irreversible and irreparable.

But in order to qualify for that role, which will revitalize and perhaps upgrade its current secondary role in the Middle East, Europe must relinquish its stereotypical views of the conflict between Israel and the Arab World, reassess its support for the now defunct Oslo Accords by recognizing its pitfalls, and devise a new policy that will regard the current Israeli–Palestinian difficulties, not only for what they are, but in the context of the whole Middle East – where whatever party is made to toe any particular line or adopt a certain policy, will have all its interests weighed before its fate is sealed.

One of the major handicaps that has so far foiled any attempt to resolve the Israeli–Palestinian rift is the fact that all parties which have touched it, have had the tendency to divide it into what they thought were 'manageable' portions, in order to resolve it piecemeal. But those 'good intentions' simply overlooked the fact that the Palestinian people, now comprising close to nine million, is one group, and not agreeable to a separate accommodation for each of its component parts (those in Jordan are Jordanians, those in Israel are Israelis, those in Lebanon and Syria are refugees without a solution, etc.). This approach did not work in the past and will not work in the future. Therefore a new concept is needed that regards the entire land of Palestine (or the Land of Israel in Israeli parlance), as one unit where the entire Palestinian people, together with the Israelis, can find solace, comfort and good neighborliness.

EUROPEAN INEPTITUDE TO DATE

Europe has been considered inept thus far to fulfill that all-important role, because of its openly 'Arab policy', spelled out and pursued by President Chirac of France for the past two decades, since he was Prime Minister under Giscard d'Estaing's Presidency. This is not the time or place to discuss the morality of that policy, for there is none in international affairs; but, even in terms of what France has lost in prestige and cash by catering one-sidedly to the Arabs, does not compare with her loss of credibility in the eyes of Israel, something that has crippled her ability to approach the situation even-handedly. This attitude – which is usually, and fortunately, moderated and counter-balanced by Britain's and Germany's fairer understanding of these processes – is, unfortunately, common to other members of the European Union, who automatically blame Israel for any clash with the Palestinians, and create a viciously hostile atmosphere, born of ignorance and bias, in their countries' public opinion and media.

Israel also recalls the Osirak nuclear reactor sold by PM Chirac to Saddam Hussein in the 1970s, in spite of Israel's protests about putting that dangerous toy in the hands of a rogue state led by a megalomaniac murderer, who had vowed to 'burn Israel' with his unconventional weapons. He showed his mettle and his evil intentions when he gas-bombed thousands of Kurds, destroyed hundreds of their villages, instituted a reign of terror in his own country, and then successively invaded first Iran and then Kuwait in his bid to enlarge his domain and use it as a launching pad against Israel and the Gulf States. When these protests were to no avail, and Iraq came dangerously close to constructing the bomb, little Israel took the daring *démarche* of mounting a pre-emptive strike against the site and destroying it, to vocal condemnation by all Europe – especially France. Even during the Second Gulf War, when Saddam became the enemy of the pro-American coalition, including France, neither the latter (or any other European country) had the decency to thank Israel for that heroic and single-handed effort. This was not considered in Israel as an example of balanced foreign policy; it was rather seen as irresponsible policy, in which others could be sacrificed for the sake of some questionable commercial gain.

More recently, against the background of the two successive Palestinian Intifadas (1987 and 2000), the image of Israel has again been blackened; not necessarily only by its conduct, but by myopic, irresponsible and biased remarks made by European politicians, which have been echoed by their media. There is talk of a 'cycle of violence', without author or origin, as if there has been no declaration of war (the Intifada) by one party against the other, and no necessity for Israel, like any other country, to protect its people. There is talk of a 'disproportionate' Israeli response. What is proportionate? Does this mean that when Palestinian terrorists blow up ten innocent Israeli civilians, Israel should do exactly the same? Israel retaliates against Palestinian military installations, usually at night when they are empty, precisely in order to save the life of the not-so-innocent terrorists who dwell there. Is real estate more important to the Europeans than innocent lives? The Israelis are accused of 'targeted assassinations'. Yes. Targeted. Either to punish those who murdered tens of Israelis and go unpunished, or to forestall a terrorist gang on its way to commit another act of murder; once again against innocent people.

Just as the USA launched missiles against Bin-Laden, or the Europeans tried to liquidate Saddam during the Gulf War, because of their proven terrorist record, so Israel retaliates against terrorists. Is there any retribution Israel can mount without being blamed – short of sitting idle and doing nothing, which would encourage more violence? How can Israel pursue a 'due process of law' when the terrorists enjoy the protection of the PA, who refuses to extradite them to Israel, and then released those from prison who had been convicted when the Intifada broke out? After the horror at the discotheque in Tel Aviv, where 23 teenagers were butchered, Israel did nothing and even declared a one-sided cease-fire, against public opinion which cried out – not for revenge, as it is usually depicted in the European media – but punishment and prevention of more atrocities. But Israel has known no peace and therefore it has no option but to attempt to stop the perpetrators. However, Europeans only regard Israel with sympathy when it absorbs beatings silently: as soon as it acts to protect itself, it is accused of 'aggression', 'out-of-proportion force', etc.

Israelis are outraged by the way that Europeans do not call the initiators of the violence (the Intifada) to order, as do the Americans. Instead, they receive Arafat with honor, thus encouraging his tendency to pursue violent means. In fact, when Ehud Barak was in power in the initial stages of the Intifada, he was in Paris for a meeting with Arafat, sponsored by the Americans, but it was Chirac who scuttled it, thus letting Arafat off the hook and permitting him to intensify his violent methods. Palestinians are frustrated? Very understandable. The Israelis are too. The whole process of Oslo was predicated on the Palestinian obligation that UNDER NO CIRCUMSTANCES would they resort to violence, and that all disagreements, including those about Jerusalem and the Israeli settlements, would henceforth be resolved by negotiations. To justify violence today for ANY REASON, is to promote it instead of extinguishing it.

Europeans do not appear to be critical of the Palestinians even when they keep changing their 'pretexts' for violence. At one point they said it was the settlements; but when Barak practically offered them the option of evacuating most of them they said it was Israel's refusal to allow in 4 million Palestinian refugees (which would turn Israel into another Arab country, something that Israel, of course, rejected). Then, they said it was Sharon's visit to the Temple Mount, which to their mind 'desecrated' their Holy Shrine – as though it were not also his. Then it was Israeli 'aggression' (which, exactly? Israel did not declare any Intifada) that prompted Palestinian violence. And now it is the issue of Orient House, which has been taken over by Israel (again a matter of real estate where no one lost his life); as if that were the trigger of violence and not its result. On the one hand, Europeans declare that they support the Mitchell and Tenet arrangements, both of which specify that negotiations should be resumed AFTER a complete cease-fire, FOLLOWED by a cooling-off period to test Palestinian intentions. But, on the other hand, they do nothing to prevail on Arafat to declare and enforce an immediate cease-fire. He has elected to force Israel to talk while he continues to shoot, against the provisions of Mitchell and Tenet, which he said he accepted. This duplicity does not impress the Europeans, who continue to welcome Arafat and finance his corrupt system and the salaries he disburses to his terrorist gangs. Only America and Britain have had the decency to sanction him for that duplicity.

One of the favorite 'tests' used by the European media to

exemplify Israeli's 'disproportionate reaction' is the body count that is relayed day in, day out, in the media. It is well known that those who attack usually suffer many more casualties than those who defend well-fortified positions. That is one reason for the higher Palestinian body-count. The other is, that when you send mobs of thousands on the rampage – purposely including children in order to awaken world disgust – against a military position manned by a few, many more of the rampaging mob are likely to succumb in the resulting mêlée than well-trained soldiers, who know something about fighting. Moreover, dozens of cases of abuse of civilians by angered Israeli soldiers have been investigated, and the culprits court-martialled and jailed. On the Palestinian side we see the mass-release of jailed terrorists; and there are mass celebrations and the distribution of sweets in the streets when a Palestinian act of terror has 'succeeded' in claiming Israeli victims, and the perpetrators are hailed as national heroes. However, Europe seems to take no cognizance of these differences of behavior, it only repeats the mantra of 'Israeli brutality', as if Israelis wake up in the morning, having nothing to do and decide to move in and pester Palestinians. If anyone is interested in peace and quiet, it is Israel; therefore all we need is the Palestinians to stop the Intifada, which they vowed they would not – because they are interested in the continuation of violence until Israel submits to their demands.

Since the beginning of the current Intifada, another phenomenon has occurred which has caused Middle Eastern violence to be exported to Europe, and for the latter to become deeply involved in it. Radical Muslim and Arab groups, new immigrants to Europe, have gone on the rampage against Jewish targets: synagogues and Jewish schools have been torched in their dozens; cemeteries have been desecrated; Jewish worshippers have been physically attacked or reviled, for the most part with impunity; in spite of the widespread distribution of hundreds of these acts in France, Britain and Germany (as well as the Americas, Russia and Australia). One could easily imagine what would have happened to those Muslim minorities had they dared to torch a church; or how they would have reacted had anyone had the audacity to desecrate a mosque. The Jews of Europe did not retaliate in kind, they just voiced their fears quietly and with dignity, a small reminder to the Europeans who respects whom and who outrages whom.

The growing numbers of Muslims and Arabs in European countries of course make them worthy targets for courting by politicians in their quest for minority votes. But these groups, while they make the best of their lives under democracies, use the freedom they have to organize and multiply, and cluster in particular areas where they become local majorities or form strong minorities, thus directly influencing their governments to further harden their attitude towards Israel. Since Israel is facing the same problem with its Arab–Muslim minority, which totals 20 per cent of the population, it may find itself in the future alongside the Europeans in battling Arab bigotry towards Jews and Muslim fundamentalists who wish to subvert the Western order. So, although for now, Europe seems steeped in a pro-Arab mood, which detracts from its position as an honest broker between the parties, there are indications that this might be reversed in the future.

THE DEBACLE OF OSLO

Once again, there has been a mammoth misunderstanding of what happened in Oslo, and its aftermath, and the famous 'evenhandedness' was discarded and the blame was placed on both parties equally, leaving them to accuse each other of causing the breakdown. It would not be amiss, therefore, to follow step-by-step the mistakes that were built in to the Oslo process, so that something else may be put in place. In Oslo, under the influence of the euphoria over the 'historical breakthrough', the parties were not aware of the many pitfalls along the way, and simply enumerated the obligations of both parties without ensuring there was an ironclad link between the fulfillment of each step and the next. And so, the parties began blaming each other from day one for violations of the agreement – and these accusations were basically true – but neither insisted that things should be put back on course before the next step was taken. And so, instead of Oslo being regarded as a confidence-building measure, it became the epitome of confidence-wrecking.

Another major pitfall was the sky-rocketing expectations that both parties raised in their constituencies; these stood in contradiction to one another, and there was no way they could be fulfilled at the same time. The Palestinians promised their people that they would get a state; that the refugees would be repatriated; that all Israeli settlements would be removed; and that East Jerusalem would become the Palestinian capital. In return, the Israelis pledged to their peace-hungry and peace-deprived people that the question of a Palestinian state would be reviewed only after five years of autonomy; that no refugees would be accepted by Israel; that the settlement issue would be discussed only in the context of the permanent settlement with the Palestinians; and that Jerusalem would remain 'for ever united under Israeli rule'. But people on both sides soon realized that these contradictions could not be bridged.

Under the Oslo umbrella Israel obligated itself to withdraw gradually from the West Bank and Gaza (the extent and pace of withdrawal was left to Israel to determine according to developments); and to allow the PA to take over the evacuated lands and to enforce its rule via a police force that was not to exceed 9,000 men (that figure was revised upwards several times), armed by weapons handed to them by Israel. The assumption was that these weapons would be used to maintain public order and to fight terrorism. Israel also undertook to provide a safe passage between Gaza and the West Bank; to allow Palestinians to work in Israel; to allow the opening of an airport and a sea-port in Gaza; and to maintain open borders with the Palestinians, assuming that mutual interest would help sustain that state of affairs.

The Palestinians obligated themselves to renounce violence unconditionally; to not allow citizens, other than the agreed-upon police, to possess or use weapons; to arrest terrorists and combat their terrorist infrastructure; to extradite to Israel for trial criminals who had sought shelter with the PA; and to ban from its territory arms such as anti-tank and anti-aircraft guns, mortars and any other lethal weapons that were not needed to maintain order or fight terrorism. The Palestinians also undertook to put an end to anti-Israeli and anti-Semitic incitement in its official media and school curriculum. All matters relating to Jerusalem, the settlements and the refugees were left to the end of the negotiating process, to be discussed as part of the permanent settlement of the conflict, whose end was perceived to be around the corner.

But, it soon turned out, in the lifetime of Prime Minister Rabin who gave the green light to the Accords, that Arafat would not, or could not, stop terrorism against Israel unless it threatened his own rule. Soon, the number of Israeli casualties from terrorist attacks following Oslo turned out to be several-fold higher than the toll from the pre-Oslo period. The Israelis rebelled against their government, asking what was the point of Oslo – if instead of producing calm and peace it increased the numbers of victims so dramatically. The PM attempted to allay those fears by euphemistically dubbing them the 'victims of peace', a terminology that was rejected outright by the people, who believed that peace should entail no victims at all. Yet, he continued with withdrawals, and with allowing safe passage, and with permitting the building of the airport and the seaport; all the while imploring the Palestinians to extradite the criminals or to jail them, to destroy terrorism, and to collect the illegal weapons – which were evident on all TV screens, when Palestinians in their cities mounted processions of all sorts; to eliminate the incitement; and to carry out the rest of their obligations. However, true to what was accepted in Oslo, he flatly rejected any Palestinian attempt to raise the questions of Jerusalem, the refugees, or the settlements, before the final status negotiations are inaugurated.

Worse, it also turned out, that while Israel was battling terrorism, and the rage of the Israeli public was mounting because the terrorism never ceased, Arafat was facing troubles of his own – not only from the Islamists who stood in opposition to his policy, but also from the populace, once it understood that Arafat's corrupt regime was siphoning off most of the international donors' money (raised incidentally by none other than Israel's Foreign Minister Mr Peres) into his and his cronies' pockets. Outraged at seeing their dreams for a better life under 'independence' shattered, Palestinians joined the terrorists. Many an Israeli employer was murdered by his Palestinian employees; the latter also began to sabotage their places of work by, for example, pouring cement into the sewer systems of completed houses that they helped build, which then had to be torn down by their contractors.

Disgusted by these developments, the Israeli public voted for PM Netanyahu in 1996, hoping for a tougher stand that would make the Oslo process more viable for the Israelis. Essentially, as expressed in his Wye Agreement with Arafat in 1998, he posited any progress of the implementation of the process on the simple slogan: 'If they give they will receive; if they don't they won't.' This meant that he was signaling to Arafat that he was now to be held accountable for every one of his deeds or the acts he allowed to unfold under his reign. Namely, there would be further Israeli pullbacks only if the weapons are collected, incitement stopped, terrorism crushed, and criminals jailed or extradited, etc. Arafat had not been accustomed to accountability by the previous regime, therefore he was recalcitrant in the face of these demands for reciprocity, which every lawyer knows is a prerequisite for implementing agreements. Instead, the Palestinians dug tunnels under Rafah to allow the massive smuggling of weapons from Egypt, and began manufacturing mortars and other 'illegal' weapons, which are now in evidence during the Intifada.

Netanyahu made one further step towards Arafat, by allowing one further withdrawal of Israeli troops from the West Bank; but, awaiting the Palestinian executions of their obligations, he stopped there, only to be accused by the Palestinians and the Israeli Left – and therefore also by Europe – that he had 'destroyed' the peace process. No one explained how it was possible to expect the Israelis alone to continue to give in while the Palestinian obligations lay in tatters. The Palestinians nevertheless had a strong trump card in their possession with which to castigate the Israelis: they had waited the entire five-year period of the 'Interim Agreement', which had expired in 1998, and they had expected by then to have their state, to see total Israeli withdrawal (which was never on the cards), to remove Israeli settlements, and to take East Jerusalem under their rule; but nothing happened.

It was hard to explain to them, and for them to understand, that their reasoning was faulty if they thought that – regardless of how they honored their own obligations – Israel's had to be implemented in full. They were like the buyer of a house who expects the house he purchased to be handed to him, as stipulated by the contract, even if he had not made the necessary payments. Then passions mounted, Israel was accused on all sides that it had not fulfilled its obligations, which was technically true, since it refused to hand in the keys as long as the house was unpaid for. The continuation of terrorism produced the mass closure of Palestinian territories by Israel for the purposes of search and prevention; and most Palestinian workers in Israel, who proved unreliable, even dangerous for their employers, found themselves out of work, which in turn fed the spiral of frustration and violence.

In 1999, Barak was elected on a platform of peace with the Palestinians and the Syrians within the year. He engaged in very intense negotiations with Arafat, trying to jump-start the permanent status negotiations instead of remaining stymied in the interim agreement quagmire. Barak believed that a quantum jump that went directly to the bottom line, was the only way out. He laid before Arafat a complete outline of what Israel offered: a Palestinian state, including most of East Jerusalem; and 95 per cent of the West Bank to be evacuated, as well as the Gaza Strip in its entirety, meaning that most Israeli settlements would be dismantled or handed over to the Palestinians. But Barak had only one condition: that Arafat sign a declaration about the finality of the conflict; namely that after that accord, the Palestinians would no longer lay any claims at Israel's door.

Apparently that was too much for Arafat. He certainly wanted the territories, Jerusalem, the settlements, etc., but he also wished to reserve the right to renew the 'armed struggle', using his improved positions after Israeli withdrawal as a launching pad to demand more. A new issue was now tabled by the Palestinians: to provide for the 'right of return' of four million Palestinians, the descendants of those 700,000 refugees from 1948. To press their point, they declared an Intifada in September 2001. This was neither 'popular' nor 'spontaneous', but carefully crafted by Arafat to force Israel to accept his diktats, which had become increasingly popular among Palestinian public opinion, due to the unrealistic over-expectations that had been cultivated in the previous seven years. Arafat was not encouraged by Europe to accept the deal, which would have allowed him to fulfill most of his dreams. Instead, he chose the road of violence as explained in the previous section.

The swing of the political pendulum again brought the right-wing PM, Ariel Sharon, to power in Israel, and he has shown great political skill in forming a government of national unity, to pursue the double course of harsh retaliation for each act of terrorism, after his own restraint in the initial months of his rule also proved in vain, while at the same time keeping the channels of negotiation open. It is clear, however, that since the base of Oslo has been eroded, it cannot serve any longer as the platform on which a peace edifice can be constructed. Here is where Europe – a Europe that is devoid of her biases and stereotypical views of the conflict – can step in with a new initiative, based on a totally new concept of the area and a new vision for its implementation. All the more so since the Americans are now reluctant to get involved in this frustrating and never-ending conflict.

WHAT NEEDS TO BE DONE?

The basic problem that has plagued all the attempts to resolve the Palestinian–Israeli dispute has been the vain and inconsiderate assumption that the Palestinian people could be partitioned into its different components, in order to settle each of them separately: a third of these people, who reside in Jordan (about three million), and who constitute more than half the population there, are said to be 'Jordanians'; the over one million Israeli-Arabs are said to be Israelis; the two million or so in Syria, Lebanon and other diasporas, are beyond everyone's concern. Only the third who have remained in the West Bank and Gaza (close to three million), have been put on the agenda of all international deliberations, including Oslo. However, if the PLO purports to speak for all Palestinians, it cannot, as demonstrated during Camp David II (July 2000), accept to settle one-third of the question by establishing a Palestinian state in the West Bank and Gaza, and abandon the other two-thirds. This is the reason that, when Barak and Arafat came very close to a deal, the stumbling bloc proved to be the right of return of the refugees; this is a non-starter for the Israelis.

Palestine, or the Land of Israel in Israeli parlance, is the same territory rightfully claimed by both parties, even as it is known under various appellations (Israel, Jordan, Palestine). It refers to what was the land of the Israelites in old times, and to the modern pattern of settlement of the Palestinians: namely, that large swath of land, partly fertile, partly desert, where the Israeli Jews and Palestinian Arabs have historically, geographically – and now, demographically – put down their roots; where they constitute the overwhelming majority of the population; and over which they stake their claims for ownership. These claims must be negotiated between the parties, the land partitioned in some agreed way, and recognized as the land of both nationalities. In other words, the solution must be comprehensive, and include the majority of the Palestinian people, not just a third of it, for it to be considered equitable and for it to last. The entire land must be put on the table for negotiation, nowhere should be excluded, neither Jerusalem, Tel Aviv, Ramallah, Nablus, Amman or Irbid.

A new peace process should be started from square one, this time at the initiative of the EU, called the Brussels Process, based on principles of equality, reciprocity and openness, and rewarded at its end by the acceptance and integration of both Israel and Palestine at peace, into the EU, in order to safeguard within the European Community the achievements of the peace accords. The suggested four principles for the Brussels Conference are as follows:

1. Full recognition of the right of self-determination and nation-hood for both parties. In Oslo the mistake was made that while Israel recognized that right for the Palestinians, it did not ask, nor did it receive, reciprocity with regard to the Jewish people. For the Israelis who were involved in the negotiations, the fact that the PLO recognized the State of Israel was sufficient. However, since Article 20 of the Palestinian National Charter denied the right of Jews to self-determination – claiming that the Jews are not a nation – it was essential to extricate from them their recognition of Israel as a 'Jewish state', exactly parallel to Palestine as an 'Arab state'. That would have not only negated Article 20 and indicated a change in the Palestinian attitude towards Jewish nationhood, it would have avoided the later claims by the Palestinians, that since Israel was in fact a bi-national state – due to the strong component of Palestinians in its midst – it was impractical to grant the right of self-determi-nation to the Jewish people. Moreover, when they started pressing for the right of return for the Palestinians once the negotiations with Israel had come to an end, it was evident that the State of Israel they had 'recognized' would in fact turn into another Palestinian state.

   So, as the question of the nature of Israel had been left in doubt, and Oslo had not provided any foolproof definition, a long struggle between Israel and the Palestinians commenced to alter the PLO Charter: this did not come to fruition, but the struggle poisoned the atmosphere of the talks, and the Palestinian demand for the right of return also erased all the progress made in the talks earlier. The issue of how the State of Israel is defined is of prime importance, because if the Palestinian interpretation is accepted it implies that the Palestinians have the right of self-determination in the West Bank and Gaza, and also in Israel, while the Jewish State has no right to exist as an independent entity. The situation is somewhat parallel to what is happening in the Balkans today, where the Albanians have their nationhood and independence in Albania, but they insist on acquiring another one in Kosovo, which is part of Serbia, and in gaining recognition of Macedonia

as a bi-national state, in which they also form part of the population. That would leave the Albanians with two and a half
countries, while the Macedonians would be denied even one of
their own.

2. Both parties have developed modern national liberation
movements, which must be mutually recognized. In Oslo, once
again, the Israeli negotiators made the error of recognizing the
PLO without demanding in return an equal recognition of
Zionism. This not only permitted the Palestinians to continue to
dub Zionism as 'racism', and to resist the General Assembly
resolution of 1991 which – with the support of the European
countries – repealed the 1975 resolution to this effect, but also
allowed the PLO Charter to stand, in spite of the Palestinian
commitment to alter it. The PLO charter does not condemn Israel
(except in one context), or the Jews (except for denying their right
of self-determination), but it viciously attacks Zionism, and vows
in 15 of its 33 Articles, to eliminate all political, military, cultural
and economic manifestations of Zionism in Palestine.

  Again, this failure of the Israeli negotiators to make the recognition of one conditional on the recognition of the other, led to
one-sided Israeli legitimation of the PLO; while Zionism, its
counterpart, remained vilified by the Palestinians. This also led
to demands by the Palestinians living in Israel that Zionism, and
its symbols, be eliminated from Israel; this is comparable to
Arabs living today in France demanding that the 'Marseillaise'
be abandoned and the country stripped of its French symbols
and culture, in order for them to feel comfortable there. This also
caused a long and unpleasant debate between the Israelis and
the Palestinians regarding the Charter; with Israel insisting that
all negative references to her in the Charter (there are none) be
excised, and the Palestinians emphasizing that they had 'only'
condemned Zionism, not Israel. Even the final attempt to force
the Palestinians to amend the Charter ended in a farce, orchestrated by the Americans; but the Charter remained in force, and
its clauses hurtful to the Israeli Jews.

3. The question of territory should also be resolved by presenting
all the pieces of the puzzle on the negotiating table. The
Palestinians cannot hope to assemble the majority of their
people under their rule – which seems to be the prerequisite for

a durable resolution of the conflict – unless they take into account the two-thirds of their people living outside the West Bank and Gaza, and seek territorial ways to accommodate the refugees among them who have been rotting in refugee camps for three generations in a row. Therefore, the territory where the single largest Palestinian population dwells – Jordan – cannot be left out of the equation. We are not talking about the 'disappearance' of an existing country, just about re-naming it and about democratizing its regime; something that the European Union ought to be the first to promote. For the Hashemite King is not a country or a people, but merely part of a regime originally transplanted from Saudi Arabia by the British; while most of the people there, who are Palestinians, have the right to rule the country because they form the majority of the population.

If indeed the king is as beloved and popular as he pretends, he can, of course, remain on his throne, by the consent of the Palestinians and not in antagonism to them, and his country can be re-baptized the 'Hashemite Kingdom of Palestine', where the King would be a mere figurehead and symbol, like the Belgian or the Danish Kings, while the true focus of power would move from the royal court to an elected government in which the Palestinians would, by definition, be the overwhelming component. It is with such a government that Israel should negotiate the fate of the territories, Jerusalem, the settlements, etc., and all the matters that pertain to a durable and acceptable settlement.

Both parties would be much more relaxed in such negotiations: the Israelis, because a greater Palestine, which could post her unlimited armed forces east of the Jordan could also afford to demilitarize the West Bank (as Egyptians did the Sinai). Thus, all weapons smuggling and other sensitive issues of security, would be removed. The Palestinians would have many more good reasons to adopt such an arrangement. First, it would allow them control of a large territory that could accommodate the refugees; second, they would achieve good neighborliness with Israel, and possibly even cooperate with it economically and technically; third, bloodshed would finally end, and construction and development begin; and, finally, the Palestinians would attain full statehood. Their negotiations with Israel would then center, not around the explosive questions of a Palestinian state, terrorism, security or the hair-splitting debates of who started what, when and where, but on the issue of how to partition real estate, how to secure access to holy places for all, etc.; all from a base of existing and self-confident secure states. In other words, the negotiations would become less ideological and qualitative, and more practical and quantitative. The experience of conflict management elsewhere has shown that the latter are much easier to settle, because they are amenable to negotiation, compromise and agreement; while the former are more absolute and locked into uncompromising positions, both religious and otherwise.

Certainly, such negotiations would not be easy, because each party would struggle to retain as much territory as possible in a zero-sum game situation. However, attractive proposals could be made to attract Palestinian interest: for example, instead of dividing Greater Palestine East–West, it could be divided North–South, thus ensuring the Palestinians continuity of territory between their domains east of the Jordan and the heavily populated Gaza Strip, and certainly between these domains and those parts of the West bank that would revert to them under the permanent agreement. Then, each party within its own boundaries, would determine any immigration and citizenship policy it pleased, within their respective sovereign territories; and both the Palestinian right of return, and the Israeli Law of Return, could be implemented without hampering, or posing a menace to, the other.

4. Once the territory was divided in whatever way agreed, there would remain the question of the inhabitants remaining in the country other than their own; namely, Palestinians who continued to live under Israeli sovereign rule and, conceivably, Israelis left behind in Palestine when the agreement entered into force. The decision to stay or move to the other state should be left to individual choice, and population movement should operate on the basis of equality and reciprocity, and provide a gradual and long-term solution in order to avoid the trauma of forced transfer of populations, as had happened to the German populations of Poland and the Sudeten after the Second World War. Three options must be offered to the 'alien' populations, on both sides (and sufficient time to make their decision):

   a. To sell their properties and move voluntarily to their mother country where they can fulfill their political and emotional needs and dreams.

b. To swear allegiance to their new country, obtain citizenship, learn its culture and language, and couple their fate and the fate of their families with its fate.

c. Do neither of the above, and simply remain as alien permanent residents in their towns and villages, with all the rights of residents, including work and social services, but retaining the citizenship of their mother country, where they can vote and exercise other rights and duties. In a situation of open borders and a peaceful, but secure, coexistence, in view of the short distances between the two states, they would be like Belgians living in the Netherlands, or vice versa.

ENDING THE CONFLICT AND JOINING EUROPE

The greatest attraction of the above plan, or a variety thereof, is that it does, on the one hand, offer the hope that a solution is possible if begun from square one, on a totally different basis, initiated by an international body that has not 'sullied' its hands in the mess so far. On the other hand it promises a reward for the completion of an agreement and the implementation of its clauses, in the form of joining the European Union. Another advantage it holds is that neither side is forced to accept the other's diktat, but both yield to the initiative of Greater Europe, which is also capable of luring the parties to accept its plan, and has the economic clout to see to it that its stipulations are respected by both sides.

This plan promises a departure from the tiring and confusing minutiae involved in the various Oslo Agreements and their derivatives: Oslo I and II, Camp David I and II, Cairo I and II, Wye Plantation I and II, Paris and Washington, Sharm al Sheikh I and II. So many agreements only mean that there has been no agreement at all; for instead of simplifying things, defining clear boundaries at every stage and promising an outcome, the tortuous minds of the negotiators ventured into inventions like 'Area A', 'B' and 'C' which complicated the implementation of what seemed to have been agreed. The result was that, instead of confidence being instilled into the two parties, they were dominated by conflict, friction and suspicion.

One negative lesson from Oslo is that it tried to tackle the complicated issues by mounting an elaborate edifice of interim agreements that were to serve as way stations for the continuation of the process; the ultimate goal of which remained undefined and nebulous. But way stations can only be built when you know in which direction the train is going. If you get off at the wrong station you can always wait for the next train; but if you board the wrong train, you reach a destination you did not intend. Therefore, a permanent settlement – which is the destination of the train – must be the negotiated goal of a new initiative; and, when reached, its implementation should be spread over several years, each station leading to the direction of the final destination.

Oslo also taught us, once again, the foolishness of what Henry Kissinger once called 'constructive ambiguity'. By this he meant that negotiators ought to find formulae with which both parties could live, even though each of them interpreted the terms differently. The famous Security Council Resolution 242 (November 1967) provides an example of this; 34 years later we have still not agreed upon its interpretation, even though everybody religiously refers to it as if it were the Gospel. Oslo and its derivatives are replete with such formulations, and no sooner had they been signed than both parties accused each other of violating the terms, because each side understood them differently and strove to enforce their version or interpretation. However, while one can reach an initial 'agreement' with this technique, soon the day of reckoning comes, when the parties have to implement the ambivalent text, and disagreement immediately ensues. Therefore, any new agreement must be clear, in terms and spirit, so as not to leave any uncertainties or loopholes.

And, finally, this is Europe's great opportunity to abandon the illusory comfort of standing on the sidelines, and to take the conflict in the Middle East into its own hands. Illusory comfort, because sooner or later, Europe will have to confront the mounting wave of terrorism in Spain by ETA, in Britain by the IRA, in France by the Corsican nationalists, in the Balkans by Albanian nationalists, among others. Therefore, it cannot simply wash its hands of the terrorist campaign to which Israel is subjected, and expect the Palestinian problem to be the only one dominated by terrorism. International terrorists assist each other and learn from each other. It is in Europe's interest to defuse the Palestinian time-bomb, then the situation in the Middle East might then serve as a model and guide, even before the ripple effects of terrorism are felt beyond Palestinian territory. If Europe does so, and succeeds, this could be one of its finest hours.

12. The Israeli–Jordan Peace Agreement: A Missed Opportunity*

ubi solitudinem faciunt pacem apellant
[wherever they sow desolation they call it peace]
Tacitus, *Historia*

Great cries of exhilaration were heard in Israel, from the Left and the Right, blurring the boundaries between government and opposition, when late Prime Minister Rabin announced to an overjoyed Israeli public the conclusion of a peace treaty with Jordan in 1994. Finally, it was said, and felt, the long-standing 'friendly' and 'intimate' relationship with the 'moderate' and 'pro-Western' monarch was formalized and institutionalized, thus eliminating, once and for all, the abiding threat of the Eastern Front.

The wall-to-wall rare consensus among the Israeli public towards this dramatic event overshadowed the deep divisions between the 'peace camp' and the 'hard-liners', and pushed to the sidelines their radically different, even diametrically opposed, motives for supporting this peace arrangement. Rabin and his group thought that the isolated Palestinians would come to terms more easily once King Hussein openly allied with Israel; the Likud and its allies hoped that by resolving the Palestinian problem within Jordan, which is home to half the Palestinian people (3.5 out of 8 million), they could avoid addressing the thorny question of Palestinian nationhood in the Territories. Both ends of the Israeli political continuum behaved as if Jordan were the main source of Israeli concerns, and they rushed to settle with it as if such a settlement would put an end to those concerns. Both were wrong on both counts.

---

* Originally published as *The Israeli–Jordan Peace Agreement: A Missed Opportunity*, ACPR Policy Paper No. 26 (Sha'arei Tikva: Ariel Centre, 1998).

THE ESSENTIALS OF THE ISRAEL–JORDAN
PEACE AGREEMENT (1994)

The Madrid Process, which opened in the wake of the Second Gulf War (1991), resulted in a series of bilateral meetings in Washington between Israel and its neighbors during 1992, which were geared to produce bilateral peace treaties. At first, at Israel's insistence and with American connivance, the Israeli delegation negotiated with a joint Jordanian–Palestinian counterpart in the search for a solution to the Palestinian issue that could meet the terms of the Camp David Accords (1978), which had recognized the 'legitimate rights' of the Palestinian people, in contrast with the 242 Security Council Resolution, which had only mentioned the need to resolve the refugee problem.

The talks soon stalled, due to the Palestinian need to lend the PLO stamp of legitimacy to the Palestinian contingent in the negotiations, something that Israel rejected out of hand. But, when a change of government took place in Israel in June 1992, the new administration decided to short-circuit the ongoing Washington talks, established a parallel channel to the PLO in Oslo, and concluded an agreement with the Palestinians behind the backs of the American facilitators of the official channel of negotiations. Newly elected President Clinton seized the occasion, aligned himself with the Rabin government's volte-face and sponsored the signing ceremony of the accords on the lawn of the White House (September 1993).

Once the Israeli government acknowledged the separate existence of a Palestinian entity, it was only a matter of time before King Hussein jumped on the bandwagon. His motives were obvious: if he could get a separate acknowledgement of legitimacy from Israel for his rule in Jordan over half the Palestinian people – which constituted two-thirds of the population of his Kingdom – the entire Palestinian problem would be handed over to Israel to resolve. He had washed his hands clean of the Palestinian 'headache' back in 1988, at the height of the Intifada, when he renounced his claim to the West Bank, which had been his fief between 1948 and 1967 and the retrieval of which he had been pursuing thereafter. He was delighted to pass on to Israel the Palestinian hot potato and to entrench himself as the legitimate ruler of Jordan with recognized interests in the Islamic holy shrines in Jerusalem.

The accords which he negotiated and rapidly concluded with Israel covered six different areas, all of which worked in Jordan's favor:

1. Border Adjustments: Three areas on the border between Jordan and Israel necessitated Israeli withdrawals as follows:
   (a) Out of the 381 square kilometers claimed by Jordan south of the Dead Sea since 1949, Israel agreed to hand over 300.
   (b) In the Naharayim area on the border between Israel and Jordan, at the convergence of the Jordan and Yarmuk Rivers, Jordan got part of the five square kilometers under dispute and turned them into the 'Island of Peace', where meetings between the populations of the parties were to be facilitated.
   (c) In the southern Arava Desert 30 square kilometers, which had been reclaimed and fertilized by Israeli kibbutzim over the years, were formally returned to Jordanian sovereignty, although they remained practically under lease in the hands of their Israeli users.

2. Water Distribution: Under the Accords, Jordan was to receive more water from the Yarmuk River than its original share, and Israel undertook to raise the necessary funds to finance the dams that were to ameliorate the storing capacity of the river. Beyond those agreements, thirsty Jordan never desisted from demanding more water from Israel's own shrinking supplies, to an extent which has necessitated dipping into the Kinneret national reservoir, itself under a severe process of depletion after many years of drought and changing climatic patterns.

3. Palestinians living in Jordan were put on the agenda as candidates for repatriation to West Palestine. This 60 per cent majority component of the Jordanian population, which is potentially inimical to King Hussein, was further increased by 10 per cent following the escape during the Gulf War of some 350,000 Palestinian refugees from Kuwait to Jordan. The rise of their ratio from 60 to 70 per cent, with the attending socio-economic problems of unemployment, crime, political unrest and Islamic inroads into the social fabric, meant that the regime had to do anything it could to negotiate them away to anyone ready to take them. Some 800,000 of them, dubbed by Jordan and the PLO the '1967 refugees' were forced onto the agenda of

negotiations and were considered as candidates for immediate repatriation to the West Bank and Gaza; while hundreds of thousands more were to be discussed in the context of the permanent settlement between Israel and the Palestinians. Worse, Israel agreed to discuss the question of these refugees in a quadripartite forum (with Egypt, Jordan and the PLO), in which it would be outnumbered, isolated and accused by the Arabs of obstructing the solution.

4. The Islamic Holy Places in Jerusalem were recognized, according to the Washington Statement of 25 July 1994, as pertaining to Jordan's 'unique historic role' in the city. That meant that subsequent to Jordan's illegal occupation of East Jerusalem for 29 years, and its removal by force from there in 1967, and after Hussein had waived his claim to the West Bank (including Jerusalem) in 1988, the Hashemites were now introduced once again through the backdoor and given a role in the city, to the detriment of Israel who claims it as her 'eternal capital' and of the Palestinians who succeeded in forcing it onto the Oslo agenda. By playing Jordanians against Palestinians in the city, Israel runs the risk of losing to both and of seeing its own authority eroded.

5. 'Security' and 'Normalization' are the key concepts which have induced the Israelis into the Accords with Jordan. The Israeli national psyche has a hard time coming to terms with the idea that Jewish independence and the recognition of Israeli security needs are to go hand in hand with any peace arrangement between Israel and its neighbors as a matter of course. Indeed, Israel's almost pathological need to seek acceptance and recognition from any quarter the world over, and at almost any price, and to rejoice beyond measure when this seems to be achieved, lies behind the great and unjustified concessions it had to make to Jordan to get these Accords. Thus, in gaining legitimacy from an autocratic king, himself in search of legitimacy, and in obtaining permission for the besieged Israelis to walk the alleys of Petra, Irbid and Karak, Israel found its aspirations fulfilled. But Israel is also unmindful that, judging from the Egyptian precedent, the peace with Jordan is not foolproof and King Hussein or his successors are likely to join anti-Israeli coalitions in the future as they did in 1967 and once again during the Gulf War in 1991.

6. Economic Cooperation – a euphemism for a one-sided Israeli line of credit, technical assistance, fund-raising and lobbying in the West for grants to the Kingdom, as well as aid in land conservation, agro-technology, water supply, industrial parks, etc. The only rewards Israel got in return were warnings of the impending economic imperialism of Israel. Tangible gains in selling Israeli products are difficult to envisage due to the inability of the Arab markets in general to purchase Israeli high-tech and other expensive products.

WHEN THE PEACE ACCORDS BECOME A TRAP

Israel's concessions to Jordan regarding land and water, the allowances in terms of fund-raising, and the lip service to the Hashemite House – in return for practically nothing – in themselves will not determine the making or breaking of the Jewish State. The problem lies with the premises underlying Israel's policy which led to that agreement regardless of whether or not it was initiated by the government or backed by the opposition. And, at the end of the process, due to the expectations we helped raise across the world, Israel will be punished, pay the whole price and get nothing in return, just as in the famous Jewish story whose lessons we have refused to heed.

As indicated above, the strategy of the Israeli government has been to shift the center of gravity from unreliable and unpredictable Arafat to 'moderate' and pro-Western Hussein, in order to dwarf the Palestinian issue; while the right-wing opposition has sustained Hussein in order to eliminate Arafat. Both were wrong; and the king has outsmarted both. He understood his problem of legitimacy in the eyes of his Palestinian majority which remembers him as the descendant of the Hashemite House whose roots are in Hijaz, Saudi Arabia. Hussein, like his grandfather Abdullah, has been taking great pains to cultivate the new Jordanian identity in Eastern Palestine, whose population consists of either veteran Palestinian Bedouins or newcomers from the West Bank and elsewhere either before 1948, or during the wars that ensued, or as a result thereof.

But, when the Israeli government lent to Hussein the legitimacy he needed for his rule, it fell into the trap of recognizing his country as 'Jordan', as if Hussein and his House were a people or a country and not merely a disposable regime, an autocratic one at that, probably in power against the will of his people, who are basically Palestinian and identify themselves as such. Had Israel insisted on the Palestinian nature of Jordan – a proposition repeatedly hailed by Hussein himself ('Jordan is Palestine and Palestine is Jordan'), a proposition supported by history, geography and demography – and demanded that the right of self-determination be accorded to the entire Palestinian people, including those in Jordan and in Israel, then Jordan, being part of Palestine and home to half the Palestinian people, would have become part of the solution of the Palestinian problem.

Under these circumstances, a 'Hashemite Kingdom of Palestine' could have been declared, with the royal house at its helm as a constitutional monarchy as long as the people there wanted it, but with the actual power in the hands of the Palestinian majority. But, since this did not happen, the entire Palestinian burden now rests squarely on Israel's shoulders out of its own choice; and since Israel cannot alone resolve this problem it becomes insoluble for the following reasons:

1. If the PLO continues to claim that it represents the entire Palestinian people, including the 3.5 million in Jordan and the million in Israel, the dream of self-determination cannot be fulfilled as long as the Palestinians are divided between Jordan, Judea, Samaria and Gaza, Israel (what are erroneously called the 'Israeli Arabs'), and the Diaspora (refugee camps in Syria and Lebanon and Palestinian communities in the West).
2. The Right of Return which is hailed by the Palestinians as one of their basic demands for a settlement, cannot be achieved in the territory west of the Jordan River which is already overpopulated and whose permanent status is still disputed with Israel.
3. Even if Israel and the Palestinians were to come to a full agreement on the extent of the Palestinian autonomy/State in the present parameters of the negotiation, this would encompass only one-third of the Palestinian people, while the other two-thirds would continue to vie for independence and to knock on Israel's door, violently or otherwise, in search of a solution.
4. A Palestinian entity west of the Jordan would insist on all paraphernalia of statehood such as a fully fledged army, which Israel cannot allow. This itself would give rise to unrest and friction due to the difficulty of policing the imperceptible transition from police to military control.

5. The Palestinian entity would remain discontented with both Israel and the Jordanian State, due to the continuum of Palestinian population in all three.
6. This no-win situation would further deteriorate due to the mounting activity of the Muslim Brothers (Hamas) in Jordan and west of the River, who are committed to rejecting partial agreements between the Palestinians and Israel, and who demand the application of *shari'a* law over the entire territory of historical Palestine as a first step toward the recreation of the universal Caliphate. The problematic legitimacy of the Jordanian, as well as the PLO, rule in East and West Palestine, respectively – while the Brothers are waiting in the aisles in both places and accumulating popularity – leaves open the question of whether Israel can conclude any permanent settlement with the governments in place on either side of the Jordan River. The lesson of Western support to the military government in Algeria and to other autocrats in Egypt, Jordan, Morocco, etc., while legitimacy was shown to belong to the Islamists there, and the ensuing killings and chaos, ought to deter any wise administration from following the same road.

The Palestinians do not care to raise these concerns in public because they are mindful of the fact that if their problem were to be settled in such a way as to include Jordan too, and their official rule were recognized there, the pressure would be taken off Israel to accord them self-determination and statehood. Jordan is theirs, as a matter of course, and it is only a matter of time before their overwhelming majority will displace the Hashemites, at worse, or co-opt them in Hashemite Palestine, at best. Therefore, they focus all their effort, military and diplomatic, on obtaining their independence from Israel so as to ensure its retreat from the West Bank, as a first step to demanding more and cashing in the rest which will fall into their lap like a ripe fig.

Had the Palestinians made clear at this point their claim over all the territories where they constitute a majority or a sizable minority, which would have meant, in fact, laying claim to Jordan as well as Israel, they would have defeated their purpose and forfeited the support they now enjoy as a stateless people. For they would then be demanding two and a half states: one in the West Bank and Gaza, one in Jordan (that they already have in all but the title), and half of Israel, which they refuse to recognize as a Jewish state, and insist on its bi-national (Jewish–Palestinian) character. Only the implementation of this dream is likely to alleviate the despair of the refugees who have been rotting in the camps for three generations, and who would settle for nothing less than returning to an aggrandized Palestine. Such talks, coupled with accusations against Arafat, that he has left them on the sidelines in Oslo, are already heard among many Palestinian quarters.

SQUARING THE TRIANGLE

The Palestinian triangle (in Jordan, Israel and the Territories) cannot be squared unless all three parts are taken together in the context of one large territorial unit called Palestine/The Land of Israel, in which Palestinian Arabs and Israeli Jews have equal part and equal right. In this perspective, Jordan, which is part of Palestine, is not only part of the Palestinian problem but also a vital part of its solution. Concluding a separate peace with Jordan constituted, therefore, from the Israeli point of view, a foreclosure of options for the solution of the core issue of Palestine. But going back to square one, even today, is not impossible.

In Oslo a tragic mistake was made of recognizing that 80 per cent of Palestine and 50 per cent of the Palestinians were King Hussein's as Jordanians, but this did not resolve the question of Palestinian nationhood. Quite the contrary, by excluding from the settlement the very components that could facilitate it, it was made impossible. There is no escape from the conclusion, therefore, that two paradoxical premises have to be adopted by both parties:

1. Only if the two parties, Israelis and Palestinians, who inhabit, have relations with, and own Palestine/The Land of Israel, openly advance maximalistic claims to the land in its entirety, i.e. on both sides of the Jordan, can they also make concessions to the other party: Israel in the East Bank and the Palestinians in the West Bank; only then do they have something to give up without precipitating irreversible damage to their very existence.
2. Only if each party recognizes the rights of the other can it also expect its demands to be heeded. Each party wants the other to be 'realistic' and accept the need to withdraw and make concessions, but unless each party also recognizes the symmetry and

reciprocity built into the mutual system of recognition of rights, no one will move to make the necessary sacrifices. Thus, rather than list a series of 'nos' to the partners in negotiations – namely spelling out the non-starters which become preconditions before any discussion was started – it is better to state the equal and parallel rights of both parties and discuss what each party is prepared to concede in order to reach a settlement. In other words, only if the Israelis and Palestinians accept the premise that each one of them owns all of historical Palestine, that is Israel, the Territories and Jordan, but so does the other too, can the negotiations begin.

Once these principles are accepted, the issue becomes one of boundaries. This vast land can be divided north–south or east–west so as to accommodate both peoples and at the same time respond to their basic needs. If the Palestinians want to keep the Hashemite House and be loyal to it, it is their affair; if the King wants to test his long-standing claim that he is beloved of his subjects and is popular with them, they would certainly consent to turn their State into the Hashemite Kingdom of Palestine, and their King into a constitutional monarch, while the overwhelming Palestinian majority retains the actual reins of power.

This would be the government, whatever its composition, that Israel would have to deal with to implement the permanent peace plan. The negotiations will be protracted, difficult and tortuous before the final boundaries are agreed upon, but when they are, everyone would understand that the lot has been drawn, the land has been divided and an acceptable peace settlement by the two peoples has been established. Because under these circumstances, the debate between the parties would be a quantitative one, about territories and assets that can be agreed upon in the process of give-and-take as a means and a compromise as an end, it would no longer be a qualitative conflict where Israel denies the rise of a Palestinian state and Palestinians refute the idea of a Jewish state in part of Palestine – something that they did not fully accept yet in spite of Oslo.

Such a Palestinian state would not be by nature, any stronger or more ill-willed than the present Jordanian State. Because if 'moderate' Jordan could attack Israel in 1967, and associate with Israel's enemies in 1973 and during the Gulf War of 1991, there is no reason for Israel to fear that a Palestinian state in the same territory and with the same demographic composition would do any worse. The fate of the territories west of the Jordan, now ruled by Israel, would then be discussed with a self-confident Palestinian government, based east of the river, for whom the West Bank and Gaza, or parts thereof, would be no more than part of Palestine, and which would therefore be more agreeable to territorial compromise to satisfy Israeli security needs. In this regard the Egyptian model could be enlightening: the Egyptians agreed in the Camp David process to demilitarize Sinai only because they could still maintain their armies along the Suez Canal and in the Egyptian hinterland.

After the partition of all Palestine between Israeli Jews and Palestinian Arabs, both populations who wish to continue to reside in the State that is not their own will be able to do so and will acquire the right of permanent residence. They will have to obey the local laws and submit to the local administrative system, but will owe their political loyalty, including citizenship, absentee vote and military service, to their own State. Thus, regardless of the exact borders between the two States, the demographic realities would matter little. In Israel, the Palestinians/Jordanians, including Israeli Arabs, who wish to reside there but maintain their national Arab identity, would continue to hold their alien passports while residing in Israel. Conversely, Israelis now residing in settlements that may revert to the new Palestinian/Jordanian entity, would act likewise. But, once the borders are drawn between the two parties, each one of them would devise and control its own immigration and citizenship policy to suit its particular needs within its own sovereign territory.

There are, however, two other concurrent (not substitute) possibilities to settle the nationality versus territory contradiction. First, people on both sides could of their own will decide to leave their place of residence, sell their property and move to the State with which they can identify and in which they can feel part of the ruling majority. It might take generations before this voluntary population transfer resulted in the demographic balance settling at a certain level permanently. If the two States agreed upon such a procedure during their negotiations, they could jointly declare their encouragement of voluntary population exchange as part of the general settlement between them. Alternatively, the alien residents could apply for citizenship in their country of residence and thereby cast their lot in with their country of choice, partake of its economic, political and cultural life, serve in its armed forces, be educated in its language, and identify with its aspirations.

THE QUESTION OF JERUSALEM

The question of Jerusalem may also be addressed within this framework, in the context of the new Jordanian–Palestinian State. Jerusalem had been the seat of the Palestinian Grand Mufti in the 1930s and 1940s, but was later relegated by the Hashemites to the status of a backwater provincial city. It re-entered the world stage as a result of its reunification in 1967 under Israeli rule and the international attention it has attracted ever since. In the Israeli–Jordanian peace accords of 1994, Jordan was again given a say in Jerusalem, due to Hussein's insistence that he regain part of the aura of the curator of the Holy Places in Jerusalem, which he had lost in 1967 and which was part of his problematic political legitimacy in the first place.

The growing centrality of Jerusalem in the Muslim world, not least of all because it is currently not ruled by a Muslim power, makes it a major stumbling block on the road to peace between Israel and the Arabs/Muslims. It serves no purpose to invoke the sanctity of the city for the Jews or the Muslims and its centrality in their respective histories, cultures, politics and religions, for such contentions, irrefutable as they may be, could immediately be countered by parallel claims from all parties concerned. No one has invented an instrument to gauge the intensity of religious feeling or the extent of political commitments. In history, and even more so in political behavior, it is perceptions that count, it is beliefs that are operationally important, it is convictions that are valid – not what we would like to see as the 'objective truth' or 'hard fact'. Therefore, the harder one attempts to prove his point in this debate, the more the other feels constrained to emphasize his own heritage and to conjure up the entire length and breadth of history to plead his case.

Putting Jerusalem on the negotiation table, whatever be the mode of the permanent settlement, not only would meet the criterion that everything is negotiable, but it could also dramatically alter the ambiance of the talks and prod the Palestinians–Jordanians to adopt the principle of sharing when the two parties are irretrievably locked in a system of mutual exclusion. The model to follow is that of Hebron, where during all the centuries of Islamic rule that preceded 1967, the Jews never had access beyond the seventh step to the Tombs of the Patriarchs, which the Muslims called the Ibrahimi Mosque. When Israel took over in 1967, and against the widespread expectation that it would act likewise and exclude the Muslims henceforth, it announced that since the shrine was holy to both Judaism and Islam, the days of worship would be equally divided between the parties. The Muslims never accepted that arrangement, continued to claim their exclusive right to the place, but had no choice but to be reconciled to reality.

Similarly, the Muslims who had built their Aqsa Mosque and Dome of the Rock on the ruins of the ancient Jewish temples, claim exclusivity for these places, stressing, among other things, that Islam had displaced both Christianity and Judaism and was the one revealed religion, and therefore no one else other than them had the right to the place. Israel, rather than inflaming the mood of Muslims across the world, decided to give in and not insist on sharing. This, in turn, has not only reinforced the Muslim claim of exclusivity, but has also induced them to expand their hold on the site by building a lower level dubbed the Marwani Mosque. If this could be reversed and the Muslims made to realize that they cannot monopolize a holy shrine which is claimed by others too, regardless of who rules the city, a long way would have been traveled towards acceptance of the other and towards coexistence in Jerusalem which could facilitate other practical arrangements. As elsewhere, no one can get everything but everyone will get something.

In the search for such a miraculous solution, many ideas have been proposed: from the internationalization of the city, to the sovereignty of the monotheistic religions over their religious sites; from a condominium of the city by Israel and some Arab/Muslim entity such as Palestine, Jordan or Saudi Arabia, to autonomous boroughs under one united municipal umbrella. Because nothing could be agreed, due to the lack of a universally accepted definition of sovereignty, autonomy, what is whose, etc., the problem was relegated to the end of the peace process. But the peace process does not seem to be served by this evasion, for the tensions are mounting and the parties are positioning themselves with *fait accompli* to prepare for the ultimate show-down. Here too, the shifting of the Palestinian center of gravity eastwards, would by necessity lessen the pressure on Jerusalem and promote other creative solutions for a Palestinian–Jordanian capital, while the Islamic sites could get recognition and autonomy on a basis of sharing as outlined above.

BALANCE OF GAINS AND DRAWBACKS

Life in general, and diplomatic *démarches* in particular, is a process of choice. It would be too easy if the choice were between good and bad, cheap and expensive, beneficial and harmful. Very often the preferred choice bears a price tag which makes its worth questionable. Therefore, one has to analyze the proposed solution in terms of the vital interests of the parties, and only if the projected benefits are not exceeded by the perceived drawbacks, does the plan stand any chance of implementation.

Israel would have to pay with territory for any benefits it might draw from such a settlement. What territory, and to what extent, will remain a subject of negotiation between Israelis and Jordanians–Palestinians. But it is clear that, having no other major tangible asset to yield, the Israelis must pay mainly in terms of land. Paying with territory, however, does not necessarily mean the complete Israeli withdrawal from the West Bank, for the Israelis could very well advance the argument that since they claim the right over all historical Palestine–Jordan, as do the Palestino–Jordanians, their readiness to yield the East Bank and retain parts of the rest is a territorial concession of major proportion. This argument, which would certainly be rejected by the Jordanians–Palestinians, who could claim a right to the same, would also allow them to advance their counter-claims and posit their own territorial demands.

Protracted negotiations might ensue, which might lead to the brink of a crisis, but ultimately an accommodation would be found, for territory is a quantitative issue amenable to concession, compromise and negotiation. In return for Israel's admittedly high payment in territory, it would stand to gain much. It could claim and retain much of the territory of the West Bank necessary for its security, and after that agreement is attained, it will remain not as an occupying power but as of right. The Palestinian Arabs remaining under Israeli rule, once they are assured of nationhood, statehood and freedom of choice as to their future, would calm down and desist from violence; the problem of Israeli Arabs, who are now torn between their country and their people, would be resolved and each individual would become the master of his own fate; Israel could then regain the image of a peace-loving and generous country, once its crucial contribution to the freedom of the Jordanians–Palestinians is recognized. Under this plan, Israel would be able to remain Jewish and democratic, free from the demographic menace, within boundaries finally recognized by its neighbors and the international community. Israel's improved image and secure border would render it an attractive place for Western Jews to settle in, and most of the present Israeli settlements in the territories would not only be maintained but they could even be reinforced and expanded when Israel's sovereignty over them is assured. The Zionist nature of Israel would become clearer and more unshakable, and her nearly homogeneous citizenry would be able, under conditions of peace and prosperity, to revive their pioneering spirit.

The Jordanians–Palestinians must also pay a heavy price: renouncing their desire for the removal of Israel from their midst; settling for the eastern side of Palestine as their main base, with incremental gains from the West Bank and Gaza; giving up the 'Right of Return' into Israel and the PLO Charter. The Hashemites will also have to yield their autocratic rule in favor of a democratically elected government where the Palestinians would have the determining voice. Certainly, no ruler has ever relinquished power of his own will, but this would be a much smaller sacrifice than the territorial and ideological concessions that both the Palestinians and the Israelis would be called upon to make.

In return, the Jordanians–Palestinians would get more than three-quarters of historical Palestine, where plenty of territory is available to resettle refugees who have been languishing in camps for the past 50 years. Already in the context of the Oslo Accords, the refugees have been raising their voice against the PA which has left them outside the settlement due to its inability to absorb them in its confined territory, and they will inevitably continue to knock on Israel's door for a solution. Unless, that is, their problem is seen to be resolved in the vast land of Palestine across the Jordan River. The Palestinians would finally have a state of their own where they can implement their aspirations and gain recognition and support from Israel as a peaceful neighbor whose vital national interests would have also been fulfilled. They would then control the fate of most Palestinians, not merely the one-third of them presently dwelling in the West Bank and Gaza; either through direct rule or via absentee citizenship for those remaining in Israel and elsewhere.

A Jordanian vital interest as such does not exist except as expressed by the King ruling that State. Since popular will, to the extent that it exists, reflects that of the Palestinian majority in that state much more than that of the King, it stands to reason that the Hashemites should yield to their people's desire. It will not be easy but it is not unreasonable, compared with the sacrifices that Israel and the Palestinians would have to incur. For the King too, the benefits are great and promising: in addition to regaining some parts of his lost territory while retaining his throne and the rule of the Hashemites over Palestine, and to gaining legitimacy for his throne and his reign from the majority of his subjects; he would also establish, finally, borders of internal peace not only with the Israelis but also with the Palestinians. He would dramatically increase his population from four to six million or more, some of whom would continue to reside in Israel but be his subjects and citizens, in addition to the refugees who would flow in in their eagerness for permanent settlement; Jordan would get access to the Mediterranean in Gaza via Israeli territory, unless the agreed upon division of the land would be along north–south lines, in which case Palestine–Jordan would be directly and permanently related to the Gaza shore.

Under these conditions, the Palestinians would at last be able to channel their talent, energies, manpower and creativity into developing their country, resettling their refugees, and cultivating their heritage and culture. They would also have a large and strong army posted east of the Jordan while their West Bank possessions would remain demilitarized so as not to pose a threat to Israel. If the Palestinian majority decides to retain the King at its head, as a constitutional monarch in the Hashemite Kingdom of Palestine, he would regain parts of his lost territories and double the numbers of his subjects with the inflow of Palestinians, or of the absentee citizens in Israel, Syria, Lebanon and the Diaspora. The King would then enjoy legitimacy as the head of Hashemite Palestine where popular will would have granted him the monarchy. He would then enjoy security and stability for his crown and would be able to devote his energies, not to foiling attempts against his rule, but to benevolent government, to economic and cultural pursuits as a reigning but not ruling head of state. He could even retain some authority as supreme commander of his armed forces; he could dissolve the parliament, nominate the government, and the like. If he is so sure about his popularity among his subjects, he could even abdicate his throne and run for election as the head of the state or the executive authority thereof. In fact, the Monarch could act like the President in the French system, while preserving the traditional regalia he is reluctant to abandon and without his authority being greatly eroded or diminished.

In this fashion, the vital interests of the parties would be fulfilled and safeguarded, and the new framework of peace would create the necessary ambiance for advancing far beyond the proposed plan once its feasibility and workability is tested and proven. Then imagination and goodwill may produce more advanced regional federations and confederations, common markets and security pacts, to respond to emerging needs. This can happen only after the Palestinians experience freedom and independence in conjunction with their Jordanian alliance and then gain enough self-confidence to relinquish some of their sovereignty to the benefit of larger units. Then reality and its needs can perhaps carry the peoples of the Middle East further than anyone has imagined. Reality is not limited by imagination.

STAGES OF IMPLEMENTATION

It is evident that parts of this plan will be attacked by both parties and other interested powers, in accordance with their purposes and perceived interests. Israel would be reluctant to discuss the abandonment of more territory and the rise of a large and strong Palestinian state independent of it; Jordan will be loath to transfer much of the Monarch's power to the Palestinians at the expense of the painstakingly cultivated Jordanian identity; the PLO will reject the plan because it undercuts its claimed leadership over all Palestinians, which under the present circumstances still maintains its hope for two and a half Palestinian states (the existing one in Jordan, the one it is claiming from Israel in the territories and the autonomy of Palestinians living in Israel). The USA and other Western powers might view the weakening of Hussein and Jordan as a blow to their interests in the Middle East, especially as there is no telling what kind of anti-Western government might come to power should the Palestinians have their way there.

However, if all parties are made to comprehend the alternatives to this proposed solution – the continued threat to Middle Eastern stability and the menace of war inherent in it – they may conclude that the proposed solution is bad but the alternatives are worse. Statesmanship consists of seizing the bad before it becomes worse, when one takes into account that the easy choice between bad and good seldom presents itself to decision-makers. Since 1967, no other alternatives, including the Oslo Process and the ensuing peace between Israel and Jordan, have become a realistic and universally agreed-upon basis for a settlement. For most of these 'solutions' have skirted the issue of the indivisibility of the Palestinian people in the three countries in which they dwell, the problem of Jordan as part of Palestine, and the equal rights of Palestinians and Israelis over all of historical Palestine.

The key nations for the implementation of this plan are the USA and Saudi Arabia, which, if convinced of its feasibility, could prevail upon King Hussein to accept it. The King and his country depend very heavily for economic and military survival. If told that the choice is either his consent to share power or turmoil that might bring about his downfall, Hussein might be amenable to accommodation, knowing that otherwise he stands to lose support on which he depends. Then, the Israelis would have to be persuaded of the benefits to them of such a plan whereby they would retain enough territory to ensure their security and keep their state Jewish and democratic.

There are, of course, double-edged considerations as to who should initiate the talks on this plan: if Israel did, it would immediately be rejected by all Arabs; if the USA did, some Arabs might reject it while others might consent to it as a renewed basis for negotiations after the waning of Oslo. If Arabs, say Egypt or Saudi Arabia, should announce the plan, it might stand a better chance. On the other hand, this plan, which is conceived as one package, has inherent in it steps that Israel might like to take unilaterally in order to promote its implementation without, or prior to, other parties' consent. If Israel publicly announced the principles underlying the plan, it would have accomplished a public relations *tour de force*, by pronouncing itself in favor of the elements the world has been expecting and breathing new life into the dwindling peace process: 'Yes' to Palestinian statehood; 'Yes' to a permanent solution of the problem experienced by the bulk of the Palestinian people, including the settlement of the sensitive refugee problem; and 'Yes' to peace on Israel's eastern border. The Arabs would then have either to accept the terms, or at least accept the need to negotiate on all or some of them; or they would have to reject them. If they accepted, the renewed negotiations would create a positive ambiance favoring a permanent peace settlement; if they refused, Israel would have stated its position in conciliatory terms and could then feel free to proceed on several fronts:

1. Launch a worldwide diplomatic and information campaign explaining the benefits of this plan to all parties, bearing in mind that if Israel spelled out the principle of Palestinian statehood in the context of Jordan, and the details of its own version thereof, the discussion on the world stage would shift from blaming Israel for its negativism to debate on the merits of the plan. Then, everyone would be put to the test: Israel for its interest, will try to pacify its eastern border and negotiate for a large Palestinian state; the Jordanians for their readiness to accommodate their own people; the Palestinians for their desire to reach a permanent solution with Israel; the Israeli Arabs for their eagerness to resolve their national problem and make their own free choice as individuals. Statements by all these parties and their reverberations across the world would indicate the degree to which each is ready to compromise, and would allow Israel to distinguish between signals and noises in pursuit of the plan.

2. Israel can, at the same time, address itself to the more than one million Palestinians under its rule and elicit their opinions as to their future relations with Israel and/or with the future Palestinian State. Those who feel that they can identify with the Jewish–Zionist State and who opt to integrate themselves fully into the Israeli system would be naturalized without delay, begin to exercise their rights and fulfill their duties, and weave their lives into the national fabric. The others, probably the majority, who would rather join the Jordanian–Palestinian State after it is established, or be its nationals while continuing to reside in Israel, would have to wait until this issue was resolved by negotiation. Once established, that Jordanian–Palestinian government would negotiate with Israel the question of Palestinian nationality for the Palestinians remaining in Israel, the issue of the final disposition of the territories, and all the issues relating to water, the Israeli settlements outside Israeli sovereignty, common borders and the contents, safeguards and modalities of the implementation of the bilateral peace between Israel and Jordan–Palestine. Arrangements would also be made regarding shared economic interests, labor markets, technical cooperation, open borders, and the like.

3. Until Jordanian–Palestinian sovereignty is established in territories that might be evacuated by Israel – and unless other arrangements were agreed upon by the parties – Israel would maintain, even increase, the pace of settlement there. The ratio-

nale is two-pronged: to press the Jordanian–Palestinians to come to terms with Israel as soon as possible, in order to bring to a halt the Israeli settlements within what they claim as their territory; but at the same time to signal to them that by settling more Israelis in those territories, Israel is exercising its claim on that land until an agreement to the contrary is reached. By so doing, Israel would be approaching parity with the Palestinian settlement in pre-1967 Israel, now amounting to over one million (in contrast with the 250,000 Israelis in the territories, including the satellite towns around Jerusalem claimed by the Palestinians as their own). When a peace agreement is reached between Israel and Jordanian–Palestine, Israelis whose settlements would fall within Arab territory would face the same choices as Palestinians in Israel: remain as resident aliens in the Jordanian–Palestinian State; sell their property and return home; or apply for fully fledged Arab citizenship.

In this respect, the Israeli settlements in the West Bank and Gaza can play a decisive role, just as the Israeli settlements in Sinai were a major incentive (not an obstacle) to peace between Israel and Egypt. It has become evident that one of the major factors behind Sadat's peace initiative in 1977 was his realization that the city of Yamit and the score of agricultural settlements in the Sinai Peninsula were taking root and expanding, and there would be no way to dismantle them unless he hurried and arrested that process. In fact, his first demand before his trip to Jerusalem was that the settlements be removed. Only when he was assured of that, did he begin to negotiate. Similarly, if the Jordanians–Palestinians are assured of a plan that would test their readiness to consider this plan in exchange for Israeli concessions, they would begin to negotiate seriously. A fear of more losses if they waited might bring them around quicker, even though they realize that many demographic and territorial changes have become irreversible.

Oslo and its aftermath has taught all parties that there is no gain to be made from 'constructive ambiguities', because the desire to satisfy everyone by wording which is interpreted differently by the parties collapses on the day of reckoning when implementation forces the signatories to the 'agreement' into a head-on collision. But, clear commitments and obligations, with a clear timetable and a series of tests along the way to ensure compliance, would not suffice. It is necessary to agree on a permanent settlement, no matter how protracted and frustrating the negotiations, and from this derive the steps for the gradual implementation. To sign up to interim steps which lead nowhere, becomes a recipe for mutual accusations and a rapid erosion of the agreement, as we have seen since Oslo. In Oslo the parties embarked on the wrong train, which did not lead to any desirable destination, and by now is running out of control and needs to be stopped immediately. If the parties want to get anywhere, they must go back to square one, put all the pieces of the puzzle on the table and begin to reconstruct the jigsaw from scratch. When they attain a compromise on the ultimate solution, all the rest will be details.

13. Armistice in Jerusalem Once Again?[1]

Although Jerusalem has changed rapidly and considerably since the 1967 War and reunification, one still has a lingering sense of the legacy of the bygone Armistice Regime. New Israeli neighborhoods have grown up as satellite towns all around the core of the city beyond the old demarcation line; development has dramatically altered the network of services throughout the city; Mount Scopus, now connected to the city by a major network of highways, has been rebuilt into a mammoth fortress-campus which accommodates the Hebrew University and the Hadassah Hospital; new roads and highways have been paved to criss-cross the city and link its new neighborhoods; what was a formidable array of military positions and fortifications has turned into sprawling housing projects; free access to the holy places of all faiths has been made available to all; new museums, shopping malls, entertainment centers and places of worship have sprouted everywhere; tourism has picked up considerably; and a general feeling of content originating from an upgraded standard of living is perceptible, in spite of the fact that the population doubled between 1967 and 1987 (from just under 300,000 in both parts of the divided city to more than 600,000 within the unified municipal boundaries).

There is, however, a sense of unease stemming from the feeling of temporariness that still hovers over the city, because things do not appear to have been settled or to have attained the finality one finds in Amsterdam or in Stockholm. There are still far too many security personnel patrolling the streets or peeking into your bag when you enter a public establishment, as if to remind you that disputes are far from settled. There are still two separate and very different cities coexisting side by side, rather than one unified municipal and socio-cultural system. Where the demarcation line used to run through the heart of the city, a north–south highway was built which, rather than unifying by transporting people rapidly from one end of the city to another, has ironically exposed the divide, like a scar which refuses to heal. The populations and ways of life do not mix: western Jerusalem has remained predominantly Jewish and Western, while eastern Jerusalem has remained prevailingly Arab, Muslim and oriental. Tensions, prejudices, suspicions and fears – which are at times translated into violence – are still rampant and necessitate special measures of caution and scrutiny, which in turn increase the level of unease.

The memories of the Armistice are also present by virtue of the many buildings and other physical features that are still there: no one over 40 can pass by the city wall on the one hand, or the towering and renovated Notre Dame, on the other, without reminiscing about the formidable military positions which had spurted out fire and death during the years of the armistice. Many open spaces still exist – like the legendary Ammunition and French Hills in the north, or Government House in the south, which were no man's land or military positions, now turned into parks or roads, or new neighborhoods or war memorials – which cannot but remind the onlooker of the dramas that unfolded there during the many incidents which eroded the armistice and then finally destroyed it. One cannot pass through what was the Mandelbaum Gate without noticing the MAC (Mixed Armistice Commission) House or the Turdjman Post, now turned into a museum, and feeling a chill down his back in remembrance of the many firing incidents, the MAC meetings, the daily crossings at the Gate or the fortnightly convoys to Mount Scopus.

And, then, there are the daily reminders of the unsettled problem of Jerusalem: political declarations, diplomatic meetings, demonstrations by one faction or another, academic symposia, learned articles and newspaper reports, which express the various views on what was done in the past and what needs to be done now and in the future, and expose the deepest strata of conflicting convictions, of contradictory narratives, of clashing hopes and of the most diverse remedies. No other world capital has seen its past, present and future so disputed and dipped in conflict, its history and fate so emotionally controversial. In other words, even though the pinnacle of a temporarily unresolved conflict – the armistice – is no more, the reigning uncertainties and disagreements still feed that spirit of the provisional as if it were still there, refusing to die.

THE ARMISTICE REGIME (1947–67)

As the negotiations between Israel and the Palestinians have been proceeding with regard to the permanent settlement of the Jerusalem issue as part of an eventual peace accord between the parties, several models have been invoked: such as internationalization; London-style boroughs under joint sovereignty; one unified city with a special status for the holy places of all religions; various modes of functional division; or a return to something approximating the divided city under the armistice of 1947–67, when East Jerusalem was ruled by Jordan, and West Jerusalem by Israel. That regime, which was supervised by the United Nations, while providing a *modus operandi* of sorts, hardly constituted a *modus vivendi* that both sides could live with. For the city was partitioned by barbed wire and dominated by military positions and fortifications, and by occasional outbursts of fire and violence, which made the threat to the daily life of its citizens omnipresent. That regime, which was temporary by definition, in view of the very nature of armistice, was also asymmetric in the sense that while for Israel West Jerusalem was its capital, East Jerusalem remained for the Jordanians a backwater border-town throughout. This meant that a huge gap developed over the years between the two parts of the city, which would make reunification very difficult: one part was modern, bustling with political and cultural activity, relatively wealthy, and steadily growing; the other was a sleepy large village, under-developed and neglected.

The talks on the permanent status of Jerusalem are changing some long-established perspectives. Evidently, Jerusalem has never been an entity or asset that could be discussed and objectively identified with one nation, culture, religion and political system; it has always been the subject of many narratives, dreams and cascades of emotions, depending on who tells the story, in what context and for what purpose. It seems, nevertheless, that the current peace process has narrowed the field of competitors to two contending approaches which have come to be acknowledged by the international community, though reluctantly: the Israelis who want to keep the city unified in its present urban boundaries, and the Palestinians who claim the eastern part of the city as their sovereign capital. The notion has become universally accepted that any agreed solution those two parties would subscribe to, will become the normative one; and, for the first time, no one else is demanding direct or indirect rule over the city or parts thereof, even though claims for specific prerogatives regarding the holy places have been voiced by church, consular, Islamic, UN and international circles.

Thus, any bilateral settlement between the parties will be tempted to look at the Armistice Regime as a precedent to learn from. It is the contention of this chapter, however, that the Armistice Model can only serve as a negative one that must be skirted and discarded as a viable option in view of its dismal failure along Israeli–Arab boundaries in general and through the Jerusalem area in particular. Some lessons and conclusions present themselves which merit consideration:

- Interim arrangements like the Israel–Jordan armistice are useless unless they lead to an agreed, gradual and clear timetable of steps towards a final accord. Leaving important clauses open for further negotiation, such as Article VIII[2] in Jerusalem, which guaranteed access to Jewish holy places and humanitarian institutions in East Jerusalem but was never implemented, is a recipe for future trouble.
- Agreements must be hammered out by the parties concerned without outside interference. Experience has shown that intermediaries are inclined to develop interests of their own, and instead of facilitating agreement they may at times aggravate existing disagreements.
- 'Constructive ambiguity' in agreements may be disastrous in the final analysis. For the problem is not to find the right wording for an agreement, but to avoid double meanings and multiple interpretations which generate crises of expectations when the parties end up with something different from what they understood, or are misled by assurances given to them. No matter how agreeable the wording of clauses may sound initially, the day of reckoning comes when formulae adopted at the negotiating table come to be applied in the real world, and the parties discover or suspect that they have been double-crossed.
- Divided cities are not viable in the long run, because the open wounds cutting through roads, communications, water and electricity grids and the very landscape of the city, remain as a negative reminder that things could be different and more normal. Naturally, in other settings, such as Berlin or Belfast, the scar in the middle of the city, which partitioned the same people and culture, and possibly families, into two halves, was crueler

on the human level. In divided Jerusalem, except for small groups that had been evacuated during the 1948 War, the partition also went along national, religious, ethnic and linguistic divides, which made the alienation between its halves less cruel, but present all the same.

- Where borders are drawn or defined, great care must be taken to avoid any vagueness, misinterpretation or faulty marking. To be respected, borders must be policed and clearly delineated. The authority for policing borders and supervising peace along them must be delegated to local commanders who know each other, meet with each other and are accessible to each other. When minor incidents are reported to higher authority, they tend to get distorted and exaggerated, and by the time the top leadership begins to deal with them, they have acquired an importance of their own and become much more difficult to settle.

- Under Arab/Islamic rule, free access to the holy places in Jerusalem cannot be guaranteed. While local Muslims under the armistice generally enjoyed freedom of worship in the Aqsa Mosque and its adjoining shrines, the Muslims of Israel were denied entry to those holy places throughout the armistice period. Israeli Christians were allowed into Bethlehem on Christmas, but Jews were totally excluded from their shrines on the Temple Mount and in other parts of Jordanian-controlled Jerusalem, in spite of Article VIII of the Armistice, which had provided differently. The issue is one of tolerance on a basis of equality and sharing, instead of exclusion and arrogance of power. In the view of Muslims, Jews have no rights on the Temple Mount and therefore they have neither claim nor right of entry to any part of the entire complex, and that view was always enforced when Muslims were in control of Jerusalem.

- During the period of the Armistice neither the UN nor any of the Great Powers sought to facilitate daily life in Jerusalem except for their own nationals. They interested themselves in the functioning of the Armistice Regime only to the extent that it served their interests. In no case did they seek permanent arrangements to replace the Armistice, nor did they call Jordan to task for disrupting the functioning of the Armistice Regime by paralyzing the main provisions of the vital Article VIII.

- Jerusalem under armistice seemed everybody's concern and everybody knew better than the Israelis and the Jordanians what should be done there, what the parties' interests in it were and what their Jerusalem policy ought to be. Seldom in the history of international relations have so many proffered so much gratuitous advice on so many issues in so limited a territory and with so little effect as the Great Powers did in relation to Jerusalem. Never before has the capital city of any sovereign country been the subject of such blatant intervention on the part of just about everybody, and never before has the sovereign government of any nation been so attentive and so sensitive about what others had to say with regard to the affairs of its capital city.

UNILATERAL SOLUTIONS ATTEMPTED BY ISRAEL

The shortcomings of the Armistice are evident. But is there another basis on which to seek a solution to the Jerusalem problem, which has remained the thorniest in the Arab–Israeli dispute? Short of re-dividing the city and exposing it once again to the agonies of the Armistice period, are there other ways of solving this quandary? Does the solution of the Jerusalem issue hinge upon a resolution of all the pending Arab–Israeli bones of contention, as some people believe,[3] or is it – as Pope John-Paul II sees it – the starting point for negotiating a settlement of the entire conflict?

The Oslo Accords of 1993 relegated the issue of Jerusalem – along with other difficult aspects of the conflict – to the final phase of the Oslo Process. This assumed that confidence-building through settling minor issues would generate enough good will to produce agreed solutions for this more difficult problem. Experience, however, showed that every step in the implementation of the Oslo Accords led to new tensions, generated new accusations, and produced new expectations likely to make negotiations over Jerusalem harder, not easier.

There was a wide convergence of opinion against the repartition of Jerusalem. Israel's unequivocal stand in this sense was backed not only by historical claims and the clear reality of Israeli predominance in the city, but also by the negative experience that had accumulated during the Armistice years. If Jerusalem were to be re-divided, or eastern Jerusalem revert to Arab rule in a context of peace, one ought to be aware of the possible consequences:

- West Jerusalem under Israel will be prosperous, free, open and thriving; the Arab-controlled east would be backward, poor, oppressed, overcrowded and neglected (compare East and West Berlin). The deprived and unemployed population of the east – just like that of Nablus, Hebron, Tul-Karem, Jenin, Qalqiliya, Ramallah and Bethlehem, which have already been ceded to the PA – will slip into Israel illegally with the connivance of the PA to seek work, at best, to steel and commit crime, at worst.
- Palestinian crime – car thefts, house and business robberies, document counterfeiting, manslaughter, rape, smuggling and drugs – within western Jerusalem will increase dramatically due to the proximity of the two parts of the city and the great attraction of the more modern, affluent and larger Israeli part. This has already happened to a great extent, but at least the Israeli police can investigate and lay its hand on the perpetrators. If the criminals were free – like in Ramallah and Nablus today – to turn East Jerusalem into their haven, there is no certainty the Palestinian police would be able or willing to curtail this population flow; or whether it would be able to loosen or tighten its control on crime according to the fortunes of the relations between the Palestinians and Israelis.
- Jewish freedom of access to their holy places, especially the Wailing Wall, might come under a renewed threat. The Mount of Olives might be desecrated again once it is under Palestinian sovereignty, and Jews no longer be permitted to bury their dead there.
- The great archaeological excavations carried out during the past 30 years, which have uncovered the ancient Jewish past of Jerusalem, will be obliterated as part of a complete Arabization and Islamization of that part of the city.
- The Hebrew University on Mount Scopus and the Hadassah Hospital, which has become the most important medical center in eastern Jerusalem, will have to close their gates once again. For, even if their existence as an enclave in an Arab environment and free access to them were guaranteed, their operation at the mercy of a foreign government would become untenable.
- East Jerusalem under the Palestinian authority might become a permanent strategic and security threat to Israel's capital city. Indeed, Palestinian fighters would be allowed to take up positions, one or two kilometers from the Israeli Knesset and government offices, from which they could threaten daily life in the city, as they did in the days of Armistice.

It is hard to imagine that Israelis would accept a reversion to this kind of situation. To make sure that they would not have to face such a possibility Israel enacted a Basic Jerusalem Law in July 1980, mandating that an undivided Jerusalem must remain the sovereign capital of Israel. This was a complementary law to the one of June 1967, which applied the Israeli legal and administrative system to East Jerusalem, thereby placing it under Israeli sovereignty as part and parcel of the rest of Israel. It was not an act of annexation because Israel did not regard itself as an occupying power in any part of Jerusalem, nor had it ever recognized Transjordan's occupation of Palestinian territory in 1948, East Jerusalem included, as a rightful expansion of sovereignty.[4] Of course, there are other points of view advanced by Arab and some Western, even Israeli, jurists,[5] but since the practical absorption of the city happened in a situation where only Israel lay a lawful claim to Jerusalem at that time, it is important to understand the reasons behind this step which were partly lessons drawn from the Armistice experience.

Israel's Minister of Justice, who introduced the relevant legislation to the Knesset on 27 June 1967, explained that what needed to be stated for the purpose of the relevant bill was that:

> The Israel Defence Forces have liberated from foreign yoke considerable areas of the Land of Israel ... which have now been under the control of the Israel Defence Forces for more than a fortnight ... The position of the State of Israel was based from the start on the principle that the law, the jurisdiction and administration of the State apply to all those parts of the Land of Israel which are *de facto* under the State control ... It was the view of the government – and this view conformed with the requirements of international law – that in addition to the control by the Israeli Defence Forces of these territories, there is required also an open act of sovereignty on the part of Israel to make Israel law applicable to them ... It is for this reason that the government saw fit to introduce the bill, which I now submit to the Knesset.[6]

Thus, in the same way as the Armistice boundaries in 1949 were determined by war rather than by the UN (whose Partition Resolution was rejected by the Arabs), the Armistice Lines in Jerusalem were also invalid the moment the Jordanian forces revoked the Armistice and went on the attack on 5 June 1967. Hence, the new territorial division of Jerusalem and the introduction of Israel law and administration into East Jerusalem were fully valid. Some further juridical analysis of the new position created by Israel's repulse of Jordan's aggression against it on 5 June 1967 may interest the reader. Western Jerusalem and its corridor to the coastal plain, as well as other parts of the country which fell outside the Partition boundaries of what was to be a Jewish state, automatically became Israeli territory as a result of the Arab rejection of Partition and the subsequent attack on the Jewish areas of Palestine. In the same way, the Jordanian attack on 5 June 1967 made legal the takeover by Israel of Jordanian-held territories which were no part of recognized sovereign Jordanian land.[7] The entire international community, with the exception of Great Britain and Pakistan, had never recognized Jordanian sovereignty over the territories occupied by Jordan's Army in the war of 1948–49 beyond Jordan's national territory.

In August 1988, King Hussein of Jordan announced publicly that he was renouncing his country's claims to territories west of the river Jordan. He did so, it is believed, out of fear that Palestinian anti-Israel rioting and violence, which were then rife and well publicized in many countries (the so-called Intifada), might spill over across the Jordan River into his country. Therefore, of the existing sovereign entities that might have laid claim to Jerusalem, only Israel remained. However, the Oslo Accords signed between Israel and the Palestinians in 1993, opened new vistas for claims and counter-claims, inasmuch as Israel agreed to discuss the question of Jerusalem as part of the permanent status of territories lost by Jordan to Israel during the 1967 combined Arab assault on Israel, best known as the Six Day War. The Palestinian position is clear: the Oslo Accords open the way for them to establish a Palestinian state, with Jerusalem as its capital. Israel opposes these ambitions and has made it abundantly clear that Jerusalem will remain united under Israeli sovereignty. In due course the signatories of the Oslo Accords were to negotiate a final agreement concerning the conditions and modalities of their co-existence within the boundaries of Mandated Palestine as defined in 1922, namely the territory lying between the Mediterranean Sea in the west, the Kingdom of Jordan in the east, Syria and Lebanon to the north and Egypt to the south.[8] The size of the territory available is very small indeed – 25,000 square kilometers. Its natural resources are very modest, to say the least. Its historic capital Jerusalem, where Judaism matured and became the fountainhead of two other monotheistic faiths, has developed a political magnetism unappreciative of Jewish spiritual and historical seniority. It will take Solomonic wisdom to structure the compromises that will allow the tiny land of the Bible to be a warm and safe home for the people of the Bible as well as a focus of religious sentiments for all the believers in the one God.

IN THE AFTERMATH OF OSLO

What remains contentious, however, is whether the city can be re-divided between two sovereignties, or whether it could remain under Israel's sole jurisdiction, while allowance is made for particular religious and political interests, which often merge into one as far as Jerusalem is concerned. Israel, drawing from its past history, and in response to cultural, religious and political domestic urges, can maintain its firm position due to the practical reality on the ground where no one seriously challenges her rule. The Palestinians, however, who claim to inherit Jordan's rights in eastern Jerusalem, as if Jordan had any valid rights there, can only voice their aspirations and press for a settlement acceptable to Israel. Having no wherewithal to implement their dreams, their leaders, notably Yasser Arafat, use the Arab–Islamic symbolism of Jerusalem to mobilize the masses behind their claims. The masses are also bound by historical memories, real or imagined, and especially by the religious fervor that has been drummed up by the Hamas Islamists in the ongoing game of Islamic one-upmanship between the PA and its most formidable opponents. Since Arafat created the PA, he invokes Jerusalem as a powerful unifying and mobilizing symbol in almost all his public speeches. On every instance, he lists all the towns so far regained from Israel and vows to 'march into Jerusalem', or to 'pray in Jerusalem' at the end of the process.

Arafat often refers to Jerusalem as *'al-Quds a-Sharif'* (Jerusalem the Noble), or *'al-Quds al-'arabiyya'* (Arab Jerusalem); the former signifying the whole of Jerusalem in Arab and Arafat's parlance in general; the latter, normally meaning East Jerusalem, namely that part of the city claimed by the Palestinians as their capital. On Christmas Eve of 1995, when he went to Bethlehem on the occasion of its handover by Israel to the PA, Arafat declared Christ to be Palestinian, implying a connection between Islam and Christianity, both under his protective wings, since they are both Palestinian.

This renders Arafat the Curator of the Holy Places of both Christianity and Islam in Jerusalem, and makes the PLO the partner of world Christianity, and not only of world Islam, in Holy Jerusalem. This, in itself, makes him a better and more universally accepted ruler of the city than the Jewish Israelis. His intentions were picked up by the Greek Orthodox Patriarch of Jerusalem, who declared to a delighted Arafat on that occasion: 'Here is the successor of Sophronius welcoming the successor of Umar ibn-al-Khattab!'[9] No one present or watching the ceremony on television could miss the parallel. Reference was made to the submission of the Byzantine Patriarch of Jerusalem in 638 to the second Caliph of Islam, Umar ibn-al-Khattab (634–44), who conquered Jerusalem and put an end to many centuries of Christian rule. Until the Crusaders, who established the Christian Kingdom of Jerusalem in 1099, the city was to remain, uninterruptedly, part and parcel of *Dar al Islam*, the Pax Islamica. Arafat liked the Patriarch's comments so much that he ordered the Palestinian press to publish it in their headlines. This became known when one ill-advised and independent-minded journalist, the night editor of the daily *al-Quds*, Mahir al-'Alami, refused to conform, and found himself arrested and interrogated in the dark basements of the security apparatus in Jericho. Arafat's eagerness to get the Patriarch's sycophancy widely publicized did not stem from his intention to humiliate him, or from his flattering comparison with Umar, but mainly from his newly acquired glamorous image as the new prospective liberator of Jerusalem.

This makes Arafat the latest link in the apostolic chain of great liberators which to date have included Umar, and then Saladin, who recaptured Jerusalem in 1187 from the Crusaders. If one bears in mind the oft-made comparison in Arab and Islamic circles between the medieval Crusader State and contemporary Israel, one necessarily comes to the conclusion that exactly as Umar had occupied Jerusalem by peaceful means through the surrender of the Christians, and Saladin by force through the conquest of the city and the expulsion or massacre of its inhabitants, so will Arafat. He will repeat that feat either by accepting the surrendering of East Jerusalem to him by the Israelis, or by pressing his call for jihad in order to capture all of it. Umar and Saladin had been celebrated as the legitimate rulers of the city following the oath of allegiance (*bay'a*) accorded them by the crowd. In Bethlehem, while the loudspeakers were enjoining the masses to deliver the *bay'a* to

Arafat, the parallel became neat, complete, inescapable. History had come a full circle.

After Oslo came the Israel–Jordan Peace Accord of 1994, which complicated the matter of Jerusalem even further. This Accord recognized the 'special historical role' of Jordan in the 'Islamic holy places in Jerusalem'; which means that after Jordan had been severed from Jerusalem as a result of its aggression in 1967, and after Hussein himself had finally renounced his occupation of the West Bank, including Jerusalem, in 1988, Israel re-introduced him through the back window. That the King needed the title of Curator of al-Aqsa – just like his much wiser grandfather – to legitimize his rule, is clear; it is difficult to see, however, how this measure will serve any of Israel's interests unless the idea is to displace Arafat's grip on the city. There was also the 'Jordanian Option', which had consisted of transferring the Palestinian Territories back to the King – in fact, returning to the situation that had obtained in June 1967 and that had served as the launching pad for Hussein's all-out attack against Israel. However, when the King himself renounced his rule in the Territories in 1988 – as a result of the outbreak of the first Intifada in 1987 – and especially after he signed a peace treaty with Israel in 1994, the whole issue became irrelevant. Since the collapse of the 'Jordanian Option', the competition between Jordan and the PLO in the city has only added to the existing problems.

The death of armistice as a viable option for governing the relations between Israel and the Arabs necessitated new and creative formulae of accommodation between the parties concerned. However, the future is seen differently, not only by Palestinians and Israelis, but also by other nations across the world. The only comprehensive and unequivocal stand in this regard, which is asserted with a credibility backed by concrete reality, is the one taken by Israel: namely, that undivided Jerusalem must remain Israel's sovereign capital. But will all the others accept that stand? Interesting variants to this option were also elaborated by Israelis[10] and others.[11] Be that as it may, this will certainly hinge on the proposed solution to two major issues: the modalities of rule over the Arabs who live in Jerusalem; and the regime that will govern universal access to all religious holy places, of all faiths, in the united city. (King Hussein, for example, spoke about an 'open city'.[12])

On the municipal government level, many suggestions have been floated around which divide Greater Jerusalem into boroughs like London, or arrondissements like Paris; which enable neighborhood administrations, Arab or Jewish, to manage their daily affairs; while an elected umbrella municipality will continue to govern the metropolitan services common to all: transportation, water, sewage, etc. Other views suggest that the present situation of one unified administration would respond to all needs if only the Arabs would vote in the elections and send their representatives to the city council. But, due to the Palestinian refusal to acquiesce in the present state of affairs, namely of a united city under Israeli rule, the likelihood that they would consent to either of these suggestions looks minimal, pending a comprehensive solution of the political issue in the context of a permanent and mutually acceptable peace accord between Israel and the Palestinians, who are regarded by many international jurists as the sovereign over East Jerusalem.

Pending the permanent settlement, however, one needs to tackle the question of the holy places; this must be regarded as separate from the issue of sovereignty, exactly as the Ministry of Education in Israel has decided not to enforce an Israeli curriculum on the Arab schools of East Jerusalem, but to allow them to pursue a Jordanian curriculum, it can do the same with holy places without renouncing one iota of Israel's sovereignty. The problem for the Israeli authorities will be to maintain the famous *status quo* from Ottoman times,[13] but at the same time also maintain equality between the various communities when their religious traditions are in conflict, and allow all contentions to be settled by courts of law. Israel's law of 1967, guaranteeing the protection of, and free access to, the holy places, is the expression of the firm intent of the Israeli Government, which is the current territorial sovereign throughout the city, to ensure that this remains the case. Territorial sovereignty, incidentally, does not necessarily mean that the State of Israel must also exert its jurisdiction over all spheres of life of the inhabitants of East Jerusalem. Education and religious worship are two such potentially independent spheres; nationality may be another.

Coming back to the Armistice Regime, which was the main focus of this study, does it bear any relevance, residual or otherwise, to the permanent settlement of the question of Jerusalem now under discussion? The most likely point of departure for such an inquiry would seem to be Article XII of the Armistice Agreement between Israel and Jordan, whose second paragraph stated simply that the 'Agreement shall remain in force until a peaceful settlement between the parties is achieved ...'[14] The peace treaty concluded between Israel and Jordan in 1994 was certainly a peaceful settlement, and it included a paragraph on the special status accorded to the Hashemites in Jerusalem's Muslim Holy Places. On the other hand, as the Jordanians have renounced their territorial claim to the West Bank and Jerusalem in favor of the Palestinians, does the peace between Jordan and Israel still satisfy the requirement envisaged in the Armistice Agreement?

This question had already come up during the negotiations of Israel and Egypt at Camp David in 1978. Those agreements had encompassed not only the Egyptian–Israeli bilateral peace arrangement, but also a second framework for peace geared to resolve the Palestinian issue, what had come to be known as the 'Autonomy Talks' between Egyptian and Israeli officials without the Palestinian participation. Egypt insisted in a letter that Jerusalem was part and parcel of the West Bank, namely the area bound on the west, north and south by the respective portions of the armistice demarcation lines. Israel, in a parallel letter, held its ground, and there the matter rested, since the Autonomy Talks were stalled in any case. An Israeli international lawyer, Y. Blum, analyzed the question in light of established treaty law whereby 'a material breach of an accord on the part of one side entitles the other side to regard the entire agreement as null and void'. Israel, he maintained, had acted formally in conformity with this rule, inasmuch as it responded to the Jordanian abrogation of the Armistice Agreement when it launched its onslaught on West Jerusalem, and along the entire demarcation line for that matter, on 5 June 1967.[15]

After that war, the Security Council of the UN, which supervised the armistice agreements between Israel and the Arabs, adopted a new resolution, No. 242, which – while freezing new cease-fire lines to replace the defunct armistice lines – also made it clear that the new situation was temporary pending the outcome of peace negotiations. This not only rendered the Armistice Regime redundant because inoperative, but created a substitute for it which was to lead not back to the *status quo ante bellum*, but to new peace arrangements. This was in effect the signature on the death writ for the Armistice Regime, by the very international institution which had devised it in the first place, even though it was never explicitly invalidated. Therefore, subsequent Security Council reservations regarding Israeli measures affecting Jerusalem, do not have to be seen as attempts to revive the Armistice but rather as a sign of displeasure at the changes effected by Israel in the status of Jerusalem (Jewish versus Islamic character, Jewish versus Arab demography, the administration of the city, the state of the holy places, archaeological excavations, etc.).[16]

On the other hand, one has to remember that the UN components of the armistice machinery have remained in being, notably United Nations Truce Supervision Organization (but not the Mixed Armistice Commissions). One may ask, 'What does this organization have to do beyond perpetuating its independent stature in a place where its primary function is no longer needed?' But this would not be the first time that the UN has wasted its limited resources on financing sinecures. Another constant element inherited from the Armistice era is the 'green line'; that is, the former Demarcation Line between Israel and Jordan, which has become the only accepted reference both within and outside Israel. In Israel there are towns, cities and villages, but beyond the Green Line they are 'settlements' and, for some European media, 'colonies'. West of the former Armistice Line you are in Israel, and east of it you are in the West Bank, Samaria and Judea; 'occupied territory', 'liberated territory', 'administered area', and what have you.

LESSONS AND SOLUTIONS

With both the UN institution extant, and the line it was assumed to have supervised still living in the memories of all sides, one should not be surprised if among the arguments advanced against Israel in the context of a permanent solution to the Jerusalem problem, the specter of the old Armistice Line is raised once again. The Palestinians, who insist that East Jerusalem be their capital, have already invoked the boundary that had divided it during the years of Armistice, as a reference for the reapportioning of the territory of the city, even if it is not physically re-divided. For the old Armistice Line remains the only ever agreed demarcation between Israel and any Arab authority in Jerusalem, even though it was traced from the start 'without prejudice to future territorial settlements or boundary lines or to claims of either party'.[17] This means that if the Palestinians come to the conclusion that they cannot otherwise extract what they want from Israel, in the context of the permanent settlement negotiations, they are likely to revive the old notion of the Demarcation Line and to demand that it be the basis for the negotiations. If they were to succeed, this is what we are likely to relive:

1. If the city is physically partitioned, once again, with barbed wire running through its heart and armed forces posted along the lines on either side, this is a recipe for friction, suspicion, tension and hostile acts. What is happening today along the temporary divide around Jerusalem and on its northern and southern approaches, may pale in comparison with the violence that Jerusalem-related emotions can provoke in the case of re-division.
2. A redivided city would mean that the western part would be wealthy and advanced, modern, stable and a hub of high-tech and international communications; while the other would be poor, overcrowded and a center of unemployment and crime which would look with envy at its more fortunate neighbor, in the way Soweto looked at Johannesburg. This is the recipe for theft, crime and robbery that would render life impossible for its population.
3. An eastern Jerusalem under Palestinian sovereignty would become the shelter for all criminals escaping from Israeli law; similar to the situation in Ramallah, Bethlehem and Nablus since Oslo.

It is then essential that whatever solution is adopted by agreement, some steps must be adopted to ensure that the city remains livable:

1. The presence of armed forces should be seriously curtailed and peace maintained by police forces of the two parties acting in unison, or at least closely collaborating through joint patrols, with direct telephone lines between the commanders and an emergency mechanism to defuse dangerous situations.
2. Each of the three monotheistic religions must be given jurisdiction over their religious sites, but clear understandings have to be reached regarding the sharing of common holy places, coordination of visitors, and limitations about access of the adherents of one faith into the sites of the other, etc.
3. Places that are claimed by more than one faith, such as the Temple Mount or the Holy Sepulchre, have to be regulated and fairly assigned to all claimants.

4. Neither the UN, nor any other international body, should be assigned the task of supervising borders or overseeing the holy places, in view of the dismal performance of the Armistice Commission during the Armistice Regime.
5. In view of the mounting wave of religious fundamentalism, which had in the past heightened the tension between the various parties and excluded certain claimants from their rights to access their holy places, it is imperative that the rules and the supervision governing the holy places, be drawn up jointly by diplomats and clergymen.

To force the issue, the Palestinians may use measured and controlled violence within the urban area of Jerusalem in order to challenge Israel's firm stand on a united Jerusalem under its exclusive rule. By so doing, they would also address the Christian world and convince it that Israel is not capable of assuring peace and stability in Jerusalem – the prerequisite for the unhindered flow of Christian pilgrims to the Holy Land. The Palestinians can also invoke the paradox that though prior to 1967, there were occasional disturbances on the Armistice Demarcation Line, peace was guaranteed for the Christians who flocked to their holy places, which were mostly located within Arab-controlled East Jerusalem. Now that the city is entirely under Israeli rule and no demarcation lines exist, the hazards for the Christian pilgrims have increased due to Palestinian discontent. It would therefore be better, according to their logic, to restore Arab control (this time Palestinian) of the city, under the protective wings of Arafat, so that the new Sophroniuses might enjoy the favors of the new Umar. In this regard, Palestinian and Christian interests converge; did not Arafat himself declare Christ a Palestinian?

The challenge to Israel would then be considerable. Patent, uncontrollable violence might draw sympathy for Israel, or at least an understanding for its need to quell it, but measured and calculated disturbances, which could be construed by the world as legitimate manifestations of discontent against 'occupation', would put Israel in an untenable situation. If it moved against the violence by force, it would surely be condemned for a 'disproportionate' reaction against peaceful citizens; if it did not, it would be blamed for its inability to ensure peace, stability and security in the holy city. In this context, the coming years may be crucial, because then Palestinians and Israelis are to have engaged in negotiations regarding the permanent settlement; if the state of the talks continues to be unsatisfactory, that could impel the Palestinians to move into action.[18]

The plight of Christians in the Muslim world has been well documented,[19] and the Christian world would certainly prefer to have its holy places protected by liberal and democratic Israeli laws than subject to the whims of some tyrant. But the matter is one not of cosy idealism but of expedient pragmatism: Christians around the world would rather find some practical arrangement that works, even if it approximates the Armistice Regime of yesteryear, than support the impracticality of Israeli democratic rule which cannot be enforced and cannot ensure the peace. The challenge for Israel, then, is to engage in legislation beyond the 1967 Law for the Protection of Holy Places, in such a way – and in co-ordination with various Christian organizations, including the Vatican[20] – that not only would there be a broad basis on which the preventive measures could be adopted in order to guarantee peace in the holy places, but there also would be an understanding about the measures necessary to restore it, should it be disrupted. Only under such conditions might the Armistice Regime be finally buried and never invoked again.[21]

NOTES

1. This was part of research later published as the book: Raphael Israeli, *Jerusalem Divided: The Armistice Regime, 1947–1967* (London: Frank Cass, 2002).
2. The Armistice Agreement was signed between Israel and Jordan, April 1949, in Rhodes. For the full text, see Israeli, *Jerusalem Divided*.
3. See Walter Eytan (the man who negotiated the Armistice Agreement), 'The Struggle for the Political Status of Jerusalem', *Monthly Survey*, 10 (October 1984), pp. 15–21 [Hebrew].
4. See O. Ahimeir (ed.), *Jerusalem: Aspects of Law* (Jerusalem: Jerusalem Institute of Israeli Studies, 1980) [English and Hebrew]; especially the articles by Y. Bar-Sela and Y. England.
5. Sarah Kaminker, 'Building Restrictions in East Jerusalem', *Journal of Palestine Studies*, 26, 4 (Summer 1997); and Kate Maguire, *The Israelisation of Jerusalem*, Arab Papers (London: Arab Research Center, 1989).
6. *Israel's Parliamentary Records*, vol. 49, p. 2420 [Hebrew]; cited by Blum, 'The Juridical Status of East Jerusalem', in Ahimeir, *Jerusalem*, p. 240.
7. Ruth Lapidoth and Moshe Hirsch, *Jerusalem: Political and Legal Aspects* (Jerusalem: The Jerusalem Institute for Israel Studies, 1994), p. 5.
8. The outburst of the Intifadah in September 2000 has further delayed indefinitely the possibility of a negotiated settlement, as the Oslo Accords went into abeyance.
9. The story was widely covered and reported by both the Palestinian and Israeli media, written and electronic.
10. See, for example, Moshe Hirsch and Debra Housen-Couriel, *The Jerusalem Problem: Proposals for its Resolution* (Jerusalem: The Jerusalem Institute for Israel Studies, 1994)

[Hebrew]; and Menachem Klein, *Jerusalem in the Peace Negotiations* (Jerusalem: The Jerusalem Institute for Israel Studies, 1995) [Hebrew].

11. For example, 'Jerusalem: City of Universal Peace', *SIDIC*, 4, 2 (1971).

12. S. Meir, 'United Jerusalem in Jordanian Eyes' *International Problems*, 29, 3–4 (Fall 1980), p. 7.

13. See Englard, 'The Status of Holy Places in Jerusalem', in Ahimeir, *Jerusalem*.

14. See the text of the Armistice Agreement, in Israeli, *Jerusalem Divided*.

15. Y. Blum, 'The Juridical Status of East Jerusalem', in Ahimeir, *Jerusalem*, pp. 25–8. See also, Y. Blum, *The Juridical Status of Jerusalem*. Jerusalem Papers on Peace Problems No. 2 (New York: United Nations, 1974), pp. 6–32.

16. See Resolution 465 of 1 March 1980, and Resolution 467 of 30 June 1980.

17. Article II of the Armistice Agreement.

18. That year was to be crucial – but, when the Camp David Conference of July 2000 failed and the Intifadah broke out in September, the talks were put on hold indefinitely. Nothing could therefore be raised, although the Palestinians said – informally – that they would demand the re-division of the city along the old lines.

19. See Bat Ye'or, *The Dhimmi* (Rutherford, NJ: Fairleigh Dickinson University Press, 1987); and Ye'or, *The Decline of Eastern Christianity under Islam* (Rutherford, NJ: Fairleigh Dickinson University Press, 1996).

20. See A. Lopez, *Israel's Relations with the Vatican, Jerusalem Letter*, 401, 1 (March 1999).

21. See Hirsch and Housen-Couriel, *The Jerusalem Problem*; and Klein, *Jerusalem in the Peace Negotiations.*

14. Conclusion: Quantity and Quality in Conflict Resolution*

ON QUANTITY AND QUALITY

In negotiations tackling difficult conflicts between nations, peoples, societies and individuals, one of the most difficult obstacles to overcome is the gap between what the parties regard as 'negotiable' in a give-and-take process, and what they deem as 'non-negotiable' under any circumstances.

This obviously means that there are issues which are relatively amenable to compromise, while others constitute *sine qua nons* or red-lines that the party in question is not prepared to cross. Why is this so?

The argument advanced here is that negotiable issues usually concern assets and other measurable objects, the renunciation of which only means material, or real estate, or monetary loss. When one senses that the sustained loss can be compensated for by gaining other assets, or that by giving up something, one gains something, one may be inclined to give and take and come to a compromise. That is a *quantitative* argument: measurable, negotiable and compromisable.

When, one the other hand, the parties advance value-related arguments, the debate goes one notch up. For 'value' is, by definition, immeasurable and may be greatly significant to one, but be totally insignificant to the other. The contested value may be moral, cultural or religious, and as such it becomes utterly non-negotiable and immutable. This is a *qualitative* debate.

It is therefore vital that the parties be aware, not only of the parameters of every problem on the agenda of negotiations, but

---

* This chapter was initially written in 1995 as a policy paper.

also of the quantitative versus the qualitative nature of these parameters. If they are aware of these distinctions, it is evident that they may accept what cannot be changed and strive to change what can be changed. Moreover, this mutual awareness on the part of both the parties might produce mechanisms of compensation whereby qualitative issues can be respected and accepted if the accepting party can get some satisfactory quantitative *quid pro quo* for its acceding to the qualitative demand of the other; or the accepting party might demand that, for its compromise on a qualitative issue, it expects, likewise, a similar concession by its interlocutor.

There would be, of course, parties to the conflict who would delegitimize others as an act of faith. If the partner is thus qualitatively disqualified, then perhaps a gradual and incremental process of quantitative concessions can offset the initial qualitative refusal of the other party to compromise.

In any process of conflict resolution which addresses itself to this procedure, if the distinction is made as outlined above, the quantitative issues would tend to be resolved first, while the qualitative ones would tend to be relegated to the end of the process. This might be a grave mistake, however, since the pool of quantitative *quid pro quos* which can act as agents for blunting the sharp qualitative differences between the parties will be depleted when the latter's turn at the negotiating table comes. Therefore, according to this scheme, it is vital to address the qualitative issues first and then mitigate them with quantitative concessions; only when the former are on the road to a solution might all the others become relatively easy to address.

TESTING THE HYPOTHESIS

The resolution of difficult contemporary conflicts, such as in Ireland and Bosnia, and the Israeli–Arab dispute, can be examined in light of the above hypothesis. There are some striking similarities between the qualitative and quantitative issues on all three fronts, although with different mixes, emphases, intensities and problems. Let us examine the two recent agreements between Israel and Jordan and Israel and the Palestinians.

Israel–Jordan Agreement

The Israeli–Jordan peace agreement, signed in 1994, included the following major clauses:

1. The return of some land to the Hashemite Kingdom, claimed by Jordan and cultivated by Israel over the years.
2. Israel agreed to allocate some of its water to Jordan.
3. Israel agreed to discuss the repatriation to 'Palestine' of Palestinians long residing in Jordan.
4. Israel recognized the special status of Jordan as regards the Muslim Holy Places in Jerusalem.
5. Normalization of relations between the two countries, which means, in essence, mutual recognition and commitment to maintain security.
6. Economic cooperation between the parties.

Israel's concessions in most of these issues are measurable and quantitative, these involve matters where Israel can pay in concrete terms in return for what it hoped would become a qualitative concession on the part of the Arabs, who had denied its very right to exist. In effect, by signing the peace treaty with Jordan, Israel agreed to surrender some of its assets (land and water), to grant economic aid, to lobby in the USA for the alleviation of Jordan's debt, and even to assist King Hussein in obtaining new military gear which might be turned against itself in some future war. Israel has also accepted the responsibility for partly relieving the Jordanian regime of the demographic burden of the Palestinians, who constitute two-thirds or more of Jordan's population. By acceding to Jordan's urge that Israel should discuss the 1967, and then the 1948, war refugees, Israel has actually taken the considerable risk of upsetting her own fragile demographic balance.

These matters cannot in themselves constitute any fatal threat to Israel. Much more importantly, King Hussein, whose grandfather had arrived in Eastern Palestine from Saudi Arabia, has sought since his establishment as king to gain legitimacy as a ruler of Jordan, although imposed from the outside. Israel then lends him this legitimacy by announcing, in effect, that he is the recognized and accepted ruler of Eastern Palestine, renamed Jordan, and of one half of the Palestinian people (three out of six million), renamed Jordanians, instead of insisting that he is the Hashemite King of Palestine, and his subjects are Palestinians. This qualitative move, which squarely pushed the Palestinian problem away from Hussein and right into Israel's own lap, was of supreme existential importance to Hussein, because his regime hangs on this recognition, acceptance, and assistance from Israel; but it is of less earth-moving import to Israel. The Israeli government, which cut the deal with Hussein, was not only interested in cultivating the reputedly 'moderate' and 'pro-Western' king (which he was not in 1967 or during the Gulf crisis), but also strove to cut Arafat down to size, by suggesting that he (Arafat) only controlled one-third of the Palestinians: those in the territories (*c.* two million). The Israeli opposition, which also approved of this treaty, believed that Hussein could be substituted for Arafat and that the former would act as an axe to topple the latter. Both were, of course, wrong. Had Israel tackled the qualitative issues of 'What is Jordan?' and 'Who are the Jordanians?', and found that they both closely related to Palestine and the Palestinians, then perhaps the problem of 'Jordan' would not have been resolved, but the much more real question of 'Palestine' would have been addressed.

Instead, Israel 'resolved' the superficial quantitative issues, unaware of, or just ignoring, the fact that King Hussein is not representative of a people or a country, but just a regime, superimposed from the outside upon Palestine and the Palestinians. Had Israel pressed for a truly representative government in Jordan, that would by necessity be 'Palestinian', with or without Hussein as a constitutional monarch, then perhaps the entire Palestinian dispute could have been qualitatively resolved. Now, it remains an open and bleeding wound awaiting a new qualitative solution, while the quantitative concessions Israel has already made might turn out to have been made in vain.

This is particularly so since opposition to peace within Jordan is widespread and mounting, especially among the solid strata which count in the monarchy's pecking order: professionals, intellectuals and religious leaders. Indeed, Muslim fundamentalists in the Kingdom, just like their counterparts in the Territories, continue to claim the entirety of Palestine (including Israel) as a *waqf* land where the Islamic *shari'a* law ought to be applied forthwith and uncompromisingly. They get political and financial support from Iran, the Sudan, Saudi Arabia and Muslim fundraisers in the West. Should they come to power in Jordan and annul the peace with Israel, what could Israel do? Start from square one? Retake the assets she has relinquished? Who would then support her?

Israel and the Palestinians

The Oslo Declaration of Principles, supplemented by Oslo II, unlike the Israeli–Jordanian accords, contained nothing permanent. They were supposed only to lead to an interim agreement, pending the negotiations, and then the application of a permanent settlement. To arrive at a permanent settlement, the parties had first to reach a meeting of minds on qualitative as well as quantitative issues, which would then be translated into a written document. However, the Oslo documents, far from reflecting a meeting of minds that was a prerequisite to an agreement, attempted to plaster over differences with a series of ambiguous statements that were immediately given to different, even contradictory, interpretations.

Israel and the PLO, unable to agree on anything substantial – that is, qualitative – except for their readiness to talk to each other, followed the road of incremental quantities, by first designating steps to be followed in order to reach interim agreements, before a permanent settlement was hammered out and agreed upon.

In order to reach an interim agreement (Oslo I and II), Israel had to pay in quantitative terms: withdrawal, partial autonomy, economic aid, compromises on water and security, and the like. And so, while squandering its trump cards to reach temporary settlement, Israel was left with few arrows in its quiver for the much more difficult qualitative permanent agreement. The argument here is not against the gradualism that is inherent in accords of this sort. Certainly, following the long and bitter conflict between Israel and the Palestinians, no one has expected a one-stroke settlement. However, only when the contours of the permanent settlement are known, discussed and agreed upon, can there be an interim arrangement that would allow the gradual implementation of the agreed principle. In the meantime, the parties could put into practice confidence-building measures to remove the obstacles separating them, to test each other's intentions and goodwill, and to study the feasibility of the coming phases. In other words, 'interim' should signify a step in the agreed-upon direction; gradualism means a step-by-step journey towards an agreed goal. Quantitative steps must follow the milestones that lead to a known qualitative target.

In Oslo I and II, no goal was specified, and therefore the very attempt to devise steps on a non-existent road, seems ludicrous. The Israeli–Egyptian peace accords of 1979 had been carried out incrementally, but their ultimate goal was known to both signatories: Israeli withdrawal from Sinai; the evacuation of Israeli settlements there; the turning over of oil fields and military airfields – all quantitative and one-sided Israeli concessions; in return for the recognition of Israel by the Egyptians and their according her diplomatic relations, normalization and security arrangements. Implementation was spread over a period of three years, but all that time, the parties knew where they were heading.

In Oslo, the goal was nebulous. The Israelis said that all was open to negotiations; the Palestinians affirmed that the interim meetings were geared to fulfill the Palestinian national dreams: nationhood; the 'Right of Return'; the uprooting of Israeli settlements; Jerusalem as their capital; etc.

The contradiction between the resolution of the Palestinians to ultimately arrive at their qualitative goals, and the equally qualitative determination of the Israelis not to let that happen, has led to the parties tackling quantitative issues only. Even the one far-reaching qualitative concession made by both parties at the outset of the process – namely that Israel should recognize the PLO in return for the latter's renunciation of its National Charter, which is reputedly committed to Israel's destruction – has so far been respected only by Israel, while the Palestinians are still procrastinating under various pretexts. Then, the whole issue was relegated to the post-election period of the PA, in the hope that the new Palestinian Council would be able and willing to amend or abrogate the basic constitutional document of the PLO, adopted by the Palestinian National Council in 1964 (revised in 1968).

All this while, the Israelis and the Palestinians were cultivating contradictory goals among their own people, for lack of an even remotely agreed-upon basis for a permanent solution. When that stage sets in, things will by necessity come to the fore; and if nothing is done to soft pedal the frustration of the Palestinians, a crash is inevitable. The Palestinians celebrated with festivities in every city in the West Bank relinquished to their rule by the Israelis. But when the ceremonies and the euphoria ran their course, and the novel becomes routine, the people will demand that Arafat implement his oft-repeated pledge that 'next will be Jerusalem, the capital of the Palestinian state'.

However, Jerusalem is only one of the stumbling blocks, about which it is hard to see how Israel or the Palestinians are going to compromise. Other qualitative issues include the Right of Return, which has not been abandoned by the Palestinians; the granting of Palestinian nationhood, strongly opposed by Israel; the withdrawal from Israeli settlements (close to 150 of them); the uprooting of Israeli settlers (close to 300,000 of them, including six satellite towns around Jerusalem), and the like.

The fact that Israel has made some cosmetic concessions to the Palestinians on some of these issues does not diminish the intensity of the Palestinian demands one iota. Quite the contrary, the fact that Israel has allowed PLO activities in East Jerusalem, including fully-fledged diplomatic activity in Orient House and the participation of East Jerusalemites in the elections to the PA, has only raised expectations among the Palestinians that 'Arab Jerusalem' can be expected to come to fruition sometime down the line, and that the more they press, the sooner it will happen. Arafat, too, has been raising the tempers and messianic expectations among the Palestinians, which leads to the concrete fear among Israelis that as passions rise, people will become impatient and they may resort, again, to violence, in order to precipitate the process.

If violence becomes the norm again, then the present cease-fire between PLO and Hamas, which is geared to push the Israelis out of the West Bank and not allow them any pretext to drag their feet, will have to end. Not only would the Hamas then feel free to resume terrorism, with popular support, in order to prod the Israelis to continue their withdrawal into Oslo III or the permanent settlement, but PLO members might also be amenable to encourage the course of violence, when they feel that diplomacy and negotiation no longer carry with them a full Israeli retreat.

A sweeping Israeli withdrawal from East Jerusalem and the settlements in the West Bank and Gaza is difficult to envisage, even under the Labor government. None other than the architects of Oslo on the Israeli side are talking about retaining all Jerusalem united under Israeli rule and annexing most settlements with a majority of settlers to Israel proper. What PLO leader can acquiesce in this state of affairs? If he did, what Hamas sheikh can consent to letting the Palestinian leadership 'sell out' Palestinian holy land (*waqf*) to the Zionist Jews, the 'enemies of Allah'? As a tactic to get more, as a base to demand more, it was politic to enter into temporary compromise with Israel; but as a permanent settlement which would put an end to Palestinian rights and dreams? Very unlikely.

CONCLUSIONS AND CONSEQUENCES

Taken in its totality, the Arab–Israeli conflict has always consisted of two elements: quality versus quantity. Israel has demanded, since its inception, to be recognized, accepted and legitimized by its Arab neighbors; the Arabs have accused Israel of taking over Arab lands and urged it to evacuate them, all of them, to the point of vanishing, because its very existence had been predicated on the 'usurpation' of Arab lands. This basic demand of the Arabs has been repeated even by some post-Oslo Palestinians, who regard the Israeli–Palestinian accords as nothing but a first step towards the elimination of Israel.

It was necessary for Israel to occupy more lands, as a result of its various wars against the Arabs, in order to convince its rivals/interlocutors of their need to talk to it and negotiate with it as the only way to recoup their lands. The new formula, which posited the 'land for peace' equation as a balanced *quid pro quo* in order to resolve the conflict, was precisely calculated to pay the Arabs in terms of quantity, in return for Israel gaining their qualitative approval. But, while this formula seemed workable with the Egyptians and Jordanians, since Israel had no designs on their lands in the first place, the Palestinians considered it totally inadequate, for the following qualitative reasons:

1. The totalistic approach to the land, based on divine promise, plays as much a role among Hamas fundamentalists as among the hard-core Israeli settlers of the Gush Emunim brand. Both the government of Israel and the Palestinian Authority could disregard their opposition and proceed with their peace process, but in both cases the public trauma and outcry would be so great that no legitimate government could ignore them.
2. Both Palestinians and Israelis strive to obtain most of the same land, in spite of the permanent settlements of the other party on that land. In short, this must be a zero-sum game: the more one party gets, the less the other will have. Zero-sum games are less likely to breed agreements and settlements; games that produce something for everybody are more likely to succeed.
3. Jerusalem is not just land; it is not only the pearl in the Palestinian crown, but a religious-cultural-historical bone of contention. Because sentiments run so high on both sides, but there is only one Jerusalem, the struggle for it becomes

inescapable and difficult.

4. The land is more limited than the demographic demand for it. The West Bank and Gaza, which are supposed to provide the territorial underpinnings of the Palestinian entity, can only accommodate one-third of the Palestinian people (two out of six million), and comprise only a fraction of the whole Palestinian-claimed territory. The unresolved problem of the outside Palestinian majority and the confinement of the Palestinian entity to a limited territory, will be a recipe for continued bitterness and discontent.

5. Palestinian economic dependence on Israel (job markets, manufactured goods, technological help, etc.) will have to continue even after any permanent settlement is reached; the huge discrepancy in the GNP (1:10 ratio) will also be hard to ignore. This means that illegal immigrants, illegal trafficking, theft and other measures of economic and social discontent will continue to jeopardize any agreement arrived at by the parties.

6. While fundamentalists also have some influence in Israel, although only marginal, in surrounding Arab–Islamic countries the profile of Islam has risen so high that either Muslim fundamentalists have taken over some countries and subjected them to *shari'a* law, or they are at least demanding a strong voice in local politics. In view of the formula, which suggests that more Islamization also means more anti-Israeli virulence, it is hard to see how these two diametrically opposed trends can co-exist.

For all these reasons, one is hard pressed to see how the present peace process between Israel and the Palestinians might end. Oslo II did not give the Palestinians more than seven West Bank towns and some of their immediate hinterland, but the bulk of the territory (70 per cent for now) remains more or less fully under Israeli control, including all Israeli settlements. What the Palestinians will do next, or how quickly and how significantly Israel will have to submit to Palestinian pressures to withdraw further, are all questions that will only be touched at the beginning of the third step of Oslo, i.e., negotiations on the final scheme.

Had Israel held on to some disposable assets, it might have been able to lure the Palestinians to continue the game. But now, those assets have nearly all been spent. Now only the qualitative issues remain: if Israel withdraws from the territories, will the Arabs grant her their ultimate recognition and thus bring about the end of the conflict? Or, on the contrary, since Israel has no satisfactory means of reward, will the Arabs continue to push her off balance and bring about her demise? Or, will the Palestinians behave like the Egyptians: take their territories back first, then disclaim the peace accords without officially abrogating them, and wait for the first opportunity to abolish them? In this situation, instead of serving as a lever for normalization and reconciliation, the assets relinquished by Israel will act as an appetizer that presses the hungry Palestinians to demand more sacrifice from themselves for the cause.

Bibliography

ARAB AND IRANIAN MEDIA

Afaq Arabiyya (Cairo)
Akhbar al-Yaum (Cairo)
Al-Akhbar (Cairo)
Al-Ahali (Cairo)
Al-Ahram (Cairo)
Al-Ahram al-Arabi (Cairo)
Al-Ahram al-Iqtisadi (Cairo)
Al-Ahrar (Cairo)
Al-Arabi (Cairo)
Al-Ayyam (Palestinian Authority)
Al-Dustur (Amman)
Al-Gumhuriyya (Cairo)
Al-Hayat (London)
Al-Islam wa-Filastin (Cyprus)
Al Quds al-Arabi (London)

Al-Ra'i (Amman)
Al-Risalah (Gaza)
Al-Safir (Beirut)
Al Sharq al-Awsat (London)
Al-Sirat Weekly (Umm al-Fahm)
Al Usbu' (Cairo)
Al Usbu' al Adabi (Damascus)
Al-Wafd (Cairo)
Al-Watan al-Arabi (London)
Egyptian Gazette (Cairo)
Kaihan (Teheran)
October (Cairo)
Palestinian Television (Ramallah/Gaza)
Rooz al-Yussuf (Cairo)
Tishrin (Damascus)

ISRAELI AND WESTERN MEDIA AND JOURNALS

Arabica (Paris)
Azure (Jerusalem)
Commentary (New York)
Educational Researcher (New York)
FBIS-NES (American Information
  Agency), Washington
France-Pays Arabes (Paris)
Ha'aretz (Tel Aviv)
*International Journal of Middle Eastern
  Studies* (Oxford)
International Problems (Jerusalem)
Israel's Parliamentary Records (Jerusalem)
Israel Televison, Channel One (Jerusalem)
Jerusalem Letter (Jerusalem)

Jerusalem Studies in Arabic and Islam
  (Jerusalem)
Journal of Palestine Studies (Beirut)
Journal of Terrorism and Political Violence
  (London)
Ma'ariv (Tel Aviv)
Med Akad (Amsterdam)
*MEMRI (Middle East Media and Research
  Institute)* (Jerusalem and Washington)
Middle East Digest (Jerusalem)
Middle East Quarterly (Philadelphia)
Monthly Survey (Tel-Aviv) [Hebrew]
Survey of Arab Affairs (Jerusalem)
Wall Street Journal (New York)

ARTICLES/LECTURES

Abd-al 'Adhim, Lutfi, 'Arabs and Jews: Who will Annihilate Whom?', *Al-Ahram al-Iqtisadi,* 27 September 1982, pp. 4–7.

Allon, Ilai, 'Negotiations in Islam', Public Lecture at Hebrew University, 3 March 1992.

Busset, H., 'Omar's Image as the Conqueror of Jerusalem', *Jerusalem Studies of Arabic and Islam* 8 (1986), pp. 153–4.Eytan, Walter, 'The Struggle for the Political Status of Jerusalem', *Monthly Survey*, 10 (October 1984), pp. 15–21 [Hebrew].

Gannor, Bo'az, 'The Islamic Jihad: The Imperative of Holy War', *Survey of Arab Affairs* (15 February 1993).

Gerber, Haim, 'Palestine And Other Territorial Concepts in the Seventeenth Century', *International Journal of Middle Eastern Studies,* 30 (1998), pp. 563–72.

Hawting, Gerald, 'Al-Hudaybiyya and the Conquest of Mecca', *Jerusalem Studies of Arabic and Islam*, 8 (1986), pp. 1–23.

Hazoni, Yoram, 'Editorial', *Azure*, 2 (1997), pp. 3–5.

Israeli, Raphael, 'Muslim Fundamentalists as Social Revolutionaries', *Journal of Terrorism and Political Violence*, 6, 4 (Winter 1994), pp. 462–75.

——, 'Islamikaze and their Significance', *Journal of Terrorism and Political Violence*, 9, 3 (1997), pp. 96–121.

Kaminker, Sarah, 'Building Restrictions in East Jerusalem', *Journal of Palestine Studies*, 26, 4 (Summer 1997).

Kister, M., 'Al-Hira', *Arabica*, 15 (1965).

——, 'The Massacre of Banu Qurayza', *Jerusalem Studies of Arabic and Islam*, 8 (1986) pp. 61–9.

Lecker, Michael, 'The Hudaybiyya Treaty and the Expedition against Khaybar', *Jerusalem Studies of Arabic and Islam*, 5 (1984), pp.1–11.

Lewis, Bernard, 'The Return of Islam', *Commentary* (Winter 1976), pp. 39–49.

——, 'Muslim Anti-Semitism', *The Middle East Quarterly*, 5, 2 (1998).

Lopez, A., 'Israel's Relations with the Vatican', *Jerusalem Letter*, 401 (March 1999).

Meir, S., 'United Jerusalem in Jordanian Eyes', *International Problems*, 3–4 (Fall 1980).

Phillips, D.C., 'The Good, the Bad and the Ugly: The Many Faces of Constructivism', *Educational Researcher*, 24, 7 (1995).

'Readings in Islamic Martyrology', *Al-Islam wa-Filastin*, 5 June 1988 [Arabic].

Wensinck, A.J., 'The Oriental Doctrine of the Martyrs', *Med Akad*, Series A, 6,1 (1921), pp. 1–28.

BOOKS

Ahimeir, Ora (ed.), *Jerusalem: Aspects of Law* (Jerusalem: Jerusalem Institute of Israeli Studies, 1980).

Alexander, Yona (ed.), *The 1988–89 Annual of Terrorism* (Amsterdam: Martinus Nijhoff, 1990).

Algar, Hamid, *Islam and Revolution* (Berkeley, CA: UC Press, 1981).

Ayoub, Mahmoud, *Redemptive Suffering in Islam: A Study of the Devotional Aspects of 'Ashura'* (The Hague: Mouton, 1978).

Babuaziz, A, and Weiner, M. (eds), *State, Religion and Ethnic Politics* (Syracuse, NY: Syracuse University Press, 1987).

Bat Ye'or, *The Dhimmi* (Rutherford, NY: Fairleigh Dickinson University Press, 1987).

——, *The Decline of Eastern Christianity Under Islam* (Rutherford, NY: Fairleigh Dickinson University Press, 1996).

Blum, Y. 'The Juridical Status of East Jerusalem', in O. Ahimeir (ed.), *Jerusalem: Aspects of Law* (Jerusalem: Jerusalem Institute of Israeli Studies, 1980). [English and Hebrew].

Chesneaux, Jean *et al.* (eds) *Movements Populaires et Societes Secretes au XIXe Siecle* (Paris: Maspero, 1970).

Elad, Amikam, 'Why did Abd-al Malik Build the Dome of the Rock?', in J. Raby and J. Johns (eds), *Bayt al-Maqdi* (New York: Oxford University Press, 1992), pp. 33–57.

England, Y., 'The Status of the Holy Places in Jerusalem', in O. Ahimeir (ed.), *Jerusalem: Aspects of Law* (Jerusalem: Jerusalem Institute of Israel Studies, 1980). [English and Hebrew].

Esposito, John (ed), *Islam in Asia: Religion, Politics and Society* (New York: Oxford Press, 1987).

Firer, Ruth, 'From Peace-Making to Tolerance Building', in R. Moses (ed.) *Psychology of Peace and Conflict: The Israeli–Palestinian Experience* (Jerusalem: The Truman Institute for the Advancement of Peace, 1995), pp. 79–86.

Gani, A., 'Afghanistan, Islam and Counter-Revolutionary Movements', in J. Esposito (ed.), *Islam in Asia: Religion, Politics and Society* (New York: Oxford Press, 1987).

Gibb, H.A.R *et al.*, *The New Encyclopedia of Islam*, 11 Vols, 2nd edn (Leiden: Brill, 1960–2000).

Gilbert, Martin, *Jerusalem in the Twentieth Century* (London: Chatto and Windus, 1996).

Goldziher, Ignaz, *Muhammedanische Studien* (Halle: University of Halle, 1989).

Hatina, Meir, *Palestinian Radicalism: The Islamic Jihad Movement* (Tel Aviv: Tel Aviv University, 1994).

Hirsch, Moshe and Housen-Couriel, Debra, *The Jerusalem Problem: Proposals for its Resolution* (Jerusalem: Jerusalem Institute for Israel Studies, 1994).

Israeli, Raphael, 'The Charter of Allah: The Platform of the Islamic Resistance Movement', in Yona Alexander (ed.), *The 1988–89 Annual of Terrorism* (Amsterdam: Martinus Nijhoff, 1990), pp. 99–134.

——, *Peace is in the Eye of the Beholder* (Berlin and NY: Mouton, 1986).

——, *Muslim Fundamentalism in Israel* (London: Brassey's, 1993).

——, *Jerusalem Divided: The Armistice Regime, 1947–67* (London: Frank Cass, 2002).

Johnson, H., *Islam and Politics of Meaning in Palestinian Nationalism* (London: Kegan Paul, 1982).

Kelin, Menachem, *Jerusalem in the Peace Negotiations* (Jerusalem: Jerusalem Institute of Israel Studies, 1995) [Hebrew].

Kodansha Encyclopedia of Japan (Tokyo and New York, 1983).

The Koran (Harmondsworth: Penguin, 2003).

Kramer, Martin (ed.), *Protest and Revolution in Shi'ite Islam* (Tel Aviv: Tel Aviv University, 1994).

Lapidoth, Ruth and Hirsch, Moshe, *Jerusalem: Legal and Political Aspects* (Jerusalem: The Jerusalem Institute of Israeli Studies, 1994).

Lewis, Bernard, *Semites and Anti-Semites* (New York: Norton, 1986).

Maguire, Kate, *The Israelization of Jerusalem*, Arab Papers (London: Arab Research Centre, 1989).

Mansur, Anis, *The Wailing Wall and the Tears* (Cairo, 1982) [Arabic].

Mashhur, Mustafa, *Al-Jihad hua al-Sabil* [Jihad is the Path] (Cairo, n.d.) [Arabic].

Masiri, abd-al Wahhab, *Jews, Judaism and Zionism* (Cairo, 2000) [Arabic].

Meirriam, J. (ed.), *Afghan Resistance: The Politics of Survival* (Boulder, CO: Westview, 1984).

Moses, R. (ed), *Psychology of Peace and Conflict: The Israeli-Palestinian Experience* (Jerusalem: The Truman Institute for the Advancement of Peace, 1995), pp. 79–86.

Nabi, E., 'The Changing Role of Islam as a Unifying Force in Afghanistan', in A. Babuaziz and M. Weiner (eds), *State, Religion and Ethnic Politics* (Syracuse, NY: Syracuse University Press, 1987).

Palestinian Authority, *Palestinian National Education for the Fifth* Grade, No. 509 (Ramallah/Gaza: Palestinian Authority) [Arabic].

——, *Our Arabic Language for the Second Grade*, No. 513 (Ramallah/Gaza: Palestinian Authority) [Arabic].

——, *National Palestinian Education for the Fifth Grade*, No. 529 (Ramallah/Gaza, Palestinian Authority) [Arabic].

——, *Our Arabic Language for the Fifth Grade*, No. 542 (Ramallah/Gaza, Palestinian Authority) [Arabic].

——, *Social and National Education for the Fifth Grade*, No. 549 (Ramallah/Gaza: Palestinian Authority) [Arabic].

——, *Geography for the Arab Homeland for the Sixth Grade*, No. 557 (Ramallah/Gaza: Palestinian Authority) [Arabic].

——, *Reader and Literary Texts for the Eighth Grade*, No. 578 (Ramallah/Gaza: Palestinian Authority) [Arabic].

——, *Composition and Summarizing for the Eighth Grade*, No. 581 (Ramallah/Gaza: Palestinian Authority) [Arabic].

—— , *Modern Arab History and Contemporary Problems for the Tenth Grade*, No. 613 (Ramallah/Gaza: Palestinian Authority) [Arabic].

——, *Geography of Arab Lands for the Twelfth Grade*, No. 650 (Ramallah/Gaza: Palestinian Authority) [Arabic].

——, *Outstanding Examples of Our Civilization for the Eleventh Grade*, (Ramallah/Gaza: Palestinian Authority) [Arabic].

——, *Islamic Education for the Ninth Grade* (Ramallah/Gaza: Palestinian Authority) [Arabic].

——, *Islamic Authority for the Eighth Grade* (Ramallah/Gaza: Palestinian Authority) [Arabic].

——, *Islamic Education for the Seventh Grade*, No. 564 (Ramallah/Gaza, Palestinian Authority) [Arabic].

——, *The New History of the Arabs and the World* (Ramallah/Gaza: Palestinian Authority) [Arabic].

Peres, Shimon, *The New Middle East* (Bnei Brak: Steimatzki, 1993) [Hebrew].

Qut'b, Sayyid, *Our Struggle Against the Jews* (Beirut, 1986).

Raby and J. Johns (eds), *Bayt al-Maqdis* (New York: Oxford University Press, 1992).

Rif'at, Ahmad, *Al-Nabi al-Musallah* (London, 1991) [Arabic].

Roy, Olivier, *Islam and Resistance in Afghanistan* (Cambridge: Cambridge University Press, 1987).

Sa'fan, Kamil, *Jews, History and Doctrine* (Cairo, 1982) [Arabic].

Sivan, Emanuel, *Muslim Radicals* (Tel Aviv: Am Oved, 1985) [Hebrew].

Taheri, Amir, *The Spirit of Allah* (Tel Aviv: Am Oved, 1986) [Hebrew].

Tlas, Mustafa, *The Matza of Zion* (Paris, 1999).

Watt, Montgomery, *Muhammad at Medina* (Oxford: Oxford University Press, 1956).

Webman, Esther, *Antisemitic Motifs in the Ideology of Hizballah and the Hamas. Project for the Study of Antisemitism* (Tel Aviv: Tel Aviv University, 1994).

Index